## PRAISE FOR
# ROBERT LEKACHMAN'S
# *VISIONS AND NIGHTMARES*

"This is an important book. ***Visions and Nightmares*** represents a significant advance in American liberal thought and should be read by everyone—liberal, conservative or assorted shades of neo—concerned about American politics."
—*The Los Angeles Times Book Review*

"An intelligently passionate brief against the Reagan Administration. A sober realism is the strength of this provocative, thoughtful book." —*The New York Times Book Review*

"With ***Visions and Nightmares***, Lekachman has established himself as the preeminent chronicler of militant opposition to Reaganomics." —*The Voice Literary Supplement*

"You've got to hand it to economist Robert Lekachman. No mush. No waffling. No fuzzy academic theories. Just unvarnished opinion." —*Business Week*

"***Visions and Nightmares*** is an angry, witty polemic that summarizes trends culled from the American public record. . . . An important, highly provocative book that raises vital questions." —*The San Francisco Chronicle*

Also by Robert Lekachman

*Greed Is Not Enough: Reaganomics*
*Capitalism for Beginners*
*Economists at Bay*
*Inflation: The Permanent Problem of Boom and Bust*
*National Income and Public Policy*
*The Age of Keynes*
*A History of Economic Ideas*

Edited by Robert Lekachman

*Keynes' General Theory: Reports of Three Decades*
*Varieties of Economics*
*Keynes and the Classics*
*National Economic Policy for Economic Welfare at Home and Abroad*

Edited by Robert Lekachman and David Novack

*Development and Society*

# Visions and Nightmares

*America After Reagan*

ROBERT LEKACHMAN

Collier Books

MACMILLAN PUBLISHING COMPANY

New York

## ACKNOWLEDGMENTS

I am grateful to my editor, Ned Chase, who actually enjoys reading books and encouraging their perpetrators; my agent, Robin Straus, who represented me professionally and pleasantly; and my friend the Reverend James R. McGraw, who guided me in the exploration of Protestant theology. It would be churlish to deny the inspiration of Ronald Reagan—the face that launched a thousand polemics.

Copyright © 1987 by Robert Lekachman
Preface copyright © 1988 by Robert Lekachman

All rights reserved. No part of this book may be reproduced or transmitted in any form or by any means, electronic or mechanical, including photocopying, recording or by any information storage and retrieval system, without permission in writing from the Publisher.

Macmillan Publishing Company
866 Third Avenue, New York, N.Y. 10022
Collier Macmillan Canada, Inc.

Library of Congress Cataloging-in-Publication Data

Lekachman, Robert.
  Visions and nightmares : America after Reagan / Robert Lekachman. —1st Collier Books ed.
    p.   cm.
  Reissued with new copyrighted pref.
  Bibliography: p.
  Includes index.
  ISBN 0-02-073710-6 (pbk.)
    1. United States—Politics and government—1981–   2. United States—Economic policy—1981–   3. Presidents—United States—Election—1984. 4. Reagan, Ronald. I. Title.
E876.L45   1988
973.927—dc19                                                87-29033
                                                                                   CIP

Macmillan books are available at special discounts for bulk purchases for sales promotions, premiums, fund-raising, or educational use. For details, contact:

Special Sales Director
Macmillan Publishing Company
866 Third Avenue
New York, N.Y. 10022

FIRST COLLIER BOOKS EDITION 1988

10 9 8 7 6 5 4 3 2 1

Printed in the United States of America

*Visions and Nightmares* is also available in a hardcover edition by Macmillan Publishing Company.

*For Eva—as always*

# About the Author

Robert Lekachman, distinguished Professor of Economics at the Graduate Center of the City University of New York Lehman College Campus, is the author of *The Age of Keynes* and *Greed Is Not Enough* (which was on the *New York Times* bestseller list), among other works, and is a prolific contributor to the *New York Times Magazine* and *Book Review*, *Harper's*, the *Atlantic*, *Encounter*, the *New Republic*, *Commentary*, and other leading periodicals. He has appeared on such television shows as "Firing Line," the "MacNeil-Lehrer Report," "Nightline," and the "CBS Evening News." He is a lifelong New York City resident.

# Contents

*Election Preface* xi

*Introduction* xxix

*Chapter 1*
Why Reagan Won 1

*Chapter 2*
It Really Was a (Nearly) Great Society 42

*Chapter 3*
After Reagan . . . Reagan 83

*Chapter 4*
After Reagan . . . Still More Reagan 117

*Chapter 5*
America Rearranged 148

*Chapter 6*
Neolibs, Technocrats, and Yuppies 162

*Chapter 7*
New Wars of Religion 205

## Contents

*Chapter 8*

The Secular Left: Hope or Fantasy?   254

*Notes*   293

*Index*   305

# Election Preface

A BUSINESS JOURNAL I choose not to name in order to shield the guilty headlined a hostile review of this book, "Didn't Ronald Reagan Do Anything Right?" An emphatic "no" was my short answer to the ill-intentioned query even before the gaudy scandals of arms for hostages, diversions of funds to the contras, Swiss bank accounts, and patriotism for profit swam before the bemused eyes of TV viewers during the silly summer of 1987. What a cast of characters! How can one forget General Secord, who saw no reason not to turn a penny or two from the Iranscam? Or his business partner, Albert Hakim, an impressario of talents so dazzling that, in time, spared from manipulating new companies and bank accounts and providing for the financial future of the North family, he could serve as Secretary of State for a day and present the First Channel, or was it the Second Channel, with a nine-point program of his own inspiration? One of the programs' major demands was the release of seventeen terrorists in Kuwaiti prisons. Another item committed the American government to termination with or without extreme prejudice of Sadam Hussein, Iraq's unpleasant tyrant. Our agents believed it irrelevant to inform Secretary of State George Shultz that his foreign policy had been hijacked. As for the CIA, his natural diffidence could not prevent General Secord from confiding his candid view that he, his partner, and a spare colonel or two could do a better job than the legions of spooks deployed by the late Bill Casey. To update Samuel Johnson, patriotism is the last refuge of an entrepreneur, particularly one whose hand is caught in the till.

In his apparently candid testimony to the Congressional

*Election Preface*

committees, George Shultz, an economist of dour mien, emerged as a hero to all but such die-hard Reaganites as Senator Orrin Hatch and his House Republican colleagues. Chairmen Hamilton and Inouye, shining their lantern in all directions, had at last found an honest man who by his own account played his piano downstairs in complete ignorance of the skullduggery afoot upstairs. Admiral Poindexter, whose fitness reports extolled his photographic memory, recalled amazingly little of the large events in which he figured. By contrast, George Shultz, from a White House standpoint, suffered an embarrassing failure to forget McFarlane's, Casey's, and Poindexter's lies and deceptions. Nor could he deny that Ronald Reagan had concealed from him all three of the celebrated findings he had signed in authorization of arms sales to Iran. As *Newsday* columnist Murray Kempton wonderingly commented, Shultz continued to look like a pudding, but who would have thought there was so much blood in that particular pudding? In one of his last columns before retirement, James Reston, longtime resident sage of the *New York Times*, thought it a pity that Shultz was not a presidential contender. As Reston compassionately forgot, Shultz's resignation threats involved turf-protection rather than principle. Only carping critics recalled the example of Cyrus Vance, who resigned as Jimmy Carter's Secretary of State because of principled disagreement with the Desert 1 attempt to rescue hostages. A successful rescue might well have reelected Jimmy Carter.

Different emotions surged through the overheated mind of a *Wall Street Journal* editorial writer on July 27. His hero was Ollie North. I quote: "Ronald Reagan clearly is gifted with Irish luck. Oliver L. North, a man he fired, has saved his presidency," presumably from soft-on-commie types like Caspar Weinberger and George Shultz. Rather churlishly, the *Journal* had not a word of praise for Brendan Sullivan, Ollie's astute and combative legal adviser. Demonstrating once more that in America anyone can become president or at least vice president, some conservatives touted a Kemp–North ticket as the best therapy for tired Republican blood and an ideal antidote to the "moderation" and "pragmatism" with which Senator Dole and Vice President Bush have been most unfairly charged.

## Election Preface

Ollie merits more than casual mention. Because of the gaudy company he kept before his president cast this "national hero"—Ronald Reagan's very words—overboard, it is easy to misinterpret his conduct and character. A retinue that stars Secord, Hakim, and Manucher Ghorbanifar—an individual of mysterious loyalties and consequently great wealth—and allots featured roles to John Singlaub, another former general turned arms-and-security entrepreneur, and a pair of Israeli munitions merchants, delightfully named Nimrodi and Schwimmer, implies a shortage of Boy Scouts. Appearances strongly suggested that in conformity to the spiritual values of the Reagan era, North condoned and perhaps hoped in the future to share the substantial cash rewards of entreprenurial patriotic endeavor.

As so often they do, appearances deceive. Ollie's role models are not to be found among Reaganite business types. Nor is he an exotic plant in a garden of bureaucratic weeds. Fairly, to comprehend Ollie, one must look beyond his instant commercialization to the very spirit of twentieth-century American capitalism. Back in 1904, Thorstein Veblen memorably identified Ollie's prototypes and analyzed with virtuosity their contribution to or subtraction from capitalism's fortunes. For the most part, Veblen defined capitalism as fierce combat between engineers addicted to technology and the production of serviceable goods, and business tycoons fixated upon profit and paper manipulation. Aided by battalions of lawyers, accountants, stockbrokers, advertisers, and public-relations wizards, the J. P. Morgans of Veblen's day frequently made more money sabotaging efficiency than promoting it.

In cheerful moments, Veblen predicted the eventual triumph of engineers, scientists, technicians, and skilled workers. In darker moods, he feared that the paladins of business enterprise would subvert honest engineers and pervert the instinct of honest workmanship implanted in us by nature in order to improve the human species according to Darwinian prescription.

Our astute Norwegian guide glimpsed a still more calamitous possibility. In the contest for power, some entrants were remnants of "older conventions," notably "soldiers, politicians, the clergy, and men of fashion." Their habits of thought, focusing admiringly upon national supremacy, theological sanc-

*Election Preface*

tion, and military glory, were formed long before the legal, natural rights, Lockean ethos of business enterprise, and even longer before the age of mass communication and self-indulgent consumption.

Just as though Veblen foresaw North's and Secord's "Enterprise," he asserted that soldiers in particular were likely to be drawn into military and commercial conflicts by the ever-expanding global reach of business enterprise and the soaring ambitions of politicians. Generals and admirals turn out to be uncomfortable allies of business enterprise; the wars that are their *raisons d'etre* propel society back "to a more archaic situation that preceded the scheme of natural rights." The business enterprisers begin by enlisting the military as their agents in the hunt for markets and profits. Before the military are done, they have attached the magnates to their chariots as they careen onward to the victory for which, as General Douglas MacArthur memorably proclaimed, there is no substitute.

The consequences, Veblen itemized with relish, were "absolute government, dynastic politics, devolutions of rights and honors, ecclesiastical authority, and popular submission and squalor." In the wake of World War I, Veblen described Kaiser Wilhelm's imperial Germany as an excellent example of an alliance of business enterprise and the military that transformed itself into a partnership between generals and engineers to the neglect of the profit aspirations of tycoons. Presciently, Veblen wondered whether a similar fate was in store for Japan, in 1919 still an American ally.

Ollie and Thorstein track together a considerable distance. Ollie is a decorated, battle-scarred veteran, avid for new conflicts, and prepared to take on Abu Nidal *mano a mano*. In his *Doonesbury* cartoon strip, a cultural artifact creepily close to reality, Garry Trudeau toyed with the vision of a boffo bout between North and Nidal in Las Vegas. Our Ollie emotionally celebrates "freedom fighters" and lays his life on the line in Teheran. He conscripts God on his side. Raised a Catholic, Ollie now belongs to a charismatic Episcopal congregation where on Sundays the faithful babble in tongues, making as much sense as Ollie's five glorious days of public testimony. These are not the calculating sentiments of a mercenary on the prowl for lucre, although an optimist like Ollie probably

## Election Preface

never excluded the possibility that geopolitical activity and old-time profit were mutually reinforcing rather than mutually exclusive as Congressional killjoys spent so much time insisting during the hearings.

As for any good warrior, Ollie's world view is Manichean. For the Devil, read Communism. For God, read America, possibly minus Congress and the departments of State and Defense. For loyalty read obedience to superiors. Ollie reminds us of that illustrative anecdote of Watergate, the confrontation between General Haig, Nixon's chief of staff, and Attorney General Elliott Richardson, an *echt* Brahmin. Haig directed Richardson to fire the meddlesome Archibald Cox summarily. Richardson demurred. Haig, astonished, reminded the Attorney General that his words conveyed a direct order of the Commander-in-Chief. Which settled the issue for ("I'm in charge here!") Haig but not for his opponent, a Harvard Law School type presumably more familiar with the American constitution than West Point alumni. Like the good general, our hero lacks patience with the traditional concept of democracy as a process interwoven with multiple, conflicting goals which more frequently demand compromises than confrontations. If the policies of Ollie's president, his commander-in-chief, require concealment, dissimulation, alteration of documents, circumvention or outright breach of statutes, shredding, and deliberate falsehood, so be it. The best of intentions— loyalty to president and God, amply justify the worst of actions. To put the matter gently, North's ethics were situational. Never lie unless it is expedient to do so. And, as Ollie pointed out, if his country didn't want him to shred documents, why did it furnish his office with a shredder?

Ollie is not unique. Our history recalls other figures who combined righteous yearning for glory in deadly combat against evil enemies, with contempt for the creaky mechanisms of democracy and the compromising politicians who manipulate them. General Douglas MacArthur once again and General George Patton spring immediately to mind. The latter believed in his own reincarnation as Alexander the Great. The former may have despaired of finding an historical predecessor up to his own standards.

However, Veblen carries us only so far in understanding

Ollie. He did not anticipate a military culture in which the martial virtues yield precedence to bureaucratic skills. Some of the black comedy of Reagan-style militarism is the reluctance of Secretary Weinberger and the Joint Chiefs of Staff actually to use the men and weapons that they have been zealously accumulating. The bureaucrats distrust the warriors, perhaps the explanation of North's comparatively modest rank for a career soldier in his early forties. Norths, Pattons, and MacArthurs these days are lucky to make full colonel. The generals and admirals have learned the ignoble arts of political infighting. They have demonstrated skill in extracting appropriations from Congress and spreading procurement contracts carefully around the fifty states, in each and every Congressperson's constituency. No wonder North saw enemies to the left, right, front, and center.

Veblen lived at the rosy dawn of the mass media before television transformed politics and popular culture. As the world now knows, Ollie is a superb TV performer. His good looks, manly bearing, intensely blue dachschund-like eyes, and melodious voice inflections project the true believer's message. No harm done that superior acting and the con arts of astute merchandising reinforce the message. This self-proclaimed David, testifying it is true with limited immunity and a fuming, insecurely leashed legal tiger at his side (the biblical David vanquished his philistine opponent without an attendant consigliere), took on the multi-headed Congressional Goliath. Ollie touched hearts if not minds with his proclamation, tirelessly reiterated, of trust, faith, courage, love of family, Marine solidarity, and the utter selflessness of each waking action. How unlike the rest of us!

For Ollie embodies in fantasy everything most Americans are not. He glories in archaic virtues better suited to earlier times. Dragged into the nuclear age, such virtues tempt their devotees into the crimes of blind obedience around which the Nuremberg trials revolved, as Senator Daniel Inouye warned. Far better for America that Ollie deposit his militant virtues in escrow here or in Switzerland and direct his considerable talents to making a good living like the rest of us banal mortals.

I have indulged myself in these reflections partly because like any other true-blue Reagan basher I derive unashamed

*Election Preface*

delight in the misfortunes of an administration that so amply merits them and many more. But the entire episode luridly illustrates two of the malignant tendencies examined at some length in this book: militarism and privatization. The nightmares of my title represent my apprehension that even after Ronald Reagan retires to his ranch, the trends that he accelerated will retain enough momentum to continue during the administration of a less ideological Republican or Democrat.

Militarism, both bureaucratic and archaic, first. The signs of it are protean. The president salutes upon mounting and debarking from his helicopter. Halftime ceremonies at college football games feature enormous American flags, precision drill teams, and military bands. The latter often are adjuncts of ROTC units, popular once more even on elite Ivy campuses. Cities compete furiously to become home ports for our 600 ship navy. Congressional doves strive vigorously to direct military contracts to their own constituencies. The Pentagon budget has ceased to grow but it has stabilized at a figure just about twice that of the final year of the Carter presidency. As the cost overruns for the lethal military toys mount, the Pentagon budget will renew its ascent. The bulk of federal research support flows to weapons development. Although some scientists have conscientiously refused to work on Star Wars, a great many of their talented colleagues—physicists, mathematicians, computer wizards and others, have cheerfully cooperated with the Pentagon, some lured by research grants, others by the intellectual puzzles to be solved, and a few, no doubt, out of genuine support for the program. Alliances between generals and scientists have been bonded in mutual interest.

Although no loyal Reaganite would concede the obvious, the long expansion that began at the end of 1982 is the child of two parents as in biology: massive tax cuts and ascending federal outlays on weapons procurement. This is military Keynesianism *pur sang*. There is no reason to refrain from quoting John Maynard Keynes directly on this issue:

> Ancient Egypt was doubly fortunate, and doubtless owed to this its fabled wealth, in that it possessed *two* activities, namely, pyramid-building as well as the search for the

## Election Preface

precious metals, the fruits of which, since they could not serve the needs of man by being consumed, did not stale with abundance. The Middle Ages built cathedrals and sang dirges.... Thus we are so sensible, have schooled ourselves to so close a semblance of prudent financiers, taking careful thought before we add to the "financial" burdens of posterity by building them houses to live in, that we have no such easy escape from the sufferings of unemployment.

No one can fairly accuse the Reagan administration of building houses for the rising proportion of the population priced out of the swollen market for accommodation. But of pyramid and cathedral equivalents we suffer no shortage. Aircraft carriers, refurbished battleships, missiles, and submarines are as useless as pyramids but infinitely more dangerous. They are much inferior to cathedrals as objects of veneration. Ideology now, as in the 1930s when Keynes wrote, cripples our ability communally to shelter, educate, and medicate our population. Too bad under the circumstances that weapons are more popular than cathedrals.

A president infatuated with his own roles long ago in war flicks, inevitably surrounded himself with military types. Bud McFarlane, Ollie North, and John Poindexter shared military careers. The marines detailed Ollie, possibly with a sigh of relief, to the National Security Council. Poindexter, a presidential appointee, served in effect on leave from the navy initially as McFarlane's deputy and subsequently as his successor. For outside help, they turned to other military types, Generals Secord and Singlaub and Colonel Dutton among others, buccaneers not bureaucrats to a man. The military's atavistic remnants were in full charge for a space of time of our foreign policy in the Middle East and Central America.

Militarization threatens our prosperity. Talented Japanese scientists and engineers develop new and better products snapped up by quality-conscious American consumers. Our counterparts work on weapons which, if we are lucky, will never be used. We devote 6–7 percent of our GNP to the Pentagon. After years of heavy American pressure, the Japanese in 1987 edged almost imperceptibly over 1 percent. The Pentagon has exacerbated this damage by its preference for single-source contracts. Defense work has become notoriously inefficient, dangerously prone to defect, and routinely far more expensive than the Pentagon and its allies among military contractors estimate. When major weapons producers venture into civilian markets, they almost invariably fail, for their consumer goods replicate the failings of their military hardware: typically they are overpriced, gold-plated, and prone to quick breakdown.

Bad enough that American living standards have become casualties of militarization. Far worse that the very existence of warplanes available for "surgical strikes," carrier task forces, and resurrected battleships, tempts frustrated presidents, eager for quick fixes to complex crises, to substitute force for the ambiguous techniques of negotiation and economic pressure. Pause momentarily to brood upon our "assets" in the single category of special forces. Army Rangers raid by parachute. Green Berets specialize in guerrilla war and counterinsurgencies. The supersecret Delta Force tries to rescue hostages. Navy Seals, as they should, make waterborne strikes. Not to be outdone by rival services, the Air Force trains its Special Operations Wing to infiltrate and conduct aerial supply missions. Trailing behind, the Marines, reluctantly modifying their commitment to suicidal landings on defended islands, have been training their elite group. Jimmy Carter's Desert 1 attempt to rescue hostages was a fiasco. The "surgical strike" against Libya did not translate to paradise 1986's number one bogeyman Muammur Quadaffi. It did kill a number of civilians including a child or two. After the Marine barracks calamity in Beirut, Ronald Reagan not only hastily withdrew surviving Americans, he ordered one of our battleships to bombard a Shiite settlement. It is no easier to indefinitely sit on bayonets than it ever was.

## 2

Privatization represents a faith that entrepreneurial, for-profit activity nearly always and nearly everywhere is preferable to public alternatives. A government program is a monopoly, unresponsive either to the efficiency pressures of normal com-

## Election Preface

petition or to the preferences of the clients ostensibly served. Clients are caught in bureaucratic webs. Customers displeased with a product, a price, or the quality of a service, cannot shift their patronage to other vendors. The sweet certainty of zealotry expresses itself in words like these:

> Public schools are almost always monopolists in their sectors and are largely sheltered from market forces. . . . They have a semi-captive clientele with little choice but to patronize the local monopoly. . . . Public schools are sheltered even further by the fact that their funding comes from political authorities via taxation rather than from parents as a fee for services rendered. Parents may complain about the quality of education, but they are not in financial control.

Thus runs the July–August issue of the *Cato Policy Report*, a libertarian organ. This is not the occasion to ponder the problems of public education, but the naivete of such statements is almost refreshing. In town and villages, parents elect school boards who set teaching salaries, hire principals and superintendents, and set funding priorities. The voters approve or, frequently, disapprove school budgets. New York City's decentralization efforts, though far from satisfactory, delegate considerable hiring and curricular discretion to school districts. And so on. Much is wrong with American education but the source of the trouble is not to be found in parental and community powerlessness.

I deal at some length in this volume with the defects and disasters that have attended efforts to convert health care into one more competitive market, animated by the bottom-line calculations of detergent giants and pet food titans. Here I need add only a few words of comment upon the ultimate, logical extension of the faith in General Secord's notorious Enterprise. In its most grandiose version, Secord, Hakim, North, Dutton, and miscellaneous allies envisaged a profit-making corporation, financed by arms sales and contributions from interested parties, capable of conducting covert operations in Latin America, Africa, the Middle East, and anywhere else opportunity presented itself. Bill Casey was intrigued by the

*Election Preface*

concept and the ineffable Admiral Poindexter thought it had good points.

With the possible exception of Albert Hakim, all parties to the Enterprise esteemed themselves as patriots first and foremost, and businessmen second. Gladly did they assume responsibility for defining the objectives of American policy. Manfully did they seek to pursue them by all available means. Unreluctantly they practiced the arts of mendacity, dissimulation, and deceit reprehended in the honor codes of West Point and Annapolis. Privatization became the tool, the operating manual that translated into action the archaic virtues uncelebrated by Veblen. No inconvenient Congressional meddling, no obstruction from pusillanimous Cabinet members, and no need to confuse the presidential mind with inconvenient knowledge about what the boys plus Fawn Hall were up to. Spitz Channell and his associates, ably abetted by Ollie, substituted for Congressional appropriations committees, and the Enterprise comprehended in embyro superior alternatives to the CIA and the Departments of Defense and State. Try as he would, President Reagan could not bring himself to condemn so imaginative an extension of the principle of free enterprise.

In the Age of Reagan, approaching its sunset, it is a sad necessity to reiterate sentiments no longer commonplace. One is that of community, the sense of outrage that human beings go hungry, children lack medical attention, the mentally and physically handicapped fend for themselves, simply because they lack the cash to shop in stores, buy Blue Cross health insurance, and otherwise perform as upstanding consumers. Allied to this civilized view is the feeling that rich societies owe their citizens protection against serious disaster—prolonged unemployment, disabling disease or accident, mental ailments, and indigent old age. Such attachment to a social minimum manifests itself in universal health protection in all advanced communities except the Union of South Africa and these United States. It animates efforts in countries like Sweden to retrain and reemploy displaced workers in declining industries. That is to say in the market economies of western Europe deference is also paid to the ties of social sympathy that bind citizens of widely differing net worth to each other.

If it does nothing else, privatization weakens the already

fragile bonds of social sympathy between Americans of differing status and situation. Weakened though it has been, the public school has traditionlly served a unifying function. So since 1935 has Social Security. More than one of the 1988's presidential contenders seems inclined partly to privatize public schools, Social Security or both. Perhaps out of the grandiose lunacy of the Enterprise will come some good in the shape of a public reconsideration of the desirability of privatization in spheres other than foreign policy.

## 3

After Gary Hart self-destructed—victim of libido, delusions of invulnerability, and media prurience—the *Nation* commissioned a poll to ascertain the presidential preferences of loyal Democrats. As of August 1987, nearly a quarter of the sample remained faithful to Gary, twice the fraction smitten by Jesse Jackson. Far behind were Dukakis, Gephardt, Biden, Gore, Simon, and Babbitt. I draw no larger inference from this measure of public political acumen than the obvious: it is just as difficult to erase a name from the communal memory bank as it is to register the name in the first place.

Those who penetrate deep into the text of this book (I salute them!) will be rewarded or amused by a small anachronism. I entertained myself for several pages by speculating on the character of the Gary Hart administration, on the assumption, plausible enough at the time, that 1988 would turn out to be a Democratic year and Hart would be its beneficiary. I need not reiterate my nominees for cabinet positions, but something ought be said about the reasons so many Democrats supported Hart. Parenthetically, if Gary Hart is ancient history, so also are the Yuppie restaurants which I trashed, where Hart supporters used to congregate. New York's wild real estate market is replacing them with even trendier clothing boutiques. The moral appears to be that he who complains about a phenomenon is likely soon to confront something worse. Repentantly, I sigh for the departed glory of Ruelles.

Although Hart managed George McGovern's calamitous 1972 presidential campaign, his role model ever since and

*Election Preface*

probably even in 1972 was John F. Kennedy. Kennedy's thousand days were by conventional political criteria at best a mixed success. If the nuclear test ban treaty and the successful resolution of the Cuban missile crisis were foreign policy triumphs, the Bay of Pigs fiasco, the Berlin wall, and the escalation of American involvement in Vietnam were counterbalancing blunders. From the last of them, the country has yet fully to recover.

Kennedy's domestic scorecard was even more dispiriting. His major tax proposal combined rate reductions and loophole closures. Congress by autumn 1963 had rejected tax reforms and was proceeding with glacial languor toward consideration of tax cuts. The outcome was in serious doubt. Similar uncertainty attended civil rights legislation. Initially both Kennedys, president and attorney general, had been exceedingly cautious. Their hand was forced by the police dogs and cattle prods wielded by the Jim Clarks and Bull Connors against Martin Luther King's unarmed practitioners of nonviolent civil disobedience. TV turned these southern sheriffs into instant villains, personification of the evils of segregation. Nor did the president's judicial appointments reveal strong liberal sympathies. The president's single Supreme Court nominee, his old friend Byron ("Whizzer") White, turned into a dependable conservative.

Nevertheless, Kennedy caught public imagination in ways that continue to resonate in national politics. From time to time, Ronald Reagan, half a dozen years older than Kennedy would have been if he had lived, finds it convenient to evoke the Kennedy legacy. One of the elements of that legacy was the appeal to idealism. The altruistic face of that idealism registered in the institutional guise of the Peace Corps. No Republican president—Nixon, Ford, or Reagan has opposed its survival. Idealism's sterner expression found voice in Kennedy's resounding inaugural pledge to pay any price, bear any burden in defense of freedom. If the triumph of freedom against the Communist threat required lower taxes, many Americans were ready to pay the price and bear the burden.

Kennedy was the spirit of vigor, a favorite word. His youthful energy and good looks concealed a bad back, a case of Addison's disease treated by cortisone, and sexual promiscuity undisclosed

## Election Preface

by media more respectful of politicians' privacy in the 1960s than in the 1980s. Youth seeks new frontiers. Kennedy located them in space. Youth is impatient with the outworn ideological hangups of aging Poloniuses. In a Yale commencement address, Kennedy declared that rising living standards, the elimination of poverty, the stimulation of growth, and allied economic issues had been translated into technical issues by the intellectual alchemy of John Maynard Keynes. Class warfare was obsolete. Rich and poor, managers and wage slaves, shared common interests.

The Kennedy heritage—unifying idealism, emphasis upon new frontiers, confidence in the power of technology, belief in technical fixes to acute issues of conflict between groups, and avoidance at all times of any ideology less global than unflinching combat against Communism in the interests of the Free World, was claimed by Gary Hart. In the jostling of Democrats for their party's grand prize, at least Senators Joseph Biden and Al Gore quite deliberately cast themselves as latter day Kennedys. Representative Gephardt's otherwise persuasive claim is vitiated by his emphasis on an old idea—trade protection. Governor Michael Dukakis possesses the strongest technological credentials. The amount of credit he deserves for Massachusetts' economic revival is disputable, but his effective partnerships among state agencies, universities, and business enterprises—in all but name an industrial policy—as well as his innovative work-welfare program, both qualify as new ideas. Conventional party wisdom insists that nearly as obsolete as Reaganomics itself are Great Society programs. Of the contenders in the summer of 1987, only Illinois' Paul Simon calls himself a liberal, looks favorably upon public job creation, and celebrates Harry Truman as his role model.

Bad ideas such as supply-side economics, original intent constitutional interpretations, compulsory pregnancy and compulsory prayer, contra aid, and balanced budget and antiabortion amendments, are politically more potent than no ideas at all or better ideas embraced with less intensity by their advocates. Come January 1989, a Democrat may quite well inherit Ronald Reagan's lease on the White House. On current form, Republicans are more likely to lose the election than Democrats are to win it. Should 1987's sluggish economy subside into

## Election Preface

unmistakable recession, the Republican's strongest selling point, the long expansion of the economy that began at the end of 1982, will be blunted. Ollie North to the contrary notwithstanding, Iranscam will be an albatross around Republican necks.

Although a Democratic president is preferable to any of the current Republicans, the blurred signals emitted by the Democratic contenders threaten the same sort of insecure, conflicted, unsuccessful presidency that afflicted Jimmy Carter and his constituents. The times call for national leadership animated by concern for diminished equity in the distribution of income, and a renewed conception of government not as a burden but as an instrument of protection for vulnerable groups. It is a mean society that defines itself as a mere aggregate of individual strivers for financial gain.

The next president at best will confront a sluggish economy afflicted by intransigent federal and trade deficits and a simmering Third World debt crisis. At worst, serious recession will compel him/her to focus upon recovery. Just because a new recession will begin in the context of an already huge federal deficit, it will be difficult to deploy the traditional antirecession techniques of tax cuts and enlarged expenditures on public jobs and social programs.

It will be hard all the same for the new president and Congress to postpone attention to at least four problems sedulously neglected during the Reagan era. One is welfare dependency. A national consensus has gradually emerged that the women who head the vast majority of long-term welfare families should be educated, trained, and either coaxed or prodded into gainful jobs in the private sector. Agreement is equally general that even modest success requires adequate day care facilities and continuation of Medicaid coverage for some period after a welfare client actually secures employment, for the kind of jobs available are likely to be at or near the minimum wage. Here ends consensus. Liberals define the key adjective "adequate" more generously than conservatives who are inclined to leave day care design (and financing) to the states. Liberals coax. Conservatives prod. On the whole, sticks are cheaper than carrots, at least in the short run. Here, as in imposition of minimum grant and eligibility provisions, the public and political debate will not soon end. But even the

## Election Preface

most frugal of initiatives will cost the feds and the states money. Our nonsystem of health-care delivery is a costly mess. Although we spend nearly 11 percent of our gross national product on doctors, dentists, nurses, hospitals, health insurers, medical bureaucrats, nursing homes, pharmaceuticals, and high-tech diagnostic devices, we leave totally unprotected by any private or public insurance some 37 million Americans, most of them employed at low-wage service jobs or their equivalent in the revived sweatshops in our major cities. Medicare is turning into a bad joke for the elderly. On average, senior citizens (nobody is old in America) must pay as large a fraction of their incomes for health care as they did before Medicare came into operation. AIDS threatens huge bills into the perceivable future.

Our Canadian neighbors allocate 8.5 percent of their smaller per capita GNP to health care but protect all residents and even tourists struck down by medical emergencies. A relative of mine on a business trip to British Columbia was hospitalized and subsequently died in an utterly unAmerican fashion. Prior to admission, no one asked him or his wife about health insurance and net worth. He received skilled nursing and medical care. No bill was presented to his widow and his body was shipped back to Maine at government expense. It may be that comprehensive health insurance even in free enterprise America will rise from the dead as the political cause of the 1990s. Even if it does not, piecemeal reactions to AIDS, nursing home costs for the rising number of the very old, and the sixth of the population now dependent upon overburdened emergency rooms and crowded outpatient clinics, will again add to government expenditures.

The scandal of homelessness highlights a third challenge to the new administration: the enormous shortage of affordable housing for low and moderate income families. Gentrification, the spread of financial services and data processing into residential areas, and the virtual cessation during the Reagan administration of federal subsidies for low-income residential construction, have combined to shrink the stock of all but luxury units during a period when demand for shelter has been steadily rising. It will be difficult for even a Republican

## Election Preface

administration completely to evade a need that reaches well upward from the poor to the middle class.

Finally, collapsing bridges and epidemic airport delays have reminded us of our deteriorating infrastructure, not only bridges and airports but also roads, sewers, water mains, water purification facilities, aging power transmission lines, and mass transit facilities. Mere maintenance will cost many billions and extension to accommodate a growing population many more.

Should time on weekends hang heavy on the chief executive's hands, he can brood over acid rain, ozone depletion, the plight of family farmers, worker health and safety, the state of public education, and, of course, a politically feasible method of raising the tens of billions of dollars required even minimally to address these unavoidable national needs. No wonder that as the summer of 1987 drew to its steamy close three Democratic heavyweights refused to enter the wide open competition for their party's presidential designation. Such has been public languor that the trio—Governor Mario Cuomo and Senators Sam Nunn and Bill Bradley have been doing better in the polls than most of the announced contenders.

A Democrat may become the next president without a liberal vision that contrasts with the conservative alternative. He/she is unlikey to make much difference as president in the absence of a coherent conception of government's role and responsibility. Toward the conclusion of this volume, I proposed Mario Cuomo as the most eloquent spokesman for a caring, responding, helping government. His noncandidacy has left a void on what passes in conservative America for the respectable political left. Too bad that no one else among the Democratic contenders plausibly fills the gap. Perhaps perception of that great truth will induce Governor Cuomo to reconsider his withdrawal.

Robert Lekachman,<br>August 1987

# Introduction

RARELY CAN THE official demise of an important political tendency be dated with the precision of 1984's electoral follies. Walter Mondale presided over the funeral ceremonies for Great Society liberalism in prime television time on July 18, 1984. To the cheers of momentarily optimistic delegates to the Democratic convention in San Francisco, he cried exultantly, "Look at our platform. There are no defense cuts that weaken our security; no business taxes that weaken our economy; no laundry lists that raid our Treasury."[1] He then proceeded to wage a calamitous campaign focused upon that enervating issue, the huge federal deficit. Mondale's call for higher taxes in an expanding economy, at a time of rising employment and diminishing inflation, possessed the credibility of a water conservation campaign in an African rain forest. It condemned him to run unpersuasively against his own personal history as well as the Democratic platforms of an entire generation. This politician famed for his caution might at least have coupled each of his tax-increase warnings with a specific catalogue of benefits purchasable out of larger federal revenues. That he did not do so registered his own diminishing attachment to the Democratic heritage of social amelioration.

Out of piety for the dead, let us recall the defining features of Lyndon Johnson's Great Society. From time to time, Americans rediscover poverty. The 1960s were such an occasion and Michael Harrington's *The Other America* was its manifesto. The war on poverty, a centerpiece of Johnsonian liberalism, combined somewhat inchoately traditional and innovative approaches. A traditional and usually convenient way to alleviate

*Introduction*

poverty is to give money, food, cheap housing, and free medical care to poor people, conditioning the transfers from the Treasury upon need and, frequently, willingness to seek paid employment or perform unpaid public services. Such initiatives as food stamps, Medicaid, more generous welfare regulations, and subsidized rental apartments extended this familiar liberal approach, caricatured by its opponents as a predilection for throwing money at problems, a sport now popular only in Pentagon circles. Considerably more novel and, in the event, enormously more risky, was the theme of empowerment—of the poor, the female, the black, and the Hispanic. Liberal social scientists perceived members of these overlapping groups as passive victims of the harsh blows of fate and circumstances, so alienated from conventional politics as to disdain voting, let alone more active organizational efforts. Unless they took their future in their own hands, the best intentioned of devices to alleviate their poverty were certain to fail to transform victims into self-supporting contributors to the Internal Revenue Service. Once poverty is contemplated as an affair of culture, individual motivation, and institutional structure, money and free services presumably alleviate hardship and soothe the public conscience, but they fail of themselves to transform poor people into thrifty, punctual, self-denying, upwardly mobile middle-class types. Better that the poor do not starve in the street, but best of all that they earn their own sustenance.

How did middle-class sociologists, social workers, psychologists, lawyers, and political scientists turn lower-class targets of their concern into mainstream participants in the labor force? One way was to make them as litigious as their more prosperous fellow citizens. As lawyers sometimes imperialistically assert, for every legal injury there must be a legal remedy. In the mid-1960s, a new cadre of poverty lawyers—young, idealistic graduates of elite law schools—found a haven in the federally financed Legal Services Corporation and a powerful instrument in class-action suits against local, state, and federal authorities for asserted violations of the rights of minorities, women, and welfare recipients. In California, Ronald Reagan as governor lost a number of contests with legal services attorneys and acquired an abiding distaste for them. As president, he has repeatedly sought to eliminate legal services, thus far without

## Introduction

congressional assent. In their brief moments of glory, warriors in this legal Children's Crusade mobilized such difficult constituencies as welfare mothers and migrant farm laborers in collaboration with George Wiley's short-lived National Welfare Rights Organization and Cesar Chavez's United Farm Workers. They trumpeted loudly the claims and rights of the poor.

Empowerment was also in the minds of the drafters of the statute that established the Office of Economic Opportunity. That magic phrase "maximum feasible participation" was to be the banner under which representatives of the poor shared power with mayors and city councils in the allocation of federal monies for urban services, job training, education, and much else. To nobody's astonishment, the mayors were not amused and did their considerable best to stack community action boards with their own tame nominees. When Chicago's puissant mayor Richard Daley protested OEC interference in his duchy, LBJ speedily instructed the agency to cease its endeavors to extend maximum feasible participation to "the city that works," as Daley admirers dubbed Chicago. Politics as usual survived in good health.

As a strategy, empowerment inevitably tended to set minorities against the dominant white, male, middle class. Affirmative action was barely acceptable during economic expansion but the slightest downturn in the economy set blacks against whites and women against men, particularly when union seniority clauses clashed with affirmative-action hiring programs. Seniority dictated layoffs strictly in accordance with length of service. This principle sacred to unions imposed the brunt of recession upon those last hired—the women and blacks briefly aided by affirmative action.

Similar struggles for power took place over the schools. Education is a major status symbol and the key to financial success. So long as schools remained segregated, the black community, as much in the North as in the South, could comfortably be placed by the white majority in an inferior position. School integration reduces white advantages over blacks for admission to the better universities and professional schools. It widens competition for jobs in major law firms and residencies in high-status hospitals. Status correlates with exclusion. In an expanding economy, ascribing high standing to

*Introduction*

members of previously excluded groups diminishes its value to educated, professionally credentialed white males. When growth is slow, the struggle for preferment turns nasty.

The Voting Rights Act transformed the political terrain of Dixie. For the first time since Reconstruction days after the Civil War, Southern blacks could safely register and vote. George Wallace, the symbol of segregation forever, the man who vowed to stand in the schoolhouse door to block integration, the demagogue who after an early defeat guaranteed that never again would he be out-segged by a rival, ran successfully for governor in the 1980s as an apostle of racial harmony, made many black appointments, and received substantial support from black leaders and their constituents. Blacks became judges, mayors, legislators, and, wonder of wonders, sheriffs. Virginia inaugurated a black lieutenant-governor, the first black holder of statewide office since Reconstruction. Somewhere in Hades, the shades of Bull Connor and Jim Clark, those unwitting allies of Martin Luther King, Jr., must be groaning piteously.

2

In a conservative polity like the United States, how on earth did even that master legislative manipulator Lyndon Johnson persuade the public to accept, if not actively support, innovations which in significant instances promoted minority over majority interests? The answer is simple enough: at Great Society feasts, places were set for almost everybody.[2] In 1964, as the "unconditional" war against poverty mobilized its troops, Congress enacted a major tax cut to the joy of prosperous individuals and major corporations. If Medicaid delivered new services to the poor, Medicare and increased Social Security pensions rescued the middle class from the dangers of crippling hospital bills and indigent old age.

Moreover, the federal government became a money machine for doctors, hospitals, and health insurers, and a job and entitlement program for middle-class professionals. For a decade and a half, there was little federal effort to slow escalation of physicians' fees and hospital-room charges at rates twice or

*Introduction*

three times those of general inflation. Appropriations for middle- and low-income housing and urban development translated into fat profits for builders and middle-class incomes for members of construction unions. The war on poverty amounted to still another set of career opportunities for middle-class planners, trainers, and specialists in all manner of individual and community problems.

Indeed, except by the criterion of Lyndon Johnson's inflated rhetoric, the Great Society was not a failure. As we shall subsequently see, a fairer verdict would identify a mixed assortment of successful, partially successful, and futile novelties. It attests to the vanished vigor of Great Society ideology that Richard Nixon made only half-hearted efforts to repeal major statutes. Even more astonishingly, the Family Assistance Plan, Nixon's legendary good deed, made income support the right of the working poor as well as that of the welfare clientele. If Congress had accepted FAP, it would have extended the Great Society further than LBJ had been willing to contemplate. In his first term, Ronald Reagan, a far more determined and consistent enemy of the Great Society, managed to terminate only one major legislative legacy of the 1960s, the Comprehensive Employment and Training Act. To give credit where credit is due, he did succeed, especially in 1981, in reducing appropriations for nutrition, housing, and medical programs and in replacing the Comprehensive Employment and Training Act, a Nixon initiative, with a private-sector substitute. And although the Legal Services Corporation, the president's favorite bête noire, survives, Reagan has appointed to its board of directors conservatives who have severely narrowed its scope of operation.

Nevertheless, few if any important politicians even in the most fervently Democratic of constituencies seek office as unqualified partisans of the Great Society. Younger Democrats, frequently dubbed neoliberals, share conservative disdain for governmental bureaucracy. After the fashion of Gary Hart, they hunt for free-market solutions to problems "ineffectually" handled by government. Three of Senator Hart's new ideas were pollution fees instead of Environmental Protection Agency regulations, Individual Training Accounts in place of public job training, and voluntary compacts between unions and

## Introduction

corporations in the interests of productivity, investment, and job protection. Years before the notion became popular, Hart advocated taxes on imported oil. Perceptions control public opinion and, whatever the evidence to the contrary, most Americans came to judge the Great Society a failure, while of course clinging fiercely to Medicare, enhanced Social Security benefits, low tuition charges at public universities, subsidized student loans, and other middle-class benefits from the same federal government current fashion ridicules and despises.

The 1960s were an age of planners, economists, and true believers in the capacity of government to improve the lives of vulnerable citizens. Halfway through the 1980s, the new national hero is the entrepreneur. By the end of 1984, Chrysler's Lee Iacocca had sold a million copies of his life story, *Iacocca*. *In Search of Excellence* preceded Mr. Iacocca's self-celebration in public favor. *Time*'s 1984 Man of the Year was Peter Ueberroth, who turned the summer Olympics into a profitable commercial venture. Humana, Health Corporation of America, American Medical International, and smaller rivals have located big bucks in for-profit hospital care. In the nomenclature of corporate health the folks who fill hospital beds are customers, not patients.

What transformed the public mood? Vietnam became a potent rival for public money and public attention, but a less-than-adequate explanation of diminishing popular confidence in government. In retrospect, much of the Great Society was a design for financial disaster. Lyndon Johnson's political pragmatism came at a high price. Sometimes the cleverest of political deals sabotages the very purposes it is designed to serve. Such has been the fate of Medicare, Medicaid, and affordable, public-supported housing. In these and other instances, Johnson bought off the opposition of physicians, hospitals, insurers, banks, and builders with federal largesse that soon ballooned at nearly exponential rates. The exaggerated expectations that facilitate congressional approval of new social innovations generate equally exaggerated criticism. The Great Society promised implausible victories at implausibly small cost to the taxpayers. No wonder that in 1976 Jimmy Carter waged as vigorous a campaign against big government and, implicitly, the Great Society as Ronald Reagan did four years later. Just as an earlier generation came to believe that the New Deal's Works Progress Administration employed millions of leaf rakers, this generation has been led to believe that the innovations of the 1960s were extravagant failures.

3

I have not written this book to celebrate the Great Society or mourn its current disrepute. My visions and nightmares are speculations upon the shape of American society after Ronald Reagan completes his second term. Will his successor—Jack Kemp, Howard Baker, Bob Dole, George Bush, Newt Gingrich, Jeane Kirkpatrick, Lewis Lehrman, or some less familiar contender for the imperial presidency—carry the Republican party to its third straight national victory, a feat unmatched by either Democrats or Republicans since the days of Franklin Roosevelt and Harry Truman? What will such a triumph mean? Our major parties have always been uneasy coalitions of discordant interests and opinions, held together by common concerns valued higher than the issues that divide the partners. Within the Republican fold are traditional conservatives devoted to balanced budgets, comfortable with a frugal welfare state, and indifferent or hostile to school prayer and crusades against abortion, pornography, Marxist professors, and pernicious evolutionary doctrines. These, however, are the very crusades most precious to Jerry Falwell's Moral Majority, an important source of Republican support. Under the capacious Reagan canopy, there are also supply-siders led by Congressman Kemp and Lew Lehrman. In their view, more tax cuts and a return to the gold standard will fix the little that is still wrong with the American economy. Nor should the militant anti-Communists be ignored. As partisans of ever-larger Pentagon budgets and increasingly overt intervention in Latin America, they mobilize the seldom latent public fear of the Soviet Union and its agents and the public weakness for *Rambo* solutions.

Can such a coalition stay together? Possibly, perhaps probably. The reactionary impulses that have propelled policy in the Reagan era may be powerful enough and the opposition to them sufficiently disorganized to withstand both possible recession and quarrels among coalition partners. In 1987 or 1988, Americans may be as patient with rising unemployment and declining real income as they were in 1981 and 1982, particularly if economic adversity spares middle America. Something presumably can be done to soothe each of the factions within the party. Renewed and more serious White House pressure on behalf of constitutional amendments mandating school prayer and prohibiting abortion might appease the Moral Majority, even if these amendments fail to be enacted. A similar campaign for a balanced-budget amendment would gratify traditional conservatives and avoid the inconveniences of the Gramm-Rudman Act. Supply-siders could well accept such symbolic action as a welcome substitute for tax increases that, according to their theology, stifle enterprise and investment. Even if the military budget grows at a slower rate, the militarists may console themselves with what has already been achieved in the rearming of America.

If the rest of this century records continuation of the Reagan revolution, it is comparatively easy, though exceedingly depressing, to sketch the evolution of social and economic policy. Although late in 1985 the Treasury unveiled a major plan to reform the tax code that lightened individual tax burdens, recouped lost revenue by heavier imposts on business, and thus won a measure of involuntary applause from startled liberals, it is likely to have been an aberration, for Treasury II, trundled out in mid-1985, excised most of the tributes to equity that lifted liberal spirits. Despite the hoopla surrounding 1986 congressional tax "reform," tax privileges, though curtailed, survive. Worst of all, the new measure all but abandons progressivity as a principle. Until just recently, even mild conservatives thought it appropriate that the wealthy contribute somewhat higher percentages of their income to the Treasury than less affluent fellow citizens. No longer.

By no startling coincidence in a Reagan official family where James Baker and George Bush ably represent Texas interests, tax loopholes for major oil and gas interests reappeared. So also did indulgences for capital gains and corporate profits. In the name of supply-side encouragement to saving, investment, and work effort, marginal tax rates, those that apply above all to individuals already excessively rewarded by 1981 tax cuts,

*Introduction*

in the top 1 or 2 percent of income distribution, will be steadily reduced. Under cover of concern that consumers spend too much and save too little, a European-style value-added tax, an outright national sales tax, an energy tax, or some combination will be promoted as a substitute for declining income-tax revenues. In sum, taxes will be heavier on low- and moderate-income families and lighter on their financial betters.

Whether or not military appropriations continue to rise at the 9 percent annual rate of the first Reagan administration, or Gramm-Rudman temporarily delays procurement plans, the Pentagon will gain weight each year and absorb larger fractions of each federal budget. Pressure upon domestic programs will thus be unabated, particularly if the gross national product grows at less than the 4 percent annual rate projected by administration optimists. The familiar targets include veterans, federal civil servants, Medicare patients, and, as ever, welfare beneficiaries of Aid to the Families of Dependent Children, food stamps, and special nutrition assistance to pregnant women, infants, and small children. In the good old cause of states' rights, these programs may well be transferred to states and localities, unaccompanied by federal funds adequate to finance them. Income tests may be applied to Medicare and veterans' medical benefits, a favorite proposal of conservative economists. Should the political winds blow favorable reactionary gusts, an ideologically conservative White House incumbent might be tempted to adopt as his own the stance of Charles Murray, whose tract against the welfare state, *Losing Ground*, proposed sweeping abolition of all cash and service benefits to the poverty population. Murray echoes George Gilder, who at the beginning of the first Reagan administration insisted that the poor require the spur of their own poverty if they are to improve their situation and join the American celebration. Eliminating programs targeted to low-income Americans will indubitably sharpen that spur and dig into a larger number of human hides. A good many once-middle-class families will join the poor. In American history, downward mobility has been the flip side of the opportunity society.

For conservatives, Social Security has been at once their largest and most difficult target. As a wandering minstrel of free enterprise for General Electric, a fervent Goldwaterite in

*Introduction*

1964, and a two-term California governor, Ronald Reagan had repeatedly declared his preference for a voluntary alternative to Social Security before he became president. Political exigency—a great many Republicans enjoy Social Security benefits—compelled him to reverse course as president and proclaim undying allegiance to the old folks' Treasury checks. His successor might not be similarly constrained. Pensions are a notoriously technical topic. One way to diminish the appeal of Social Security and shrink the number of its advocates is to offer newcomers in the labor force a choice between Social Security and individual retirement accounts under some appealing rubric like Freedom of Choice. In the long run, there is no surer method of eroding public support and converting public pensions into a program for the low-income elderly. Once Social Security ceases to be a universal program, it will share the vulnerability to media and political assault now focused upon welfare, food stamps, and other means-tested programs. As the maxim in the social welfare community runs, programs for poor people are poor programs. They automatically divide poor people from the rest of the community.

In a Reaganite future without Reagan, unions will continue to lose members and representation elections as pragmatic American workers conclude that collective action can do little to combat corporations determined to maintain or achieve union-free environments. Conservative presidents will reinforce worker perceptions by additional appointments of antilabor federal judges and members of the National Labor Relations Board. William Rehnquist's promotion to Chief Justice and Antonin Scalia's appointment to the Supreme Court are bad news for unions. Universities and the media will become more and more dependent for support upon the corporate sector. The ambit of civil rights and civil liberties will shrink. In the conservative future, something very like the British Official Secrets Act will limit public information about the more questionable activities of their political masters.

My nightmare emphatically is not the emergence of an American version of fascism. Plutocracy, not fascism, is the word of choice for a society whose dominant values are commercial and military. The conservative vision of the future

*Introduction*

resembles the America of Calvin Coolidge, one of Ronald Reagan's favorite presidents.

## 4

Nightmares fortunately convey uncertain resemblances to reality. There are benign visions of the future, also deeply rooted in American history. God may demur from Jerry Falwell's claim that great wealth is His way of rewarding those who put him first. The Moral Majority habitually blesses Ronald Reagan and George Bush for good measure as divine instruments. But there is an alternative religious voice, that of liberal Protestants echoing the social gospel, radical Protestants living in voluntary poverty among the poor people whom they serve, Jews who cleave to their faith's traditional addiction to social justice, and Catholics who identify in the gospels and papal encyclicals injunctions they must heed to pursue enlightened public policies even when they thwart the financial interests of powerful business interests.

Just after the 1984 presidential election, the American bishops issued the first draft of a pastoral letter, *Catholic Social Teaching and the U.S. Economy*. A shortened second draft, released in 1985, added some words of praise for American capitalism but otherwise, if anything, strengthened the bishops' emphasis upon social reform and government action to promote social justice. Bishops and archbishops themselves administer huge properties. Their natural allies are the affluent businessmen whose contributions keep Catholic hospitals and parochial schools open. Nevertheless, their interpretation of Catholic doctrine and tradition impelled them to take the risk of offending powerful members of their own community. Indeed, the pastoral letter's emphasis upon serving the needs of the poor as the highest of public priorities, its assertion that "increased participation in society by people living on its margins takes priority over the preservation of privileged concentrations of power, wealth, and income," and its unqualified claim that "meeting human needs and increasing participation should be priority targets in the investment of wealth,

## Introduction

talent, and human energy," echo contemporary liberal devotion to full employment and public provision for the poor.

The bishops moved to the left of conventional Great Society liberalism in their distress over inequities in the distribution of income, wealth, and power and their willingness to use government as an engine of direct job creation. Much against current economic and political fashion, they reasserted the 3–4 percent unemployment targets of the 1960s and recalled from general neglect the 1978 Humphrey-Hawkins Act—a measure which set unemployment targets subsequently ignored by both Carter and Reagan. For a spell, until political reaction compelled him to reverse course, Lyndon Johnson was willing to redistribute political power within local jurisdictions. He never for a moment endorsed outright egalitarian redistribution of income and wealth.

It is unwise to exaggerate the bishops' power to lead their own constituency, let alone the non-Catholic majority, in the direction of social justice. In fact, a few days before the pastoral letter was released for general circulation, a self-styled lay commission on Catholic social teaching and the U.S. economy, headed by the financier William Simon and the theologian Michael Novak and including such notables as Clare Booth Luce, Alexander Haig, the Harvard political scientist James Q. Wilson, and Peter Grace of the Grace Commission Report on the federal government and its wicked ways, issued its own defense of American capitalism and its suggestion that the bishops had a good deal to learn from the triumphs of businessmen, perhaps more than the latter had to learn from the bishops.

The lay commission was courteous. William Buckley's *National Review* was outraged. Its December 14, 1984, issue, a collector's item, warmed up with an unsigned editorial verdict that "What the American Catholic bishops are engaged in, to put it starkly, is the evisceration of their own moral and intellectual authority. They are squandering capital, to change metaphors, which they did not earn, and which has been accumulated over many centuries by much better men and women than they." Further along, that scourge of the left Tom Bethell judged that "For the most part the letter is economically illiterate—but then so are many economists." Mr. Buckley

*Introduction*

himself had of proprietor's right the last word: "What is objectionable and un-Christian here is the overall tone of sullen resentment toward the most productive, the most democratic, the most generous-spirited, and yes, the most egalitarian nation on earth. It is egalitarian because its prosperity depends on the equal protection of the weak and the strong that forms the basis of property rights. These rights in turn cannot emerge without the Christian belief that all are equal in the sight of God." The bishops failed to understand that God is a capitalist.

To speak temperately, the Catholic community is divided. So also are Protestants as they struggle to formulate their own reactions to ascendant doctrines of wealth. And although Jews voted two to one for Mondale in 1984, they were probably more disquieted by Reagan's flirtation with the Moral Majority's agenda than by his assault upon the welfare state. This is only to record the obvious—that conservative materialism elicits celebration in the ranks of the religious whatever bishops, priests, ministers, and rabbis say to the contrary.

The importance of the bishops' valiant cry for social justice is in the future if and when the political pendulum swings from right to left. Franklin Roosevelt entered the White House in 1933 endowed with neither program nor ideology. During the 1932 campaign, he attacked Herbert Hoover as a big spender and promised to balance the federal budget forthwith. How little do politics change! When like a sensible national leader he responded to the desperate needs of bankrupt farmers, foreclosed homeowners, and armies of unemployed men and women, he borrowed what he could, where he could. Both the Social Security Act of 1935 and the National Labor Relations Act of the same year built upon pioneering legislation in Wisconsin. That state's social welfare experiments in the 1920s were the fruit of a productive alliance between politicians and academics. The LaFollettes—Robert *père* and *fils*, and brother Philip—for a generation ran the state through their chosen instrument, the Progressive party. On the Madison campus of the University of Wisconsin, John R. Commons, Selig Perlman, and their colleagues patiently devised the administrative mechanisms for the delivery of old-age and unemployment benefits and a body of labor legislation suitable for adoption on the national stage. The moral? Should the

*Introduction*

moment arrive, in 1988, 1992, or later, when a progressive politician becomes president, he or she will urgently need help.

Help of at least two varieties. The first is programmatic. In 1981, Ronald Reagan and his allies could draw upon the labors in the wilderness of two decades of conservatives. Periodicals like Irving Kristol's *The Public Interest* explored notions such as cost-benefit analysis, negative income taxes, and pollution fees. As a young congressman, David Stockman himself wrote a much-quoted article entitled "The Social Pork Barrel," which documented with many horrible examples the wastefulness and misdirection of federal attempts to succor the poor. In the fashion of social science, the journal's contributors made the case against school busing, federal job-training efforts, community action, and affirmative action. They advocated privatization of public services; deregulation of airlines, trucking, and financial services; and, more generally, the superiority of market over bureaucratic solutions to almost any given problem.

Conservative think tanks—the American Enterprise Institute, the Hoover Institution, and the Heritage Foundation among others—sponsored libraries of detailed inquiry into the workings of the welfare state and, equally important, equally detailed conservative alternatives. Periodicals like the Heritage Foundation's *Policy Review* and the American Enterprise Institute's *Regulation* and *Public Opinion* aired conservative attitudes and proposals. For liberals, the lesson is clear. Unless they do their homework as faithfully as did the diligent conservatives, they shall miss opportunity when it knocks at their door. Politicians who rely upon liberal intellectuals will be disappointed if their ideologues perform less efficiently than their opponents'.

In office, presidents need programs. To get elected, they need simple, appealing themes, the very opposite of the negative Mondale obsession with budgets and deficits. Peace, prosperity, patriotism, and freedom from government meddling—Ronald Reagan's themes—are excellent slogans. The time may come when other excellent political cries—justice, equality, and community— will have their vogue as supplements to them. Then the bishops' pastoral letter and similar documents from other religious groups will offer a Democratic contender the sort of assistance needed to win an election. It

*Introduction*

remains to be seen whether secular liberal and radical intellectuals will use their time of exile as productively as did their conservative antagonists.

5

Charles Peters, founder and editor of the *Washington Monthly*, apparently coined the term "neoliberal," albeit to his subsequent regret. The parentage of "yuppie" for young urban professional and "yumpie" for young upwardly mobile professional is uncertain. Although their numbers are smaller than their notoriety, yuppies are prominent in the neoliberal fraternity and sorority. What distinguishes neoliberals from other beasts in the political and ideological zoos is their preference for market solutions to problems best handled, in the view of conventional liberals, by government. Their affection for the private sector appears to ally them with the neoconservatives. Senator Bill Bradley's and Representative Richard Gephardt's FAST (fair and simple) tax-simplification scheme departed sharply from traditional liberal attempts to increase the tax burdens of the affluent by imposing high marginal personal income tax rates upon large incomes. It did not seek additional revenue to fund social programs. It did endeavor to diminish the number of investment and personal decisions influenced by the tax code and thus free markets to do their thing—allocate investment and human effort in the most productve direction. No good neoconservative need demur from so laudable an objective.

Neoliberals edge perilously close to neoconservatives also in their distaste for the warm rhetoric of class conflict and their confidence in adroitly crafted technical solutions to issues of environment, health, employment, taxes, and similar dilemmas. Income redistribution, full employment, comparable worth, comprehensive health protection, and other passions of the left place low or nowhere on their agenda. Neoliberals come closest to emotional warmth when they extol the promise of hi-tech. Their young constituents are concentrated in sectors of the economy most affected by computers—biotechnology, health care, fiber optics, financial services, data processing,

## Introduction

and, increasingly, the operations of both offices and factories.

Nevertheless, in two significant respects neoliberals part company with their sometime allies. They temper their confidence in the magic of the marketplace with a willingness to deploy government in the service of faster economic growth and less painful shuffling of people and communities from declining to expanding industries and activities. Under the rubric of "industrial policy," some economists and a few politicians have endorsed adaptations of Japan's approach to promising industries: preferential access to credit; outright subsidy; exemption from antitrust restraints on joint research; cooperative efforts among unions, corporations, and public authorities; and tax favors. On the very moderate left, Robert Reich and Lester Thurow propose a judicious balance of favors to corporations with new managerial responsibilities for job training and social services.

An astute, slightly cynical journalist highlighted the fuzziness of "industrial policy" in the following virtuoso dictionary definition:

> *n.* 1. Economics: a systematic response on the part of government to economic distress (sp. unemployment) resulting from dislocations caused by changing domestic and international circumstances. 2. any of the operating parts thereof, including industrial banks [*q.v.*], tripartite committees, etc. 3. the activities that make up an i.p., such as protection from imports, tax relief, disincentives to expansion by producers of undesirable, outdated and/or uncompetitive products [see STEEL]. 4. Politics: [Dem.] a program offered in an election campaign as an alternative to Reaganomics [*q.v.*] or to replace the New Deal [*q.v.*] while assuaging public concern or fear aroused by frightening economic change. 5. a program of action to hasten the transition from basic industry to high technology in an orderly fashion. 6. [Repub.] a method of destroying the foundation of an economy by importing foreign concepts that are not transferable [see MITI]. 7. central planning.[3]

During the 1984 presidential primaries, Gary Hart for a time teetered on the verge of advancing industrial policy as a major theme. Robert Reich's *The Next American Frontier* attracted Walter Mondale among its appreciative readers. But for major politicians, industrial policy is a treacherous issue. Opponents have been known to liken it to Soviet-style five-year plans. Promoting the virtues of hi-tech without losing support from the beleaguered employees of rust-bowl industries requires considerable virtuosity. No wonder that thus far it has been economists, industrial union leaders, a few businessmen, and miscellaneous scribblers who have played most enthusiastically with industrial policy as an alternative to both old-style liberalism and Reaganomics.

Still, if nature continues to abhor vacuums, Democrats in quest of winning issues in 1988 may well find themselves impelled to pick up industrial policy. For them, it may be the only game in town. As Walter Mondale's experience demonstrated, the voters prefer the real thing—a genuine to an ersatz conservative, particularly when the true conservative promises low taxes and continued prosperity and the imitation offers to balance the budget (who really cares?) by raising taxes. Democrats will get nowhere pretending that they are meaner than Republicans. Their party's history attests to the fact that few find the impersonation convincing.

The second distinction between neocons and neolibs focuses on the welfare state. By and large, members of the two factions share old-fashioned conservative criticisms of existing social programs as wasteful, administratively cumbersome, and poorly targeted. With fewer reservations than neoconservatives and, of course, far fewer than the social Darwinists within the Reagan official family, neolibs accept the reality of social distress and the responsibility of government to alleviate it. National health may return as a neoliberal issue less because of the inequities of health care exacerbated by current attempts at cost control than because these restraints on hospital treatment and limitations of private insurance benefits in the not-so-long run are more likely to increase than diminish health care's share of the GNP. The emergence of an underpaid proletariat of surplus doctors may persuade the traditionally conservative medical profession that there are fates worse than government employment. If welfare reform again surfaces as a public issue, neoliberals are likely to return to some sort of federally administered negative income tax as a replacement for the anarchy of the existing nonsystem. Although neoliberals are unlikely to appreciate his company, Jimmy Carter was the first neoliberal president and his scheme for welfare reform, the ineptly titled PBJI (Program for Better Jobs and Incomes) was a technocrat's answer to the puzzle of reconciling work incentives and a decent level of assistance to the needy.

It is easy to scoff at neoliberals and even more tempting to dismiss their followers as a small, trendy group of young urbanites who have received more media attention (yuppies proliferate in television and on newspapers) than they deserve. Yet their alliance with hi-tech, their distrust of bureaucratic solutions, and their confidence in "pragmatic," nonideological responses to the needs of the voters all echo popular American beliefs.

What the neoliberals urgently require for 1988 is a candidate as attractive as Jack Kennedy, himself in some ways a precursor of neoliberalism. Can the neoliberals sweep into the Oval Office? Possibly. Can they cope successfully with the management of the American economy? The answer, for reasons to emerge in due course, is probably not.

6

What, finally, of the secular left? Can that left rise again? It might be more accurate to phrase the question simply, Can the left rise for the first time as a political winner at the national level? Shouldn't wistful democratic planners, income and power redistributors, social democrats, and left liberals recognize the futility of their dreams and enroll in supply-side academies for the ideologically handicapped?

Such fashionable despair as these queries imply is both unwise and a self-indulgent counsel to quietism. Consider that former loser Ronald Reagan. He launched his presidential campaign in 1964 when he delivered a famous speech in flaming support of Barry Goldwater, whose premature Reaganism was as soundly thrashed by Lyndon Johnson as George McGovern and Walter Mondale were beaten by Richard Nixon and the finally triumphant Ronald Reagan. For sixteen years, Reagan held firm to a set of principles that, in the 1960s and the first half of the

*Introduction*

1970s, were derided as those of the kooky far right. Kooky or not, to an astonishing degree the public has come to accept these very articles of Reagan faith as conventional political wisdom. Democrats who dream of regaining the White House by imitating Republicans delude themselves.

Nor will a politically victorious alternative to the conservative "opportunity society" define itself as something simply different from currently popular deification of businessmen, competition, and allegedly free markets. Renewed recession and unemployment may tarnish the public reputation of corporate titans without persuading the voters that the politicians waiting eagerly in the wings will perform better than those occupying center stage. The fate of the left in Great Britain should suffice to warn believers in the pendulum theory of politics that losers don't become automatic winners after the public sours on politicians too long in power. Mrs. Thatcher won a resounding victory in 1983 after presiding for four years over the highest levels of unemployment since the Great Depression. She was aided of course by a popular little war in the Falklands, much as Ronald Reagan benefited from the Grenada invasion. And her opposition was conveniently split between the Labour Party and the Liberal-Social Democratic Alliance. But the split itself testified to the bankruptcy of a Labour Party riven by conflict between its moderates and radicals. It was indeed that exercise in fratricide that drove Labour eminences like Shirley Williams and Roy Jenkins out of the party in which they had spent their political careers and inspired them to take the risky decision to form a new party. No comfort to opponents of Mrs. Thatcher that the Alliance and Labour collected considerably more votes than did her Conservatives. As in the United States, pluralities are all that are needed to win elections.

This is only to reiterate the necessity of developing an agenda, organizing an effective coalition of forces, and inspiring coalition members. Where are the troops? They are numerous but disorganized and frequently at odds among themselves. They include middle-class activists on environmental and nuclear issues; progressive trade unions like the machinists and auto workers; women in the labor force increasingly animated by the rallying cry of comparable worth; Jews, blacks, and Hispanics; liberal communicants of the churches and synagogues;

xlvii

and the neighborhood groups, sometimes in the spirit of Saul Alinsky, who mobilize against construction projects like New York City's Westway, nuclear power plants like Long Island's Shoreham, and the flight of steel mills from the industrial Midwest. In Washington, the spirit of the 1960s is not even a spectral apparition, but in cities and towns the aging heirs of the 1960s and many young recruits remain faithful to the vision of grass-roots change and participation.

The question still nags: how are the partisans of disparate causes ever to get together? Environmentalists detested Westway, but members of construction unions supported it as a source of new jobs. Within unions, men and women frequently clash over the incompatibility of affirmative action and seniority rules; comparable worth soon may become equally divisive. Secular liberals and radicals who applaud the bishops' criticisms of the performance of the American economy detest official Catholic doctrine on abortion and contraception. Women and civil libertarians diverge over the regulation of pornography. Blacks and Jews quarrel over affirmative action. The AFL-CIO takes a harder foreign policy line than otherwise compatible liberal academic intellectuals judge acceptable. So it goes in the ranks of the undisciplined army of the left.

Under Reagan, the conservatives got their act together, but it is always easier for the party of property to unite beneath the standard of profit and wealth, allies otherwise distasteful to one another. Partisans of change traditionally have a harder time agreeing upon the kind of change they want most. Do the bishops have the winning strategy for the inchoate left? I don't think so. The eminent, earnest, and evangelical economist Alfred Marshall reluctantly concluded that it was prudent to rely upon the strongest, not the highest, of human motives— self-interest rather than altruism. As admirable and often moving as the pastoral letter is, with its emphasis on alleviating the plight of the poor as a first priority of public policy, that emphasis is unlikely to appeal to neoconservative Ben Wattenberg's unpoor, unblack, and unyoung majority. At least implicitly, the bishops call upon the prosperous to share their good things with the less fortunate. Self-sacrifice is rarely popular, especially in a society that glorifies consumption.

Yet there are issues and even passions, the theme of this

volume's final chapter, susceptible to harmonizing the diverse interests of a winning anticonservative coalition, issues more significant to most or all elements than the matters upon which they continue to disagree. Among them, full employment is by far the most important. Here is an objective capable of attracting even conservatives who fret over welfare cheating and welfare costs, liberals who agonize over power, and the Catholics who follow the lead of their hierarchy in deploring the powerlessness of the poor and the inequitable distribution of income and wealth in Reagan's America. The Mondale campaign's most glaring weakness was total absence of credible commitment to the full-employment targets of the Humphrey-Hawkins Act.

Full employment—the 2½–3 percent unemployment that introductory economics textbooks a generation ago advanced as a minimum in a free society—improves working conditions for blue- and white-collar workers and strengthens their unions. It converts the largely failed promises of affirmative action into genuine jobs and promotions for women, blacks, and Hispanics. It facilitates a tempo of economic growth rapid enough to give impetus to comparative worth and minimize disruptive impact upon male workers. Any economy that tacitly accepts 7 percent joblessness as its measure of full employment opts for frightened employees; constant pressure upon pay scales; conflict among such potential allies as young, older, male, female, white, and black workers; and a tilting of the interest group balance even more one-sidedly in favor of large corporate employers.

Bankers, economists, conservative legislators, and other partisans of sound money gravely warn that full employment is inflationary. The appropriate response to this partially justified caveat, of course, is controls over key prices, wage bargains, and profit margins, either directly or via tax-based income policies that reward economic actors who exhibit wage or price restraint with tax refunds or punish the willful with tax penalties.

Full employment greatly reduces, although it cannot entirely eliminate, welfare dependency. Here the not excessively expensive corollary to full employment is the sort of reform vainly floated by the Nixon and Carter administrations, a negative income tax whose benefits extend beyond welfare recipients to fully employed but badly paid members of the working poor, hovering around the poverty line. Last time around, powerful opponents of welfare reform concentrated much of their criticism upon the inclusion of the working poor. Quite accurately, they scented the heresy of mild income redistribution. But what is wrong with that, so long as care is taken to redistribute from the top to the bottom fifth in income?

Welfare reform promises to unite the working poor and the welfare population. If anything, however, it intensifies the resentment of better-paid manual workers and the middle class proper. For that resentment, part of the treatment is, at last, comprehensive health care, a thriftier option, as will later be seen, to our present wildly expensive combination of nonprofit and for-profit hospitals, health insurers, entrepreneurial doctors and dentists, and public subsidies. Medicaid is the most valuable and most expensive of benefits to the poor. Those not quite poor enough to qualify understandably resent the privileges of those only slightly worse off than themselves.

Who will pay? In the first place, welfare costs will decline as will food stamps and unemployment compensation transfers within the context of steady-state full employment. In the second, a slimming diet for the Pentagon will release large sums for more sensible expenditure than enlarging the Weinberger collection of deadly toys. And finally, genuine tax reform crafted to collect fair shares from corporations and affluent individuals will pour huge new revenues into Treasury coffers.

Compassion is a luxury of the prosperous. A fully employed economy shrinks the number of losers, enlarges the company of winners, and enables the latter at small personal cost to treat the former generously. A fully employed economy makes labor scarce and employers solicitous. Almost certainly the route to greater workplace autonomy is not imitation of Japanese quality circles. It is the guarantee of a job to every willing worker.

In relying upon self-interest as the strongest of human motives rather than altruism, higher but weaker in his esteem, Alfred Marshall was frequently but not invariably correct. Reagan's 1980 victory could with some stretching be interpreted in the grammar of self-interest, although only by ignoring the affront to national pride daily reiterated by the Iranian hostage crisis. The man did promise lower prices, more jobs, and rising

*Introduction*

living standards to voters disconcerted by soaring inflation, lofty interest rates, and unemployment high by the criteria of the 1960s and 1970s. Individual calculation of financial gain fails to explain Ronald Reagan's 1984 landslide, which encompassed farm states injured by falling crop prices, industrial states where unemployment rates were particularly high, union members who ignored the administration's hostility to organized labor, and women who forgave the president his opposition to the Equal Rights Amendment and the remainder of the feminist agenda. Mr. Reagan's masterly deployment of traditional emotions, America as Number One, America uniquely the land of opportunity, and America as that shining city on a hill, exempt from the mean passions of mere Europeans and Asians, simply swamped the calculus of self-interest. On the Republican horizon looms no 1988 candidate who approximates Reagan's virtuosity in the mobilization of political passion. For Democrats, Mario Cuomo seems best able to combine individual selfishness and aspirations to the general welfare. Successful politicians at the national level, as 1984 once again demonstrated, do not win on purely economic grounds. The greediest of our number like to think themselves capable of high-minded conduct.

*Chapter 1*

# Why Reagan Won

IN LATE 1965, a middle-income taxpayer, in point of fact a university professor like myself, could buy a new eight-room colonial with two and one-half baths on one-third of a casually landscaped acre in Stonybrook, hard by the aspiring Graduate Center of the State University of New York at Stonybrook, Long Island, for a mere $24,000. In those dear, dead days beyond recall, the better-than-tolerable terms on which bourgeois comfort could be purchased included a 95 percent mortgage over a thirty-year term at a fixed rate of 6 percent, for in the financially unsophisticated 1960s no one in America had heard of variable-rate mortgages. I write out of the additional recollection that I grumbled at 6 percent as a usurious increase over still-lower rates in the recent past and mourned the 4 percent, zero-down-payment mortgages available right after World War II under the GI Bill of Rights. Even harder to believe, property owners didn't expect to double their money in two or three years, and move on to grander houses on ever-bigger lots in suburbs of rising prestige. When, three years later, I tired of the bucolic life and returned to the security of the West Side of Manhattan, I disposed of the house at a profit of merely $4,000.

I shall return shortly to the economy of the 1960s, but it is well to digress for the moment and recall how that decade is now recalled by those who lived through it and share their boring recollections with the unhearing young. Much more colorful events tend to blot out mundane economic statistics. Seldom were the times more tumultuous. Events crowded upon each other in a fashion bewildering to staid types fresh from the placidity of the Eisenhower reign of the 1950s. Civil rights marches and political assassinations, mass anti-Vietnam demonstrations in Washington and occupation of university presidents' offices and computer centers by militant student activists, urban commotions starring militant youths and enraged welfare mothers, the flowering of the women's movement and gay rights agitation, the police riot in Chicago at the 1968 Democratic convention, and more, much more, all turned the evening news programs into serial melodrama, more exciting than any episode of "Hill Street Blues" ever managed to become.

The young and the outrageous, overlapping categories, vied with each other to offend straight America. Students for a Democratic Society, which started as a rational movement of the semi-Marxist left, drifted into the futile violence of the Weatherpeople. Blacks and whites collaborated in the early history of the Student Nonviolent Coordinating Committee, but mounting black rage expelled whites and junked peaceful resistance as a tactic. As Martin Luther King, Jr., had warned white moderates in his 1963 "Letter from a Birmingham Jail," his powerful call for civil disobedience to unjust, racially discriminatory legislation and practice was all that protected the white majority from the violence of Malcolm X, Eldridge Cleaver, Huey Newton, Bobby Seale, and other black partisans of direct action, grouped as Black Muslims or Black Panthers.

Drugs spread from inner-city ghettos, where they could be ignored or even tacitly endorsed as diverting idle teenagers from gang warfare into chemical stupor, to middle-class high schools and then junior highs. Jack Kerouac and Allen Ginsberg celebrated in prose and poetry the states of consciousness attained by judicious doses of LSD and other hallucinogens. Timothy Leary, a lecturer in psychology, strained Harvard tolerance beyond its limits by preaching drug liberation in classrooms. Such are the oddities of American culture that two decades later, after serving a prison sentence, Leary toured the college lecture circuit in tandem with G. Gordon Liddy, himself a penitentiary veteran for his role in the Watergate caper. In Suffolk County, New York, at 5 A.M., the sheriff and two score deputies armed with shotguns descended on the Stonybrook dormitories on the hunt for drugs, publicity, and political gain. Until the fickle media shifted their attention,

Stonybrook was dubiously celebrated as the drug capital of the collegiate university—a distinction that it probably did not merit. Middle America was as morbidly fixated upon the wild conduct of the young as it was two decades later upon the shenanigans of the wealthy and powerful.

Suffolk County's finest did discover drugs in the dormitories as well as some decidedly irregular rooming arrangements. For the young, at least those in the colleges favored by media attention, not only scorned alcohol and tobacco, their parents' placebos, in favor of pot and harder stuff; they openly flouted the professed morality if not the actual conduct of the older generation. Birth-control-pill protection against undesired pregnancy seemed to sever the connection between sexual gratification and procreation and complete its link with sheer hedonism. Middle-class parents grew accustomed to their children's live-in boy- and girlfriends. Many homosexual as well as straight couples formed long-term relationships as staid as matrimony. On the wilder fringes of the feminist movement, some "progressed" from assaults on male chauvinist pigs to serious reservations about heterosexuality as an organizing social principle.

Little was sacred. Bumper stickers advised motorists to "Support Your Local Police—Give a Cop a Bribe Today." Draft resisters burned their cards publicly. Some sewed American flags to the seats of their pants. There were lawyers prepared to defend such conduct as symbolic speech protected by the First Amendment, legal reasoning unacceptable to that aging paladin of the First Amendment, Supreme Court Justice Hugo Black, who declined to merge speech and this kind of action.

Nevertheless, for the conventional, the Supreme Court was a problem of its own. Still dominated by Chief Justice Earl Warren—whose appointment Dwight Eisenhower came to regret as his biggest presidential blunder—and his liberal colleagues, it sponsored disruptions in traditional social and institutional customs. One series of decisions edged close to the definition of welfare as a right rather than an exercise of public charity, a momentous semantic shift. Charity can be reduced or withheld at the option of givers, but rights invoke constitutional guarantees of due process and invite judicial review of welfare agencies' administrative procedures. A second line of cases expanded civil rights enforcement, putting teeth into school-integration efforts by mandating busing and validating affirmative action as a remedy for sexual and racial discrimination in employment. But probably nothing enraged conservative critics of the Court and boomed the sale of "Impeach Earl Warren" bumper proclamations more than famous decisions like *Gideon*, which affirmed the right of an accused felon to a lawyer; *In re Gault*, which extended adult legal protections to juvenile offenders; and, most of all, *Miranda*, which required arresting officers to inform freshly arrested prisoners of their right to remain silent and obtain legal counsel. If anything infuriated critics as much as *Miranda*, it was the famous (or notorious) exclusionary rule. That rule excluded from criminal trials evidence illegally gathered by the police. To hear opponents of the rule, it annually set free armies of armed felons primed to make the streets, subways, and buses combat zones.

Enough? There was more. Allegedly doctrinaire liberals interpreted separation of church and state in ways without constitutional mandate. According to such scholarly critics as Richard Morgan,[1] the Court, in its misguided attempts to keep unbreached Jefferson's "wall of separation" between religion and politics, unfairly excluded children enrolled in church-sponsored schools from such benefits as bus transportation, lunches, and special education. Not content with this imposition of unwarranted financial burdens upon the parents of children in Jewish day schools, Catholic parochial schools, and Protestant academies, the Court took to undermining the disciplinary authority of public school principals and teachers. As the indictment complained, the Court, by creating children's rights as something akin to due process in criminal proceedings, tied the hands of school administrators. To expel, suspend, or consign to a special school a disruptive pupil was to invite a lawsuit all too eagerly conducted by the rights-inebriated litigators of the American Civil Liberties Union and their allies in the federally funded Legal Services Corporation.

Partisans of the Warren Court were pleased that its liberal majority had, at last, thrown the cloak of constitutional protection over the shoulders of blacks, women, children, criminals, the disabled, and other previously unfairly exposed groups of

## Why Reagan Won

Americans. Opponents were no less certain that the Court had almost frivolously undermined the authority of the police, churches, schools, and elected public officials. Willingly or not, Earl Warren and his colleagues had contributed mightily, in the words of political scientist Richard Morgan, to "disabling America." Those who deplored the Warren Court and all its works often viewed the rights explosion as little more than a contest between professional elites—on one side older lawyers representing traditions of institutional authority, and on the other young legal tigers recently sprung from Ivy League law schools and eager to make their mark quickly as challengers of almost everything conservatives held precious.

For some the collapse of authority and moral standards was signaled by student occupation in 1968 of several Columbia University buildings, including the administrative center, Low Library. The spectacle of bearded, presumably drug-taking students and their female companions screaming obscenities at the "fuzz" and inviting police reprisals which, when they came, were predictably excessive, bewildered and depressed middle-class parents. The disorderly scene enraged working-class mothers and fathers who could not afford to send sons and daughters to Columbia or to Harvard, where a rerun of the Columbia melodrama occurred a year later. On both campuses, the police, blue-collar in class origin, took comprehensible pleasure in cracking the skulls of pampered, middle-class adolescents who failed to appreciate their own good luck at attending America's best colleges and universities. At Harvard they had waited three centuries for their crack at retributive justice. Where had these upper-middle-income adolescents acquired the sheer bad manners to rummage through Columbia president Grayson Kirk's office and smoke his cigars? What gave incompletely educated college students the right to junk university curricula and substitute "relevant" courses of their own devising? Tenure and promotion decisions were difficult enough without student participation in their making.

As in any social movement, the liberation and empowerment themes of the rebels contained good sense alongside weird doctrine and offensive conduct. Civil rights for blacks were disgracefully late in arriving, a century after the Civil War. Sexual discrimination did and still does unfairly handicap women in the job market. Particularly in the South, welfare was administered punitively as though to be in need deprived the poor of the ordinary protections of citizenship. If, as optimistically advertised, universities are communities, there was a reasonable case for enlisting students in the governance of campuses. All too frequently these good causes were sabotaged by fringe extremists, flamboyant blacks overturning capitalism on the evening news, equally photogenic women advocating liberation through lesbianism, anti-Vietnam demonstrators taunting the police as pigs and fascists, and so on.

Success in American politics requires recruitment of allies, not public contempt and derision of potential friends. This was a truth perceived by young supporters of Gene McCarthy's antiwar candidacy in 1968. Beards were shorn, hair was cut, and attire tidied so that the independent voters of New Hampshire that snowy March would pause and heed the soft-spoken case for their hero. "Clean for Gene" was a sacrifice worth the making. Such are the cultural ironies that numerous McCarthy supporters thought he was a Vietnam hawk, possibly because he looked and sounded even more respectable than the participants in his children's crusade.

The enthusiasms of the 1960s crested in 1972 in the nomination of George McGovern. Senator McGovern was, and no doubt is, a man of strong religious conviction and powerful belief in the traditional virtues of marriage and the family. Mr. McGovern represented South Dakota, a conservative state inclined to select Republicans for public office. He had been a university teacher and he possessed an earned doctorate in history. The man was as straight as it is bearable for a human being to be, possibly even straighter. But his political record made him the candidate of the crazies along with the sensible. His early opposition to the Vietnam War, his advocacy of civil rights for blacks and homosexuals, his sympathy for the women's movement, and his endorsement of a version of a negative income tax to replace welfare all resonated agreeably in the ears of new-era liberals. Unfortunately for the senator, it was the fringe of radicals, acting out their bizarre passions, who, at the Democratic nominating convention, preempted prime television time to demonstrate and denounce, and thus compelled their candidate to deliver his acceptance speech at 3

A.M., long after the hard-working electorate had flicked the set off and retired to their beds.

For a great many middle- and working-class Americans, Democrats and Republicans, the politics of the 1970s and 1980s registered their revulsion against the outrages of the 1960s. Ronald Reagan's tough handling of the California campuses enhanced his popularity. In the same state, S. I. Hayakawa's defiance of radicals at San Francisco State College propelled him into the United States Senate. Reagan very nearly snatched the Republican nomination in 1976 from Gerald Ford, a sitting president. Even in the wake of Watergate and Ford's politically disastrous pardon of his disgraced predecessor, Richard Nixon, Jimmy Carter barely edged Mr. Ford out. A born-again Christian, an advocate of prayer and opponent of abortion, a partisan of smaller government, and a professed outsider in Washington, Mr. Carter could not disclaim support from blacks, activist women, and the remainder of the still-active fringe constituencies of the fevered past.

And despite the hesitancy of his domestic policies, Mr. Carter did undeniably appoint a great many feminists, blacks, consumer advocates, and miscellaneously liberated types to the bench, the regulatory agencies, and the executive branch of government. Out of their crowded cubbyholes, Naderites emerged, blinking, into the sunshine of power and decent salaries as custodians of auto safety, worker protection on the job, honesty in advertising, and candor in stock flotations. Bad enough in the eyes of Republicans, conservative Democrats, and true believers in competition, red in tooth and claw. Even more outrageously, the man also refused to participate in crusades against abortion and for school prayer. He tolerated pub crawling on the part of some of his helpers. No excuse that he prayed daily, agonized publicly over his shortcomings, and taught a Sunday school class all during his four years in office. No matter that Ronald Reagan seldom attended church, was on poor terms with some of his own children, and had been divorced from his first wife. As Jimmy Carter would not, Ronald Reagan sang the songs of "Christian" America and recalled his fallen-away followers to a golden age of strict sexual morality, temperance, neighborly charity, upstanding individualism, and public prayer. Perhaps the public prefered Ronald

Reagan's easygoing inconsistency to Jimmy Carter's pious effort to lead his daily life in as close proximity as possible to the injunctions of the Gospels.

At the end of the 1970s, the breakdown of conventional morality; the prevalence of crime and drug abuse; the sense among the mature and elderly that the young were out of hand; the general loss of confidence in teachers, politicians, businessmen, lawyers, doctors, the military, and the clergy; the renewed menace, real or contrived, of the Soviet Union in Afghanistan and Central America; and the disorders of the economy all seemed to merge as a psychodrama of general drift and disorder. Nobody seemed to be in charge. Jimmy Carter's notorious "malaise" speech, in effect an admission of his own inability to mobilize the groups which had elected him, was scarcely calculated to reassure the electorate that their president commanded men and events. Conceivably, if the hostages in Iran had been released before the 1980 election or if the rescue mission had succeeded instead of collapsing in disarray, the country's and Mr. Carter's morale might have recovered. As events actually unrolled, the voters turned gratefully to a candidate of transparent optimism and self-confidence. Ronald Reagan then and later never gave a sign of inability to cope with either domestic or foreign responsibility. At the end of four years in office, he looked younger than he had in January 1981. By contrast, his chief of staff, James Baker, had aged a decade. As the joke went, the president had delegated aging, like other onerous tasks, to his helpers.

Only economists believe that financial self-interest is the single or even the major explanation of personal and political behavior. People respond to patriotic appeals and to the Moral Majority's agenda of "social" issues. They are concerned about the adequacy of police and fire protection, the quality of public education, and the behavior of their children. Graffiti in the subways affront New Yorkers as symptoms of social disorder. Violence and pornography on television attract legions of viewers and offend legions more, two groups whose membership overlaps. This is to say that those who interpret the rightward drift of American political sentiment essentially as a cultural phenomenon may have grasped the root of the matter.

These so-called "social" issues were perhaps as powerful in

1976 as in 1980, but they did not suffice to win nomination for Ronald Reagan or victory for Gerald Ford. People do not vote only their pocketbooks, but they are unlikely to neglect entirely the impact of the economy upon their personal finances. Hence there is an alternative or at least complementary hypothesis deserving of exploration. It focuses upon the fortunes and misfortunes of working families in their daily lives as employees, home buyers, and shoppers in supermarkets and showrooms. It suggests that the emerging conservatism of the 1970s and its triumph in the 1980s reflect economic dislocation at least as much as social and cultural disaffection.

2

Men and women on factory and office payrolls fared well in the 1960s, a rare decade of steady economic growth unmarred until 1969 by recession. In 1977 prices, workers in the private economy averaged a $165-weekly wage in 1960. Ten years later the figure had climbed to $183.20, an 11 percent improvement. Production workers in manufacturing fared substantially better. Their pay increased from $183.50 in 1960 to $208 ten years later, a nearly 14 percent advance. When more generous medical and other fringe benefits are counted in, a worker who filled the same position for ten years was substantially better off in 1970 than in 1960. In Detroit and other auto centers, high school graduates, diplomas in hand, walked into General Motors and Ford employment offices and, like their fathers, uncles, and brothers before them, got assembly-line jobs, which, after a brief probation, promised middle-class incomes for semiskilled labor until retirement. A union card came with the job. The United Automobile Workers had an enviable record of improving the pay and benefits of its members, as did other industrial unions in the 1960s in steel, machinery, glass, electrical equipment, and rubber tires.

In the 1960s, prices behaved themselves and inflation was generally dismissed as an un-American affliction. If the 1967 consumer price index is taken as 100, prices stood at 88.7 in 1960, edged upward in seven years 1 or 2 percent each twelve months to the 1967 figure, and even after the inflationary impact of Vietnam touched 116.3 in 1970. In those primitive times, acceleration of inflation between 1967 and 1970 to 5 percent each year alarmed financial markets and political analysts. Gentle inflation confers upon the public the blessings of sound currency, confidence that a dollar will buy this year much what it bought last year and will most likely command next year. When unions bargain for 3 percent wage gains, the extra money is real, not an inflationary mirage.[2]

To rising incomes and sound money was added steady employment. In the period's worst year, unemployment for all workers averaged 6.5 percent. This was 1961, the first year of John Kennedy's thousand days. The activists in the Kennedy administration greeted the figure with alarm and as the occasion for vigorous response. For the rest of the decade, unemployment never exceeded 5.5 percent. For four consecutive years— 1966–69—fewer than 4 percent of the labor force were jobless, just about the minimum amount of "frictional" unemployment possible in a market where people are free to leave jobs, small businesses can close or open without restraint, and a tiny minority lack salable skills even in an active labor market. Low unemployment strengthens unions and diminishes the fears of workers. If pay or working conditions displease, other employers are hiring.[3]

As usual, blacks fared less well. In those four years, 1966–69, of particularly low general unemployment, their incidence of joblessness ranged between 6.4 and 7.4 percent, numbers that, nonetheless, in the 1980s were taken as encouraging for the entire labor force. Textbooks and politicians regarded 3–4 percent general unemployment as genuine policy goals. Much of the job-training efforts of the Kennedy-Johnson era were directed at minority workers in the hope of narrowing and ultimately closing the gap between them and the white majority.

Until late in the decade, tax burdens were comparatively tolerable, the personal income tax was mildly progressive, corporations paid substantial sums to the Treasury, and payroll taxes to finance Social Security were light. The contrast between the 1960s and the 1980s is sharp. Millions of Americans, earning low or moderate incomes, now pay considerably more in Social Security contributions for their retirement than the Internal Revenue Service collects as personal income tax. The

1986–87 rate, 7.15, is scheduled by 1990 to reach 7.65. By contrast, in 1960 only 3 percent was subtracted from paychecks and, although this figure had risen to 4.4 percent by 1968, much larger increases were to occur in the years that followed. By 1981 the Social Security levy had crept inexorably up to 6.65. In contrast to personal income taxes, the Social Security tax is highly regressive. Because it applied only to wages and salaries under $4,800 in 1960, but rose to a maximum of $7,800 by 1970, it collected a far higher percentage of income from moderate and low-income earners than from their more affluent brethren. Thus an employee who earned exactly $7,800 paid $374.40 toward Social Security in 1970. Someone earning ten times as much also paid this sum, and consequently was assessed at one tenth the rate of the poorer citizen. Moreover, the higher one is on the income scale, the larger is the percentage of gross income derived from dividends, capital gains, royalties, rent, and interest, none of them subject to Social Security tax.[4] In the 1960s, Social Security deductions were an annoyance and a tax inequity but not yet the burden they were soon to become.

For ordinary folks, personal income taxes changed very little during the 1960s. The 1964 tax act, initiated by John Kennedy late in 1962 and pushed through Congress early in 1964, somewhat reduced tax liabilities and the 1968 tax surcharge slightly increased them. But the tax bite was comparatively gentle and, perhaps more important, grew more savage only very slowly. Thus, after 1964 and before 1968, a 14 percent rate applied to the first $1,000 of taxable income (after exemptions and deductions), edged up to 15 percent on the second thousand, 16 percent on the third, 17 percent on the fourth, and 19 percent on additional income between $4,000 and $8,000.[5]

At these rates, in the noninflationary context of the period, bracket creep was scarcely a problem. No blue-collar worker could sensibly boggle at opportunities for weekend work at time-and-a-half rates on the ground that the IRS would mulct him of a substantial fraction of his extra earnings. For that matter, higher-paid doctors, lawyers, and executives needed to earn more than $52,000 in taxable income before taxes on the portion of their income in excess of $52,000 exceeded 50 percent. During the 1960s, the personal income tax was a progressive but far from confiscatory levy that extracted slightly higher percentages from the prosperous than the less fortunate majority. The 70 percent rates at the top of the tax schedule vastly exaggerated the actual impact of personal taxation. Exemptions for dependents, generous allowances for business expenses, deductions for mortgage interest and property taxes, acknowledgment of charitable contributions, and a great many more imaginative tax-saving loopholes diminished actual tax payments by the affluent far below the severe numbers in the tax tables. Still, the apparent steepness of the rate structure—the populist gap between 14 percent at the low end and 70 percent at the top of the income pyramid—soothed the general public and cost the rich amazingly little. No one loves a tax collector, but popular rebellion against taxes awaited the 1970s and 1980s.

In the haze of retrospect, the 1960s often appear in the media as an era of profligate spending on social programs of dubious merit, wastefully administered and targeted at undeserving and deserving recipients indiscriminately. Closely inspected, official statistics related a less exciting and more complicated tale. Of course, the global figures appear to support critics of the welfare state who fear for the solvency of the fisc. In 1980 dollars, federal outlays on social insurance, education, public aid, veterans' services, and health and medical care rose from a modest $73.6 billion in 1950 to $129.9 billion in 1960, $281.9 billion in 1970, and $492.2 billion in 1980.[6] These expenditures amounted to only 3.7 percent of the gross national product in 1950, 4.9 percent in 1960, but an impressive 7.8 percent in 1970, and a majestic 11.5 percent in 1980. Care needs to be taken. Indeed the statistician's favorite sport of disaggregation must be indulged as an aid to comprehension. In 1950, Social Security was a fledgling, a decade and a half old. Not many over-sixty-fives were eligible for benefits, and the ratio of workers to pensioners was high. Naturally, as time passed, the number of beneficiaries rose and the ratio between working contributors and retirees dropped. Moreover, in the mid-1960s, Medicare came into existence as a supplementary benefit to Social Security retirees. The pensions and medical care of Social Security do indeed improve the condition of the elderly poor, but their beneficiaries are heavily middle class. Pensions and Medicare whose costs dominate social spending consist very substantially of transfers within the middle class, from its younger to its older members.

How significant were these essentially middle-class programs in the social welfare expenditure explosion? Still in 1980 dollars, total federal expenditures on social insurance, education, and public aid amounted to $73.6 billion in 1950, $129.9 billion in 1960, $281.9 billion in 1970, and $492.2 billion in 1980. The sums are impressive even if they are adjusted for a larger population. Let us perform that adjustment. The cost per capita of social welfare (as ever in 1980 dollars) was $480 in 1950, $712 in 1960, $1,354 in 1970, and $2,140 in 1980. Does it not make the flesh creep to realize that between 1950 and 1980, just thirty years, considerably less than half a lifetime, expenditures by each of us on social welfare had considerably more than quadrupled?

Perhaps so, but look again where the checks flowed. Social insurance at $101 per capita in 1950 was about 21 percent of social expenditures. Enlarged to $263 per capita ten years later, it was nearly 37 percent of 1960's $712 per capita total. By 1970, the comparable numbers were $507 per person for social insurance, $1,354 for total social welfare, and a 37.5 percent share for social insurance. By 1980, per capita social insurance was $994 of the entire social welfare expenditure of $2,140—over 46 percent of the total. One might apologize for the dreary arithmetic were it not essential to correct the widespread conviction that in the 1960s and the 1970s lavish subsidies to the poor bankrupted middle America. Rich Americans rent politicians. Middle Americans vote. Poor Americans remain home on election day. The political payoffs shovel whipped cream to the wealthy, pastry to families of moderate income, and crumbs to the poor.

Other fruits of expanded New Deal programs and fresh Great Society initiatives flowed to the middle class. Medicare, veterans' benefits, and federal subsidies to elementary and high schools lightened middle-class burdens. And, of course, new programs required the services of credentialed, middle-class professionals of many kinds—job trainers, psychologists, social workers, program evaluators, lawyers, and administrators. There was, as the ancient gag ran, money in poverty, just as nowadays funding is ample for inventors of ever more esoteric weapons.

Nor did the first Reagan administration trim appreciable federal subsidies to the middle class. The *Wall Street Journal*, whose record of opposition to federal spending is unblemished, examined early in 1985 the ways in which an imaginary family in Sacramento, California, lived the better for federal initiatives.[7] In this journalistic fable, Mr. "Center," a rock-ribbed Reaganite, earns an annual income of $40,000 from the sale of insurance. The Centers had a college-age daughter. They paid low electricity rates because the Sacramento Metropolitan Utility District bought 25 percent of its power from the federal government. Mrs. Center wanted to open a delicatessen to be financed by a loan guaranteed by the Small Business Administration. The Centers borrowed money at subsidized interest rates to send their daughter to the University of California. The daughter's Amtrak fares to and from her campus covered only a third of the cost of service. The remainder was a federal subsidy. A small airline serves Sacramento. Without still another federal subsidy, it would probably discontinue the Sacramento route. Federal support of mass transit keeps bus fares down for the Centers. The family enjoy summer camping holidays in Yosemite National Park. They are delightfully inexpensive, a mere three dollars admission charge for the family car and seven dollars per night for a campsite. Reagan's 1986 budget proposed tripling these heavily subsidized fees. The local hospital will be compelled to raise charges to private patients if the percentage of Medicare reimbursement is reduced from the 80 percent of the amounts currently charged private patients. Finally, if revenue sharing were eliminated, Sacramento would lose the $5 million now used to support part of the $45 million fire-fighting budget. The city's manager predicted that "We wouldn't just lay off firefighters. We would probably cut the money from our parks and recreation programs and our libraries, defer the maintenance of roads, that sort of thing. It would be a real blow." Few middle-class families, no doubt, pause to compute the value of the benefits they derive from the federal government. They are exceedingly substantial.

It is possible, nevertheless, to overstate the case. Although a

## Why Reagan Won

large percentage of a growing welfare state's disbursements went to the middle class, not astonishing in a middle-class society, something new did happen in the mid-1960s. Lyndon Johnson's war on poverty, at least for the time being, transformed public perceptions of what it meant to be poor. The older conception of poverty featured individual misfortune or inadequacy. The generous were expected to relieve misfortunes.[8] Most inadequacies were the deserved consequences of laziness or other weaknesses of character. The dustman in George Bernard Shaw's *Pygmalion* mordantly skewered Victorian attitudes that sought to distinguish between the deserving and the undeserving poor. Hearken to his philosophy:[9]

> What am I, Governors both? I ask you, what am I? I'm one of the undeserving poor: that's what I am. Think of what that means to a man. It means that he's up agen middle-class morality all the time. If there's anything going, and I put in for a bit of it, it's always the same story: "Youre undeserving; so you cant have it." But my needs is as great as the most deserving widow's that ever got money out of six different charities in one week for the death of the same husband. I don't need less than a deserving man: I need more. I dont eat less hearty than him; and I drink a lot more. I want a bit of amusement, 'cause I'm a thinking man. I want cheerfulness and a song and a band when I feel low. Well, they charge me just the same for everything as they charge the deserving. What is middle-class morality? Just an excuse for never giving me anything.

Were a fifth of the American population really victims of either bad luck or their own shortcomings? Once the federal government defined the notion of a poverty level and began to count the number of people below it, it turned out that in the midst of general affluence there were large numbers of people still badly fed, wretchedly housed, and poorly clothed. To say in the buoyant emotional climate of the mid-1960s that they were mostly personal failures was unpopular. When, in 1965, Daniel Patrick Moynihan released a report on the black family that emphasized connections between poverty and female-headed families, charges of racism caused the Johnson administration in which Moynihan served to disavow findings that, to vociferous critics both black and white, appeared to blame the victims of racial discrimination for their own troubles. It followed that poverty must be rooted in the social and political context of racism, sexism, and a distribution of influence and power that militated against the success in particular of the urban poor. In Mayor Daley's Chicago, even in Mayor Wagner's New York, school, protective, and other services were scanted in low-income neighborhoods and unfairly concentrated wherever the affluent congregated. City hall pays attention to slum dwellers only when ghetto violence, gang wars, and drug traffic threaten respectable neighborhoods.

If poverty is society's fault, society ought to amend its failings and do its best to compensate those neglected in the past for their losses of opportunity, income, and status. For a spell in the 1960s, a genuine political response to poverty enlisted the support of numerous solid citizens abruptly sensitized to the institutionalized injustices of their community. A generation ago, public perception of social problems led to serious efforts to resolve them. One remedy was statutory attention to such civil rights as fair housing; nondiscriminatory hiring and promotion; voting; equal access to motels, restaurants, and other public accommodations; and desegregated schools. The general public, outside of the South at least, was ready to embrace civil rights legislation. As later events demonstrated, Northerners no more than Southerners were convinced that appropriate remedies included numerical goals for the hiring of women and blacks, or mandatory busing for the objective of school integration.

In sheer financial terms, legislative and judicial affirmation of civil rights is inexpensive. Other responses to poverty cost money. Title I of 1965's Elementary and Secondary Education Act targeted funds to inner-city, lower-income school districts. Head Start was designed to help the preschool children of the poor catch up with the luckier progeny of the middle class. Food stamps and special nutritional aid to pregnant women, infants, and young children ameliorated dietary deficiencies. Medicaid began as free medical care for those below the poverty threshold. A variety of expensive programs sought to provide decent housing. Both residential and nonresidential job-training efforts were initiated.

## Why Reagan Won

In the 1960s, when most of these innovations were just beginning, their dollar cost was comparatively small. As late as 1970, food stamps were only a $577 million federal budget item. Ten years later, their cost had ballooned to a figure in excess of $9 billion. In 1960, half a decade before the enactment of the Elementary and Secondary Education Act, one of that ex-schoolteacher Lyndon Johnson's favorite projects, the federal government furnished $868 million in subsidies to cities and states. That sum trebled by 1965 and more than doubled between that year and 1970. By the time Ronald Reagan was campaigning against Jimmy Carter in 1980 on the theme of big government, subsidies to public schools stopped just short of $13 billion.[10] The sums register the normally rapid rate of growth in new programs, a bulge in the number of school-age children and, after 1973, acceleration in inflation rates. Still, the raw numbers did tend to reinforce public perception that government was growing faster than taxpayer capacity to finance it.

Or inspect that most horrible illustration of cost escalation, the health sector. Health and medical programs cost the federal government a modest $604 million in 1950 when Harry Truman was president. They nearly tripled to $1,737 million in 1960 at the end of the Eisenhower years. By 1965 they were approaching $3 billion, by 1970 closing in on $5 billion, and in 1980 exceeded $13 billion.[11] Federal Medicare costs rose from $6.2 billion in 1970 to $57.5 billion in 1984.[12] Medicaid cost the federal government $2.6 billion in 1970. By 1984 the figure had swollen to $20 billion.[13]

One way of simplifying this buzzing confusion of numbers is to inspect the rate of increase in federal social expenditures after allowing for inflation. In 1973 prices, 1966 federal spending rose 18 percent over the preceding year. In succeeding years ending in 1974, rates of increase were 10, 9, 8, 15, 11, 12, 5, and 8.[14] True, once more much of the money flowed to middle-class recipients, but there were well-publicized exceptions, the most resented among them public assistance, a category which includes cash benefits, free medical care, food stamps, and social services. Between 1965 and 1969, in constant dollars, public assistance rose 90 percent and between 1970 and 1974 an additional 82 percent.[15] It is fair to say that in the fifteen years between the mid-1960s heyday of the Great Society and the watershed 1980 presidential election, welfare-state benefits expanded at unprecedented rates most of all for the middle class but very significantly as well for the poor.

What should be made of this record? Let us postpone to the next chapter any effort to assess the success of Great Society initiatives, and here measure the American version of the welfare state by international criteria. To begin with, despite Great Society additions to New Deal social benefits, the American welfare state in 1980 was by European criteria an incomplete, irrational, and ungenerous affair. The Union of South Africa and the United States are alone in the industrialized world in their failure to offer health protection to the entire population. Only the Soviet Union and South Africa incarcerate comparable percentages of their population. The Great Society's quarter loaf was free or nearly free care for the elderly (Medicare) and for the poor (Medicaid). In the late 1970s and 1980s, the percentage of medical care covered by Medicare steadily declined and the proportion of low-income families eligible for Medicaid steadily diminished.

We treat children in particular much less generously than is the Western European and Scandinavian habit. One careful inquiry[16] focused on vulnerable families, those with working and nonworking single mothers, low earners in one-earner families, the long-term and short-term unemployed in one-earner families, and families with four or more children. The authors contrasted these families with typical one- or two-earner families. Representative incomes from both groups were then compared. In Sweden, a single unemployed mother of two young children received support from the government equal to approximately 94 percent of an average unmarried production worker's earnings. For France, the figure was 79 percent and for Germany 67 percent. New York, historically the most generous state, provided 55 percent, and Pennsylvania was in the top third in the generosity rankings at 44 percent.

Moreover, Sweden, France, and Germany all provide universal children's and housing allowance. Public assistance standards are national instead of our irrational, bureaucratically cumbersome, and expensive patchwork of state-set benefit levels, work requirements, and widely varying administrative standards. Nowhere is the contrast between Western Europe and this country sharper than in the handling of unemployment compensation. The European objective is maintenance of an unemployed worker's normal living standard or a close approximation of it. In France and Denmark, unemployment benefits last as long as three years. Here they expire at the end of six months, except when Congress enacts emergency extensions of thirteen or at most twenty-six weeks. Much higher percentages of the unemployed are eligible for benefits in Europe than in the United States, and the benefits themselves are more generous. Swedish payments replace 78 percent of a worker's normal income, Austrian 70 percent, and West German 63 percent. The corresponding American figure is 44 percent.[17]

Not many Americans collect social statistics as a hobby. Sports records are considerably more popular. Even if more Americans were equipped to contrast European and American practice, they might deny the domestic relevance of European experience. A question that became increasingly popular in the 1970s was whether the country could afford the welfare services it was offering, however parsimonious these might seem by European criteria. The burden of social expenditure is bearable even when in absolute dollars it increases rapidly if the economy is growing at least as rapidly and if there are no urgent competing budgetary demands upon the federal government. Between 1960 and 1968, the economy did expand steadily without recession and until 1967 without inflation. After that date Vietnam expenditures continued to grow even more steeply than they had in late 1965 and 1966. Congress, in 1968, after dragging its feet for more than a year, raised taxes. In 1969, the first recession in nearly a decade raised unemployment and slowed growth. OPEC's successful price coups in 1973 and again in 1979 produced that malign combination of unemployment and inflation dubbed stagflation by Paul Samuelson. Real incomes stagnated and refused to resume normal rates of expansion in the Reagan years.

It is one thing, as in the mid-1960s, to combine expanding Social Security and a war on poverty with a substantial tax cut, and quite another to ask workers of moderate incomes to pay marginal tax rates as high as 35 or 40 percent on incomes artificially enlarged by inflation. This is to say the cost of social welfare escalated at politically the worst of possible times. Social welfare became an expensive tax burden just when in the 1970s average families found themselves coping with tight budgets, spells of layoff, inflation, and energy shortages. Many middle-class families thought of themselves as poor. Many of their children perforce contented themselves with smaller cars and housing accommodations than those of their parents.

Again, other people's troubles rarely console one. In Europe, stagflation was a more acute problem than here at home. For one thing, until North Sea oil began to be pumped in significant quantity, Europe was far more dependent on OPEC than was the United States. OPEC's epic redistribution of global assets in its own favor was certain to generate dislocation in the best managed of economies. Richard Nixon, Gerald Ford, and Jimmy Carter were more unlucky than maladroit in the conduct of economic policy. Ronald Reagan was the heaven-blessed legatee of OPEC's declining market power in the 1980s as energy conservation reduced demand for OPEC fuel and new wells came into operation outside of cartel control.

This is all very well in retrospect. What ordinary citizens knew in the disordered 1970s was that prices seemed to rise daily in supermarkets. Fuel costs compelled them to swap their beloved gas guzzlers for small, boxy compacts and subcompacts. Property taxes escalated as assessors took account of rising property and home prices. And the federal income tax, usually amplified by state and sometimes municipal levies, took bigger pieces out of inflation-shrunken paychecks.

Whom to blame? In 1968 it was Hubert Humphrey's misfortune to be vice-president in an administration that had turned the Vietnam War into a national calamity and Richard Nixon's great good fortune to be in a politically plausible position to promise an end to that conflict. In 1976 it was Gerald Ford's bad luck to be held responsible for the economic disorders that followed OPEC's 1973 quadrupling of energy prices and Jimmy Carter's opportunity to win as a critic of Ford policies. Fickle fate turned the tables on Jimmy in 1980. Many of the same things Carter had boringly said about Ford were now repeated far more effectively by Ronald Reagan about him. Truth without affect rarely elects or reelects presidents.

3

America is the land of pragmatism, the word and the philosophy that were the coinage of William James. As a philosophy, pragmatism is America's single claim to originality. Pragmatists are problem-solvers. To criticize rarely suffices. Critics are challenged to propose their own, presumably superior solutions to dilemmas ill-handled by officeholders. Demolition justifies itself only by the promise of subsequent construction. Ideas and proposals are the province, the customary role of intellectuals, located until recently somewhere on the liberal or radical political left. In his classic collection of essays, *The Liberal Imagination*, Lionel Trilling asserted that "In the United States at this time liberalism is not only the dominant but even the sole intellectual tradition. For it is the plain fact that nowadays there are no conservative or reactionary ideas in general circulation." Trilling immediately warned that "This does not mean, of course, that there is no impulse to conservatism or to reaction. Such impulses are certainly very strong, perhaps even stronger than most of us know. But the conservative impulse and the reactionary impulse do not, with some isolated and some ecclesiastical exceptions, express themselves in ideas but only in action or in irritable mental gestures which seek to resemble ideas."[18] Trilling wrote his preface in 1949. Three years later Dwight Eisenhower ended the Roosevelt-Truman era but accepted the legacy of the New Deal and never sought seriously to repeal its innovations in social legislation, and assorted subsidies and protections to farmers, unions, homeowners, and bank depositors.

It was not that the men and women in Eisenhower's official family or Republican allies in Congress and state legislatures lacked conservative impulses or refrained from "irritable mental gestures." In their different styles John Foster Dulles and Joe McCarthy were professional purveyors of such gestures. What was missing was any large, generalized conservative sentiment as a counterpoise to the combination of moral stance and social ideal that Trilling took to define liberalism. Trilling, deploring the absence of strong conservative opposition worthy of liberal steel, quoted John Stuart Mill, who recommended that liberals pray for conservatives in words like these: "Lord, enlighten thou our enemies . . . sharpen their wits, give acuteness to their perceptions and consecutiveness and clearness to their reasoning powers. We are in danger from their folly, not their wisdom: their weakness is what fills us with apprehension, not their strength."[19] The opposition of the powerful mind of a Coleridge, argued Mill, could only strengthen liberals by exposing their weaknesses and complacency.

As Trilling was completely aware, nineteenth-century liberalism centered its hopes of human enlightenment and material progress in individual action, not government intervention. Mill, Gladstone's "saint of liberalism," took a view of human nature, though softened at the edges, that was essentially Benthamite. Men and women were rational creatures who, if properly educated, could make their own intelligent choices with minimal guidance from others, still less from government. People calculated pleasures and pains in accordance with that utilitarian strain in English thought which Bentham erected into a system.[20] As economic actors, workers gravitated toward higher-paid, pleasanter jobs and away from inferior alternatives. Farmers and businessmen sought the most profitable markets. By proper education, ordinary wage slaves could be converted to the great Malthusian truth that the only cure for poverty was limitation of human numbers. Once enlightenment spread to the working class, its members would marry late and bring fewer clamoring mouths into a world hard-pressed to feed them.

Grown-ups, with the notable exception of women, were responsible for their own welfare. An ardent feminist, Mill attacked the subjugation of women by men. It was only their dependent status that justified in Mill's eyes state intervention to regulate the working hours and conditions of women. For, as Mill reiterated, the general rule of economic life ought to be laissez-faire: free trade between England and the rest of the world, free choice of occupation and employers, free dissemination of ideas. Freedom promised more than rising living standards. It was the only route to the unfolding of human potentialities. Mill was more concerned about the intellectual and cultural condition of the average Briton than about his command of comforts and luxuries. Mill's liberalism in self-confident Victorian Britain was seamless. He was certain that progress toward universal rationality would make his fellow citizens as free politically, culturally, and intellectually as they were in the universe of commerce and contract. His vision extended far beyond the limited maximization objectives of the economists with whom he was raised.

Not that he rebelled against political economy. Mill's father, James, was a follower and popularizer of David Ricardo. As a child, John Stuart Mill knew Ricardo and Bentham and imbibed the clear truths of classical economics from them, Malthus, and the grandparent of their doctrines, Adam Smith. By mid-century, when Mill published his own *Principles of Political Economy*, the dominant text for more than a generation, almost every literate Englishman took for granted the virtues of economic liberty and the responsibility of each adult to enter into voluntary bargains with other adults. Mill's conception of liberalism was powerfully individualistic, though more substantially modified than he admitted by such exemptions from the sway of laissez-faire as support for public education, factory acts, and subsidized emigration.

Indispensable to it was confidence in the capacity of a laissez-faire economy to provide sustenance for its members. Here Mill took comfort from Say's Law. Jean Baptiste Say, a French disciple of Adam Smith, argued early in the nineteenth century that under the rule of free competition capitalist economies automatically reached equilibrium at full employment of men, resources, and machines. Why, after all, should a rational soul endure drudgery in a factory or shop save for his urgent need for the wages that could purchase food, clothing, shelter, and the pleasures of existence? He and his fellows were the market for the goods in the stores. Entrepreneurs could rest confident that the wages they paid would return to them as demand for goods.

Thrifty families saved part of their income. But saving was as much spending as direct expenditure on food and clothing. Once deposited in banks, savings were speedily loaned to businessmen who spent them on raw materials acquired from farmers, machinery that increased the incomes of other businessmen, and new workers who promptly spent their wages. Savers made their deposits because banks paid them interest. The banks could do so because they charged borrowers still higher interest. Employers in general could be certain that they could enlarge their operations and increase their sales up to the point where there were no more people to be hired, no more raw materials to be processed, and no idle machines to be started up.

Businessmen inevitably make mistakes. They produce too much of one item or too little of another. They set prices too high, so that customers flee, or too low, so that merchandise disappears before it can be replaced. However, wherever competition reigns, mistakes are almost self-correcting. Workers who lose their jobs offer their services at lower wages and promptly identify new positions. Factory owners shift from unpopular to fashionable products. Retailers run sales when their inventories begin to accumulate. Lower wages and prices stimulate renewed employment and production, and the economy expands to the limits of its capacity. The less-alert businessmen become insolvent. Stubborn workmen, unwilling to work at lower wages, remain unemployed until they yield to the logic of the market. Competition rewards the intelligent and the efficient and penalizes the incompetent. What better prescription for ever-increasing productivity and ever-improving material standards of life?

Shorn of Mill's concern for the quality of human life, and bereft of his respect for intellect, the rugged individualism of the Coolidge-Hoover era could claim at least a limited, economic kinship with nineteenth-century liberalism. Mill would not have cheered the decade's vulgar exaltation of wealth and the assurances from financiers that every man could be a millionaire if he steadily purchased common stock in Wall Street. The best authorities were certain that the bull market, unlike all previous bull markets, would last forever and ever.

Probably most citizens in the Coolidge era believed that each person was responsible for his own welfare. Thrifty folks saved to tide them over brief spells of unemployment and to prepare for old age. The adult children of the thriftless were responsible for their profligate parents. Churches and private charities cared for orphans and the mentally and physically handicapped. State intervention was minimal and properly so. It did not diminish Calvin Coolidge's popularity that he slept ten hours each night and supplemented his nocturnal rest with afternoon naps. No one, least of all the prospering business community, wanted an active governmental presence. The role of government was to cut taxes and get out of the way of thrusting businessmen. A somnolent president was an ideal White House occupant.

The individual autonomy exalted by the creed of rugged individualism was compounded of some fact and a good deal of myth. Loaded down by debt, farmers were victims of the vagaries of weather and foreign markets. Clothing and textile workers who lost jobs in the shrinking garment trades of New England and New York had few alternatives and no transferable skill. Small businessmen teetered on the brink of insolvency. For the average family to share in the consumer celebration meant heavy borrowing. Burdened by home mortgages and car-installment payments, few families could survive financially intact even a short stretch of idleness. Southern blacks sharecropped under conditions akin to peonage. The Ku Klux Klan regularly lynched "uppity" blacks. Anti-Semitism and anti-Catholicism were as popular in upper-class as in blue-collar circles. Ivy League universities enforced tight quotas against Jews and other undesirables.

To dignify it beyond its deserts, rugged individualism was one of those noble lies praised by Plato as myths that bind classes together and promote political stability. So long as the poor blame their poverty on themselves, they will leave the rich secure in their possessions. For once suspicion spreads that the rich bear responsibility for the deprivations of the poor, no millionaire can rest comfortably in his bed.

What turned rugged individualism into a term of derision and transformed the content of liberalism was of course the seemingly endless stagnation of the Great Depression. Who was autonomous in the 1930s? Not the hordes of unemployed, more than a quarter of the labor force in 1932 and 1933. Desperate men and women roamed the streets and rode the rails in search of nonexistent jobs at almost any wage. Not farmers who destroyed crops in fields because market prices were lower than the cost of transportation between farms and grain elevators. Not respectable, middle-class homeowners unable to meet mortgage payments. Banks drove farmers off their farms and expelled families from their homes. Not even autonomous, as it turned out, were America's arrogant industrialists whose clamor impelled Congress to enact and Herbert Hoover to sign the Smoot-Hawley Tariff Act, the steepest barrier to imports in American history.

Few were exempt from the hardships of economic shipwreck. Most Americans, pragmatic rather than ideological, turned to government for help. Roosevelt himself believed in fiscal prudence, balanced budgets, and individual initiative. He had campaigned against Hoover in 1932 as a big spender and promised once in the White House to slash the federal payroll and eliminate Hoover's deficits. Fortunately for his constituents, he was an indifferent student of neoclassical economics at Harvard and a politician of rare virtuosity who responded seriatim to the needs of the voters. Farmers got the Agricultural Adjustment Act to prop up crop prices. Businessmen got the National Industrial Recovery Act, a confused and chaotic experiment in corporate planning. Millions of the unemployed were put on Works Progress Administration payrolls. A new Homeowners Loan Corporation averted mortgage foreclosure. The Federal Deposit Insurance Corporation shielded savers from the consequences of bank failure. The Tennessee Valley Authority brought new payrolls and new hope to much of the South. The 1935 Social Security Act for the first time borrowed European provisions for the elderly, the unemployed, and the down and out.

By European criteria the American welfare state might have been a rickety, parsimonious, grudging affair, but it represented, all the same, a sharp break with the tradition of independence and self-reliance so recently in vogue. By the end of World War II, the foundation of classical economics, Say's Law, had crumbled under the continued demonstration that modern economies were anything but self-adjusting, that indeed the sort of equilibrium they attained was at persistently low levels of employment and activity, not at Say's cheerful full employment. This large-scale demonstration that Say had it wrong was complemented by the spreading popularity of the theories of John Maynard Keynes.

Keynes demonstrated as a matter of abstract analysis as well as of experience that full employment was an unusual phenomenon. Persistent unemployment, he maintained, was the direct result of too little spending. Either consumers, investors, or government bought too little to provide employment for the entire labor force. Unemployment ceased to be an individual responsibility: it was the result of mysterious macroeconomic maladjustments between the inclinations of investors and the behavior of savers. In the Keynesian universe, thrift ceased to be a virtue and became a vice, for there was no assurance that savings deposited in banks would pass rapidly into the hands of investors. Banks might be too timid to lend. Investors might be too gloomy to borrow. Where the pragmatic Roosevelt reacted to the pain of his constituents, Keynes justified intervention on grounds of high principle. Indeed, if there were persistent tendencies toward underemployment in mature economies, it was the government's obligation to create public employment as an ongoing activity.

Keynes not only sanctioned, indeed demanded, government intervention to create income and jobs—the tools of fiscal and monetary policy familiar to college students and readers of business sections in the newspapers—he also gave powerful impetus to the welfare state. If thrift more frequently than not generated unemployment and shuttered factories rather than new investment and economic growth, then politicians were wrong to stimulate saving. It followed that income maintenance in old age, illness, unemployment, and disability became even more clearly public responsibilities, and not merely on humanitarian grounds. These were the folks most likely to spend all or nearly all the public benefits that they received.

Keynesian liberalism registered itself immediately after World War II in the passage of the Employment Act of 1946. Although it was a much-watered-down version of a proposal that initially embraced a mild form of planning, the statute did accept public responsibility for the pursuit and maintenance of "maximum" employment. The words "full employment" were excised from the initial draft as too inflammatory. Institutionally, two new bodies came into being, the Council of Economic Advisers in the Executive Branch and the Joint Economic Committee of Congress.

The council has precisely as much influence on national economic policy as the man in the Oval Office grants it. In the 1960s, particularly in the three Kennedy years and the first of the Johnson years, economists were highly regarded. Walter Heller, as chairman of the Kennedy council, by all accounts, not excluding his own, succeeded in educating his master into the mysteries of fiscal policy. If the young president were to keep his promise to get the country moving again, then growth rates in output and employment needed to accelerate. All that was needed, as good Keynesians knew, was new spending by government, a substantial tax cut, or a combination of the two. The 1964 tax cut was widely acclaimed as a triumph of an idea—the central Keynesian advice to politicians that they can manipulate the economy so as to evoke from it desired levels of activity, income, and employment. *Time* paid John Maynard Keynes the tribute of placing him on its cover. By 1973, Richard Nixon was calling himself a Keynesian, a signal to some that Keynesian economics must be in trouble.

The 1964 tax cut was successful. Economic growth did pick up speed and unemployment did decline. There was a connection between a buoyant economy and the public reputation of government. Here was persuasive evidence visible in larger paychecks and rising living standards that the politicians and their economic helpers really knew what they were doing. As Walter Heller exuberantly put it in 1966, "Economics has come of age in the 1960s. Two presidents have recognized and drawn on modern economics as a source of national strength and presidential power. . . . The paralyzing grip of economic myth and false fears on policy has been loosened, perhaps even broken. We at last accept in fact what was accepted in law twenty years ago . . . that the federal government has an overarching responsibility for the nation's economic stability and growth. . . . These are profound changes. . . . And they have put the political economist at the president's elbow."[21]

Presidents understandably like to hear that they have new power, and none was more likely to be thrilled by the good tidings than Lyndon Baines Johnson, at last able in the White House to make the mark on history commensurate with his outsized ego. The Great Society—a phrase, horrified conservatives quickly discovered, coined by Graham Wallas, a leader of the English Fabian Socialists—was inevitably trumpeted in Texas-sized rhetoric, but it was a natural extension of New Deal liberalism. Most of the enduring innovations of the New Deal offered continuing benefits to the middle class. The poor had little in the way of savings to be insured. The Federal Housing Administration guaranteed mortgages for middle-class homeowners. Social Security benefits flowed overwhelmingly to the middle class and the top tier of blue-collar workers who collected larger checks for longer survival periods than lower-paid colleagues, particularly black, whose life expectancies were considerably shorter.

As a social vision, modern American liberalism is inclusive. It aims to diminish as near to zero as human ingenuity and political goodwill can manage the number of people shut out of decent jobs, effective schools, and comfortable housing. As usual, the gap between vision and political practice is discomfortingly wide. The New Deal, whose political health was hostage to an uneasy coalition of northern liberals and southern racists, ignored the black community and kept civil rights off its agenda. Frances Perkins was Roosevelt's Secretary of Labor, but the New Deal seldom placed women's issues high among its priorities. As for the poor, their problem was purely and simply lack of income. Once the economy revived, their skiffs would surely rise in the company of the larger craft of the more affluent.

LBJ's innovation was his attempt to bring into the American celebration blacks, women, and the millions of low-income families who somehow survived on the margins of society. In American terms, LBJ took an enormous gamble when he tried to embrace within the American celebration marginalized minorities. Great Society strategies promised to help the deprived, but they also implicitly threatened the traditional advantages of the prosperous, especially in the troubled school arena. Compensatory education and Head Start were designed to narrow the advantages middle-class parents offer their children over the progeny of the poor. Job training was to supply marketable skills and repair gaps in literacy. Community-action programs and legal services were to raise the poor out of their

## Visions and Nightmares

habitual political inertia. Model Cities and other housing programs were to eliminate slums. Medicaid was to supply free medical care of middle-class quality to low-income patients. Civil rights and voting rights legislation promised the black community access to public facilities, political office, jobs, and housing on equal terms with whites—at last. The Great Society rejected biblical advice that the poor were always to be with us. The empowerment of the powerless resembles a zero-sum game: more for the poor means less for the affluent.

To sum up, liberalism in the 1960s was optimistic, technical, and, in retrospect, a trifle utopian. Optimism centered upon perception of government as competent and responsible. The economists were not the only experts in possession of sharp-edged policy tools for presidential wielding. Sociologists and psychologists thought that they understood the culture of poverty and the etiology of crime and juvenile delinquency. This was the glorious moment of community-action strategists, urban planners, educators, counselors, motivators, social workers, and job trainers. In the social-work community, young radicals ridiculed the casework ethos that, from the time of Jane Addams and the settlement house movement she mothered, focused on the troubles of individual clients. Clients were troubled because an unjust and uncaring society had failed them. It followed that the appropriate social-work mission was one for activists who could lead the way to a transformed society and the elimination of social pathology. In retrospect, the Great Society went both too far and not far enough. Its empowerment visions frightened conventional liberals. What would professional credentials be worth when the poor took their fate in their own hands? Actual compromises on LBJ's part with entrenched professional and business interests in the design of Medicare, Medicaid, and subsidized housing added vastly to program costs and tagged liberals with the stigma of fiscal profligacy that continues to handicap Democratic presidential candidates.

Manifestly reach exceeded grasp. For one thing, the theorists knew less than they claimed to know. For another, for all the sound and fury, funding, particularly for the more innovative Great Society programs, was always inadequate. For a third, the most radical aspect of the Great Society, its attempt to politicize the urban poor, generated effective sabotage and outright hostility from the city halls of the land. Finally, Vietnam soon diverted both funds and public attention to Southeast Asia and away from inner-city ghettos. Whom the gods would destroy they make leaders of a democracy engaged in an unpopular war.

Nevertheless, there were in the 1960s and even in the early 1970s few if any respectable conservative alternatives to liberal economics and liberal confidence in government action. The monetarists and free marketers, led by Milton Friedman and his Chicago associates, were respected members of the economists' guild but a distinct professional minority. Keynesians continued to hold the high professional ground. Conservatives grumbled at the costs and asserted failures of social programs, but as the young David Stockman indignantly pointed out in 1975, congressional Republicans soon joined their Democratic opponents in voting appropriations which flowed into their constituencies for the benefit of their own supporters.[22]

Grumbling rarely suffices. However effectively housing, job training, mental health, or other federal programs were criticized, however substantial was the evidence that misconceptions of design as well as waste and mismanagement weakened their impact, conservatives were unlikely to eliminate or even seriously to curtail existing efforts unless and until they defined plausible alternatives to them. This was especially true of the sums expended on income maintenance for the poor and elderly. The parallel is close between the situation of conservatives twenty years ago and liberals in this decade. Congressional liberals have repeatedly failed to check the escalation of the Pentagon budget because they tacitly accept the conservative diagnosis of the Soviet threat, because military spending flows into their states and districts, and, most of all, because they fail to articulate convincingly any way to counter potential and actual Soviet designs other than continued accumulation of old and new weapons. So once it was for conservatives in the arena of social policy.

Not now. The not-so-long march to power that culminated in the ascendancy of Ronald Reagan drew its intellectual ammunition from the musings of a growing collection of publicists, sociologists, political scientists, cultural observers, and economists. The label applied to them and willingly accepted only by Irving Kristol, the most prominent of their number, is "neoconservative." What appeared in their early days to distinguish the neos from plain vanilla conservatives was reasonable civility of tone, reliance upon social science evidence, and exploration of more efficient alternatives to failed governmental strategies in any number of policy areas—school integration, job equality, housing, health service delivery, and so on. Central to their strategy was developing techniques of policy evaluation at least arguably neutral in their application. A casualty of their success in the Reagan era has been precisely the restraint that helped propel them to the seats of authority.

Among the numerous periodicals spawned by the new conservatives, it is convenient to take as a leading example one of the earliest and most influential, *The Public Interest*. Its co-editors were Irving Kristol, a Trotskyite as a City College student, subsequently an editor of *Commentary* and a severe critic of the critics of McCarthyism, and still later founding editor along with Stephen Spender of *Encounter*, published in London and secretly financed by the CIA; and Daniel Bell, once labor editor at *Fortune* and subsequently an Ivy League academic initially at Columbia and then at Harvard. The first issue appeared in the fall of 1965. "The aim of *The Public Interest*," said the editors, "is at once modest and presumptuous. It is to help all of us, when we discuss issues of public policy, to know a little better what we are talking about—and preferably in time to make such knowledge effective."[23] Kristol and Bell quoted approvingly Walter Lippmann's definition: "The public interest may be presumed to be what men would choose if they saw clearly, thought rationally, acted disinterestedly and-benevolently,"[24] like, presumably, the journal's editors and contributors. This typically Olympian statement casually disregarded cultural, class, and financial distortions of any human being's capacity to act disinterestedly and benevolently. The editors seemed to hark back to Plato's philosopher-kings, graduates of training rather more demanding than City College in the late 1930s where Bell and Kristol practiced adolescent polemics.

It attested to the difficulties of filling the periodical with high-quality alternatives to liberal remedies for social ills that the first dozen issues relied heavily on well-known liberals and even temperate radicals with records of respectable treatment of Karl Marx. One of the latter, Robert Heilbroner, joined Robert Solow, a card-carrying liberal MIT economist, in discussing the alleged threat to jobs represented by automation. A symposium on financing higher education drew upon the opinions of Clark Kerr, who headed the University of California during Ronald Reagan's gubernatorial years, and cherished academic freedom honorably enough to incur the wrath of both Ronald Reagan and Ed Meese. Christopher Jencks and David Riesman furnished two articles on Catholic colleges. Kenneth Boulding, a highly regarded liberal economist of suspicious pacifist tendencies, brooded over scarcity. Among other noted names in the liberal community or among the moderate left were Alvin Schorr and James Tobin, later to be a Nobel laureate, debating the merits of a negative income tax; the political scientist Samuel Beer on liberalism; and the anthropologist Elliott Liebow on fatherless children.

As the years passed, *The Public Interest*'s stable of dependable neoconservative contributors grew sufficiently large so that liberals appeared in its pages less and less frequently. And many of the regulars were as well known to general readers and as highly regarded by their peers as the established liberals. Steady contributors included Nathan Glazer, a former liberal who criticized affirmative action as a form of discrimination; James Q. Wilson, a Harvard expert on crime; Roger Starr, later to become a member of the *New York Times* editorial board, and a close observer of housing and urban affairs; William Gorham, a leading exponent of cost-benefit analysis; George Gilder, Jude Wanniski, and Paul Craig Roberts on supply-side economics; another Harvard political scientist, Samuel Huntington, on defense issues; the Harvard economist and controversial Reagan Council of Economic Advisers chairman Martin Feldstein on inflation; John Bunzel on comparable worth; Aaron Wildavsky on party politics; Thomas Sowell on black education; Daniel Patrick Moynihan on a variety of themes; and a great many other writers drawn from universities, the political arena, and the ranks of free-lance intellectuals. Their tone was frequently combative but almost always rational, practical, unillusioned about the potentialities of human behavior, and ever more entranced by the performance and potentialities of American capitalism.

The journal has been by no means free of rhetorical overstatement and polemical bias. What has won it attention and grudging respect even from opponents of its positions has been its characteristic emphasis upon social science evidence as a preferred analytical mode. Reliable evidence of human behavior is a tricky affair, subject to challenge and controversy. *Public Interest* writers have analyzed government reports, performed their own quantitative studies, organized seminars to evaluate seminal documents like the first Coleman Report on the public schools, and dissected bureaucratic regulations and Supreme Court decisions.

Much of a random issue's contents consists of sharp criticism of existing policies, among them affirmative action, school busing, environmental protection, subsidized housing, welfare, judicial sentencing practices, public education, and the finances of Social Security. More often than not, emphasis is not upon elimination of programs which maintain incomes or services for vulnerable groups, but instead upon more appropriate evaluation of program efficiency, if possible on the basis of actual experiment. Cost-benefit analysis received considerable attention in the journal. The cost-benefit analyst proceeds from the simple assumption that a program that costs a lot more than the estimated dollar value of its benefits is a bad program. The moral might be to seek the benefit in a more effective manner. Thus, in principle, one might compare the costs and prospective benefits of several modes of reducing traffic casualties: seat belts, air bags, higher minimum ages for drinking, fines for failure to belt up, mandatory jail terms for drunken drivers, or some combination of these possibilities.

It's not easy. Here is how William Gorham, a former Assistant Secretary in charge of program evaluation at the old Department of Health, Education and Welfare, put it in *The Public Interest*:

> The problems of benefits measurement . . . are not just technical; they are conceptual. It is far from obvious how the benefit of most health, education, and welfare programs should be defined. For example, Title I of the Elementary

and Secondary Education Act provided special funds to local school districts for the education of deprived children. What is it that we want to measure? Should we test the children to see whether their reading comprehension, or their arithmetic achievement, has improved faster than would have been expected? Should we ask them whether they liked school any better or felt more confident of their abilities? Should we wait and see whether they drop out of school less frequently, commit fewer crimes as teenagers, or go in greater proportions to colleges? Or shall we wait a decade or two and see how much they earn as adults, and whether, in fact, the cycle of poverty has been broken?

Nor was this the end of Gorham's difficulties:

> Even if we could conceptualize and measure the benefits of particular programs, there is the fact that benefits of different programs go to different people. Shall equal benefits to different individuals in the population be weighted equally? Is it equally important to raise the educational attainment of a suburban child and a slum child?

And so on and on.[25]

To Gorham's and the editors' credit, they did not underestimate the complexities of public-policy evaluation. Indeed, with friends of the technique like Gorham, enemies were not really necessary. But these very complexities were weapons against the best intentioned of federal interventions. A sensible alternative to expensive social programs of conjectural merit, argued *Public Interest* analysts, was the well-designed experiment. Such an experiment was in fact conducted on the vexed theme of income maintenance. The problem for both liberal and conservative critics of welfare was to design a mode of assisting those in need at tolerable financial cost and without undermining incentives to seek jobs. In thinly disguised form, ancient yearnings to separate the unworthy from the worthy poor surfaced yet again. One approach was the negative income tax. A leading NIT proponent has been Milton Friedman, who in 1962 proposed to substitute cash grants for welfare payments, food stamps, subsidized housing, and miscellaneous social services. Here is Friedman's summary of his scheme's merits:

> The advantages of the arrangement are clear. It is directed specifically at the problem of poverty. It gives help in the form most useful to the individual, namely, cash. It is general and could be substituted for the host of special measures now in effect. It makes explicit the cost borne by society. It operates outside the market. Like any other measure to alleviate poverty, it reduces the incentive of those helped to help themselves, but it does not eliminate that incentive entirely, as a system of supplementing incomes up to some fixed minimum would. An extra dollar earned always means more money available for expenditure.[26]

For free-market partisans the heart of the matter is the challenge of reconciling altruism, an often overrated sentiment, with the precious structure of personal incentive to productive effort and the equally vital liberty to spend as one chooses. Would ordinary humans, afflicted by Original Sin or original neurosis, bother to work at boring, repetitive jobs in the presence of an adequate guarantee of income in idleness? Friedman's response featured preservation of work incentives, first by making cash grants small and second by making certain that any individual improved his situation by accepting paid employment. Hence, for a 1962 family of four (when the poverty line was $3,000), Friedman's maximum grant was $1,500, half the poverty level, when no one in the family was working. If a grant recipient rustled up a part-time or ill-paid job, he or she would pay a tax of 50 percent on earnings. Someone fortunate or enterprising enough to locate a $3,000 job would surrender his or her entire $1,500 federal grant. But a $2,000 job would improve the jobholder's situation. His total income would rise from $1,500 to $2,500—the grant plus $1,000. The arithmetic of a grant at half the poverty level in combination with a 50 percent tax on any earnings guaranteed improvement in total income up to the point earnings touched the poverty level and the federal grant vanished.

Here seemed to be a neat solution to the nasty dilemmas of welfare. So neat indeed that it appealed to liberals like Yale's

James Tobin, who in 1966 formulated a considerably more generous version of the NIT. But how could one tell what basic grants and what tax rates on earnings affected the behavior of actual, living, cross-grained, relentlessly individual, breathing, sentient human beings? It was this uncertainty that helped scuttle Richard Nixon's variation upon Friedman-Tobin themes. Under the guidance of his domestic counselor, Daniel Patrick Moynihan, Nixon briefly cast himself in the role of Disraeli, the compassionate Tory who united rich and poor. Rumor went so far as to insist that Nixon had actually read Robert Blake's biography of Disraeli. Nixon's Family Assistance Program (FAP) was in fact centered upon an NIT. Who could tell how the poor would react or how much the program's costs would be? For this and other reasons, notably the opposition of conservatives who thought the scheme dangerously liberal and liberals who were outraged at Nixon's rhetoric and the low level of grants, FAP twice won favorable votes in the House of Representatives and twice died in the Senate.

It had a sequel. Congress funded a series of experiments in New Jersey, Pennsylvania, Indiana, and Washington State. Over a three-year period, researchers mostly from the academic world divided urban and rural subjects into control and experimental groups, offered the latter varying cash grants ranging from half the poverty level to considerably above that figure, and then brooded over the work behavior of their subjects. As might be anticipated, the experts continue to argue over the meaning of their findings. Daniel Patrick Moynihan, by now senior senator from New York, interpreted them pessimistically, as demonstrating a substantial negative impact on work effort as grant levels rose and, disquietingly, also promoting family breakup. Others were relieved that such negative impacts were comparatively limited. Some inveterate egalitarians even upheld the right of mismated, impecunious couples to split just like their middle-class betters and the glitzy characters in "Dynasty," "Dallas," and "Falcon Crest." And some wondered, harking back to Hawthorne effects, whether the experiment demonstrated anything at all. The abiding lesson of that famous inquiry[27] was that social experiments alter the conduct that they examine. People really can distinguish between real life and social science.

Social scientists who engage in policy evaluation tend to design studies likely to reinforce their own preferences and prejudices. Thus David Armor's survey of the impact upon scholastic achievement of school busing for purposes of racial integration demonstrated negligible gains for black youngsters. Liberals just as predictably challenged methodology and results. In the pages of *The Public Interest*, argument raged over educational achievement in general, the effectiveness of efforts to rehabilitate criminals, the costs and benefits of constructing New York's West Side Highway, the lessons of San Francisco's BART (Bay Area Rapid Transportation), the effectiveness in achieving their objectives of such federal agencies as OSHA and EPA, the economic and other merits and drawbacks of an all-volunteer military, the failed promise of methadone treatment of heroin addicts, and "The Rehabilitation of Punishment" as a response to crime.

Whatever the merits in given instances of its contributors' evidence and analysis, conservatives indisputably were setting the evaluation agenda for liberals and the latter were failing to counterpose equally authoritative, equally well argued, analyses of their own. *The Public Interest* has no liberal counterpart. The nearest approximation, Irving Howe's *Dissent*, harbors a high ratio of cultural and ideological commentary to the limited amount of social science inquiry in its pages. All very well in France where this style of writing is admired. Not so well in the United States where measurement and quantitative evidence are most valued.

Just to add to liberal discomfiture, journals on the right began to proliferate, among them the American Enterprise Institute's *Regulation* and *Public Opinion*, and the Heritage Foundation's *Policy Review*. A rising tide of monographs from these and other conservative think tanks also offered practical alternatives. These tended to substitute market remedies for bureaucratic ailments. Why not imitate the West Germans and meter pollution instead of setting unenforceable standards and struggling through the bureaucracy and the courts to impose them? Set the meter charges high enough and corporations will decide for themselves that it is cheaper to acquire filtration devices than to pay the emission bills. Conservatives (and some liberals) picked up on Milton Friedman's proposal to offer parents vouchers redeemable at schools of their choice—public, religious, or independent. Competition should improve the public schools. If it fails to do so, then other segments of the educational market will properly flourish. Vouchers are equally applicable in markets for health and housing. Why not give an eligible, low-income family a voucher redeemable for medical care or shelter of its members' own choice? Two important values are advanced: the efficiency encouraged among vendors by enhanced competition, and the freedom of choice accorded to the poor.

Similarly, cogent logic dictated unleashing the magic of the marketplace wherever it was thwarted by government regulation. Here was the argument that stimulated the Carter administration's deregulation initiatives in air travel and trucking. Its promise impelled the Reagan administration to push ahead in the financial and health sector. In the 1984 presidential primaries, two of Gary Hart's new ideas were Individual Retraining Accounts and pollution fees instead of attempts to regulate emission levels. The former was simply an extension of the voucher notion to men and women who wanted to acquire a new skill. Their vouchers were redeemable at the training or educational facility of their own choice. Here in fact is shared terrain between neoconservatives and neoliberals.

For better or, as I shall later argue, worse, the unleashing of competition not only in formerly regulated industries but also in the public sector is restructuring the manner in which all kinds of services are being delivered. Humana, Hospital Corporation of America, and smaller for-profit health operators have opened new hospitals and purchased old ones from cities like Louisville and universities like George Washington. By leasing offices to doctors in medical buildings adjacent to their hospitals, they have diminished the cherished image of independent entrepreneurship among medical practitioners. The doctor who refers too few patients to the Humana hospital fails to get his lease renewed. In another area, a private, for-profit corporation monitors minor offenders who are sentenced to house arrest. A device attached to the offender's ankle reports his location and guarantees that he will stray no more than seventy-five feet from his premises. States and cities are contracting with corporations to run prisons. At least one community has substituted a private security force for its own police.

I do not propose at this juncture to evaluate these phenomena. What is unmistakable is the force of confidence in free-market superiority to other forms of organization. What is worth reemphasizing is the distinction between this ethos and the sentiments of, say, libertarians. The latter propose to shrink government as near to invisibility as possible. Neoconservatives and their frequent allies, the neoliberals, propose to deliver social services more efficiently and therefore less expensively. They do not advocate elimination of public education or public services. They want to widen their variety and improve their quality.

If Lionel Trilling were still alive, he might be tempted to transpose liberal and conservative. It's the conservatives who now have a grip on powerful and attractive notions and the liberals who flounder feebly, their own faith in New Deal and Great Society programs weakening almost embarrassingly.

## 4

The time was right. The tunes were prepared. The minstrel had long advertised his availability for engagement. Ronald Reagan's charm, his rhetorical generality, allowed him to gather under the same, huge political tent traditional conservatives; neoconservatives; hard-line anti-Communist Democrats like Jeane Kirkpatrick, Michael Novak, and Ben Wattenberg; once-liberal Jews convinced that Reagan would be a firmer supporter of Israel than Carter; and the recently energized fundamentalists organized in Jerry Falwell's Moral Majority a.k.a. the Liberty Foundation. His professional performer's skill in projecting optimism, patriotism, traditional values, and the promise of endless bounty from an economy revivified by free enterprise contrasted as sharply with the gray personalities of Carter and Mondale as any casting director might have hoped.

In the age of television, elections increasingly are plebescites. Presidents and prime ministers speak directly to the voters over the heads of print columnists and their own party apparatus. Plato harshly criticized the direct democracy of Athens because it was the most demagogic, not the most rational, speaker who carried the day. Direct democracy condemned Socrates, the man judged the wisest of the Greeks by the oracle at Delphi. Fortunately, we do not sentence criminals or declare war by the immediate vote of the television audience. We do seem to elect our presidents and lesser officials much as the Athenians exiled unsuccessful generals and executed annoying philosophers. Soothing syrup appeals to the voters more than bitter truth.

*Chapter 2*

# It Really Was a (Nearly) Great Society

IS THERE ANYONE out there who believes that the Great Society DID NOT fail?

Conservatives of all varieties, neolibs, and the 1984 Democratic presidential nominee unite in trashing Lyndon Johnson's legislative progeny. Often the indictment is generic: government lacks the capacity to achieve the lofty goals of social policy formulated by Great Society planners. Reagan ideologues are convinced that private enterprise can better government's performance in just about every traditional function, including prisons, health services, fire protection, medical laboratories, geological surveys, maintenance, protective services, data processing, and transportation.[1] No war on poverty can end in victory so long as poor families are locked into lower-class attitudes of thriftlessness, immediate gratification, and skepticism about the benefits of education for themselves and their children.[2] Fragmented black families deprive male adolescents of authoritative paternal role models.[3] It is as hard to improve the culture of poverty as to convert the hierarchical managers of our great corporations to the merits of workplace democracy. Compensatory education is an inspirational notion, but Head Start and special programs for inner-city schools are pitiful substitutes for the cultural advantages middle-class moms and dads routinely lavish upon their children. Moral: don't waste effort, sympathy, and money on the recalcitrant poor.

As revisionist historians tell the tale, maximum feasible participation of the poor was a still more outré notion. The romantic utopians in Sargent Shriver's Office of Economic Opportunity had their sequences reversed. Middle-class people know how to manipulate the political process. Political apathy is one of the characteristics of poverty. When the poor acquire middle-class attitudes, they will shed their poverty even before their incomes ascend to middle-class size. Then and only then will their political participation become feasible. Moreover, middle-class reformers ought to think twice or thrice before stirring up class and racial passions of the sort that exploded in the urban riots of the 1960s. Just see how peaceful the cities are now that ghetto dwellers have come to understand that all they can anticipate from the Reagan administration in the way of social programs is more prisons and more police. In the Reagan era, housing for the law-abiding poor is a matter of indifference, but prison construction to accommodate lawbreakers is a booming industry.

Even if less grandiloquent criteria are applied to the Great Society, its critics judge it a failure. The Job Corps, probably the most successful Great Society training initiative, places only 35 percent of its alumni in conventional, private-sector jobs that are retained for decent periods. At $15,200 per year in 1984 prices, it costs as much to train an adolescent in a Job Corps installation as to send a potential yuppie to Harvard. Medicare and Medicaid costs have ballooned to budget-busting size. OMB budget battlers have shifted so much of the medical burden to the pensioners and the poor that the former now pay out of their own pockets as large a percentage of their incomes for medical services as they did in 1964 before Medicare came into being to relieve them of the financial anxieties of ill health. Most pensioners purchase expensive private medical insurance to supplement inadequate Medicare coverage. To make matters far worse, Medicare fails to pay for the soaring nursing-home and home-care needs of the seventy-five plus cohort of the old-old, an increasingly large segment of the population.

Education? For two decades federal funds have subsidized public elementary and secondary education and for a similar period paid Pell grants, work-study stipends, and subsidized loans to college students. The National Science Foundation, the National Institutes of Health, and the Pentagon have funded billions of dollars of university research. The results? In the mid-1980s, streams of reports from foundations and presidential commissions complain variously about the failure of the schools to convey basic literacy and numeracy to their students. Elite universities place embarrassing percentages of entering freshmen in remedial English classes. The universities themselves are faulted for turning themselves into educational cafeterias and trade schools to the neglect of their obligation to transmit the cultural tradition of the West. Celebrating his confirmation as Secretary of Education early in 1985, William J. Bennett mused aloud that he might offer his son, when he attains college age, $50,000 in lieu of four years in the Ivy League. With $50,000, the young man might in short order become a prosperous entrepreneur. At Harvard, his father darkly suspects, he might waste four precious years, not to mention stand the risk of falling into bad, radical company. Justifying his administration's plan to remove more than a million students from existing loan, grant, and work-study programs, Bennett suggested that the cuts "may require, for some students, divestiture of certain sorts—stereo divestiture, automobile divestiture, three weeks at the beach divestiture."[4] Belatedly, colleges are rushing to restore a semblance of intellectual discipline by instituting new common requirements or new core curricula, and frequently discovering that only a minority of their faculty are either willing or able to teach anything but their own specialties.

The lesson, sneer critics of social policy, ought to be visible to the meanest intellect. Even when the objectives of public action are specific and modest, such as the delivery of health care, education, and training to segments of the population who need these services, the government falls lamentably short of its aspirations, achieves what it does at inordinate, ultimately insupportable cost, or, worst of all, actually damages and enlarges dependent clienteles. Bennett appears to believe that less support to higher education will improve college curricula. Thomas Sowell, a leading black conservative economist, argues that affirmative action has retarded black upward mobility and shaken the self-esteem of middle-class blacks, uncertain whether their advancement was merited or arbitrarily decreed by federal quotas. Odd that the progeny of successful Ivy League parents

## It Really Was a (Nearly) Great Society

who gain preferential admission (affirmative action?) to the Stanfords, Harvards, and Yales that offer a competitive edge and occasionally a good education into the bargain to their graduates seem entirely capable of bearing the burdens of nepotism. They have been known to complain bitterly at the injustice of it all when nepotism did not suffice as an admission ticket.

The central charge against government, of course, stems from the conservative and neolib obsession with markets. It is their article of faith that these cherished institutions in all, or very nearly all, circumstances operate more efficiently, more sensitively, more flexibly, and inevitably less expensively than do government bureaucracies. It follows that even when the taxpayers desire publicly funded services, the private sector ought to be their preferred providers. Reduction of social protection is not necessarily the point of privatization. The Heritage Foundation, an impeccably reactionary think tank with excellent Reagan administration connections, has occasionally scolded conservatives for their emphasis upon reducing the flow of social, health, educational, and other public services. Instead, conservatives should be demonstrating how privatization can furnish as many or more services, of higher quality and at lower cost. At the local level, sanitation, protective, and other basic functions can be contracted out by competitive bidding to for-profit entrepreneurs. At all governmental levels, vouchers redeemable for health, housing, educational, and other services will offer recipients free choice among public, nonprofit, and for-profit providers. Why shouldn't low-income parents in Harlem enjoy similar diversity of choice of schooling for their youngsters as high-income types in Beverly Hills, Scarsdale, or Great Neck?[5] At their kookiest, Heritage types insist that government produces nothing of value, a serious knock at our armed forces, FBI, and CIA. All government does is shuffle around the taxpayers' hard-earned dollars, after subtracting an unconscionable percentage for bureaucratic overhead.

No more than random attention to the media suffices to collect a garland of instances in which public authorities have adopted an appropriately low posture in deference to the entrepreneurial sector. It was Humana, only recently weaned from its practice of calling the patients in its hospitals "customers," that lured Dr. William DeVries from the University of Utah with the promise of more generous funding for his artificial-heart experiments. As mentioned earlier, Humana and smaller operators are restructuring the health sector; acquiring voluntary, university, and municipal hospitals; attaching doctors to their hospitals by offering short-term office leases in nearby medical buildings; venturing into health insurance; and starting free-standing, outpatient medical and surgical centers in shopping malls.[6] Early in 1985, Humana owned eighty Medfirst clinics in thirteen states.[7]

No need to give up hope of training the unskilled and semiliterate just because federal specialists are ham-handed. Back in August 1984, according to a glossy kit hailing the event, "Ohio governor Richard Celeste (D) today visited the Third National Bank to applaud the early success of Ohio Works, a new Cleveland/Dayton-based division of America Works, a private corporation which recruits and trains entry-level workers for business from the ranks of those currently dependent on public assistance." The governor, a liberal in a conservative state, proceeded to claim that "America Works creates the capacity for a real public/private partnership where everyone benefits, and the success of Ohio Works in Dayton will lead the way for duplication in other cities where dependency on welfare is high, and where the government, recipients, and the taxpayers can be relieved of economic pressure through real jobs."

Third National was the first local business to contract for the recruitment, screening, training, and on-site supervision services offered by Ohio Works. The bank filled thirteen jobs with women previously on welfare. Everybody is enthusiastic: "This is not a social service program," boasts Ohio Works president Barbara Hayde: "We contract with employers to provide highly motivated people who want real jobs, for real pay, who can meet real expectations." Mitchell Sviridoff, who achieved fame as an urban planner in New Haven two decades ago, now heads and celebrates the Local Initiatives Support Corporation, "a national nonprofit lending and grant-making institution founded in 1980 to draw private-sector financial and technical resources into the development of deteriorated communities and neighborhoods."[8] Two presidents deplored the scarred landscape of Charlotte Street in the South Bronx, but it was LISC that in the midst of blight implausibly constructed ninety-one ranch houses, proudly maintained by their owners. Unfortunately no other builder has followed the example of LISC. Ninety-one families live better: the need is decent shelter for at least a million people in the five boroughs of New York.

Our heavily armed society now employs more private security guards than ordinary policemen on municipal payrolls. Super-patriots fund a small private army to fight for democracy side by side with Nicaraguan contras. The next step should be dazzlingly clear to libertarians. The Pentagon, a notoriously incompetent agency prone to the acquisition of fancifully priced coffeemakers, wrenches, and toilet seats inter alia, cries for privatization. Let General Motors, Exxon, IBM, and their peers get a chance to bid for pieces of the Pentagon as the only way to save on weapons procurement by offering the same bottom-line incentives as are now popular for prisons, hospitals, schools, and other public services. A private contractor might have hesitated to send marines to Lebanon for fear of damaging less than completely depreciated human assets, unless of course they were covered by appropriate private insurance. Similar computations might inhibit future Grenadas. No reason to exclude intelligence gathering and covert operations. That innovative corporate leader Harold Geneen, as boss of the International Telephone and Telegraph Corporation (ITT), offered the CIA $1 million to accelerate the overthrow of Allende in Chile. Because of pride, limited vision, fear of public reaction, or adequate funds of its own, the CIA declined ITT's help. No reason why large corporations who routinely engage in industrial espionage against rivals should not enlarge their operations in the national interest, at market prices, and replace the CIA, FBI, Defense Intelligence Agency, National Security Agency, and still more obscure spy enterprises.

2

Public-service entrepreneurship is fashionable, but it is quantitatively small. How rapidly it will grow depends in part on the durability of the nation's conservative mood and for the rest on how successful the entrepreneurs are. There are small public job-training programs that serve as useful models for entrepreneurs. The simple trick is in creaming the population. Enroll the most eager, the least educationally deficient, and the most teachable as your job trainees and you too can report high rates of placement, as has inevitably been the triumph of the Reagan administration's single jobs program, the meagerly funded Jobs Partnership Act, which was designed to create private-sector jobs only. What is to be done for the less teachable, more deficient, and least eager? There's the population no profit-seeker is likely to touch.

In the winter of 1986, New Yorkers enjoyed an instructive example of privatization in action. The city's Parking Violations Bureau had delegated to private companies collection of unpaid tickets. As the entertaining scandal unfolded, it became clear that the way to get such contracts was to pay off appropriate officials and politicians. In an otherwise dreary winter, an ambitious federal prosecutor and several local district attorneys jostled each other on the corruption trail. The borough president of Queens resigned his office and subsequently committed suicide. The Democratic party leader in the Bronx appeared to have enriched himself by hustling city contracts for at least one company in which he owned stock and stood to profit. A momentarily chastened Mayor Koch was reduced to reiteration of his own personal honesty and compelled to admit the dread possibility that he himself had committed some administrative blunders. In Yonkers and numerous other communities, private collection of garbage has been credibly suspected of mob control or infiltration. A skeptic could scarcely fail to note that the invariable citation of garbage collection as a triumph of privatization just might imply that it stands alone as a shining example of private enterprise and efficiency.

Prudent citizens unafflicted by ideology might hesitate before vaulting upon the entrepreneurial bandwagon to see whether there is anything at all to be said for the social policies of the 1960s. Start with an unlikely source, the 1985 *Economic Report of the President*.[9] I quote: "Evidence that poor people with hypertension can benefit from free medical care comes from a 'natural experiment' in which some adults were terminated

## It Really Was a (Nearly) Great Society

from the California Medicaid program in 1982. Blood pressure levels among terminated people with hypertension increased significantly during the six-month study period, compared with a control group."[10] And: "A growing consensus also suggests that infant and prenatal care can improve health outcomes."[11] One study showed that neonatal death rates (deaths of infants in the first twenty-eight days of life) were reduced by the Medicaid program. Another study found that women who seek medical care earlier during pregnancy suffer fewer miscarriages and stillbirths. Their babies are more likely to be normal weight than infants born to mothers who have received no prenatal medical attention. Medicaid, concede the three erudite economists responsible for the *Report*, has "improved the access of poor people to physicians and hospitals."[12] But it is startling to juxtapose the *Report*'s overall conclusion

> ... Medicaid has successfully met its legislated objectives. The primary emphasis of Medicaid was intended to be on persons whose economic status is beyond their control— dependent children, and the elderly, blind, and disabled. Access to medical care for these groups has markedly improved and with it have come improvements in the health of the poor.[13]

with this statement:

> Because of Medicaid's multiple criteria for eligibility, about twelve million people with income below the federal poverty threshold in 1980 were ineligible for Medicaid. At the same time, about five million of those eligible had annual family incomes at least twice the poverty standard.[14]

To non-Reaganites it would appear to follow that the health of twelve million poor people would improve if the multiple eligibility criteria were simplified. If anyone in the White House had read this report of departing economists, he might well have been appalled at this subversive implication that a social program ought actually to assist more instead of fewer people.

Social Security, by light years our most popular social program, dates back to the New Deal. But major enlargements of benefits and coverage were legislated in the 1960s and 1970s. How should this belated imitation of Otto von Bismarck's policies in the 1880s and Lloyd George's British innovations early in this century be evaluated? As its measure, *The Economic Report* compares the finances of the elderly and their juniors. The news is good:

> Thirty years ago the elderly were a relatively disadvantaged group in the population. That is no longer the case. The median real income of the elderly has more than doubled since 1950, and the income of the elderly has increased faster over the past two decades than the income of the non-elderly population. Today, elderly and non-elderly families have about equal levels of income per capita. Poverty rates among the elderly have declined so dramatically that in 1983 poverty rates for the elderly were lower than poverty rates for the rest of the population.[15]

For this dramatic shift, the despised feds deserve major credit: "Social Security benefits are the principal source of income for the majority of elderly Americans. Benefits comprise about 40 percent of the income of the elderly, and for 59 percent of the elderly households they make up at least 50 percent of their income."[16] Children have supplanted their grandparents as the age group most likely to suffer poverty and privation. Some ingenious logicians on the political right have argued not that benefits directed toward children and their families be increased, but that pensions for the elderly be curtailed, so that young and old can unite in poverty. Old-fashioned grumblers just might argue that the incidence of poverty is disreputably high in all age groups.

As usual, facts matter much less than mythology. Americans simultaneously feed upon a menu of federal and state benefits, angrily resist attempts to curtail them, and persevere in their distrust of bureaucrats bearing gifts. In the early 1960s, some 27 percent judged that "government is run by people who don't know what they're doing." By 1980, the figure was 63 percent. Nearly 80 percent of the public in that year were convinced that the government was wasting large sums of the taxpayers' hard-earned dollars.[17] Evidence rarely overwhelms emotion, let alone prejudice sedulously fostered by anti-government candidates for the presidency and lesser offices. Nevertheless, the evidence merits systematic inspection, category by category.

## POVERTY

In all situations more promising than the absolute nutritional deprivation of Ethiopian famine or Nazi concentration camps, poverty is contextual. Some people are poor because their community defines others as prosperous. So it has always been. The extravagances of the poor outraged eighteenth-century English mercantilists inflamed with the desire to keep wages low the better to compete for markets with French and Dutch rivals, much as our own free marketeers advocate lower blue-collar wages and benefits the better to match foreign competition. Here was one social commentator's list of the extravagances:

> 1. snuff-taking, 2. tea drinking, 3. ribbons, ruffles, silks, 4. dram drinking.
>
> Have not extravagance in these articles contributed greatly to make labor and the servant's wages run so high? . . . From whence it follows a great loss of hands to our manufacturers and agriculture; extravagant high wages and great expense of labor, and obstruction and diminution of our trade at home and abroad.[18]

Or savor the comments of the well-known agricultural expert, travel writer, and all-round pundit Arthur Young on the same theme: "The employment of women and children is drinking tea with white bread and butter twice a day; an extremity that may surely be called luxury in excess! No wonder rates are doubled."[19] One could hardly start too early in combating the natural laziness of the poor. Here is a respected eighteenth-century clergyman's prescription:

> When these children are four years old, they shall be sent to the county workhouse and there taught to read two hours a day and be kept fully employed the rest of their time in any of the manufactures of the house which best suits their age, strength and capacity. If it be objected that

at these early years they cannot be made useful, I reply that at four years of age there are sturdy employments in which children can earn their living; but besides, there is considerable use in their being, somehow or other, constantly employed at least twelve hours in a day, whether they earn their living or not; for by these means we hope that the rising generation will be so habituated to constant employment that it would at length prove agreeable and entertaining to them.[20]

President Reagan has not yet endorsed child labor as the therapy of choice for juvenile delinquents, but his notorious anecdotes featuring the use of food stamps to acquire vodka and welfare queens chauffeured in Cadillacs from welfare center to welfare center truly echo eighteenth-century distrust of the poor.

As living standards in the industrialized West rose during the nineteenth and twentieth centuries, the deprivations of poverty become increasingly psychic. Most Americans define poverty as income less than half the national average. That figure, more than $13,000 in early 1985, spells prosperity in Spain, Greece, and Israel and affluence in Pakistan, China, Bangladesh, and most of the rest of the world. The poverty line itself is a statistical artifact of the 1960s, a suddenly required quantitative gauge of success in the war against poverty much as in the same period body counts measured the proximity of light at the end of interminable Vietnam tunnels. A Washington civil servant, Mollie Orshansky, noted that American families in the 1960s typically spent one-third of their income on food. She then added up the prices of the items of a food basket that provided balanced nutrition for a family of four and multiplied by three. Probably not a real, live American family could tolerate the tasteless items in the low-cost diet or get through the week without an occasional beer (not included), pack of cigarettes (not included), or feeding of popcorn (not included). Still, Dr. Orshansky's invention, updated for inflation and adjusted for family size, continues to be our definition of poverty. It is undoubtedly a standard that substantially understates the size of the poverty population. For one thing, most

## It Really Was a (Nearly) Great Society

### THE POVERTY POPULATION: SELECTED YEARS[22]

| Year | Number Below Poverty Line | Percentage of Population |
|------|---------------------------|--------------------------|
| *All Races* | | |
| 1960 | 39.9 | 22.2 |
| 1965 | 33.2 | 17.3 |
| 1970 | 25.4 | 12.6 |
| 1975 | 25.9 | 12.3 |
| 1980 | 29.3 | 13.0 |
| 1981 | 31.8 | 14.0 |
| 1982 | 34.4 | 15.0 |
| 1983 | 35.3 | 15.2 |
| *White* | | |
| 1970 | 17.5 | 9.9 |
| 1975 | 17.8 | 9.7 |
| 1980 | 19.7 | 10.2 |
| 1983 | 24.0 | 12.1 |
| *Black* | | |
| 1970 | 7.5 | 33.5 |
| 1975 | 7.5 | 31.3 |
| 1980 | 8.6 | 32.5 |
| 1983 | 9.9 | 35.7 |

families now spend a quarter or less of their take-home pay on food. Multiplying the minimum food budget by four would substantially but realistically add to the millions now officially allowed to call themselves poor. For another, statisticians ignore persuasive evidence that low-income families pay higher prices than their middle-class neighbors. They have access to fewer supermarkets and lack the cash to take advantage of occasional quantity discounts and store sales.[21]

Whatever its flaws, the poverty line does offer a convenient way to compare numbers over time.

No, the unconditional war against poverty did not end in total victory, but in 1978, midway in the despised Carter administration, the 11.4 percent incidence of poverty for the entire population was just a trifle more than half the 22.2 rate for 1960 inherited by John Kennedy from the Eisenhower administration. Failure was sadly blatant for blacks whose incidence of poverty diminished only slightly prior to the

Reagan administration and since then has climbed faster than that of whites. No reason to wonder that over 90 percent of black voters in 1984 supported Mondale-Ferraro. Although nothing good supposedly occurred during the Carter years, halving poverty could well stand as a substantial accomplishment.

The official statistics which record only cash income substantially underestimate the actual improvement in the situation of the poor wrought by federal intervention—food stamps, other nutrition programs, subsidized housing, and especially Medicaid. By the second half of the 1970s, the percentage of the population below the poverty line declined to a range of 4–8 percent from 1960's 18 percent, once noncash benefits are taken into account. As one careful analyst summarized the record,

> When one takes all income except that transferred to individuals through governmental programs, census evidence for 1965 indicates that about 21.3 percent of the public would have been living in poverty; in 1972, again considering all sources of income except that received from governmental programs, census figures show that about 19.2 percent of the public would have been living in poverty, about one-tenth less than 1965. Thus, the private sector, in these times of substantial economic growth, reduced the percentage of Americans living in poverty by about one in every ten Americans; and exclusive of government programs, even in 1972, almost one in five Americans would still have been living in poverty.[23]

Growth manifestly did not suffice in the 1960s and 1970s to ameliorate the lot of the impoverished elderly. Although real per-capita disposable income rose 24 percent between 1965 and 1972, the percentage of male-headed elderly families below the poverty line declined only slightly, from 57 to 51 percent. The figure was the same in both years for female-headed elderly families, 45 percent.[24] Nor did growth do much for either white or nonwhite female-headed families younger than 65, for "Exclusive of the government's programs, a slightly *higher* proportion of these female-headed families found themselves in poverty in 1972 than in 1965. Forty percent of these

## It Really Was a (Nearly) Great Society

families lived in poverty in 1972, an increase of 4 percent over 1965."[25] Denied as its necessity is by eminent conservatives from President Reagan on down, government action is the only exit from financial poverty available to millions of the elderly and more millions of female heads of families and their young children.

For many Americans, poverty is an occasional, recurrent affliction rather than a persistent condition, the result more often than not of unemployment or illness. Between 1969 and 1978, a quarter of the American population endured at least one year of poverty.[26] Of the "persistently poor," those below the poverty line at least eight years, four out of ten are disabled, three are over sixty-five, six are in female-headed homes, and 62 percent are black.[27]

The record might well suggest that programs as partially successful as the cash grants and noncash services introduced or enlarged since 1964 ought to merit expansion. Why should twelve million Americans below the poverty line be excluded from Medicaid by the Byzantine complexity of the eligibility rules? Why in half the states should cash welfare grants be denied to families in which both fathers and mothers are present? Why should nutrition and medical aid targeted at low-income pregnant women and infants be trimmed? Why should the disabled be harried to demonstrate that they remain incapable of sustained employment? Why not enlarge the supply of subsidized housing, instead of complaining, in the Stockman fashion, that because more low-income families are excluded from such accommodation than are among the small minority who enjoy its benefits, the federal government should not supply low-income housing at all? In 1981, French, West German, and Italian social programs amounted to 30 percent of public spending. Even before Reagan cuts in such programs and symmetrical enlargements of military spending, we devoted only 21 percent of our budget for such wimpish objectives.[28]

The conservative response is predictable. The Europeans, so the indictment charges, now endure high unemployment and slow growth because they have protected citizens too well and diminished incentives to enterprise and job shifts. Moreover, to say that the Europeans are spending more by no means logically implies that we are not spending too much on ill-conceived attempts to treat publicly maladies susceptible only to the cure of individual will and effort. Although the poverty gap in 1982 was approximately $45 billion, some $101.4 billion was federally targeted at the poor—food stamps, housing assistance, AFDC, low-income energy assistance, child nutrition, Supplemental Security Income, Medicaid, unemployment benefits, and earned-income tax credit.[29] Ergo: some money must have flowed to families not officially defined as poor, people who craftily lurked slightly above the poverty line. But money is low on the list of conservative grievances. Conservatives fret over work incentives, perverse encouragement to immorality and idleness, and the entire culture of poverty. They worry as well about "a temptation for citizens in free economies committed to generous welfare programs to go too far in enhancing the power of the central state. As in the Parable of the Foolish Virgins, good intentions are not enough; the lamps may have insufficient oil."[30]

Always there is the need to separate the unworthy from the worthy poor. As the concerned Catholics of the lay letter point out, ". . . income grants would not solve the unemployment (and underemployment) problems of at least eleven million poor persons over fifteen years of age who, on the record, do wish to work for their own self-reliance. Yet even sufficient job creation would not help all the poor. As a human problem, poverty calls for human and personal involvement. That efforts to overcome it must be aimed, in part, at self-esteem and, where possible, self-reliance is the ultimate ground of personal dignity."[31] True enough, but scarcely a logical reason to deny financial relief to the needy.

Moreover, there is a good deal of evidence that the link between reasonably liberal benefits and diminished work effort is extremely tenuous. If all the major programs were repealed, as Charles Murray advocates, hours worked might rise 1 percent. Moreover, in the wake of the surge in social benefits after 1965, American unemployment rates climbed less than in other Western nations.[32] All available evidence persuasively implies that unemployment and welfare dependency correlate weakly with benefit variations for unskilled and poorly educated workers. For at least a decade, from the mid-1970s on, welfare grants in real terms declined. Yet welfare dependency increased. School dropouts historically found entry-level factory jobs. As American deindustrialization inexorably continues, these are the very jobs whose number has stagnated or actually declined in urban centers like New York, Philadelphia, and Detroit in the wake of corporate departures to low-wage, anti-union Sunbelt and foreign havens.

## NUTRITION

It is one of the assorted illogicalities of American politics that hunger and malnutrition exist side by side with the vast surpluses generated by the nation's farmers. The food-stamp program began at least as much out of the hunt by farm-state legislators for outlets for towering mountains of cheese and grain, and overflowing lakes of milk annually depressing farm prices, as from concern for the poor. In 1967, a team of nutritionally sophisticated physicians funded by the respected Field Foundation toured the country. The group reported:

> Wherever we went and wherever we looked, we saw children in significant numbers who were hungry and sick, children for whom hunger is a daily fact of life, and sickness, in many forms, an inevitability. [Many of these children] were hungry, weak, and apathetic. Their lives were being shortened. . . . They were suffering from hunger and disease and, directly or indirectly, they were dying from them.[33]

Temporarily in a shockable mood, the public responded with indignation and politically effective pressure for expansion of food stamps and child nutrition benefits. No comprehensive figures of national improvement exist, but in 1977 the Field doctors revisited the Bronx, Appalachia, Mississippi, and Texas. Dr. Raymond Wheeler of the Charlotte Medical Center reported:

> There can be little doubt that significant change has occurred since 1967. . . . Nowhere did I see the gross evidence of malnutrition among young children that we saw in 1967. . . . It is not possible any more to find very easily the bloated bellies, the shriveled infants, the gross evidence of vitamin

and protein deficiencies in children that we identified in the late 1960s.[34]

Approximately 83 percent of food stamps flow to people who otherwise would be below the poverty line.[35] Once more an appealing group (suffering children), a media event (the Field Commission Report), and the interests of a major producing group (the farmers) happily combined to generate a genuinely enlightened social policy. With perverse disregard of distinctions between success and failure in social policy, the Reagan administration has been doing its considerable best to reverse the progress of two decades. Early in 1985, the Physicians' Task Force on Hunger concluded a year-long inquiry with the charge that "Hunger is a problem of epidemic proportions across the nation. While no one knows the precise number of hungry Americans, available evidence indicates that up to twenty million citizens may be hungry at least some period of time each month."[36]

Twenty million is a conservative number. There were in 1984 15.5 million Americans below the poverty line who were not receiving food stamps, and another eight million just above that line also without nutrition assistance. Since 1980, the amount of free food distributed has soared by 700 percent. Already worse than that of many other nations, the American infant mortality rate in the first Reagan term of office ceased to decline. From 1982 to 1985, over $12 billion has been extracted from food stamps and child nutrition programs.[37] In the Reagan era, nothing fails like success in social policy and nothing succeeds like failure in weapons procurement.

## HEALTH

Let us start cheerfully. The majority of Americans have good, or moderately good access either to a physician or a clinic. One survey, conducted by the Robert Wood Johnson Foundation, puts the figure at 90 percent. And 80 percent saw a physician at least once in the preceding year.[38] Children under seventeen receive more than average medical attention.

## It Really Was a (Nearly) Great Society

The historic gap between rural and urban America has all but closed.

Here end tidings of joy. Ten percent of the population—24.5 million persons—when in need of medical help must rely upon overcrowded, understaffed hospital emergency rooms. In poorer urban neighborhoods, the percentage is far higher. As usual, the black situation is bleakest: "Black families were much less likely than white families to obtain care when they needed it. They are sharply more dissatisfied with hospital emergencies; they rate their own health status less favorably, and they—more than any other ethnic group—believe the health care system in America needs to be rebuilt."[39] Hispanics, though less well off than average Americans, endure a smaller gap than blacks between them and the majority, white population.

To be poor in America is as inadvisable medically as it is in every other respect, save aspiration for canonization. The poor assessed their health as bad. They reported twice the average chance of not getting needed care. The unemployed also fare badly. Most employers terminate health benefits within thirty to sixty days of layoff. Adults and children in families whose heads were not in the labor force also suffered more illness and more difficulty in getting medical attention than the nation at large. Some 18.6 million people, over 8 percent of adults, are uninsured. Of this number, nearly a quarter have neither a regular doctor nor any other regular source of medical attention. The more limited the education of an adult, the worse is his or her health and access to care. In the year of the survey, one out of seven Americans suffered a medical emergency and 5 percent reported difficulty securing emergency care. Serious, chronic illness hits one family in ten. For a fifth of these families, treatment costs are a significant financial burden.

Like so many of the solemn endeavors of social science, the Johnson study confirms the conclusions of common observation. Any society that stubbornly rejects comprehensive health care will not treat decently or even adequately its most vulnerable members. In terms of class, with which Americans are uneasy, the medically unserved or underserved population is low in income, sketchy in education, loosely connected with the mainstream labor force, and black, Hispanic, or unemployed. The rhetoric of American medicine trumpets the best oooooof care for all—a logical contradiction. The reality is an increasingly class differentiated system or nonsystem of health-care delivery. The *Wall Street Journal* drew the logical, free-market inference from the pervasive inequality of national income and wealth. People who can afford it have every right to state-of-the-art surgical and medical attention, private rooms, VIP suites, and gourmet meals. In this spirit, the newspaper editorially applauded a certain Dr. Oldham who is marketing for profit Dr. Steven Rosenberg's experimental cancer therapy. For a mere $19,200, paid in advance, this public spirited physician's Biotherapeutics Corporation will apply treatment at Memphis Baptist Hospital.[40]

But unnecessarily bad as health-care diffusion was in 1985, it was considerably worse a generation ago, before Medicare and Medicaid. In 1963, for example, one out of five persons below the poverty line had never, as far as he or she could remember, been examined by a doctor.[41] In 1963, 56 percent of the poor had seen a doctor during the preceding twelve months. By 1970, this figure had risen to 65 percent. In both years, 71 percent of members of high-income families had visited physicians in the preceding year. Moreover, by 1970, only 8 percent of the poor reported that they had never seen a doctor. Even more startling was the number of visits by rich and poor patients to doctors in 1970. The poor, whose health is worse than that of the rich, went 4.9 times per person to doctors' offices, the rich only 3.8 times.[42]

The best news of all concerned infant mortality. Among the poor, it plummeted over 33 percent between 1965 and 1975. The spectacular decline for blacks, twice as fast as for the general population, was from 40.3 per thousand in 1965, to 30.9 in 1970, and 24.2 in 1975.[43] For Reagan theologians, the very success of Medicare and Medicaid in improving the health of the elderly and the poor justified funding curtailments for both programs and shifts of financial burdens increasingly to elderly patients. For liberals, the equally evident lesson was, or should have been, the desirability, even the cost effectiveness, of liberalizing eligibility for Medicaid, reversing the erosion in Medicare, and moving toward comprehensive health care.

*It Really Was a (Nearly) Great Society*

## HOUSING

A long time ago, toward the end of the Roosevelt-Truman era in 1951, Congress enacted a major housing statute, the Taft-Ellender-Wagner Act, which set as its goal a decent home for every American family. Its inspiration was not Marxist. Senator Robert Taft was the dominant conservative Republican leader of the period. Senator Ellender was an influential moderate Democrat and Senator Wagner's name adorned a handful of New Deal innovations, notably the Wagner Act, as the National Labor Relations Act generally is called. Reassuringly, the senator was a splendid product of machine politics, Tammany-style. It is hard to recall that in those days even conservatives recognized the necessity of federal action to supplement a private market flagrantly incapable of providing shelter of reasonable quality at tolerable expense for working-class and low-income families. As it turned out, Congress in succeeding years invariably provided funds for fewer units of public or publicly subsidized construction than the targets of the 1951 Act required. Moreover, as has been true in the health sector, disgraceful percentages of federal funds have been skimmed off the top for the benefit of developers and landlords. In large cities, desperate shortages of affordable apartments exist for most renters except the genuinely affluent. High interest rates, slowly rising or stagnant real incomes, and escalating land and construction costs have substantially shrunk the percentage of Americans who can afford to purchase a single-family detached house on its separate plot of land—the American dream.

All this said, it remains true that, in substantial tribute to federal programs, housing quality for most families has substantially improved since 1940. In that year 20.2 percent of the population lived more than one person to a room, the standard definition of overcrowding. For blacks, the figure was twice as large. Decline has been steady, to 16 percent in 1950, 12 percent in 1960, 9 percent in 1970, and 5 percent in 1976. A similar shrinkage in substandard housing—houses or apartments with no hot running water, no or inadequate plumbing, and in great physical disrepair—has occurred. In 1940, nearly half the population endured existence in substandard units. In

1950, slightly more than a third, in 1960 a fifth, in 1970 slightly more than a tenth, and in 1978 only 8 percent of the population were still condemned to substandard housing.[44]

As the dates imply, federal intervention in the shelter market dates back to the New Deal. Lyndon Johnson's Great Society enlarged funding, experimented with new subsidy tactics, briefly floated the notion of Model Cities (one of the many casualties of Vietnam), and ended federal support for racially segregated construction. Federal funding for housing increased during the Nixon years as it did for most other New Deal and Great Society programs. Yet again the Reagan administration mounted the first successful conservative attack on the federal role in a market vital to the welfare of low, working-class, and lower-middle-income families.

## JOB TRAINING

In the 1950s and 1960s manpower specialists and general economists wrangled inconclusively over the best way to reduce unemployment, then considered much too high when it approached 5 percent. According to one school of thought, the solution was located in stimulus to the economy—the enlargement of aggregate demand for goods and services beloved of all true-blue Keynesians. When bodies are in short supply, employers will hire the unskilled, the semiliterate, the slow-witted, and the surly. They will redesign jobs to suit lower-quality workers and provide at their own expense whatever training may still be needed. The experience of World War II was taken by the partisans of aggregate demand as one of those "natural" experiments that occasionally demonstrate a theory's validity. In Studs Terkel's "good war," some thirteen million men and women at the peak of the American effort were wearing uniforms and millions more were producing guns, tanks, aircraft, ships, uniforms, and infamous tins and packages of C and K rations. Nevertheless, on the home front, civilian standards of living actually improved.

What made possible the provisioning and munitioning of the most lavishly supplied armed forces in all history and simultaneous civilian prosperity was to begin with an enormous

## It Really Was a (Nearly) Great Society

increase in aggregate demand for goods and services on the part of the federal government. The Treasury's green checks gurgled in soothing streams to military contractors, who rummaged through the population for people to hire. They found them. Some were the 4-Fs, men rejected for military service for physical or psychiatric shortcomings. Others were felons on parole or probation. More or less reformed alcoholics were welcomed. Attracted both by patriotic duty and the lure of high wages, legions of women left homes and entered factories and shipyards. Retirees rejoined the labor force. Employers trained and organized their motley recruits. Moral: job qualifications decline as the number of jobs to be filled climbs and the supply of recruits shrinks.

Advocates of the alternative, structuralist position dismissed World War II as a special case inapplicable to peacetime circumstances. The full or over-full employment of 1941–45 occurred in an atmosphere of total mobilization which generated public support for rationing and wage and price controls. These controls held in check a potential inflation which otherwise would surely have resulted from massive stimulus to the demand for every available person and raw material. Since automobiles and consumer appliances were produced, if at all, in very small quantities, consumers had less reason to spend and more incentive to save than the advertising and marketing hype of a consumer society normally permitted. In more placid times, attempts to hire the least qualified push up wages initially at the bottom and then throughout the compensation structure. Wages, 70 percent of business costs, are passed on speedily as higher prices. Unqualified workers are expensive. Pay them even minimum wages and they add to costs, set off wage demands from unions, and soon evoke from the Federal Reserve the sort of restrictions on credit and money creation that abort inflation and plunge the economy into recession.

Pumping up aggregate demand was in the structuralist view an expensive, disorderly way to employ the minority of workers unattached to steady jobs. A far superior route to the Nirvana of high employment and stable prices focused upon the skills, education, and attitudes of the persistently unemployed, the people who even in boom times can't seem to gain secure footholds in the labor market or, worse, never tried to gain them or, having tried, gave up and became permanent dropouts. These structurally unemployed youths and adults sometimes are simply in the wrong place—economic backwaters like Appalachia, rural Maine, and the declining steel towns of the Monongahela Valley. Young people in the Youngstowns of the Middle West, former homes of thriving steel mills, are less and less likely to find starting jobs if they don't leave town. Their fathers, like workers in Detroit auto plants displaced by robots and Japanese competition, and New York City garment operatives dislodged by foreigners and nonunion Southern factories, lack salable skills. Often individual difficulties derive from educational and attitudinal deficiencies. High school dropouts and even high school graduates who are functionally illiterate and thus incapable of following written instructions, or lack arithmetic skills, make poor candidates for the clerical, data processing, and financial-sector jobs that have led employment growth even as opportunities in manufacturing have stagnated or actually declined. If, in addition, they resist instruction, arrive persistently late for work, and tend to be chronically absent on Mondays and Fridays, their prospects are even dimmer.

The challenge of job training is complex. As the examples suggest, no single response avails. High school graduates of normal ability and attitude in depressed regions with few prospects of revival should be encouraged to migrate to prospering parts of the country much in the manner of their forebears and contemporary legal and illegal migrants from the rest of the world to the United States. The educational and spiritual dropouts among their age-mates who are jobless in economically thriving communities may require specialized training in residential settings after the model of the Job Corps. Older workers in declining industries will derive small comfort from relocation unless they are helped in acquiring new skills. Nor will they benefit without such skills from the capacity of some regions, notably southern New England, to shift from low- to high-tech specialties.

With varying commitment and success, national administrations of both major parties from the 1950s to the Reagan era have supported job training efforts, sometimes with heavy dependence upon direct government efforts, sometimes, as in

## It Really Was a (Nearly) Great Society

the Reagan model, in cooperation with private employers. The most massive and extensive of these initiatives, the Comprehensive Employment and Training Act of 1973 (another major example of Great Society initiatives extended by Democratic Congresses in the Nixon administration), concentrated staff and money upon young and minority clienteles, and enlisted as contractors local governments, voluntary organizations, private entrepreneurs, and community organizations. Under one CETA title, actual public jobs were created. The Act's deliberate decentralization allowed municipalities under budgetary pressure on occasion to divert CETA funds for the payment of policemen, firefighters, sanitation personnel, and other regular employees. Hard-pressed mayors ingeniously converted CETA into a form of federal revenue sharing, effectively subverting the program's objectives.

Numerous studies, many employing cost-benefit analysis, have examined the effectiveness of various training modes. In the mid-1970s, a pair of sympathetic analysts concluded that "Extensive measurement and evaluation of the effectiveness of manpower training have not yet yielded any conclusive answers, but this is more a reflection on the state of the art of measurement and evaluation than on the performance of manpower training. The evidence of success is extensive even if subject to reservations."[45] Few of the studies, for one thing, pursued the careers of training graduates long enough to make judgments on long-term benefits.

Occasional studies did extend over longer periods. One particularly thorough project examined the work histories between 1973 and 1978 of 1,136 Baltimore-area workers after their CETA involvement. Sixty percent were black and an even larger percentage members of groups traditionally hardest hit by unemployment. The Johns Hopkins team took seven years to complete their study and concluded that employment of former CETA participants significantly increased. Of the group who had been jobless an entire year before they began CETA training, 40 percent got jobs as soon as they graduated. Over half—56 percent—had jobs within six months. The record was even more encouraging for the entire 1,136. Nearly half—46 percent—went to work as soon as they ended CETA training, 59 percent within a month, and 66 percent within half a year.

*Visions and Nightmares*

Strikingly, CETA graduate rates of employment continued to rise despite increasing unemployment in the Baltimore area. At the end of the five-year period, the number of CETA graduates on job hunts had diminished to 6 percent.[46] During the five-year study period, the wages of CETA alumni improved from an initial 70 percent of average Baltimore wages to 89 percent by 1978.

Additional inquiries attested to the special effectiveness of institutional training. Surveying experiences in Boston, Denver, San Francisco, and Oakland, two veteran analysts concluded:

> Across all cities and programs, and despite unfavorable economic conditions, the average enrollee in an institutional training program was substantially better off in terms of employment stability and earnings because of his program participation. The lower the pre-training wage rate, the greater the wage and earnings gain was likely to be.[47]

Even conservatives accept Head Start, which powerfully influences the outcome of subsequent job training by intervening early enough in life to encourage the educational achievement and appropriate attitudes toward work needed for eventual economic success. Head Start serves approximately 300,000 preschoolers a year, only 20 percent of eligible low-income children.[48] A well-designed analysis of Head Start's effects on youngsters in fourteen programs concluded:

> In comparing children who participated in Head Start with those who did not, the study found that children who participated before the age of six were about 60 percent less likely to be assigned to special education classes in grade school or high school . . . were about 45 percent less likely to be held back a grade . . . exhibited a seven-point increase in IQ scores as an immediate result of the program, with a long-term increase on average of about half that; had more favorable perception of the quality of their schoolwork when in high school than did their non–Head Start cohorts; and were more likely to want to pursue higher education at a college or university.[49]

Head Start has won the rhetorical endorsement though not a high level of financial support of the Reagan administration,

## It Really Was a (Nearly) Great Society

otherwise spiritually in tune with eighteenth-century attitudes toward poverty.

In sum, innovative Great Society programs, older New Deal efforts amplified by the Great Society, and extension of Great Society initiatives in the 1970s were in many, if not most instances, reasonably successful. They did not eliminate poverty, train all the unemployable for jobs, house every family decently, ensure a balanced diet for every child and adult, or supply easy access to skilled medical and hospital treatment to the poor as well as the rich. Welfare dependency, though far less pervasive than alarmists assert, does exist. Disquieting rates of teenage unemployment, particularly among minorities, attest to unsolved dilemmas of education and attitudinal transformation. Yet the liberal impulses of the 1960s were not foolish. The billions of dollars that were appropriated generated measurable improvements in health, nutrition, education, and housing. On the gritty research evidence, more, not fewer, tax dollars ought to be devoted to routinely denigrated attempts to train the unskilled, educate young children, enlarge the supply of low-cost housing, improve the diet of pregnant women and infants, and widen access to high-quality medical care. To say so appeals not merely to compassion. Children who mature into productive workers pay taxes, stay out of jail and drug clinics, and improve the competitive position of American industry in world markets. Investment in human capital—as economists describe education, dental and medical care, job training, and the remainder of the agenda of social policy—pays large dividends. One might even seriously describe such expenditures as rather more cost-effective than most of the Pentagon's weapons-procurement efforts.

### 3

Why are these prosaic accomplishments ignored, discounted, or disputed? One set of answers was supplied a dozen years ago in a special issue of *The Public Interest* entitled "The Great Society: Lessons for the Future." Lance Liebman, one of the contributors to this neoconservative journal, put the situation like this:

It is convenient to categorize the standard explanations for the failure of domestic reform in the 1960s. They fall into four overlapping categories: 1) things improved, but not enough to meet the rise in expectations. This, the Banfield thesis, recently amplified by Wattenberg and Scammon, is certainly true with regard to some physically measurable physical amenities such as the percentage of families with indoor plumbing or a refrigerator. 2) There are things we do not know how to do. Teaching poor children to read competently may be an example. There may simply be no public program, at any cost, that can achieve this result. 3) The instrumentalities that deliver urban public services are inefficient. For example, New York City spends $49 to collect a ton of garbage while private carters do it for $17.50. Civil service unions, legislated pensions, poor wage bargaining, and inadequate supervision contribute to this higher cost. 4) Adequate resources were not provided. This means money, which was in insufficient supply because of the Vietnam War but also because the middle class resisted taxation. And it means more than money. Some policy goals—greater influence for the poor in local decisions, or more jobs on the police force for blacks—would have been costly to persons and groups benefiting from the status quo. Resources of some sort were needed to overcome their objections, and these resources were not forthcoming.[50]

It is wise to tackle obliquely alleged social policy failures, taken for granted by Liebman a dozen years ago. Late in 1984 and early in 1985, the pollsters reported spreading public optimism. Their respondents felt better about the state of the nation. They were more cheerful than they had been in the recent past about their own prospects. Even blacks who had least to celebrate were on the whole optimistic. Public euphoria strangely contrasted with an ample assortment of glum economic statistics. Unemployment was just as bad as it had been when Reagan stepped into the Oval Office for the first time as its legitimate occupant. In much of the industrial Midwest, depression conditions persisted with no relief in prospect. The gradual disintegration of OPEC plunged Texas, Oklahoma, and Louisiana into financial disarray. Staggering under an

## It Really Was a (Nearly) Great Society

unmanageable burden of debt, high interest rates, and low world prices for their surpluses, farmers were marching on Washington and the state capitals of the farm belt. The percentage of the population below the poverty line had crept upward during the Reagan years. For most factory operatives and service workers, wages rose more slowly than prices. The percentage of the labor force in unions continued to decline.

Was the public under the spell of collective illusion, convinced that the tattered economy was genuinely clothed in the gaudy raiment of boom times? There is a less fanciful and more plausible explanation in easy reach. Optimism about one's personal future depends directly upon one's expectations. At times in the last two decades, it was reasonable to expect annual increases after inflation in wages or salaries of 5 or 6 percent and a fair approximation of guaranteed lifetime employment in major corporations. Two recessions in the 1970s, stagnation or decline of average incomes, the reemergence of inflation as a major uncertainty in the planning of family budgets, and Carter administration policy vacillations colluded to dampen hopes of growth without cease. The 1981–82 mini-depression accentuated new career and income uncertainties. More yuppies live in smaller spaces, drive thriftier cars, depend on two incomes, and postpone marriage and children than did their parents in the 1950s. They seem grateful for job opportunities somewhat more plentiful in the 1980s than they were a decade earlier.

At cruel cost to the unemployed, their families, and the merchants with whom they dealt, the Federal Reserve's calculated monetary sadism did break inflation's grip. When recovery began in late 1982 and continued in 1983, 1984, and 1985, relieved Americans saluted the first marks of general and individual stability in very nearly two decades. Numerous men and women were left out of the celebration and even for the luckier majority, family incomes continued to rise largely because more and more women joined the labor force as the source of second incomes. Fewer families could afford new homes than in the 1960s or even the 1970s, but possibly an even smaller number now expected to be able to afford them. Humbler expectations are more readily gratified in the real world. Ronald Reagan's very considerable achievement, therefore, was in lowering general expectations to the point where economic performance actually outpaced the public's hopes. Habitually, conservatives perform this feat more adroitly then their liberal antagonists.

What a contrast to Lyndon Johnson! His soaring rhetoric briefly mobilized public support for the Great Society and propelled a mass of legislation through Congress in 1964, 1965, and 1966. The bill for the rhetoric was paid in highly unrealistic expectations of the speed and completeness of the bewildering variety of Johnson's innovations. How pathetic to point to the sort of successes examined a few pages back! Idle and dangerous teenagers still abounded. School and job training dropout rates were depressing. Poverty lingered. Affirmative action did not rectify in a decade the heritage of three centuries of slavery and discrimination. Head Start and extra federal funds for ghetto schools did not instantaneously and miraculously compensate for middle-class advantages. Well, then, the Great Society was a failure. *Quod erat demonstratum.* After a losing season or two, football coaches get the chop. Victory, not character building, is the objective of crazed alumni. Americans, fanatically addicted to sports, expect results as quick and decisive on the occasions when they indulge liberal presidents and acquiescent Congresses in social experiments.

The roots of the Great Society's collapse in public esteem were quintessentially political. The programs that the Reagan administration has refrained from assaulting and those that have been successfully defended against such assaults have been mostly, if not quite entirely, those held precious by politically powerful constituencies. Despite his long record of criticism of Social Security and his preference for private pension schemes, Ronald Reagan as president, after one early stab at benefit curtailment, felt compelled to declare his undeviating attachment to the financial security of the old folks. Nor has the president threatened the continued existence of the Federal Deposit Insurance Corporation, the Securities and Exchange Corporation, the Federal Housing Administration, or even the Environmental Protection Administration and the Occupational Safety and Health Administration. The final pair have indeed been severely harassed but the case of EPA is educational. The first Reagan administrator, Mrs. Anne Gor-

## It Really Was a (Nearly) Great Society

such Burford, did her best to weaken enforcement and enlist the cooperation of the business community. But public clamor and its translation into congressional investigation and pressure compelled her to resign. The president found it expedient to recall William Ruckelshaus, the first and generally respected EPA administrator, to his old position, where he did much to restore agency morale and appropriate regulatory practices.

Social Security, the most nearly universal of benefit programs, enjoys far from unexpectedly the strongest and most pervasive public support—pensioners, members of the labor force contemplating retirement, and their children and grandchildren concerned altruistically about the welfare of parents and grandparents and selfishly about the possibility that in the absence of Social Security the elderly would depend upon the young. In increasingly cramped apartments and houses, the threat of squeezing in the old folks is quite enough to enlist their juniors under the Social Security banner. The Federal Deposit Insurance Corporation, which insures deposits up to $100,000 and in practice pays off all depositors, is almost as universal as Social Security. In 1984 and 1985, depositors in Ohio and Maryland savings institutions, backed only by state insurance funds, got a costly reminder of the risks attached to inadequately regulated and guaranteed banks when major bank failures drained state resources and threw unfortunate depositors on the mercies of legislatures. A very large majority of Americans have bank accounts. Although only a minority own securities, they are an influential and prosperous group with a strong interest in unrigged securities markets. Moreover, a great many ordinary citizens own stocks indirectly via pension funds. Two generations of home buyers have acquired homes equipped with Federal Housing Administration mortgage guarantees. Deregulation translates into loss of protection and financial security. In the instance of telephone service, the country has learned, in the wake of American Telephone and Telegraph's breakup, that the sequel has been expensive, confusing, and disruptive for individuals and business enterprises. AT&T was a regulated monopoly, a very nearly universal service, which gave the country a phone system unexcelled anywhere in the world. Free-market zealots fixed something that wasn't broken.

The more nearly universal a government program is, the

better it is likely to be because its clientele includes middle- and upper-class beneficiaries whose voices are heeded by public officials. In sad contrast, programs for poor people tend to be poor programs above all because poverty is frequently more despised than pitied. And because beneficiaries are explicitly separated from the rest of the population, they are at best viewed as objects of charity and at worst as expensive charges upon the public at large. Whenever the political pendulum swings to the right, means-tested programs become highly vulnerable to the assaults of budget warriors. As David Stockman confided in 1981 to a *Washington Post* friend, his first budget proposals contained curtailment of many public subsidies to businessmen, operators of private aircraft, yachtsmen, and other prosperous citizens. These fell quickly by the wayside. The cuts that were acceptable in congressional eyes were in welfare, food stamps, nutrition programs, job training, and Medicaid—all directed at the sixth of the population below the poverty line. With considerable reason, working-class families scrambling to make ends meet on incomes not much higher than the poverty line resented paying taxes to improve the situation of families who often, in their opinion, refused to help themselves. It is easy to stigmatize minorities, to blame the victims in sociologist William Ryan's apt phrase. It is much harder, as Jimmy Carter discovered, to blame majorities. They tend to include me, you, and the rest of the neighborhood. The buck stops and stays with the middle class.

It is usually politically feasible to skew benefits toward a worthy segment of the polity but not in the direction of a stigmatized group. Corporations and affluent individuals link tax cuts, which enlarge their net worth, with new investment, job creation, and the public interest. The connections may be elusive, but so long as the public swallows such justification, the rich and powerful can rest comfortably in their waterbeds.[51] Even when conservatives form governments in Western Europe, they do not eliminate or seriously curtail family allowances—they flow to all parents, rich, middling, and poor. They are treated as ordinary income, but tax collectors claw back a portion of the allowances from the prosperous. Nowhere, even in Margaret Thatcher's Britain, has a conservative government endeavored to dismantle a national health system: too many

## It Really Was a (Nearly) Great Society

middle-class and wealthy citizens use its services. Public housing in England, council houses and flats, is a much larger percentage of the English than the American housing inventory because eligibility does not depend upon small income as it does in the United States. No stigma adheres to British occupants of subsidized housing.

This is to say successful social interventions cover substantial proportions of the population—100 percent is best. Stable majorities render them all but invulnerable to sabotage. More precariously, programs that help minorities—farmers, failing corporations, the wealthy—can at times enjoy political triumph if their beneficiaries are skillful enough in asserting the congruence of the public and their special interest. Programs at highest risk favor relatively small, stigmatized groups—unwed mothers, teenage school dropouts, or the targets of racial prejudice. The success of Reagan's assaults against income maintenance, nutrition, medical, housing, and other benefits for the poor attests to the existence of this hierarchy, just as the 1981 tax cuts represent linkage, as triumphant as it was fictitious, between further enrichment of the already wealthy and more rapid economic growth.

A familiar conservative charge against Great Society tactics was an alleged tendency to throw money at problems instead of designing appropriate, presumably free-market, solutions for them. Some evidence supports this line of criticism. However, there is a much stronger explanation of policy misadventure. Close inspection of two quantitatively important sectors of government spending, defense and health, leads to the conclusion that major responsibility for the waste and mismanagement supposedly inseparable from governmental bureaucracies actually attaches to the private sector. In these two fastest-growing portions of the federal budget, disastrous alliances between public funding and normal, profit-maximizing entrepreneurial behavior have damaged the reputation of government, diminished efficiency, and sparked taxpayer revolts against paying the bills for grossly overpriced weapons, medical technology, and health care.

Consider defense first. Each year in a drama as stylized as a Kabuki play and nearly as interminable, Congress and Defense Secretary Caspar Weinberger wrangle over the defense budget.

Mr. Weinberger stoutly asserts that not a dollar can be subtracted from the $300 billion shopping list without endangering national security and encouraging Soviet aggression. The Doles and the Domenicis who lead the Senate's Republican majority insist that defense must take its lumps if the year's budget-reduction target is to be met. How else will farmers, Amtrak passengers, subway and bus riders, parents of college-age children, beneficiaries of Medicare and Social Security, and many, many others be induced to accept smaller numbers on Treasury checks? Congress threatens to cancel the MX and the B-1 bomber, and slow the Navy's progress toward a six-hundred-ship fleet. Mr. Weinberger reveals his plans to close bases in the districts of the more vociferous critics of Pentagon appropriations and turn off the floodlights that illuminate the Washington Monument. President Reagan weighs in with thinly disguised imputations against the patriotism of Pentagon critics. Critics retort with additions to the familiar list of fancifully priced toilet seats, coffeemakers, wrenches, and hammers. The Pentagon responds that the critics don't understand the cost-accounting principles of overhead allocation, and anyway all these horrible examples were uncovered by relentless internal investigation by the Pentagon's own sleuths who have saved the taxpayers billions of dollars.

By the time a weary and jaded Congress at length adjourns as autumn leaves turn red and gold, all weapons systems survive, no bases are closed, and Pentagon appropriations after inflation rise a couple of percentage points less than Mr. Weinberger initially described as essential to the defense of the Free World. It turns out to the astonishment of none that the Pentagon has exaggerated the inflation rate and the cost of energy supplies and has been unable into the bargain to spend all the money that Congress had previously authorized. All sides declare victory. Congress has cut the budget, but no member of that body has been politically injured by the loss of defense jobs. The Pentagon has preserved every single one of its redundant missiles, aircraft, and dubious researchers into defenses against Soviet warheads. Defense contractors discreetly celebrate. All players prepare costumes and rhetoric for the new season only two or three months away.

The scenario plays to indulgent audiences despite, or perhaps

## It Really Was a (Nearly) Great Society

because of, the cynicism of the performers. Defense spending is cherished in communities plagued by persistently high unemployment even in allegedly prosperous years. Unions, merchants, local developers, and defense contractors have little trouble persuading the fiercest congressional critics of military spending that Pentagon production or base operation in their constituencies is vital to the safety of the republic. Members of Congress who endorse nuclear freezes simultaneously lobby to get New York, Boston, or Newport designated as home ports for recommissioned World War II battleships armed with cruise missiles. For its part, the Pentagon has astutely spread defense business across the country, in nearly every congressional district. A few strategically placed telephone calls to bankers, merchants, and local union officials can whip up opposition to budget limitations overnight. In the absence of concrete plans to convert defense plants into civilian production, who can blame workers for clinging to their jobs and businessmen for coddling their customers?

Curtailing the Pentagon appetite would be a challenging job for dietitians in the Office of Management and Budget even if unemployment approximated full employment (3–4 percent) levels. But there is an institutional source of enormous financial waste that is more susceptible to remedy. This is the symbiotic relationship between major defense contractors and the Pentagon. In all but legal form, Grumman, General Dynamics, and a handful of their peers are subsidiaries of the Pentagon. An exceedingly high percentage of weapons-procurement contracts is negotiated by this exclusive brotherhood without competitive bidding. New weapons dreamed up by defense contractors enlarge the empires of generals and admirals in the Pentagon. Rival deadly playthings proposed by other contractors also win Pentagon endorsement and congressional funding. While they are on active duty, high officers preside over growing budgets and more numerous subordinates. Upon retirement in their forties or early fifties, lucrative posts await them in the defense industry. Only fools or saints are at all likely to deal harshly with potential employers of notorious generosity.

Defense reformers periodically agitate for diminished placement of contracts with chosen producers and more open, competitive bidding. But even if competitive bidding were the rule instead of the exception, and retired generals and admirals were debarred from employment by weapons producers, quantities of waste would be generated by frictions between these two huge bureaucracies, military and corporate. Haggling between them (for their mutual benefit) delays design decisions, multiplies the number of reviewing authorities, encourages mid-course alterations, stretches out procurement, ultimately produces gold-plated weapons subject to frequent breakdown under combat conditions, and, inevitably, adds enormously to cost overruns in this dreadfully inefficient sector of the economy.

Even for the mentally healthy and the ideologically unhysterical, the world is a dangerous planet. Total disarmament in the foreseeable future is as fanciful as Star Wars defenses against nuclear attack. This is not to say that adequate defense cannot be financed far less wastefully. The solution—more instead of less government—is as delightfully simple as currently it is politically unpopular. John Kenneth Galbraith has cogently argued the merits of nationalization. I can do no better than cite his words:

> The combined power of the two bureaucracies would be usefully reduced by converting the large specialized weapons firms into full public corporations.... The government would acquire their stock at recently prevailing stock market valuation. Thereafter the boards of directors and senior management would be appointed by the federal government. Salaries and other emoluments would henceforth be regulated by the government in general relation to public levels; profits would accrue to the government; so also would losses as is now the case.[52]

The defense industry is an expensive hybrid. Though privately owned, weapons producers already do most of their business with government, collect working capital and progress payments from the Pentagon, and use large amounts of federally owned plants and equipment. The government absorbs losses and, as with Lockheed, lumbers to the rescue when bankruptcy threatens. As between corporate and public bu-

## It Really Was a (Nearly) Great Society

reaucracy, there are good reasons to prefer the latter. Its executives come cheaper. Their motives are less exploitive. And Congress and the media habitually oversee government activities with more enthusiasm and less pressure from campaign contributors or major advertisers than they do those of private corporations.

Defense is neither a social service nor a special favorite of the Great Society. But the parallels between it and the cost of health services are illuminating. The medical equivalent of weaponry is hospital technology. Between 1977 and 1982, Medicare costs per patient rose 107 percent, 19 percent a year. One-third of that increase related to medical technology. The quantity of services per patient rose 25 percent, and their price increased considerably faster than the general inflation rate.[53] The Medicare program frequently introduces expensive new devices and sets an example for other third-party providers. Indeed, the most spectacular opportunities for thrift are located in the sprawling agglomeration of health services.

Evidence accumulates that, although at nearly 11 percent of our gross national product we devote far more resources to the health sector than societies which guarantee universal access, like Great Britain (5.5 percent) or Canada (about 8 percent), we do not get our money's worth. Despite starvation of health appropriations by British conservatives, key indicators such as infant mortality and longevity register better performance by the British Health Service than by our own curious blend of cottage-industry private practice, corporate entrepreneurs, private health insurers, and public funders. Hospitals refuse to accept uninsured patients not out of sadism but in terror of bankruptcy. Carole Horn, a Washington, D.C., internist, tells the poignant story of a young patient whom she suspected might be suffering from cervical cancer. A freelance writer, the young woman would not allow Dr. Horn to take a Pap smear because, if malignancy were discovered, she would not be able to get medical insurance. Without it, she had no hope of paying for expensive treatment. Her physician sent her away with a prescription for an antibiotic.[54] On the other side of the medical equation, Humana funds controversial, artificial heart implants as an admitted publicity device; huge malpractice settlements escalate insurance premiums and doctors' fees; and enormous sums are expended to prolong by weeks or months the tormented lives of the terminally ill.

The Reagan solution to the crisis of medical costs is no surprise: it is its response to all problems in all seasons. Make health care competitive like other markets. Its proposed ceiling on tax exemptions for employer-financed health benefits would, the argument runs, compel employers to prune their benefit menu and impel employees to shop for less expensive care. Reagan health planners favor offering the elderly vouchers exchangeable for either Medicare or privately provided care. Competition, as salutary here as in politics and other blood sports, would improve efficiency and minimize costs in all sectors of the health industry. The major cost control of the 1980s is reimbursement to hospitals according to diagnostic-related group category. Hospitals get fixed sums for the care of patients according to the diagnostic-related group (DRG) into which an individual falls. If treatment costs less than federal reimbursement, the hospital keeps the difference. If it costs more, it must absorb the loss. Thus, market incentives encourage hospitals to discharge patients as soon as they can safely maintain themselves at home. In earlier, more foolish times, incentives were perverse. The more hospitalization totted up by the hospital administrators, the larger the Medicare reimbursement checks. The economists, accountants, and budget specialists who invented DRG prospective payment evidently labored under the strange illusion that the average American yearns to be hospitalized and once successful, resists discharge.

It is early to evaluate the success of the DRG adventure in medical accounting. Two drawbacks already are apparent. Where diagnosis is complex or uncertain, physicians will naturally select the one which justifies the most tests and the longest reimbursable hospital stay. This is a new ailment: DRG creep. Possibly more menacing to patients and in the long run more expensive is pressure to prematurely discharge patients who may then have to be readmitted in twenty-four or forty-eight hours with expensive complications. Moreover, a flourishing bureaucracy of discharge planners and peer-group second-guessers of physicians' admission and diagnostic decisions inflates hospital costs, wastes expensive time, and adds

## It Really Was a (Nearly) Great Society

unneeded complexity to an already insanely complex set of financial procedures.

Free marketers delude themselves. The health market is genuinely different from purchases of securities, groceries, appliances, cars, and package tours. The professionals that most closely resemble physicians and other health workers are funeral directors. When any supplier—physician or funeral director—holds customers captive, he controls both sides of the transaction. Doctors, not their apprehensive patients, compose medical menus. No wonder health is as expensive as it often is elusive. In 1929, its purveyors collected 4 percent of GNP. That percentage inexorably rose, to 7.3 percent in 1970, 9.4 percent a decade later, and, as already noted, currently nearly 11 percent.[55] For three decades, the cost of health care has relentlessly soared at rates two or three times those of inflation in general. Americans have paid for more than they got.

Yet, by the end of the 1980s, a burgeoning surplus of physicians projects a ratio of patients to doctors akin to that of Israel. In a competitive market, extra suppliers drive prices down. In health care, competition tends to drive costs higher instead of lower. Not only may physicians impose unnecessary costs upon patients as the number of the latter shrinks, but out of desperation hospitals join the dollar hunt. Hospital administrators compete for physician and patient favor by installing the very latest in medical technology, even when it duplicates existing facilities in nearby institutions. Early in 1983, for example, two hospitals in Columbia, Missouri (population 65,000), were both seeking approval to install magnetic resonance X-ray machines, then still in an experimental stage. In New York City, Memorial Hospital, although connected by a tunnel with New York Hospital, insisted on acquiring its own magnetic resonance imaging device. So, pace Kurt Vonnegut, it goes.

To the extent that analogies to more conventional markets actually apply to health care, they are likely to be accompanied by social pathology. Astute merchants profit by segmenting their customers and concentrating their marketing efforts upon the most affluent. Profit-making corporate health providers pursue a variant of the technique. Major operators like Humana, Beverly, National Health Care, American Medical International, and Hospital Corporation of America acquire and operate chains of nursing homes, hospitals, dialysis centers, and shopping mall drop-in clinics on "sound" commercial principles. These, of course, dictate avoidance of low-income, elderly, and chronically ailing patients. The upwardly mobile young are gratifyingly prey to acute illnesses that require lucrative but brief surgical interventions and hospital stays. For several decades, their incomes will rise and their children provide a second generation of customers. Creaming of this market diminishes support for public facilities unused by middle-class patients. In urban America fewer and fewer inhabitants can claim their own family doctors; emergency rooms in voluntary hospitals divert the medically indigent to municipal hospitals; and health delivery seems poised to return to the two-track or possibly multiple-track system from which Great Society legislation temporarily rescued it: superb care for the affluent, good care for the middle classes, cheap and inferior care for the poor.

In short, health providers, at intolerable financial cost, have ill-served the poor and vulnerable and often disappointed even the prosperous. As far back as 1970, *Business Week* commented sharply on a situation that since then has steadily worsened:

> Most of U.S. medical care, particularly the everyday business of preventing and treating routine illnesses, is inferior in quality, wastefully dispensed, and inequitably financed. Medical manpower and facilities are so maldistributed that large segments of the population, especially the urban poor and those in rural areas, get virtually no care at all—even though their illnesses are most numerous and, in a medical sense, often easy to cure. Whether poor or not, most Americans are badly served by the obsolete, overstrained medical system that has grown up around them helter-skelter. . . . The time has come for radical change.[56]

Celebrants of market capitalism routinely claim that their cherished ideal maximizes both efficiency and freedom of consumer choice. In nonmedical markets, celebration is loudest on the part of the winners. In the medical sphere, there are more losers than winners, notably the unemployed and their

## It Really Was a (Nearly) Great Society

families, pensioners, and the working poor. For all parties, American health care is painfully expensive, and outrageously capricious in its allocations of benefits and costs.

Sensibly inspected, American health care represents a failure of a bastardized public-private system which channels financial rewards to health providers and inflicts financial penalties upon the tax-paying public. The cure is not vain pursuit of an entirely private, competitive market. For reasons already stated and sufficient, health care neither echoes the characteristics of markets for consumer products and services nor is likely to be publicly accepted as close kin to these markets. An appropriate response rectifies Lyndon Johnson's fateful 1964 error: the deal he cut with health providers to permit them to rip off the Treasury in return for graciously refraining from sabotage of Medicare and Medicaid. The answer is comprehensive health care.

Sensible types class national health insurance with antitrust as just another lost cause. Franklin Roosevelt rejected health protection in the 1935 Social Security Act, possibly to avoid the fierce opposition of a much more powerful American Medical Association, partly because the framers of the Act had sketchy backgrounds in health coverage. After 1948, Harry Truman got precisely nowhere in his renewed advocacy. For an instant during the Nixon era of ambiguous domestic and global ideology, a conservative version of comprehensive coverage appeared politically feasible: the moment passed. As a candidate desperate for the endorsement of the United Automobile Workers, Jimmy Carter pledged priority for comprehensive coverage. Instead he opted for welfare reform, contemptuously rejected by Congress.

In Reagan's wake, nevertheless, the elusive goal may yet be reached, either as a version of the British salaried service, the Canadian public-private negotiated compromise, extension of existing health maintenance organizations (HMO's), or a mixture of these elements. For in spite of sabotage from organized medicine, health maintenance organizations have good records of reducing hospitalization rates and curtailing average hospitalization stays. Their success and that of state services elsewhere in the world raise the possibility of an effective coalition for universal health protection. Its members could reasonably include ordinary middle-class families disaffected by the cost of incompletely reimbursed care; large employers exercised by ever steeper Blue Cross–Blue Shield premiums paid on behalf of employees and their dependents; cities lumbered by expensive care for the indigent; and, strategically crucial, a large, annually increasing cadre of young doctors menaced by contracting pools of patients, heavy educational debts, the huge costs of solo practice, and barriers erected by established, older doctors against admission to hospital practice.

For newly qualified doctors, the choice more and more often is not between private and salaried medical practice. It is between the Humana and the public payroll. At least 40 percent of physicians are already salaried employees of health-care corporations, HMOs, the armed services, or the Veterans Administration. In the past, the entrepreneurial drive of doctors has been mitigated by the medical tradition of altruism. Such altruism is far less likely to be fostered in corporate than in public environments. To maximizers of bottom lines in corporate medicine, poor people are of no interest except as burdens to be avoided. Established practitioners no doubt will cling to the entrepreneurial independence that has rewarded them lavishly. However, their interests and those of younger colleagues already diverge and soon will diverge more widely and more openly.

I have focused upon the vital health sector as a major instance of the sort of market failure that cries for public correction. With equal merit, the defense sector, public utilities, and housing for all but the affluent can be treated in the same way. The failure of Great Society liberalism lay in its bargains with the private sector that generated enormous public expenditures and an inadequate flow of services to that public. The next wave of liberalism to succeed must be considerably more radical. It must embrace public action as a necessity, as the only means to economical delivery of the essentials of civilized survival.

## Chapter 3
## After Reagan . . . Reagan

THE CEMENT THAT holds societies together is mixed from a recipe of many ingredients. Only one is economic. Myth, prejudice, personality, fear, and passion more often than not sway a voting population seldom more than half the eligible electorate in directions opposite or indifferent to undiluted material interest. To anointed politicians—Franklin Roosevelt, Dwight Eisenhower, John Kennedy, and Ronald Reagan— much is forgiven. Credit adheres to them. Blame is diverted elsewhere. However, in the biennial and quadrennial elections that legitimate presidential and congressional action, the voters, other things equal, tend to retain incumbents when they are reasonably satisfied with their jobs, incomes, and prospects of financial improvement. Republicans lost congressional seats in 1982 at the end of the sharp mini-depression of 1981–82. President Reagan swept to landslide triumph two years later in an expanding economy. The public responds within the context of recent experience. In 1983 and 1984, laid-off workers were being recalled and new jobs were being created in numbers large enough to generate monthly declines in unemployment rates. Inflation had declined to a modest 4 percent, high if personal memory reached back to the early 1960s, but low by comparison with the opening years of this decade. Interest rates, though steep in historic terms, were considerably lower in market if not in real terms than they had been at the beginning of the first Reagan administration. One knew where one stood in making important family choices of residence, autos, appliances, and education. The appearance of stability after turmoil might well have been deceptive, but it was no less reassuring for that possibility.

To reiterate the truism that economics influences voting preferences is of course not to claim that men and women correctly interpret their own interest. As practiced by political consultants and media wizards, the political arts approximate exercises in deception, cynically designed to confuse rather than enlighten undecided voters. Blue-collar workers who cast ballots for Ronald Reagan endorsed the most anti-union chief executive in more than half a century and an administration unwilling to alter policies which attracted a continuing flood of foreign imports that have deprived millions of well-paid American jobs and exerted severe downward pressure upon wages in both union and nonunion plants. Farmers flocked to the Republican banner fully aware that Reagan's farm policies were premised on diminishing federal aid and movement toward "free" markets. Women gave Mr. Reagan a majority of their votes even though his administration has imposed its severest budget cuts on the nutrition, health, welfare, and educational programs that particularly affect women and children. They ignored or discounted the president's opposition to the Equal Rights Amendment and his agents' sabotage of family-planning programs.

Quite possibly, women, farmers, and factory workers understood their family budgets every bit as accurately as their financial betters, but attached greater weight to some of the other ingredients in the social cement. Important among them is patriotism. That sentiment is complex, at its best devotion to ideals of openness, opportunity, and civil liberties, at its worst the boastfulness of a chauvinism that exalts all things American and derogates all things foreign. It is flattered by the large collection of gold medals won by American athletes in the 1984 summer Olympics. Gymnast Mary Lou Retton became an instant heroine and Peter Ueberroth, who managed the event at a profit, an immediate if temporary 1988 presidential possibility. The "liberation" of Grenada proved to be wildly popular as an affirmation of American strength, briskly executed at small cost in lives and treasure. Prudent exclusion of

## After Reagan . . . Reagan

the media shielded the public from the Pentagon's blunders, failures of coordination, and erroneous destruction of a hospital.

The wasteful Pentagon buildup derived support from the durable anti-Communism of solid Americans and created numerous jobs in defense plants strategically located in almost every congressional district: the more wasteful the project, the larger the volume of employment generated. The Lebanon fiasco and the death of nearly three hundred marines were discordant notes in the Battle Hymn of the Republic, but the administration quickly withdrew from a no-win situation and gave itself credit for a good try. No American politician has lost credit by standing up to the Russians. The contrast between Carter's protracted hostage agony in Iran and Reagan's seemingly crisp military operations in Grenada was as sharp as it was unfair. Several Americans were in fact held as hostages in Lebanon during the 1984 presidential contest, and the Reagan administration did no better in extricating them than the allegedly wimpish Carter folks. Even Mrs. Thatcher criticized the Grenada invasion as a breach of international law. No matter. Carter lost in Iran and Reagan won in Grenada. Winning is better than losing. Show me, as that legendary football winner Knute Rockne pithily commented, a good loser and I'll show you a loser.

The United States lags behind only the Soviet Union and the Union of South Africa in the percentage of its population behind bars. We are number one in teenage pregnancies. In a typical week, more people are murdered in New York City than in the whole of Japan. Television is a wasteland of violence, infidelity, fraud, corruption, and pornography. Filmmakers fiercely resist a G-rating for their flicks as fatal to box-office attraction. Handguns are widely distributed and used with an abandon appalling to foreigners. But larger percentages of Americans profess belief in God and attend religious services regularly than in any other nation in the non-Communist world. God is invoked by politicians and enlisted as sponsor of professional football contests. There is a Fellowship of Christian Athletes. Senators and members of Congress precede meetings with lobbyists and fundraisers with well-publicized prayer breakfasts.

Just possibly, our society ranks number one also in hypocrisy. No doubt it is kinder, but unfortunately less accurate, to say that Americans prefer to think of themselves as moral and religious, however distant their conduct as citizens, husbands, and wives may stray from self-image. Walter and Joan Mondale are the children of ministers. Their family life has been exemplary. Mr. Reagan is once divorced, and twice married. His relationship with his children is cool. He does not attend church or arrange for religious services in the White House. But his grasp of the symbols of piety has been as masterly as his deployment of patriotic impulses. His vociferous support for a constitutional amendment promoting prayer in public schools is a virtuoso exercise. There is slender hope that Congress would support by the necessary margins such an amendment and an even smaller probability that three-quarters of the states would ratify it. All the better for presidential purposes. A majority of Americans tell the pollsters that they approve of school prayer. The practical difficulties of composing actual prayers in a theologically diverse society need not be faced, of course, so long as Congress, the states, or the Supreme Court present unleaped hurdles. In the meantime, the president can typecast himself in his favorite role, as champion of spiritual values, and his opponents as essentially irreligious types, secular humanists, or opponents of parental influence over the education of their sons and daughters.

As with prayers, so with the agonizing issue of abortion. In the debate over this profoundly divisive question, Mr. Reagan has clearly occupied the semantic high ground. To be pro-life is far more attractive than to be merely pro-choice. Increasingly, members of the second group find themselves on the defensive against fetuses in bottles and films that purport to demonstrate that fetuses in their mothers' wombs feel pain just like you and me. The issue blends easily into the patriarchal bias of the Reagan official family, their belief in masculine authority, and their consequent unwillingness to concede feminists' claims of women's control over their own bodies. In a public burst of candor, White House chief of staff Donald Regan asserted during the 1985 Reagan-Gorbachev Geneva summit that women were more interested in summit fashions and personalities than in serious masculine issues like the throwweights of nuclear missiles. A playful (female) television interviewer subsequently embarrassed Mr. Regan by asking him to define throwweight. He had severe feminine difficulty in doing so.

Right-to-life fervor allies itself to adult anxieties over personal safety. Although the fact may be of little comfort to frightened urbanites, the incidence of violent crime has actually been declining in recent years, mostly because the number of young males, the majority of the offenders, has been shrinking. As legions of reformers have fruitlessly argued, effective gun control might do more than any other single governmental intervention to save lives. Nevertheless, even after his own near-assassination, President Reagan reasserted his unswerving opposition to such legislation. The gun evidently plays an important role in the masculine psyche. The National Rifle Association is so significant an electoral lobby that Congress has dithered over effective restrictions upon the sale of armor-piercing ammunition for which no legitimate use has been identified by anyone.

In the conservative view, the best way to control crime is to support the police, lengthen prison terms, advocate capital punishment, hail a Bernard Goetz as a hero when he shoots four youths in a subway car, build more prisons, and attack the courts. Our prison sentences are already longer than those in most other countries. Evidence is utterly lacking that capital punishment deters homicide any more than long prison sentences discourage lesser criminals. The number of perpetrators released because arresting officers violated *Miranda* rules is exceedingly small and the quality of police work has probably improved since the courts began to disallow confessions beaten out of suspects by thugs in uniform. Again, however, Mr. Reagan, Attorney General Meese, and other administration operatives appeal to strong human emotions, not to controversial statistics and dreary constitutional debates. We all want bad people locked up. Many of us want the worst among them gassed, electrocuted, or lethally injected. Yearning for revenge has not vanished from civilized hearts. The news of an execution has more than once set crowds to cheering in the streets. If states sold tickets to executions, they would fetch high prices and help balance state budgets, particularly if they were also broadcast on commercial television.

Along with lesser breeds, Americans practice individualism but simultaneously enjoy group action. A century and a half ago, Alexis de Tocqueville marveled at the American propensity to invent new voluntary organizations on almost any pretext. The noted historian Daniel Boorstin speculated that even shared tastes for consumer goods, product communities, tighten the bonds of fraternity. Undeniably we all belong to "statistical communities." As Boorstin phrases the notion, "when a California suburbanite calls himself a member of a 'two-car family,' he is using statistics as a mirror; he is putting himself in a Statistical Community, tactfully implying that he shares other characteristics with other substantial Americans."[1] The thought of common citizenship among gobblers of Big Macs or Whoppers, smokers of True, drinkers of California chablis, drivers of Chevrolets, and fanciers of McIntoshes, videocassette recorders, compact discs, and Polaroid cameras has its ludicrous side. But Boorstin's gloss upon de Tocqueville is serious social commentary. The Bud which is for you, the time that belongs to Miller, the conversations among strangers about the comparative merits of brand-name products—these and their like are testimonials to a sharing of the symbols of common citizenship, much like the national addiction, at last diminishing, to "Dallas" and "Dynasty."

In a manner even more effective than his appeals to piety and patriotism, Ronald Reagan has convinced a large majority of his constituents that he embodies in himself the tastes, the beliefs, the attitudes, the intuitive responses, that they perceive as defining and uniting Americans. Political prudes sniff at tales that the president sets aside his briefing papers in favor of an evening of television with dinner served on trays for himself and Nancy. Most of us know just how he feels—how many times have we been guilty in our humble way of similar flights from duty? The man avoids church and simultaneously blows the trumpet for public piety? At least he says the right things. We all know how far our own practice departs from our professions. Our president shares our taste in products. He knows what entertains us. He avoids faux pas like scheduling his own inauguration in conflict with the Super Bowl. He knew better than to accept the six debates the Mondale side wanted. They would, he averred, bore the public. Right he was.

Multitudes had their troubles remaining awake during the two yawners actually inflicted upon them by the public-spirited League of Women Voters.

Again the contrast with his predecessor is sharp. More than most politicians and most people, Mr. Carter struggled to make his conduct conform to his faith. His promise never to lie to the American people; his conduct of Sunday school classes during his presidency; his celebrated *Playboy* disclosure that he suffered from lust in his heart; his revelation that when he and Mrs. Carter quarreled, they resolved their anger by kneeling in prayer on opposite sides of the bed; his agonized efforts to make human rights an integral part of American foreign policy; his ill-advised scolding of the voters as victims of spiritual malaise—all this registered discordantly in the ears and eyes of the public. Carter told us that there was a good deal of room for improvement in the way we led our lives. Reagan loves us just as we are. To be American is to be as near perfection as mere humans are likely to reach. Flattery will get you anywhere, even into the Oval Office.

Such small blemishes as mar the fair countenance of America the beautiful, the land of opportunity, the protector of freedom fighters in Nicaragua, Angola, and Afghanistan, Europe's shield again Communist tyranny, are subject to simple remedy. Take the government off our backs. Cut taxes. Lift onerous environmental, health and safety, and product-reliability regulations that add to corporate costs and handicap American exporters in the fierce competition for world markets. Salute mergers of gigantic corporations into megaliths. Remind the citizens that America is about opportunity, not governmental guarantees of cash and benefits without individual effort or merit. Affirmative action insults, or should insult, American tradition. Horizons are unlimited, wealth unbounded for individuals, not groups. Affirmative action, therefore, cuts against the grain of national character when it sets hiring and promotion targets for blacks or women as groups.

Societies live by their myths, the noble lies Plato advocated in *The Republic* as essential to social peace and class harmony. Our myths exalt individual action, legitimize gross inequalities of income and wealth as reflections of differences in human effort and attainment, despise losers, and attach small value to public intervention and group solidarity. Blue-collar opposition to unions as organizations addicted to the maximization of the wealth and power of union leaders rather than improvement in the lot of union members registers deep attachment to the credo of individualism as well as, in some instances, justified suspicion of the behavior of union officials. Nothing so well expresses the total absence of worker solidarity than the willingness of union members to tolerate lower wages for newcomers who fill jobs identical to those of veterans. When the going was good, truck drivers expressed little resentment at the lavish lifestyle of a parade of presidents stretching back to Dan Tobin and continuing with Frank Fitzsimmons, Jimmy Hoffa, and the current occupant, Jackie Presser. Why shouldn't they grab whatever they could, so long as they passed out the smaller prizes of hefty wage and benefit improvement every year or two to the boys and a few girls behind the steering wheels? American unions routinely cross each other's picket lines. During the 1981 flight controllers' strike, members of other unions calmly reported for work as usual.

There is a further point. Much as upset small children rush for comfort to their mommies, Americans troubled by social disorder and uncertainty about their own finances and job security seek paternal presidential reassurance that traditional values and traditional myths can reassert themselves. Vietnam, rebellious college students, upstart women, obstreperous Arabs, stagflation, Watergate, the Ayatollah, the scandalous exit of one president and the perceived ineffectuality of his two successors: all dented American confidence in themselves and their institutions. Public opinion researchers reported in the 1970s that rising percentages of the population distrusted lawyers, doctors, politicians, corporate executives, college teachers, and, name them, the practitioners of any trade, profession, craft, or mystery. Very little remains of professional comity. In time past reluctant to criticize colleagues publicly, doctors now routinely testify against each other in malpractice trials. Lawyers certify the negligence and incompetence of their peers. A client sued Melvin Belli, the so-called King of Torts, in reprisal for a lost suit. Mr. Belli then sued the associate in his firm who had actually handled the case.

The keen insight of retrospect suggests that the flight to the

## After Reagan ... Reagan

familiar began even before the 1960s drew to their tumultuous close. Richard Nixon promised peace with honor in Vietnam; renewed devotion to God, family values, and the work ethic; and stern treatment of drug offenders, violent radicals, and other opponents of law and order. His only complete term was marked with contradictions. In his Disraeli phase, his then domestic counselor Daniel Patrick Moynihan sweet-talked him into sponsorship of fundamental welfare reform. The environmental movement gained sufficient momentum to push important legislation through Congress; the Environmental Protection Administration is a product of the Nixon years. Social Security benefits rose steeply and, although welfare reform perished in the Senate Finance Committee at the skilled hands of Senator Russell Long, Congress enacted the Supplemental Security Income Act which greatly improved the financial situation of the blind, the disabled, and the impecunious elderly whose Social Security benefits were too small for sustenance. Deceived by Nixon's nasty rhetoric and unwilling to forgive the man for earlier misdeeds, liberals infrequently noted that money for social programs was far more generously dispensed in the conservative 1970s than in the progressive 1960s.

Nixon's crushing defeat of George McGovern in 1972 was widely interpreted as a rebuff to the alternative lifestyles of gays, drug users, abortion advocates, communards, and amateur revolutionaries. But for Watergate, a complete second Nixon term might have consolidated the conservative reaction to Great Society liberalism and installed Republicans again as the natural majority party as it had been between the Civil War and the New Deal. The presidency of Jimmy Carter, nearly as accidental a sequel to Watergate as the Ford caretaker years, restored momentum to a conservative reaction punctuated and interrupted by the gaudy burglaries, dirty tricks, and gamey tapes of the Watergate conspirators. Carter's stab at welfare reform never progressed from committee consideration to the floor of either the House of Representatives or the Senate. In violation of a campaign pledge, his administration never presented health legislation extending coverage to the entire population. Carter's few domestic successes were conservative. Congress accepted deregulation of the airlines and trucking industries. It endorsed enlargement of Pentagon budgets. It colluded with administration operatives to draw the teeth from the Humphrey-Hawkins Balanced Growth and Full Employment bill. When Congress passed energy legislation, its centerpiece was the creation of a synfuels boondoggle calculated at the time to rival defense contracts as a source of easy corporate profit.

One should not either oversimplify or overstate the liberal case against Carter. He was not willing, like Ronald Reagan, to purchase lower inflation at the cost of deep recession. Although personally opposed to abortion, he did not convert his own preferences into a public crusade. Devoted Baptist though he was, he refused to endorse prayer in the public schools. In the 1970s—the 1990s may turn out differently—even a moderate Democratic occupant of the White House paid political attention to the AFL-CIO and the concerns of minorities.

In short, the ground was better prepared for Ronald Reagan in 1980 than in 1976 when voters in Republican primaries narrowly preferred Gerald Ford, a traditional conservative, to the siren songs of their tempter in the cause of rugged individualism. It is quite possible, even probable, that the sequel to Reagan in 1988 and possibly in the remainder of this wretched century will be continuation of tendencies visibly powerful in his era.

Yet there are many disharmonies in the Reagan chorus, notably between singers of supply-side hymns of joy and prophets of the conservative social agenda—compulsory prayer and compulsory pregnancy. Considerable dissension exists within the corporate community over trade and tax policy. Populists of the right favor cuts in personal tax rates, even if corporations end up paying more. The supply-side gospel according to Jack Kemp is opposed by traditional business conservatives whose ideal tax rate on corporate earnings is zero or negative. Even so, the coalition may be held together by patriotic stimuli—judicious reinvigorating doses of Grenada. In this nightmare, military Keynesianism will continue to prop up the economy, enlarge profits, and provide jobs. A discreetly masked revival of racism will reawaken barely dormant white prejudice. The endless dream of wealth just might consume the psychic energies of yuppies and their more numerous fellow travelers. Allied with dreams of wealth is a culture of consumption epitomized by the bumper sticker "Born to Shop." Crusades against radicals and criminals will offer alternative diversions to small military adventures. Reagan's army embraces overlapping cadres of the godly and the greedy. Possibly no other Republican can keep these free spirits together. One should not underestimate the skills of our politicians. The Republican coalition surely embraces participants no more different in temperament, economic interest, and personal qualities than Franklin Roosevelt's amalgam of Southern racists, urban political bosses, furious farmers, and militant trade unionists.

The parallel to South Africa is alarming. Of course, there are no official Bantustans in America. A few middle-class blacks will win nomination as honorary whites, much as Hitler had, in World War II, elevated his Japanese allies to brevet Aryan status. As ever, our inner cities will play their role as informal Bantustans. Both our foreign and domestic policies will place growing emphasis upon officially sanctioned violence—by the police in the cities and by the CIA and the armed forces in Central America and elsewhere. Gradually the boundaries of unpenalized, unpopular expression will narrow. Universities will come under the heavy influence, perhaps the de facto control, of the government agencies and major corporations which fund them. Congress will be coaxed by a series of real or contrived spy scandals and leaks of sensitive information to enact a version of the British Official Secrets Act. Recent routinization of lie-detector tests is an excellent first step. A second is the clamor for universal drug testing. Critics who point to the unreliability of polygraphs miss the point. Polygraphs and urinalysis are instruments of social control, tests of a bureaucrat's or an employee's docility in the presence of humiliation. Causing less furor, the federal government will simply collect fewer statistics on such annoying topics as poverty, infant mortality, unemployment, farm foreclosures, and business failures. What information is gathered can be rendered less accessible and more expensive to users. Most of the 1980 census is on computer tapes, unlike all preceding census materials, which are readily available in libraries with the bindings of old-fashioned books.

# 2

In this and the next chapter, I propose to examine this dark prospect under several dispiriting rubrics:

1. Privatization of public services and its corollary, the substitution of vouchers for publicly funded services.

2. De-unionization and its corollary, continued downward drift of the wage structure.

3. As a consequence of (1) and (2), an increasing distance between the top and the bottom of income distribution and shrinkage of the middle strata.

4. Militarization.

5. Conversion of Social Security into a means-tested program, partly by ever-heavier taxation of benefits and mostly by offers of individual retirement accounts as alternatives to Social Security.

6. Dismantling by the courts, populated at all levels by large numbers of Reagan nominees, of much of the legal protection of individual rights added during the 1960s in the sunny time of the Warren court. Rehnquist, Scalia, and O'Connor are a formidable, comparatively youthful Supreme Court reactionary bloc. Unqualified ideologues like Daniel Manion are nominated for positions on the Court of Appeals.

## PRIVATIZATION

Efficiency is the prime value of standard economics, a subject, in the sage words of the Ayatollah Khomeini, "fit only for donkeys."[2] Group solidarity and universality of benefits either clash with efficiency or, at most, exist as sociologists' notions of little interest to the professional economist. Upstanding economists despise sociology. One prominent Stanford practitioner of the donkey's discipline stops reading any economic article in which the word so much as appears. In competitive markets, the comparative efficiency of participants is measured for enterprises by profitability and for their employees by market-driven variations among wages and salaries. Sellers enlarge market shares by improving old products, introducing new ones, increasing reliability, and cutting price. Workers win promotion and larger rewards as they demonstrate skills of value to employers. From the queues of job seekers, employers select first those best qualified by work history, education, and skill, and proceed in orderly fashion down the line to successively inferior candidates, the worst of whom must continue to seek jobs better suited to their meager qualifications.

Employees seek to please employers. Employers, for their part, must gratify customers on pain of lost profit and eventual bankruptcy. Competitive markets are mechanisms sensitively attuned to the changing tastes of customers. They penalize incompetent businessmen and lazy workers. They reward enterprises that cut costs and respond most rapidly to the shifting preferences of buyers. Entrepreneurs gamble huge sums on new products in the hope of providing a product that their customers had been blissfully unaware that they craved. Until children and their parents saw them, they had no better notion that Cabbage Patch dolls were an absolute necessity than that ballpoint pens, color television, and video recorders were essential items in the well-equipped household. The endless variety available to American, European, and Japanese shoppers is the envy of visitors from socialist societies. Even the anguish of choosing a long-distance telephone service or a money-market fund is no more than a temporary inconvenience. The best telephone service and the most lucrative money-market or mutual fund will win the day. Defeated rivals will slink off the economic stage, licking their wounds.

What a sad contrast government shamefacedly presents to the glittering bazaar of private enterprise! Civil service rules inhibit corruption. They also stifle innovation, shield time servers and incompetents, and enmesh citizens in rolls of red tape. Assured of lifetime tenure, bureaucrats need not treat citizens in search of licenses, permits, and information with courtesy or dispatch. Your local Bureau of Motor Vehicles as the only source of operators' licenses and car registrations behaves with the indifference and arrogance of any other monopolist. Internal Revenue Service computers routinely fail. Refunds are endlessly delayed. Innocent entrepreneurs receive impolite threats of prosecution for taxes they don't owe. Letters of apology also are delayed. En route to maximum profit, private monopolists are compelled if not to satisfy their customers, at least to avert active mutiny. Few monopolies are permanent. Public utilities, our most prominent monopolists, need new capital. The terms upon which they acquire it correlate closely with the market's judgment of efficiency and profitability. Moreover, private monopolists must fear entry of rivals much in the fashion of telephones, once the exclusive domain of AT&T and now open for grabs by numerous thrusting rivals.

Public agencies are exempt from the bottom-line discipline of the market. In most instances, they offer services and products free of charge. Even when fees are levied, they represent political rather than economic decisions. Bureaucratic imperatives encourage empire-building. Agency directors judge their place in the pecking order by the number of subordinates under their control. It follows that effective bureaucratic managers maximize employment rather than efficiency. It is difficult to evaluate the efficiency of any enterprise that either gives away or artificially prices its output. The national income statisticians in effect surrender when they estimate the value of public services according to the cost of labor, materials, rented space, and other inputs. The result inevitably is perverse, for the larger the inputs the more valuable the products are alleged to be.

It is accordingly imperative that government's role be severely curtailed. An administration felicitously guided by economists will actively encourage competition. It will hasten to enact the kind of regulations which compel enterprises to internalize external costs, that is to say force polluters either to cease polluting or, preferably, impose escalating fees upon them as the quantity of pollutants rises. Although government has an obligation to assist the helpless, it should do so in ways which interfere least with market incentives. Finally, there is a category of public goods that fall into the province of government. For the most part, these are items which cannot readily be produced for profit, such as administration of justice (though even here some exceptions exist),[3] or those from which the public cannot be excluded even if they do not contribute to the cost of creating them. Defense is the most notable example. Willy-nilly pacifists, anti-nuke crusaders, and those too poor to pay federal income tax are as completely defended as the richest and most bellicose of their neighbors.

In a variety of ways, privatization began to gain momentum, like such key elements of the Reagan agenda as deregulation and acceleration of weapons procurement (the infamous MX was a Carter favorite), in Jimmy's administration. Its advocates claim that privatization not only saves money by substituting flexible market structures for rigid bureaucracy, it also widens consumer choice. Tuition tax credits for the parents of children enrolled in private or religious schools increase the diversity of eductional programs, a good thing. They impose heavier pressure upon public schools to meet stronger competition, a better thing. Best of all, they dismantle local monopolies long enjoyed by public schools. To no article of faith are economists more strongly attached than their utter certainty that monopoly any place, any time connotes inefficiency, sterile repetition of outmoded production and delivery techniques, and corresponding absence of innovation.

Where is the line to be drawn between private and public operation? Apparently not in the vast health industry. Employment in hospitals nearly doubled between 1966 and 1979, but the rates of growth differed notably by type of ownership. Employment in public hospitals rose a mere 58 percent, in the nonprofit voluntaries 90 percent, but in the profit-making sector a dramatic 130 percent.[4] An even more rapidly expanding health specialty, nursing home facilities, now operates nearly 80 percent for profit.[5] Humana, Hospital Corporation of America, and American Medical International, the largest for-profit hospital operators, continue to acquire nonprofits, municipal hospitals, and even university-affiliated medical centers like that of George Washington University, in Washington, D.C.

Out there, of course, there are carping critics like Dr. Arnold S. Reiman, editor of the *New England Journal of Medicine*, who asserts that "The for-profit hospitals avoid services that are not profitable, even though they may be of use to the community. . . . Hospitals make money on short-term illness, preferably elective surgical procedures on otherwise healthy, relatively young people. They like short stays and a lot of diagnostic studies. They don't like patients who need labor-intensive care, like burn patients, or the chronically ill, or elderly patients. That's expensive."[6] And, of course, as a price of progress toward market efficiency an occasional patient dies. When Humana opened its new Louisville hospital in May 1983, it announced that it would not include a burn unit. Soon afterwards Norton-Kosair Children's Hospital, a nonprofit unit that for nine years had treated burn patients, announced that it could no longer afford to accept adult burn patients on whom it had lost $400,000 during the preceding year. The sequel?

> The inevitable happened. On June 23, 1983, a fifty-year-old woman was severely burned in an explosion on her houseboat in the Ohio River. She was picked up by an ambulance provided by Meic Inc. of Jeffersonville, Ind., across the river. Brenda K. Noon, the ambulance dispatcher, said in a memorandum that she called Norton-Kosair while the ambulance was on the way there. "I in turn advised Unit 237 Norton's will not accept the patient," she wrote. The patient was then sent to the Humana Hospital–University and died of smoke inhalation."[7]

The local furor caused by the incident impelled Humana to open a burn unit, an action no doubt consoling to the vicitm's relatives and friends.

As chain spokespersons concede, hospital charges frequently rise in the wake of takeovers, particularly of rural county hospitals, populated mostly by paying patients. In Collin County, Texas, voters rejected a bond issue to raise funds for its county hospital. American Medical International bought the hospital and promptly hiked charges 20 percent. As Dr. Ron Anderson, administrator of Dallas's public Parkland Hospital put it, "What the County Commissioners couldn't do, raise taxes, A. M. I. did with a hidden tax, by raising charges."[8]

Are the hospital chains truly more efficient? Do their economies of scale and business-school managerial skills really more than compensate for inflated executive salaries and generous stockholder dividends? These are early days in a market almost daily transformed by political and corporate maneuver. Nevertheless, none of the available inquiries reaches conclusions inspiring to free-market zealots. A 1984 study conducted by the Hospital Research and Educational Trust, an American Hospital Associate affiliate, concluded that in the 272 hospitals studied there were no significant efficiency differences between public and for-profit units. A California analysis echoed this judgment: "Given equal responsibility, accountability and amounts of money, government-operated public services have nearly always been shown to be equal to or better in quality than privately operated ones."[9]

Still another California survey, which compared charges by fifty-three chain hospitals, seventy-eight independent proprietary hospitals, 114 voluntary nonprofits, and thirty-five public units, discovered that the chains' inpatient bills were 24 percent higher than those of the nonprofits. There was no indication that patients received better medical care for their money. As in California, so in Florida. The state's Hospital Cost Containment Board study covering 1980–84 recorded 11 percent higher charges in profit-seeking hospitals and, belying efficiency claims, 4 percent higher operating costs.[10]

Communities lured into deals with the for-profits often live to regret them. Wyoming County Community Hospital in Warsaw, New York, for example, terminated its contract with the Hospital Corporation of America because the financial problems that seemed to justify recourse to the private sector persisted. As Douglas Bliss, the hospital board's chairman, unhappily conceded, "We had problems before they came, and they got worse when they were here."[11] Public hospitals in Greene County and the town of Cuba, also in conservative, upstate New York, decided not to renew management contracts. The alleged magic of the marketplace apparently diminishes neither the cost of patient care nor the soaring prices attached to ever more exotic advances in medical technology.

If our current festival of private enterprise continues, a thousand studies heaped high to the heavens will not slow privatization in the health sector because its benefits are less financial than they are sociological. One of the tribulations of hospitalization is the sort of people one meets. In the next bed may restlessly toss someone of the wrong color, occupation, lifestyle, or income. Privatization promises better company. Treatment in a strategically located Humana hospital warrants continuation in sickness as in health of safe, middle-class suburban life. Your fellow patients fit snugly into your own class niche. Their education, jobs, income, and opinions are just like those you encounter in your car pool or on the commuter train. Critics of corporate hospitals justifiably complain that they cream the population, consigning difficult people and their complicated ailments to public and voluntary units. Of course. The critics have identified the major attraction of private hospitals to those creamed. Who prefers skimmed milk to cream?

To the degree that purveyors of hospital care turn themselves into extensions of consumer culture, they attract customers attuned to the familiar arts of advertising and marketing. At the beginning of 1985, there were approximately 2,300 immediate- or urgent-care centers, conveniently located either in shopping malls or nearby free-standing buildings. In the spirit of Adam Smith if not of Hippocrates, these operate as entrepreneurial ventures. Of the 2,300, eighty-three were Humana Medfirst Clinics, twenty-nine Flashner Medical Partnership Doctors' Officenters, twenty-three Centra Units, eighteen Instant Care centers managed by National Medical Enterprises, to give appropriate recognition to some of the more prominent operators.[12] After all, an appointment usually is necessary with a physician in private practice. Emergency room visits entail long delays in disagreeable environments and potluck assignment to a doctor who happens to be on duty. In pleasant contrast, one can stroll into a shopping mall medical office and secure quick treatment for a mild flu virus, a migraine headache, twisted ankle, minor burn, or stomach upset from lunching at one of the mall's fast-food emporia. One-stop service. A credit card is acceptable for quick settlement of the bill. Like their hospital companions, immediate-care centers overtly appeal to the imperatives of efficiency and profit and covertly respond to the claims of class and status.

As Dr. Gerard Anderson of Johns Hopkins temperately observed, "You will find them in a Westport, a Stamford or a Greenwich but not necessarily in Harlem."[13] For the middle-class customers, the benefit is above all convenience. Typical immediate-care centers are available for business seven days a week, 365 days a year, twelve-to-sixteen hours daily. Group practices, let alone solo operators, keep bankers' rather than retailers' hours. Fees usually compare favorably with conventional charges. For young doctors, there are financial temptations. At age thirty, Dr. Bernard Corbett closed his private practice and enlisted in MedCenter, explaining that "It's becoming more competitive and it's become increasingly expensive for a young physician to set up his own practice. With these urgent-care centers you can go into practice, but you don't have to worry about money and the front office. There is someone else doing that."[14]

One fears that Dr. Corbett is naïve. If he does not attract enough customers, he will rapidly discover that the folks in the front office who tend to worry more about their money than Dr. Corbett's will either replace him with a more enterprising healer or shut the office down. For the MBAs who increasingly control hospitals, nursing homes, and HMOs, medical services are indistinguishable from other products. The tests they dare not fail are financial, not ethical. Humana and its major rivals define instant-care centers as conduits into their hospitals, much as private physicians send patients to voluntary units.

The correlation between cash and the quality of health care has always been uncomfortably high in America. Nevertheless, until recently official rhetoric and, to some extent, actual public funding operated to check the sorting of patients by income. Before the United States began to deindustrialize, major corporate and some public employers offered health coverage generous enough to pay almost all hospital room charges and physicians' fees. Employees freely chose their own doctors. The latter sent patients to hospitals as their medical judgment directed. Medicare was designed to relieve the elderly of the bulk of their health-care costs. Still-employed and retired blue-collar workers and their families shared physicians and hospital space with more affluent types.

In the ways just discussed, privatization enlarges the impact of income and wealth upon the quantity and quality of medical care. There is more to be said. Responding to competitive pressure, and taking advantage of union weakness, corporate America has launched a major offensive against employee health benefits. Strategies feature mandatory second opinions, channeling to outpatient surgery, limitations upon reimbursable hospital sojourns, and preferred provider plans which restrict or penalize free choice of personal physicians. Medicare pays a diminishing fraction of pensioners' medical expenses and propels rising percentages of the elderly into the Medicaid system after they exhaust assets during extended nursing-home stays. It scarcely helps matters that the Reagan administration proposes to eliminate federal regulation of nursing homes.

Privatization redefines health care. No longer is it a basic human right, its status in other advanced societies. In the new order, customers choose health care products much as they shop for cars, refrigerators, and microwave ovens. The four thousand employees of Quaker Oats in and around Chicago have been presented with a booklet listing charges in forty-four hospitals for such procedures as normal delivery of babies, tonsillectomies, and cardiac catheterization. Prudential Insurance and an employers' organization, the Midwest Business Group on Health, compiled the information. Quaker Oats toilers pay 15 percent of their hospital bills. If they heed the booklet's message, they can henceforth minimize their hospital charges by shopping around for the cheapest facilities and, unmentioned corollary, doctors who enjoy admitting privileges into them. Totally rational patients will change doctors if necessary to minimize costs. Zenith challenges its seven thousand workers in Glenview, Illinois, to save on maternity costs: "Having a baby: can you beat the average"? A true challenge to prospective parents. Zenith's health-care newsletter helpfully lists delivery prices in twenty-five hospitals. At fifteen of them average costs for normal deliveries exceeded the Zenith average maternity bill.[15] Do the cheaper hospitals offer inferior care? Zenith does not evaluate hospitals, it prices them.

Operating on conventional business principle, profit-making hospitals grab for larger market shares in competition with nonprofits by segmenting their customers. For those who can afford them, VIP suites and gourmet cuisine are available. Elsewhere all available corners will be cut. Nurses will become more productive. Translation: the ratio of patients to nurses, aides, and attendants will rise. Patients will be prematurely discharged when insurance or Medicare reimbursement threatens to run out. Interns and residents will work even longer hours than is the barbarous medical tradition. Pressure upon medically insured workers and their families to pay more of their own health-care bills reinforces shopping by price. It also saves money in the short run for employers and employees because cost-conscious families will hesitate to consult doctors for seemingly minor ailments. In the not-so-long run, some of these ailments will turn serious, entail days or weeks of incapacity for work, and much larger medical bills.

Those voluntary hospitals that survive will unavoidably cut costs in much the same fashion as their corporate rivals. Nonprofits and for-profits will do their best to dump financially unrewarding patients upon chronically overcrowded and underfunded municipal facilities. As market medicine dictates, indigent, elderly, and chronically ailing patients will get the care they merit—as little as possible. As President Reagan is fond of saying, America is back—to the era of public and private charity.

I have lingered so long upon the health sector because of its life-and-death significance and its sheer size—some 11 percent of the gross national product, nearly twice the Pentagon's share. Privatization is not confined to health services. It extends far beyond garbage and bill collection to the criminal justice system. Even Adam Smith, the saint of minimal government, legitimized public administration of courts. In America it is unwise to underestimate the entrepreneurial imagination. By 1984, private, profit-making enterprises owned or managed about two dozen major correction facilities, according to an American Correctional Association estimate. Its authors guess that the number will rise rapidly. Incarceration strikes the Nashville-based Corrections Corporation of America as an activity ripe for market discipline. Its president proclaimed that "Our basic mission is to provide correctional services to government in an efficient, cost-effective manner."[16]

Take Dennis E. Bradby as a corrections pioneer. He runs the Silverdale Detention Center, housing 325 prisoners serving long terms for felonies as serious as murder, county offenders enjoying Silverdale hospitality for less than a year, and a handful of drunk drivers drying out during mandatory forty-eight-hour penalty sessions. The facility is located on the edge of Chattanooga, Tennessee. Along with his forty-six subordinates, Bradby wears a camel-colored sweater bearing the insignia of the Corrections Corporation of America. Perhaps to comfort the inmates, nobody is called a guard; they are all "resident supervisors." The Corrections Corporation has rivals. Buckingham Security Ltd. even now is constructing a $20 million, 715-cell, maximum-security penitentiary north of Pittsburgh. It will specialize in child molesters, individuals in protective custody, and other hard cases menaced by members of the general prison population.[17]

Why profit-making prisons? Their advocates point to numerous virtues. Corporations avoid cumbersome state contractural procedures. Thus a facility constructed in four years by a state agency might open in six months under corporate inspiration. Private managers can freely hire and fire without sabotage from civil service rules or incompetent patronage hacks. As in any other new industry, enterprises tend to be innovative, vigorous, and lean in managerial style. Private prisons may actually be more humane than public alternatives. The Reverend Thomas Sheehy, liaison for the Catholic diocese of Galveston-Houston with an immigration detention center managed by the Corrections Corporation of America, declared that "If I had my choice of this private organization, or it being run by the Immigration and Naturalization Service, I would take this private organization. They're much more humane. The guards haven't been in the business that long, so they're not calloused."[18]

Is the public, issues of law and equity aside, getting a good bargain when government shrinks and private contractors assume new responsibilities? There is excellent cause for skepticism. Corporate newcomers to the criminal justice market, for example, will no doubt pursue the successful strategy pioneered by space contractors: bid low on initial contracts and, once customers are locked into personal and business relationships convenient to all parties, raise prices sharply. Competition is as inadequate a safeguard here as it has been in Pentagon procurement. Municipalities and states which consign construction and management of new prisons to corporate entrepreneurs will rapidly discover that they have as little alternative to private operation as the Pentagon does in dealing with a single source of a weapons system. Illustrative of the ailment is the Pentagon's intermittent suspension of General Dynamics as the recipient of new contracts. Invariably eligibility is restored just in time to qualify the contractor for still another lucrative helping of military appropriations. A government-corrections, a government-research, a government–health care partnership seems fated to replicate the expensive history of the military-industrial complex, complete with conflicts of interest on the part of bureaucrats who plan to move into the very private sector with which they officially deal, much as generals, admirals, colonels, and commanders smoothly shrug out of their uniforms into corporate pinstripes as extravagantly rewarded vice-presidents of General Dynamics, Martin Marietta, General Electric, Rockwell, and smaller clients of the Department of Defense. Ossified corporate bureaucracies wage phony war against their ossified government counterparts. Imaginative accounting is part of the game. As an impediment to economic efficiency, a single Pentagon-industrial complex is more than enough.

Private prisons and private jails threaten civil rights as well as state and local solvency. Resident counselors will shortly become as calloused as traditional guards. Prisoners will have even less protection against brutality and arbitrary discipline than they do now. Some enterprises already in operation do not inspire confidence in wholesale privatization of the corrections system. The Danner Corporation operates a Houston facility that lodged sixteen stowaways in a windowless twelve-by-twenty cellar. One of the aliens tried to escape while their guard took a telephone call. A second guard, untrained in the use of firearms, proceeded to kill one inmate and wound another. In his previous career as warden of the Lewisburg Penitentiary in Pennsylvania, one of the brothers who founded Buckingham, another corporate operator, was among a group of prison officials who were charged with inflicting cruel and unusual punishment upon two inmates in their charge.[19]

Are corporate managers willing or, if willing, able to protect the constitutional rights of their involuntary customers? Can states delegate such protection to private entities? At least one jurist, Chief Judge John Singleton of the Federal District Court in Houston, has held that the Immigration and Naturalization Service could not constitutionally surrender its responsibilities to aliens to private contractors. In his blunt language, "Because both immigration and detention are traditionally the exclusive prerogative of the state, it is evident that the actions of all the defendants were state action within the purview of the public function doctrine."[20]

The final and most powerful charge against corrections privatization is ethical. Imprisonment punishes its human target. The rule of law prescribes fair trial in open court before anyone can be deprived of personal freedom. The men and women who administer punishment are state agents, responsible to elected public officials and elected or appointed judges. Private prisons, like private hospitals, are driven by profit maximization, not sensitivity to the needs or rights of prisoners or patients. As Princeton political philosopher Michael Walzer has asked, "Is this punishment or economic calculation, the law or the market?"[21] Patients in corporate hospitals might raise a similar issue: is this test, procedure, or medication required for my benefit or that of stockholders and top managers?

Job training for profit should also be on the suspect list. For various reasons, government-sponsored programs have received mixed reviews. In time of fiscal crisis, CETA funds were diverted from job training to the support of the police, fire protection, education, and sanitation operations. It is too soon to evaluate the Reagan Job Partnership experiment. Can the profit maximizers train workers at lower cost and guide them into more permanent jobs than public alternatives? They are trying.

The Ohio Works experiment earlier noted has expanded into other states. Additional corporate trainers have entered the market. Good luck to all of them. But the evidence of success is slender, anecdotal, and suspiciously subject to the familiar allegation of "creaming." All job-training veterans know how to generate a flow of inspiring results. Simply recruit welfare recipients who are newcomers to dependency, suffer the smallest educational deficits, possess reasonably good work histories, and, with morale reasonably intact, lust for new jobs. It is comparatively easy to persuade employers to gamble on such people, especially because they can collect tax benefits as a salute to their public spirit. Of course, many or most of these new employees would have found jobs for themselves. Cost-benefit calculations are certain to deter corporate trainers and motivators from dipping very far down into the pool of the long-term jobless. Equally unlikely clients are those who lack basic reading and arithmetic skills, motivation, and any but casual work experience. For this population, success rates are low and per-capita expenditures high. From one point of view, the Job Corps' 35 percent success rate is an inspiring outcome. Corporations want quicker, cheaper, and more predictable results. Residential programs of the Job Corps variety are expensive. A price tag of $15,000 or so for a year's training is unattractive to bottom-line calculators.

For all its obvious and potential failings, privatization is a spreading affliction. At least one community has replaced its police force with a private security company. Numerous towns and cities have delegated fire protection and garbage collection to private operators. Entrepreneurs run airport control towers. Dun and Bradstreet and smaller credit agencies screen applicants for federal loans, grants, and contracts. Administration plans include shrinkage of the Veterans Administration hospital system and substitution of private alternatives, among them corporate hospitals. The Office of Management and Budget wants private insurance companies to manage, among other federal efforts, Medicare, Medicaid, and federal crop insurance. The results already are impressive. The federal government bought $100 billion of private commercial services in 1980. The comparable 1985 figure is $173 billion.[22]

Is government really that bad? Is private enterprise that good? So far the evidence against the first and on behalf of the second is almost entirely of the for-instance variety. Skeptics note how often privatization freaks cite a New York City comparison of the costs of private and public garbage collection. Can it be that other examples of private efficiency are scarce? Nonetheless, for better or worse, more Reagan entails more privatization.

### VOUCHERS

Vouchers, a firm ally of privatization, distinguish themselves from the latter by their emphasis upon widening the market for public services rather than simply substituting private for governmental suppliers. Vouchers are special-purpose currency. When they are issued by the Housing and Urban Development department or local housing authorities, landlords will accept them because they are redeemable in normal, all-purpose money. In the largest existing voucher program, supermarkets trade groceries for food stamps and subsequently redeem them in cash. It would be simpler to give the cash in the first place to those eligible. Politicians and their constituents hesitate to embrace this administrative simplification because they suspect that in the absence of restrictions upon the use of income transfers, some parents would divert food money to drugs or alcohol. Similar reservations apply to housing and medical care. In effect, vouchers, their supporters argue, judiciously compromise between two important objectives: the welfare, of the recipients, especially of children, and the substitution of free consumer choice for government direction.

Vouchers reinforce privatization by shifting demand from government bodies to individual beneficiaries. In the absence of voucher mechanisms, government usually pays food, medical, housing, or education bills for beneficiaries. Once vouchers enter the scene, government continues to pay the bills but—crucial change—no longer directs individuals to a specific supplier. Low-income families offered accommodation in a public-housing market are excluded from the remainder of the housing market. Vouchers allow such families the freedom to shop for the best deal already enjoyed by more prosperous fellow citizens. The lines are long when surplus cheese is distributed. Food stamps by contrast enable cheese-haters to buy other nutrients in more dignified, less time-wasting settings. Real people shop in supermarkets, not in government warehouses.

To enthusiasts, privatization and vouchers promise to restore consumer sovereignty over no-choice services offered by government not only to the welfare population but middle-class America as well. On the supply side of the market, privatization substitutes bottom-line business efficiency for expensive and cumbersome state bureaucracy. On the demand side, individuals will enjoy an approximation of the free choice they expect and receive in a consumer society.

Vouchers flourish in the current nurturing conservative

environment. However, their rationale extends backward in time at least to 1962 when Milton Friedman published his free-market manifesto, *Capitalism and Freedom.* In it, Friedman attacked compulsory public education as at worst a monopoly and at best an unfair competitor with private alternatives. In small communities, the public school usually is the only school. In larger communities, parents who prefer religious or independent institutions pay twice, once when they get the school tax bill and again when the alternative school bill arrives. As usual, the heaviest burden falls upon low-income parents who are aware that public schools in their neighborhood fall short of their expectations but lack the resources either to move to areas where schools are better or meet private school charges.

The present arrangement is as inefficient as it is unfair. Good teachers are discouragingly underpaid and bad ones grossly overcompensated. Civil service and union rules make it virtually impossible to dismiss incompetent performers. Teaching attracts a disproportionate percentage of mediocre college graduates. In school districts where many parents send sons and daughters to religious or independent schools, bond issues for public school construction or improvement frequently get, understandably, voted down. Consequently, present tax and financing procedures weaken both public and private education, frustrate parent preferences, and encourages continued mediocrity.

For Friedman, the remedy is blindingly obvious. Here it is, in all is stark simplicity:

> Government could require a minimum level of schooling financed by giving parents vouchers redeemable for a specified maximum sum per child per year if spent on "approved" educational services. Parents would then be free to spend this sum and any additional sum they themselves provided on purchasing educational services from an "approved" institution of their own choice. The educational services could be rendered by private enterprises operated for profit or nonprofit institutions. The role of government would be limited to insuring that the schools met certain minimum standards, such as the inclusion of a minimum

common content in their programs, much as it now inspects restaurants to see that they maintain minimum sanitary standards.[23]

Just as parents shift back and forth between McDonald's and Burger King, they could register serious dissatisfaction with one school by transferring a child to another one. As churches, secular groups, and profit-seeking entrepreneurs crowd into the school market, standards will rise everywhere, not least in the public sector. Fair competition is the best way to revitalize any monopoly.

Dr. Friedman is our most notorious free-market conservative. He is also an extraordinarily imaginative social theorist. But his vouchers have appealed also to liberals and radicals who accuse public education of cheating the children of the poor by lowering their expectations and directing them into low-paid, routine jobs. Radicals addicted to school decentralization and community control tout vouchers as a technique for the empowerment of slum denizens and welfare mothers. For a few years in the late 1960s and early 1970s, the political left and the political right seemed simultaneously intrigued by vouchers as a weapon against cost-raising and choice-limiting bureaucracy (the conservative complaint) or an assault upon a system which offered only small futures for the children of the poor (the radical indictment). In this period, a minor cottage industry populated by sociologists, lawyers, economists, and miscellaneous foundation types designed and redesigned voucher schemes in attempts to maximize choice and avoid short-changing low income families.[24]

Despite, perhaps even because of, erudite advocacy by conservatives, liberals, and radicals, Congress has refused to fund school vouchers nationally. Public school teachers and their organizations have effectively lobbied against state and local experiments. The Heritage Foundation, fervent in its admiration of vouchers and other free-market devices, has lost hope in Congress and urged pressures upon presumably more pliable state legislatures. Minnesota has actually enacted a school voucher measure and California may follow suit.

More empirical evidence exists in favor of vouchers than in support of privatization. Especially in housing, large-scale voucher demonstrations have tested the device. During the 1970s, the Department of Housing and Urban Development sponsored an Experimental Housing Allowance Program (EHAP). Thirty thousand families in twelve cities participated. EHAP furnished vouchers to experimental groups and compared their behavior with that of control groups who did not receive vouchers. The outcome was encouraging. During 1974, in Pittsburgh, a standard-quality two-bedroom apartment rented for $4,155 annually in a public-housing project. Comparable private space paid for by a voucher was available at a mere $1,869, 45 percent of the public figure. Somewhat to the astonishment of project planners, low-income families called for little help, shopped efficiently, and thus secured good value for their (or the government's) money. In one economist's opinion, "At least in the majority of housing markets, vouchers seemed better for everyone—taxpayers, recipients, and housing suppliers—than public construction and operation of low-income housing."[25]

However, the experiment was less successful in inducing participants to spend more of their income on superior housing. Only 20 percent of the vouchers' dollar value was devoted to more or better space. Families preferred to spend more on food, clothing, and medical and dental care, worthwhile budget targets but not the one anticipated by the experiment's planners. Given the opportunity, those who participate in social experiments will prefer their own objectives to those of the experimenters. Why ever not?

Other voucher demonstration projects echo EHAP findings. The Special Supplementary Food Program for women, infants, and young children (WIC) supplies a narrow range of nutritious foods to a low-income clientele at especially high medical risk. It cost 10 percent less to distribute these items in ordinary supermarkets than at public health clinics. There are two important qualifications. Supermarkets might tempt women to buy popular but not necessarily the best food items. And supermarket distribution severs an important link to the health-care system.[26]

Voucher funding of medical care for the low-income population similarly balances merits and defects. It is 40 percent cheaper to pay physicians on a conventional fee-for-service basis than to employ salaried physicians in the National Health Service. Nevertheless, vouchers, Medicare, and Medicaid in fearful array have proved incapable of attracting physicians to low-income rural and urban communities, particularly when they are distant from medical centers, teaching hospitals, and professional colleagues. As a condition of their enlistment, National Health Service doctors can be directed to underserved environments.

Vouchers have been far less effective in job placement. A wage subsidy to private employers as inducement to hire from such difficult groups as welfare mothers, parolees, and detoxified alcoholics or drug addicts is in effect an employer voucher. Its sponsors promote wage subsidies as cost-effective substitutes for expensive social programs. For conservatives, new private jobs are invariably ideologically preferable to public jobs initiatives. Under the terms of the Federal Targeted Jobs Tax Credit (TJTC), private employers can claim a tax credit of up to $4,500 for each ex-convict, welfare recipient, handicapped individual, or disadvantaged teenager they employ. Unfortunately few enterprises have taken the trouble to qualify. Employers have hired new staff without determining program eligibility and subsequently filed claims for people whom they hired in ignorance of the wage subsidy's existence. Even when generously subsidized, the business community by and large rejects the role of social program agent.[27]

This mixed record naturally does not deter free-market zealots, Moral Majoritarians, school-tax resisters, and opponents of all varieties of state action, among others, from fervent insistence upon substitution wherever at all possible of vouchers for public programs. Heritage Foundation publications envisage the universalization of school vouchers as the reward of a long march through state legislatures and gubernatorial executive mansions. Voucher imperialism extends to Medicaid. Heritage sees virtue in offering low-income families vouchers worth specified sums with which they would freely select "cost-effective providers." If voucher claimants opted for health maintenance organization care, they might save 10–40 percent on private physicians. Odd to hear conservatives endorsing the very HMOs which not so long ago they denounced as tantamount to the practice of socialized medicine. Yesterday's socialism, in dynamic America, is today's cost-effective market mechanism.

Like privatization, vouchers are votes of confidence in private markets as superior not only to government but also to religious, charitable, and cooperative modes of service delivery. Save for ideologues, the gulf separating voucher imperialism and privatization from market reality is embarrassingly wide and deep. Free-marketers implicitly or explicitly assume rough parity of resources and power between buyers and sellers. Such parity is notably lacking for poor families hunting for medical attention, decent housing, and high-quality public education. Precisely because builders have been unwilling to construct low- and moderate-income housing, claiming they cannot get satisfactory profits on their investment, federal and state agencies from the 1930s onward have built public housing and have subsidized rents.

Similar market failures encouraged Lyndon Johnson and a liberal Congress to inaugurate Medicare and Medicaid. The crazy-quilt system or nonsystem of health-care delivery—fee-for-service physicians in private practice, voluntary and municipal hospitals, and individual medical insurance—left far too many Americans entirely or substantially unable to pay for serious illnesses or even routine care. With reluctance, mainstream economists concede that when important private markets falter, a legitimate case for public provision can be made.

Markets fail more frequently than economists and conservatives prefer to admit. They falter wherever producers are poorly organized to satisfy the needs of substantial fractions of the population. They fail wherever the heritage of racial discrimination segregates blacks and other minorities in low-income ghettos unattractive to doctors and developers and uninviting to teachers and school administrators. They fail yet again when underpaid, poorly educated families lack information, time, mobility, and cash to engage in the sophisticated shopping recommended by designers of voucher schemes.

The promise of a Medicaid voucher practice will not lure physicians to Bedford-Stuyvesant, the South Bronx, the hollows of Appalachia, or the rural slums of Mississippi and Arkansas. Unless newly qualified M.D.s have wisely selected rich parents, their initial priority will be rapid repayment of debts incurred during their seven or eight years of medical school and residency. In New York, where housing vacancies are almost nil and a large homeless population includes adults employed as messengers, restaurant workers, and other badly paid service jobs, rents for the humblest shelter are out of reach of many hard-working men and women. School vouchers, at least at the $600-per-child level suggested in Reagan proposals, will open only the worst of private schools to eligible families. In New York and elsewhere, where the demand for high-quality private education exceeds supply, vouchers will simply push school fees higher.

Civilized communities alleviate the anguish of illness, indigent retirement, and unemployment. Our welfare state, at its best a cut-down version of European practice, has been eroded by Reagan's assaults upon housing, medical care, food programs, welfare, veterans' benefits, and compensatory education. For Reaganites, vouchers constructively distance government still further from direct responsibility toward vulnerable groups. Families whose voucher fails to cover their entire health needs will perforce do without medical attention. Presumably they were imprudent shoppers and thus responsible for their own misfortunes. In financing vouchers, prosperous taxpayers will be encouraged to think that they have discharged their obligations to the unfortunate.

Vouchers assuage the conscience of the community in matters of quality and equity. Although every sentient creature knows that some doctors, veterinarians, dentists, hospitals, schools, and teachers are better than others, politicians, administrators, and the public are squeamish about clear definition of some public facilities and public employees as excellent, others as acceptable, and the remainder as inferior. By imposing the burdens of choice and ignoring its limitations for the poor upon the consumers of services, communities are absolved from responsibility for the consequences of inadequate funding.

Vouchers crucially alter the funding process. An eligible Medicaid patient has a chance to get the treatment that his ailment requires. Participating physicians and hospitals can count on government reimbursement. It is harder and harder to qualify for Medicaid coverage, but that coverage once

## After Reagan . . . Reagan

conferred is an entitlement. In any voucher system, the amount of money for which a voucher is traded will drift away from the needs of its recipient. How much federal money Congress appropriates for vouchers will become part of interminable budget wrangles and trade-offs among health appropriations, the ever-voracious Pentagon, farmers, and many, many other claimants.

In the Reagan ice age, Social Security, our most successful welfare program, will not long remain invulnerable to attack. Preliminary skirmishes have already occurred. In 1983, Congress accepted the Greenspan Commission's advice to tax half the benefits of prosperous pensioners. If half, why not all? And if affluent senior citizens don't need monthly supplements to their ample resources, why pay them at all? This line of analysis terminates in redefinition of Social Security as just another means-tested benefit, eligible for budgetary surgery.

Social Security notoriously is an intergenerational transfer. Young and mature workers subsidize their elders, expecting that when their own golden years arrive, they will be subsidized even more generously. Why, ask conservatives, should not newcomers to the labor force be given the chance to maximize their retirement income by astute investment of payroll deductions? Conveniently at hand are individual retirement accounts, catering to many tastes. Risk-takers can gamble on equities. Prudent types can opt for triple-A corporate or municipal bonds. The truly cowardly can ease their anxieties by concentrating on federal securities. Of course, low-income types, irregularly employed workers, women moving in and out of the labor force, and the self-employed are unlikely IRA customers. They will continue to depend on Social Security, transformed into another stigmatized welfare program and funded and administered accordingly.

In social policy, universal coverage explains popularity and longevity. No need to accuse voucher fans of deviousness. Their yearning for efficiency and free consumer choice is probably the consequence of graduate school economics. That training has focused upon competitive markets. Those markets, as John Stuart Mill declared in 1848, are all that define economics as a science and separate it from sociology, history, and political science.

Social policy is too important to be left to economists. "Free" health, education, and housing markets threaten to dissolve historically fragile ties of community. Segmentation of services; conversion of medical care, decent housing, and adequate education into so many additional commodities available in quantities and qualities determined by income and wealth; and denial of a public interest in minimum levels of the essentials of existence for all define more than an uncaring society. They threaten the social stability upon which corporations and other income maximizers depend.

Of this chapter's specters, this is the most terrifying. But more terrors await the stout-hearted in our next chapter.

*Chapter 4*
# After Reagan
## ... Still More Reagan

THE SCOPE OF privatization, broadly defined as substitution of private for public activity, is global. In Great Britain, the durable Mrs. Thatcher has sold off state-owned enterprises and publicly owned rental units to their tenants. She has starved the British Health Service and encouraged private, commercial alternatives to it. She seeks to replace or supplement pensions for the elderly with various individually funded investment alternatives, cousins to American individual retirement accounts. In the Communist world, China has been flirting with private enterprise. Even the new leaders of the ossified Soviet Union seem timidly poised to undertake imitations of the market experiments long familiar to Hungarians and Yugoslavs.[1]

If both Marxists and democrats perceive in privatization greater efficiency and wider consumer choice, why should Americans criticize the Reagan administration's version of policies whose enthusiasts transcend ideology? Caution is advisable, not least for privatizers. Important differences separate the United States from both Western European democracies and the Communist bloc. Our public sector in 1980 was already smaller than that of other privatizing communities. The federal government owns no airlines, steel mills, or auto plants. Its only medical facilities are veterans' hospitals. Public housing constitutes only a tiny fraction of the entire housing stock. There is no American equivalent of the British Broadcasting Corporation or similar tax-funded French and German TV channels and radio stations, save our underfunded and increasingly commercial public broadcasting system. Its frantic fundraising rivals the hardest of commercial pitches. Although it is the reluctant proprietor of Conrail and Amtrak,[2] the Department of Transportation is trying hard to sell Conrail and starve Amtrak into either profitability or bankruptcy.

A frugal creation, our welfare state already relies heavily upon private suppliers—doctors, Blue Cross–Blue Shield and other insurers, corporate hospitals, nursing homes, child-care facilities, and nonprofit social welfare organizations under either religious or secular sponsorship. Such as it is, our public sector is a mixed economy, heavily influenced by private entrepreneurs.[3] American privatization thus begins at a stage far more advanced in the direction of private enterprise than most of the rest of the world. Further privatization threatens to dismantle basic functions of government; devolve federal responsibility on states, cities, and private charities which lack adequate resources; substitute means-tested for universal social provisions; and attach the stigma of welfare to new human targets.

An important exception to this administration's flight from responsibility is the military sector, that marvelous example of wasteful collaboration between corporate and Pentagon bureaucracies. Its baroque activities merit attention in themselves and as warnings of privatization yet to come in other governmental ventures.

## MILITARIZATION

In 1955, the Pentagon made off with a generous 11.2 percent of our gross national product. At the 1968 peak of Vietnam involvement, that percentage actually was lower—9.9 percent. Almost every year between 1969 and 1979 inclusive, the Pentagon's share declined, reaching a low in the latter year of 4.9 percent. Then, in 1979, the Soviet Union invaded Afghanistan, an event which impelled President Carter and Congress to increase military appropriations substantially. The incoming Reagan administration accelerated the pace of military buildup contemplated by its predecessor. For the years 1980–84 inclusive, the rising GNP percentages were, respectively, 5.2, 5.5,

6.1, 6.5, and 6.7.[4] In constant dollars, actual military expenditures rose in those five years 6.6 percent, 3.5 percent, 3.5 percent, 4.5 percent, and 2.8 percent.[5]

As Defense Secretary Caspar Weinberger and lesser officials accurately note, the United States, by post–World War II criteria, currently devotes a comparatively modest proportion of its resources to armaments. Here ends the good news. All the percentages measure a country growing in population and economic scale. In 1955 there were just under 166 million inhabitants of the then forty-eight states. The GNP in 1955 was $675.5 billion.[6] Three decades later, the GNP had ballooned to $1,639 billion.[7] The 6.7 percent share for military expenditures in 1984 was a proportion of an economy nearly two and a half times its 1955 size, or more than a sixth of 1955 GNP.

Although Gramm-Rudman may slow expenditure of the next trillion or two of weapons procurement, present trends threaten even faster enlargement of the arms budget both in actual dollars and as a percentage of GNP. The composition of military expenditures has significantly altered. Between 1970 and 1984, personnel costs slightly more than doubled. In the earlier year they were 36.2 percent and in the later year 27.9 percent of Pentagon outlays. Weapons procurement and research and development have been the areas of fastest growth. Still in current dollars, procurement outlays tripled and research and development commitments somewhat more than tripled. Procurement crept upward between 1970 and 1984 from 26.3 percent to 27.1 percent and R&D from 8.8 percent to 10.6 percent.[8] These trends are likely to accelerate because new weapons come on line traditionally embellished by vast cost overruns; rising expenditures on R&D spur invention of ever more expensive lethal toys; and the administration's Star Wars plans amount to open-ended commitments to lavish research and development of highly problematical new technologies. At worst, Star Wars will evoke similar efforts by the Soviet Union and an accelerating arms race.

One of the entertaining aspects of 1985 budget arguments in Congress was expert dispute over the exact scale of Pentagon obesity. By the middle of that year, forty-six of the one hundred largest military contractors were under investigation for miscellaneous billing frauds. Defense Secretary Weinberger, a trained accountant, announced that he had found $4 billion rattling around in Pentagon cash registers not needed for current programs, a tribute, he modestly admitted on "Meet the Press," to the Pentagon's splendid management, increasing emphasis on competition, and relentless harrying of executives who charged off haircuts, dog-kennel fees, and country club dues to the taxpayers.[9] As a suitable reward, the Secretary asked only that the $4 billion be tacked onto the 1986 Pentagon appropriation. Four-hundred-dollar clawhammers, $1,600 coffeemakers, and $600 toilet seats are chock-full of human interest, raw meat for the media and undemanding public entertainment. But as the Packard Commission reported early in 1986, these horror stories divert attention from really expensive, multibillion-dollar scandals—interservice rivalries which inspire unneeded duplication of weapons systems and gold-plating, enriching to weapons producers but frustrating to the grunts in the field.[10] Our procurement policy shrinks the number of tanks and planes actually produced, and reduces the reliability of the few that actually come into service. Cost-plus contracts have consistently rewarded defense contractors with profits far higher than those that can be earned in civilian pursuits. True Reaganites, defense contractors customarily pay few or no taxes. General Electric, a generally profitable enterprise, has exploited tax loopholes to collect refunds on taxes never paid.

The actual improvement in defense capability purchased by the dollars that began to be thrown at the Pentagon in the second half of the Carter administration is so startlingly small that hawkish senators like Georgia's Sam Nunn and Arizona's Barry Goldwater have been moved to cry foul. After inflation adjustment, the Pentagon, during 1982–85, spent 75.4 percent more for aircraft than in 1977–80 and added just 8.8 percent more planes to its inventory. The figures for missiles are 91.2 percent more dollars and just 6.4 percent more weapons. Tanks, anyone? For 30 percent more deliveries the Pentagon disgorged 147.4 percent more dollars.[11]

How do such things happen? Part of an explanation can be inferred from the educational odyssey of a certain Navy captain, Robert F. Doss, charged in 1969 with developing an anti-radar

## After Reagan . . . Still More Reagan

missile to protect American planes against North Vietnamese anti-aircraft fire. The missile was to be operational by the mid-1970s, and at $30,000 per copy cheap enough to hurl in large numbers against enemy batteries. A dozen years later, the High-Speed Anti-Radiation Missile (HARM) still had not been delivered. In the meantime it had gained weight, complexity, and susceptibility to malfunction. Current price? A cool million per shot.[12] HARM hurt only the taxpayers. By the time HARM became available, we were engaged in no war worthy of its participation.

The more important weapons procurement becomes in the Pentagon budget, the more difficult it is for Congress or, for that matter, a president with priorities different from Mr. Reagan's, to curb the voracious appetites of generals, admirals, and defense contractors. Weapons programs are multiyear commitments, hard to stop once made. Congress has never rejected a serious presidential weapons proposal. Frequently, the Pentagon has been unable in a given fiscal year to spend all the money legally available to it. Of its 1984 $320.6 billion appropriation, the Pentagon, try as it did, could not sign contracts for $43 billion, nearly 22 percent of the total.[13] Congress, in other words, can trim funds for training, maintenance, and personnel, at predictable damage to the combat effectiveness of men in uniform. It has limited influence over the growth elements of the budget—weapons and the R&D certain to incite agitation for still more weapons. Annual disputes over the rate of increase in defense appropriations disguise the lessons of current history, the most dispiriting of them that in the end any weapon dreamed up by a hustling Pentagon supplier will be funded, if not this year, then the year after or the one after that.

As more than one cartoonist has imagined, the Pentagon is not far away from perfecting its ultimate weapon, a contraption assembled from components produced in each and every one of our 435 congressional districts. Examples abound. Admire the Pentagon's astute distribution of 1983 contract awards of $118,744,000,000, nearly $119 billion, up from $104 billion in 1982, and a mere $88 billion in 1981. Not a single state, nor even the District of Columbia, was left out. As usual, California, at $26-plus billion, led the way, followed at a respectful distance by New York ($9.6 billion), Texas ($8.2 billion), Virginia ($7.1 billion), Massachusetts ($6.3 billion), and Missouri ($5.6 billion). But even sparsely populated Wyoming ($39 million) and South Dakota ($42 million) got their consolation prizes.[14] Military contracts employed 133,359 Californians and nearly 63,000 Texans. These contracts spelled the margin between prosperity and recession for merchants, developers, bankers, and blue- and white-collar workers in large numbers of communities.

No wonder anti-Pentagon congresspersons fight fiercely to preserve military contracts in their own districts and resist all proposals to close superfluous military installations. Defense work is all the more precious because unemployment rates remain high even during economic expansions. Scarce job opportunities cement alliances of unions, defense contractors, and host communities. Few phenomena, aside from Sly Stallone in *Rocky V, VI,* or *VII* or *Rambo II, III,* or *IV*, generate as much chauvinistic emotion as new military payrolls. It is common knowledge that military spending creates fewer jobs than almost any alternative disbursement of public money, but when the real choice is not between military and civilian expenditures but between military and no expenditures, defense jobs in the real world constitute a net gain to a large part of the population. In an administration intent on shrinkage in all manner of health, nutrition, housing, and income-maintenance endeavors, and quite willing to designate 7 percent unemployment as a normal condition, the defense budget is the only jobs program in town. Was it really wise in 1983 to deliver nearly $11 billion of weapons to the rest of the world, up more than $2 billion from the previous year?[15] Pragmatic folks know that arms exports enlarge factory payrolls, just like less lethal items.

Nowhere does this pathology rage more furiously than in the Star Wars program, a perfect example of a useless, destabilizing, expensive, and job- and grant-generating boondoggle for engineers, scientists, and defense contractors. Although the March 23, 1983, speech in which President Reagan proclaimed his Strategic Defense Initiative (Star Wars) resonated with claims of novelty (SDI "holds the promise of changing the course of history," "of providing new hope for our children in the twenty-first century," "of rendering . . . nuclear weapons impotent and obsolete," "of rising above dealing with other

## After Reagan . . . Still More Reagan

nations and human beings by threatening their existence"),[16] the Chief Executive, as ignorant of relevant history as of most current events, had simply revived proposals for an anti-ballistic missile seriously considered and rejected by both Lyndon Johnson and Richard Nixon, neither noted for wimpish conduct of foreign affairs and defense policy. Both presidents demurred at probable costs and the near certainty that, like all the other "impregnable" defenses on record, ABMs would be overwhelmed by improvements in offensive weapons. Such considerations induced President Nixon and our Soviet adversaries to sign an ABM treaty in 1972 which renounced all but a few ABMs and continued to rely upon the doctrine of Mutual Assured Destruction, whose by-now acceptable lunacy Star Wars subverts.

In George Ball's somber words, President Reagan "initiated a project that, if successful, would require renunciation of the ABM treaty. . . . In addition he set in motion forces that seem almost certain to trigger a further acceleration of the nuclear arms race, eliminate the last hope of controlling the weapons spiral through agreement, and seriously jeopardize the confidence and support of our NATO allies."[17] As eager for contracts, exotic technology, and new jobs as Americans, West Germany (with visible reluctance) and England (with Mrs. Thatcher's audible enthusiasm) have signed on as junior partners.

No one knows how much this science fiction fantasy will ultimately cost. The space shuttle tragedy of 1986 should serve as a somber warning against excessive reliance upon advanced technology and "infallible" computers. There are no signs that the disaster diminished administration devotion to missile defense. In presidential fantasies, Star Wars contemplates destroying not merely most Soviet missiles but all of them. Scientific imaginations let loose to dream have sketched a number of technological possibilities. Lasers and particle beams are swift enough to destroy enemy missiles soon after they are launched if they start from points not too far away from their launching sites. These weapons might be mounted on numerous orbiting battle stations, weighing one hundred tons each, revolving around our planet in numbers sufficient to attack all Soviet rockets. Or scientists might build many earth-based lasers whose beams would bounce off relay mirrors, orbiting at 24,000 miles above the earth onto "fighting" or "mission" mirrors in low orbit. These would then redirect the energy beams at the rising enemy boosters. The mirrors would have to be kept optically perfect and capable of changing their angles with complete accuracy in fractions of a second under the direction either of their own sensors or of battle management satellites in geostationary orbit 24,000 miles above. Since pre-positioned mirrors would be easy targets, some preliminary thought is being given to mirrors that would be carried collapsed on rockets and would be "popped up" at the first warning of an enemy attack.[18]

Enough. Not quite. Still another techological fix involves "popping up" lasers mounted on rockets during the three to five minutes enemy missiles are being boosted into the atmosphere. Interceptors would have to be fired from submarines off the coast of Siberia or near European Soviet Russia. Of course once the boost stage is passed, defense becomes enormously more difficult because a single SS-18 can release at least ten warheads and many decoys. From a thousand Soviet silos could emerge potential targets in the hundreds of thousands. Which ones would be real, which chaff or clouds of infrared-emitting aerosol? On the correct answer would depend the lives of some tens of millions of Americans. No second chances are conceivable. The temerity, the sheer hubris in the minds of the sponsors of Star Wars should have amazed and terrified sane observers even before investigations into the causes of 1986's space shuttle crash revealed just how flawed was the simpler technology deployed in space launches. What odds that this infinitely more complex system will be infallible? One stray missile suffices to slaughter fifteen or twenty million people quickly and many more later and more painfully.

Why are conservative American politicians and some of our NATO allies moving in the direction of funding or participating in this dangerous adventure? Why is the scientific community split over the feasibility and desirability of serious research and development of technologies so conjectural and so expensive? Motives vary. The hard anti-Communist right in Congress and such media allies as *Commentary*, the Heritage Foundation's *Policy Review*, and William Buckley's *National Review*, the daddy of them all, insist that past arms-limitation treaties have worked to the disadvantage of the United States, in part because the Soviet Union has violated them and in part because we deprive ourself of an arms race which we can win. The Soviet Union is too weak an economy to match an all-out American armament drive, and because of their economy's limitations Soviet leaders will in time be compelled to cry uncle and accept genuine disarmament. For defense contractors, prospective profits set saliva flowing.

Physicists, mathematicians, systems analysts, and economists share a professional deformation. Their techniques dissociate them from reality and focus their attention upon the solution of entrancing puzzles. Robert Oppenheimer, eloquent opponent of nuclear escalation as he became, could not restrain his initial admiration of the hydrogen bomb as a sweet piece of science. Full employment for themselves and enhanced public esteem operate as insidiously upon physicists as they do on mortals of lesser intellect. European scientists naturally want their share. Scientists are an intensely competitive caste. European entrepreneurs seek a shot at the new technologies on the Star Wars horizon. About the best to be anticipated from this confluence of interests is endless research but no breakthrough toward plausible defense. The moment of that breakthrough is the instant of maximum danger to human survival. Bettors against Star Wars are highly unlikely to survive to collect their winnings.

I have lingered upon weapons and the research that multiplies their number and costs. But military expenditures quietly escalate for other reasons as well. Take the matter of military pensions. After twenty years of service, an army colonel can retire still in his early forties, find another job (perhaps with a defense contractor with whom he dealt while in uniform), collect benefits currently worth $590,000 over his remaining lifetime in addition to his salary, and upon his second retirement enjoy, in addition to military benefits, Social Security and a corporate pension. Skilled specialists such as nuclear engineers and computer scientists, trained at public expense, improve their finances substantially by putting in their twenty years, taking their pension benefits, and running to the most eager private employer. Military retirement is the second most expensive federal retirement program funded entirely out of general tax receipts. No panic in the White House or Congress over trust-fund bankruptcy like the 1983 blitz against Social Security. No trust fund involved, just withdrawals from federal accounts already severely in deficit. Medicaid, the most expensive of currently financed federal transfers, benefits more than 20 million low-income Americans. There are only 1.4 million military retirees, a number certain to rise rapidly. The projected $18.3 billion cost in 1986 is 34 percent higher than the 1981 figure. Unfunded liabilities at $208 billion (1983) are up 58 percent since 1979.[19] This lavish retirement benefit costs more than food stamps, AFDC, or SSI, each of which aids far more vulnerable clients, the vast majority of them women and children.

Nor have we reached the end of military extravagance. The Veterans Administration spent its $25.6 billion on hospital and medical care ($8.9 billion); pensions, insurance, and burial benefits ($14.4 billion); education, training, and rehabilitation ($1.4 billion); housing ($244 million); and miscellaneous purposes ($751 million).[20] The questionable quality of the medical care offered by a grateful country received national attention after the conviction by a naval court of Commander Billig, nearly blind in one eye, who nevertheless persistently performed delicate open-heart surgery upon patients who ungratefully died in numbers large enough finally to evoke action by the physician's superiors.

A generation ago, President Eisenhower warned his constituents in his valedictory address against the military-industrial complex. He didn't know the half of it. It is by now a military-industrial-scientific-educational-union-veteran complex. Programs create interests. Interests enlarge programs. The Reagan administration has so entangled most Americans, in lesser or greater degree, in the prosperity of the Pentagon that reversal of this momentum will be horrifyingly difficult for succeeding administrations. By now, armament has comparatively little to do with national defense but a significance vital to the financial comfort of defense contractors, university science and engineering departments, workers in weapons plants, veterans, and the communities that live on one or several of the above.

Quite aside from the foreign policy bullying that the defense buildup encourages in Latin America and elsewhere, it has been documented in the work of Seymour Melman, John Ullman, Marion Anderson, and others that it siphons off to the least efficient sector of the economy talented scientists, engineers, and technicians who in luckier Japan improve efficiency and quality in industries which, in world markets, have demonstrated their capacity to defeat American rivals. During the 1983–86 economic expansion, productivity improved less than is usual during upswings of the business cycle, despite lavish "supply-side" tax breaks, hands-off antitrust division attitudes toward mergers and acquisitions, and effective euthanasia of the agencies that regulate business. Productivity puzzles the experts, but common sense suggests that the researchers and technicians who work on weapons cannot improve the civilian technologies with which Japan, unwilling to spend even 1 percent of its gross national product on defense, has terrorized the capitalist world. Our growth industries seem to be defense, fast foods, and financial services which consume increasing percentages of the leisure time of their purchasers.

Empires in decline console themselves with ritual reassertions of claims to hegemony over foreigners. Suez in 1956 was the last spasm of British and French assertion of authority over the lesser breeds. Evidently Vietnam did not effectively inoculate Americans against the same virus. Ronald Reagan's vendetta against the Sandinistas, his ludicrous proclamation in May 1985 of a state of national emergency as legal justification for the imposition of an embargo against this tiny agrarian community of three million impoverished souls, and the ambiguity of the congressional response all attest to the persistence of imperialistic yearnings in the national political ethos. Residual imperialism justifies armaments. Armaments lure their proprietors toward imperialistic intervention. The alleged, pervasive threat of Communism legitimates American meddling just as effectively as the menace of spreading capitalism justifies Soviet flexing of military muscle.

*Visions and Nightmares*

Give credit where it is unexpectedly merited. The man who pointed to the ultimate destination of current defense procurement trends happens to be Norman R. Augustine, a vice-president of Martin Marietta, a leading defense contractor: "In the year 2054, the entire defense budget will purchase just one tactical aircraft. This aircraft will have to be shared by the Air Force and Navy three and one-half days each per week, except for Leap Year, when it will be made available to the Marines for the extra day."[21]

DEUNIONIZATION

American unions never achieved the legitimacy and popular support that they have enjoyed in England, Germany, and Scandinavia. At the peak of their influence in the 1950s, unions counted as members less than a third of the labor force. By the mid-1980s, that fraction had declined to less than a fifth, and close observers predicted that if present trends persisted no more than 10 percent of workers would belong to unions by 1990. Nor are the members of this minority part of the labor force aristocracy. As two acute analysts summarize the demographics, ". . . the probability that a worker will be a union member is greater if that worker is male, nonwhite, over twenty-five years old, with no formal schooling beyond high school, living outside the south, and employed in a blue-collar job, in transportation, mining, manufacturing, or construction."[22]

For union partisans, the flip side of the picture is intensely depressing. Women, young workers, white males, the technically educated, and the hordes now engaged in paper manipulation as data processors, claims evaluators, bank and brokerage employees, sales personnel, and clerks: these are growing constituencies unattracted by unions with some important exceptions, the most notable among them teachers and state, county, and municipal workers. Still, the numbers are no occasion for cheer. In order of size, the 1980 union ranking follows:

| Teamsters | 1,891,000 |
| United Auto Workers | 1,357,000 |
| United Food and Commercial Workers | 1,300,000 |
| United Steelworkers | 1,238,000 |
| State, County, and Municipal Workers | 1,098,000 |
| Electrical Workers | 1,041,000 |
| Carpenters and Joiners | 789,000 |
| Machinists | 754,000 |
| Service Employees | 650,000 |
| Laborers International | 650,000 |
| Communications Workers | 551,000 |
| American Federation of Teachers | 551,000 |

In addition there are 1,684,000 members of the National Education Association, a professional grouping behaving more and more like an ordinary trade union.[23]

Why have unions been losing ground? A popular explanation is demographic. The labor force contains rising percentages of workers resistant for one reason or another to collective action—women who regard themselves as full-time wives and mothers and intermittent collectors of paychecks; young workers who, however inaccurately, define factory and clerical jobs as way stations to professional or entrepreneurial independence; working-class conservatives hostile to the social agenda of the national movement; and people not convinced that unions will deliver benefits substantial enough to justify monthly dues. This structural explanation is less than convincing. Why should women and young workers resist unions in the United States more than they do in Western Europe? Why do the opinion polls record women at least as favorable to unions as men? Why in universities like Yale and Columbia have unions coalesced around the issue of comparable worth—demands that in equally skilled and responsible jobs women receive rewards equivalent to those of male workers? Why do teachers and civil servants flock to unions and white-collar employees in the private sector stay away from them? Do unionized public school teachers regard themselves as less professional than unorganized bank tellers or stock exchange clerks?

Like any other institution, unions are prisoners of their history. In the nineteenth century the Knights of Labor pursued a strongly political agenda and cherished a vaguely socialist, anticapitalist vision. In competition with the American Federation of Labor, led by Samuel Gompers, they steadily lost ground and vanished from the historical stage. The catchy single-word response, "More," attributed to Gompers to the question "What does labor want?" actually misrepresents the AFL position if "more" is taken to mean simply higher wages and benefits. For AFL unions, notably in the garment trades, were pioneer supporters of factory legislation, workmen's compensation, unemployment insurance, and other social programs. In their present time of troubles, unions persist as the only large membership groups in favor of progressive social change.

It is of course also true that mainstream American unionism has focused upon bread-and-butter issues of immediate financial concern to the dues payers. Implicitly and often explicitly Gompers and after him William Green, George Meany, and Lane Kirkland have declared their allegiance to capitalism. From the Spanish-American War through Korea and Vietnam to Grenada, unions have rallied to the flag and taken hard-line, "pro-American," and, since the Bolshevik revolution in Russia, anti-Communist positions. During the McCarthyite hysteria of the 1950s, the AFL-CIO patriotically expelled unions like the mine, mill, smelter, and electrical workers, whose leaders were colored red or perhaps only a suspicious pink. Even in the Reagan era, unions have acted as agents of administration foreign policy in Central America and Western Europe.

During the deep 1981–82 mini-depression, television astutely caught the confusion of blue-collar attitudes. A made-for-TV flick entitled "Heart of Steel," filmed with *cinéma-vérité* realism in a grim but unidentified midwestern steel town, focused upon a plant closing. In its wake, the hero, demoralized by this threat to a standard of life which supported the mortgage on his house and the payments on his pickup, took to drink, child abuse, and wife beating, much as though the producers had conscientiously inspected Harvey Brenner's findings at Johns Hopkins that unemployment correlated closely with these and such other indices of demoralization as psychosomatic ailments, mental breakdown, homicide, and suicide. In disgust, his wife leaves him and takes the children with her.

A bright idea soon strikes him and his drinking buddies.

## After Reagan . . . Still More Reagan

Management justifies its shutdown and layoffs on the ground that the mill is no longer competitive with Japanese rivals. How to refute this slander of American workers? They break into the mill, guarded only by a lonely watchman. Raw materials are conveniently available. A flick of a switch restores power. Challenge: produce in a shift as much or more finished steel as the Japanese with their modern equipment do. Everyone works hard, but as the shift's end nears, energy diminishes and the goal appears tantalizingly out of reach.

Help is at hand. Our hero unfurls an enormous American flag (only disloyal viewers might wonder where it comes from) in full sight of the workers. A mighty cheer rises toward Old Glory, adrenaline surges, and with a last mighty effort the loading docks are stacked high with enough metal to confound both the Japanese and the managers who questioned the work ethic of red-blooded American workers. For all hands, morale is restored. True, management refuses to reopen the mill, but our hero, reunited with his family, is last seen waving goodbye to wife and children. He is off in his pickup to Texas, a pioneer in the American grain, eager to make his mark in the golden Southwest.

Our mass media can tolerate individual bitterness against negligent or unfeeling corporate managers, much as Soviet newspapers and magazines routinely criticize bureaucratic corruption and inefficiency. Television is predisposed to treat sympathetically the victims of layoffs on an equal-opportunity basis with abused children, homeless adults, and AIDS patients. Anyone who watched only the first half of "Heart of Steel" could readily have interpreted its message as serious criticism of the quality of management of a major American industry as well as highly adverse comment on the absence of public policies to create alternative employment or train displaced workers in new skills better rewarded by changing labor markets. A stranger to commercial television might just possibly have inferred a popularization of Marxist theories of class conflict.

We know better. With an abrupt shift of perspective, the problems of the hero and his friends become personal. It is their obligation and responsibility to pick themselves up from the floor and demonstrate their manhood, first as steelworkers and then as family providers willing to travel anywhere in search of new jobs and new lives. The viewing audience presumably breathed sighs of relief. Nothing wrong with capitalism. Nothing wrong with our hero either. Sure, there are rotten apples in corporate boardrooms as in other locales of ill repute, but the dear old competitive system really works. No one need censor our free press. Of its proprietors' own accord, it as effectively buttresses capitalism as the controlled Soviet media prop up socialism.

The media oversimplify, even caricature the lives and attitudes of their addicts. In doing so, they also influence public attitudes and public behavior. In "Dallas," "Dynasty," "Falcon Crest," and their clones, businessmen frequently figure as villains, sufficiently exotic to be distinguished from real-life chief executive officers. Conservatives from time to time complain about this media bias. Television treats union leaders far worse: it ignores their existence. Only exceptionally have unions legitimized themselves in the eyes of members as social institutions, more than mere bargaining agents who in return for monthly dues negotiate more generous contracts, protect members from arbitrary discipline, and settle their grievances. No doubt some of that failure stems from complacent union leadership, uninterested in organizing workers in untraditional fields and unresponsive to the shifting priorities of their own membership. No doubt also that the well-publicized corruption and criminality of a small handful of unions and union leaders have tarred the entire movement. The Reagan administration has found it politically convenient to solicit successfully the support of the Teamsters, the largest and possibly the most corrupt American union, rather than apply criminal sanctions to sound conservative Republican Reaganites.

On this score, unions have had a bad rap. Although as large, profit-seeking enterprises, newspaper owners naturally side with management, their editorial policy is not usually virulently anti-union. Newspapers have simply failed to cover labor news at all, save when sensational events like strikes and indictments offer excuses for headlines. The endless Anglophile soap operas on public television—"Upstairs, Downstairs," "To Serve Them All My Days," "The Jewel in the Crown," "Mountbatten," "Brideshead Revisited," and "Brothers and Strangers"—focus

## After Reagan . . . Still More Reagan

on the world of the upper class in another time and a different place. The single exception, "When the Boat Comes In," a gritty series chronicling an English union leader's career after World War I, was least publicized and never revived, possibly because working-class characters and their leaders were portrayed sympathetically and equipped with motives as complex as those of their social and financial betters.

The fact is that American unions are overwhelmingly honest. Benjamin Civiletti, Jimmy Carter's Attorney General, estimated that racketeers exercise influence over three hundred union locals out of approximately 65,000.[24] Evidence is ample that larceny and fraud are far more prevalent in the business world than they are in union circles. *Fortune* magazine, no enemy of corporate America, surveyed in 1980 some 1,043 major corporations in search of bribery, criminal fraud, illegal political contributions, criminal antitrust violations, or all or several of the above. It discovered at least one major delinquency committed by 117, or 11 percent of the group: "In total there were 208 citations covering 163 separate offenses: ninety-eight antitrust violations; twenty-eight cases of kickbacks, bribery, or illegal rebates; twenty-one instances of illegal political contributions; eleven cases of fraud; and fifty of tax evasion."[25] The American Management Association, another pro-business source, estimated in 1975 that the sums involved in commercial bribery and kickbacks were in the $3.5 billion–$10 billion ranges; securities theft and fraud, $5 billion; embezzlement, $4 billion; arson for profit, $3.5 billion; insurance fraud, $2 billion. The total, $18 billion–$24.5 billion, was somewhere between 1 and 2 percent of the 1975 gross national product.[26] Only 3 percent of blue-collar workers sensed any corruption in their own union.[27] One wonders what the comparable result would be for white-collar and managerial employees in *Fortune*'s assortment of corporate malefactors. On the available evidence, corporate America is our least law-abiding institution, far more blatantly scornful of the rule of law than either unions or politicians.

Images shape reputations. The cigar-smoking, paunchy union "boss" has been as reliable a cartoon symbol as Uncle Sam and John Bull. Indeed, George Meany, who for decades led the AFL-CIO, could have sat as the model for the caricature. In truth, the national organization offers its top officers unusual job security. Only four men in more than a century—Gompers, Green, Meany, and Kirkland—have served as president. But none of them has possessed the powers imputed to a "boss." The AFL-CIO is a confederation of entirely independent national or international unions (the adjective justifies itself by the existence of Canadian affiliates). On its executive council sit potentates who derive their power from steelworkers, machinists, carpenters, and so on, not from the national organization. Rarely can even a George Meany, let alone a Lane Kirkland, impose his will on this strong-minded group. Much as a baseball or football commissioner acts as the agent of autonomous club owners, the titular head of the AFL-CIO speaks and acts for the organization only when he has achieved consensus among its important figures. Yet the AFL-CIO expelled one of its largest affiliates, the Teamsters, on grounds of corruption and gangster influence. Has anyone heard of a business group censuring a member convicted of systematic check kiting like E. F. Hutton, serious antitrust violations like General Electric and Westinghouse, or defense-contract manipulation like General Dynamics?

At lower levels of organization, unions are far more democratic than their corporate opposite numbers. As Freeman and Medoff summarize available research,

> According to the results of several surveys of union members by the University of Michigan Survey Research Center, unions are closer to the "bastion of democracy" model than to the "union boss" model. First, a large proportion of union members participate in union activity. . . . While attendance at any particular meeting may be small, within a two-year period about three-quarters of the members went to meetings at one time or another, roughly three-quarters voted in union elections, while 16 percent were elected to, nominated for, or chosen for a union office.[28]

At the local level, officials lead precarious lives. Somewhere between 20 and 60 percent are rudely ejected from their positions after each election.[29]

Until very recently at least, still another stereotype asserted the great, even ominous power of unions. Big labor and big

## After Reagan . . . Still More Reagan

business frequently were treated as equal threats to the public interest. The 1980s have interjected a more nearly realistic appraisal. Unions have been compelled to accept wage and benefit cuts in order to preserve jobs. They have imperiled their own future viability by accepting two or several tier arrangements for new workers. That elusive ideal, solidarity, a song sung with mounting self-consciousness at the close of union meetings, is not promoted by contracts that pay teamsters, pilots, and many other groups different wages for identical work. But even when unions enrolled as members higher percentages of the labor force than they do now, even during the brief era of corporate-labor détente circa the 1950s and 1960s, unions fared poorly in pursuit of their own particular agenda. They failed to block anti-union legislation in 1947 (the Taft-Hartley Act) and 1959 (the Landrum-Griffin Act). Nor could they halt the spread of state right-to-work laws which seriously impede organizational efforts in eleven southern states, four western states, and five central states. In the 1970s, Congress refused to override President Ford's veto of a common situs picketing bill, the AFL-CIO's top priority at the time. In 1978, when a Democrat occupied the White House and Democrats basked in the glow of comfortable majorities in both the Senate and the House of Representatives, Congress rejected an exceedingly mild labor-law reform measure aimed at corporate sabotage of union bargaining efforts presumably legalized in 1935 by the National Labor Relations Act.

Unions have been most successful when they supported legislation important to wider constituencies than their own. From the 1930s onward, the union movement has provided troops for the New Deal and Great Society. Without them, it is dubious whether Medicare, Medicaid, food stamps, federally subsidized low-income housing, and other social programs could have survived the powerful opposition of fiscal conservatives, organized medicine, the Chamber of Commerce, and other business groups. Political liberals who often join their opponents in dispraise of unions would do well to ask where else is to be found mass support for progressive legislation.

Aside from employers, no group has been more hostile to unions than economists. A majority of their number prefer weak unions to strong unions and no unions to weak unions.

Their hanging verdict is a logical consequence of the profession's traditional myopia. To be a mainstream economist is to be thoroughly socialized in the model of society as a large number of markets, in varying degrees competitive. In such markets, profit-maximizing entrepreneurs, wage-maximizing employees, and welfare-maximizing customers so act as to improve efficiency, reward innovation, pay the best wages to the most productive workers, and respond with exquisite sensitivity to the tastes and preferences of shoppers. Perfect competition—an economist's utopia in which hordes of small sellers face even larger numbers of customers aware that sellers deal in identical products—distantly resembles the American economy. Advertisers exercise considerable ingenuity in differentiating their products from those of rivals. Monstrous corporations dominate manufacturing and retailing. They do their best to shape consumer tastes, not merely respond passively to them. Nevertheless, enough competition survives among products like toothpaste, patent medications, and big-ticket items like autos and major appliances so that economists can more or less plausibly claim that even the largest operator in a particular market has only incomplete control over price and sales volume. True, General Motors can raise its prices without losing all of its customers, the situation in a perfectly competitive market. But it will lose some of them and, conversely, it can sell more cars at lower prices.

Economists charge that unions distort labor markets. Powerful unions raise wages above competitive levels and thus restrict employment. Union contracts narrow managerial discretion, impair factory flexibility, and slow productivity improvement. Contract clauses that require layoffs in strict order of seniority compel retention of possibly less energetic older workers and furloughing of their more productive juniors. Work rules prohibit the sort of redeployment of effort that enhances efficiency. Worst of all, union contracts impede wage cuts during recessions and, for that matter, slow wage increases during booms. This is to say that like any other monopoly, an effective union increases the rewards of its beneficiaries at the expense in this instance of unorganized workers. In sum, unions are guilty of the equivalent of Murder 1 in the criminology of economics: they misallocate resources.

*After Reagan . . . Still More Reagan*

So much for the economists' narrow vision of the universe. The facts are more interesting. There *is* a gap between union and nonunion wages and benefits, but it is a gap whose consequences are, from an egalitarian standpoint, more nearly benign than malignant. In organized enterprises, the union presence compels management to establish the sort of due process in hiring, firing, and discipline that lowers quit rates, improves morale and productivity, and reduces absenteeism and sabotage. Unions stimulate managerial attention to research and development. Workers in unionized enterprises are more productive than unorganized brothers and sisters. Nonunion plants frequently emulate union wage scales and benefits or even improve upon them in order to keep unions out. In organized enterprises, unions have narrowed differentials between white- and blue-collar earnings as well as between older and younger workers, an egalitarian thrust sadly reversed in the concessionary economic environment of the 1980s.

Little of this reasonable case for unions less as instruments of social justice than as efficiency-enhancing institutions seems to have registered among economists, overwhelmingly middle-class types unencumbered by job experience in factories and offices. Unfortunately typical of their attitude is MIT professor Martin L. Weitzman's well-received 1984 tract *The Share Economy: Conquering Stagflation*.[30] He proposes a solution to the problem of persistently high unemployment. After all, just two decades ago, standard introductory economics texts defined 3–4 percent unemployment as full employment. In a market economy that encourages free entry into and out of product and labor markets, people between jobs, seasonally laid off, or hunting for initial employment would even in boom times account for the 3–4 percent frictionally but temporarily without work. In the 1960s, measured unemployment varied between 3.5 and 5.5 percent. The latter figure made even conservative politicians apprehensive. Moreover, high employment coincided with nearly stable prices until late 1966, when escalating Vietnam expenditures and Lyndon Johnson's reluctance to ask Congress for the tax increases needed to pay for them set off inflationary forces.

Economists go with the flow. Exponents of their guild's conventional wisdom teach that when unemployment drops below 7 percent, wages and prices stir, inflation heats up, the Federal Reserve clamps down upon the supply of money and credit, and, presto, the economy subsides into a recession akin to the 1981–82 episode during which unemployment soared to nearly 11 percent. As even economists perceive, such episodes are hard on the unemployed, the merchants and bankers who deal with them, and the communities in which they are concentrated, but their impact upon the economy is alleged to be nonetheless salutary because it forces both workers and employers to revise their expectations of ever higher wages and prices. Chastened unions accept wage and benefit cuts. Manufacturers and retailers cease to mark up prices and in desperate cases actually reduce them. Thus the way is smoothed for renewed expansion. Corporate boards ax incompetent executives. Ill-managed enterprises file bankruptcy petitions. Very much as a hefty dose of castor oil cleanses the human body of impurities, a good recession tones up the economy and smoothes the path to efficient recovery. These adjustments of course would be speedier in the absence of unions, which inevitably slow down painful, essential change.

The 1981–82 mini-depression was a powerful enough cathartic to gratify the sternest theorist. But the recovery that ensued embarrassingly contradicted the economic fable just recounted. By the middle of its third year, it was visibly tiring. The collapse of oil prices and general decline in interest rates early in 1986 pumped renewed life into a faltering recovery. It remains an expansion that has failed to alleviate an unemployment rate that in February 1986 was identical with that of early 1981. If the scandal of Reagan's early May 1985 visit to the Bitburg military cemetery in which forty-eight SS troopers were buried had not overshadowed the economic agenda that occasioned his European trip, more comment would have been addressed to the president's discomfiture over urging upon Europeans the supply-side tax cuts, deregulation of business, and celebration of enterprise which supposedly had restored the bloom to the cheeks of the American economy. In point of fact, a suspicious pallor was replacing the rude health recently visible on the face of capitalism. A clear sour note even when the going was better was sounded by the monthly unemployment figures. They stuck in the vicinity of 7 percent. In booming

## After Reagan . . . Still More Reagan

New York City, where office space and luxury apartments may soon be rented by the square inch, the jobless figure has been usually 2 percent or more higher. Minority teenage idleness exceeds 50 percent. During earlier and more naïve times, 7 percent was taken by presidents and smaller political animals as a crisis figure. In the worst month of the severest of three 1950s recessions, unemployment touched 7.6 percent, only inconsequentially higher than the rate now stoically accepted by respectable, fully employed economists as their tacit definition of full employment. February 1986's 7.3 percent civilian unemployment figure in the fortieth month of an unusually long economic expansion deserved to be memorialized as a major failure of Reaganomics.

Thoroughly socialized members of the profession, it is by now superfluous to add, have no patience with soft-headed remedies for unemployment like the Humphrey-Hawkins bill, a dead letter at the instant in 1978 when Jimmy Carter reluctantly signed it into law. Taken seriously, the statute would require Congress to create enough public employment to fill the gap between willing workers and the number of jobs available in the private economy. Economists are professionally skeptical about the value of public activity, undisciplined as it usually is by the harsh imperatives of market competition. Inefficiency is a sufficiently grave charge by itself. Even more devastating is the asserted connection between public-job creation, the menace of revived inflation, and its certain sequel, a curative recession sponsored by the Federal Reserve cheered onward by the applause of the financial community.

What ought an economist to do? It is time to return to our Cambridge instructor. Weitzman has a bright idea which has attracted the fancy of the *New York Times*, among other eminent authorities. In his small, comparatively well-written volume, he offers an elegant variation upon Japanese practice. In that booming society, large employers—the Toyotas, Sonys, and Nissans—extend lifetime employment guarantees to their lucky employees. The third of the labor force blessed with them may from time to time be asked to change jobs or even be loaned to other organizations, but their paychecks never stop so long as their behavior is good. However, when times are bad, as even in Japan they occasionally are, annual bonuses shrink from the third or half of annual wages routinely disbursed in booms to little or nothing. In effect, Japan, Incorporated, keeps people working by cutting wages and benefits. When labor costs fall, Japanese enterprises cut prices and increase sales. Thus it is that alone in the industrialized world, the ingenious Japanese operate a full-employment economy—the scourge of the universe, without inflation and without recession.

If they pay attention to sound economic advice, Americans can do as well. Here, explains Weitzman, is how. Imagine that a General Motors production worker costs GM $24 per hour. On sound calculation of marginal costs and marginal sales receipts, GM will hire additional men and women up to the moment when the last worker inscribed on the payroll adds no more than that sum to its revenues from sales. There is a small complication. On average, assume that GM actually derives $36 in sales per hour of work. The $12 difference covers overhead and profits. Then if one more worker adds less than $36 but still must be paid the standard $24, GM's margin for overhead and profits will narrow. Now vary the situation after this fashion: "Instead of having each employed worker receive a wage of $24 per hour, the UAW and GM agree that each of the (say) 500,000 employees will receive as compensation a two-thirds share of GM's average revenue per worker. In effect, the UAW is allowing GM's revenue pie to be sliced into two pieces, a two-thirds piece going to labor and a one-third piece to management."[31]

The definitional shift is crucial. GM continues to add new workers because each one costs only $16 in direct wages—the two-thirds of $24 promised regardless of the corporation's profitability. GM reaps an $8 profit. But new workers will collect paychecks of the same size as those earlier hired. The rabbit in Weitzman's analytic hat is downward adjustment of all wages. Here is the arithmetic. Let an extra worker enlarge GM revenue from $18 million to $18,000,024. Total labor cost, however, rises only from $12 million to $12,000,016 ($2/3 \times$ $18,000,024). As the sequel, hourly pay for *all* 500,00l employees declines by $8,500,001 or from $24 to $23.99998. If substantial fractions of corporate employers and their unions adopt this principle of compensation—a wage guarantee plus a revenue share—wages will fluctuate over the business cycle more than they do now, but so will prices. When both wages and prices are more flexible, that is, more sensitive to rising and falling consumer demand, then average rates of unemployment will be much lower.

As Weitzman's inebriation with his patented panacea mounts, he claims that it is capable of transforming industrial relations and inducing employers to treat workers with the same solicitude as they now show to customers who are free to buy from rivals whenever they are dissatisfied with a product's characteristics, quality, or price. The argument is cogent, or would be if in fact banks, department stores, and other vendors actually did treat customers with the solicitude Weitzman imputes to them. When warm bodies are plentiful, employers tend to consider actual and potential hired hands as interchangeable as raw materials or machine tools. All unknowing, personnel offices exemplify the power of Marx's notion of undifferentiated, homogeneous labor. Workers who quit can readily be replaced with equally productive human materials. Share compensation tends to make labor scarce. Since each additional employee costs an employer less, management will add new workers until the limits of plant capacity are reached. Men and women displeased with working conditions will, in this high-employment environment, find superior alternatives in other enterprises. Alert employers accordingly will identify their own interest in a humane factory or office environment. The last blots on the fair face of capitalism will disappear: unemployment will cease to be a problem and worker dignity will become a reality.

As Lester Thurow accurately commented, Weitzman's quick fix may be the ultimate yuppie idea. Were it not for the claims of professional comity, he might have been tempted to comment that of all yuppies, economists probably are the most simple-minded, the most prone to believe in the existence of technical solutions to intricate social and economic problems. Ours is an economy, to begin with, in which corporations do not adjust to changing markets in obedience to textbook precepts. During the disasters of 1981–82, GM and its rivals extracted important concessions from the United Auto Workers at the same time as GM announced new and lucrative bonuses payable to top managers, presumably as rewards for blackjacking the union.

Only a tidal wave of derisive publicity compelled the company to withdraw its bonus plan for repairs. Then, for good measure, the industry raised instead of lowered sticker prices on new models and leaned on the Reagan administration, ostentatiously devoted to free trade, to impose "voluntary" quotas on exports of Japanese Toyotas, Nissans, and Hondas to the American market.

Weitzman has nothing to say about the role of management in his share economy. When sales and profits slump, Japanese enterprises cut most deeply the rewards of executives, a practice likely to promote solidarity between ordinary wage slaves and their supervisors. Does Weitzman really expect American workers to hold still while the compensation of their masters soars at rates several times their own? What reaction is human to episodes like GM's behavior in 1981–82?

Weitzman refrains from direct attacks upon unions. The logic of his argument, however, implies in the first place that under conditions of more or less permanent labor scarcity unions are unnecessary: the self-interest of employers will generate steady improvement in workplace conditions. But, in the second place, as Weitzman from time to time hints or asserts, the most important explanation of persistent unemployment is allegedly excessive wages exhorted by strong unions from compliant employers. This is a singularly inadequate explanation of the historically high rate of unemployment that has marred the 1983–86 expansion. Real wage rates in manufacturing have in most industries declined, but output has failed to increase and prices have not been cut.

Emphasis upon high wages as the major cause of unemployment neglects managerial incompetence, the scandalous overpayment of bungling chief executives, paper entrepreneurialism,[32] and the notorious failure of steel, autos, and other basic industries to adopt advanced technologies frequently invented by Americans but widely diffused only in Japan and West Germany. At the beginning of this century, Thorstein Veblen presciently speculated upon the clash between the mechanical efficiencies of mass-production factory techniques and the wasteful sabotage of financiers, lawyers, stock speculators, accountants, and other practitioners of paper manipulation. In 1985, American productivity actually declined, despite tiresome, inflated claims for computers; unleashed banks and securities firms; deregulated truckers, airlines, and communications; and the supremacy of American business education. Veblen would have enjoyed this verification of his theory that the saboteurs of capitalism are not radical workers but respectable asset-redeploying, three-piece-suit-adorned corporate managers, ignorant of engineering but highly skilled in the merger and acquisition arts.

Weitzman imagines an American economy whose managers yearn to reduce prices, only to be thwarted by the rigidity of labor costs and the intransigeance of short-sighted union leaders. In his tale, full employment is only attainable when markets are free and prices and wages are flexible. Little in the pricing strategies of major corporate actors reveals attachment to downward price flexibility. Unions lured into share economy schemes might well discover that wages really did decline but that employment increased very little. Their members, often already displeased with union efforts, are unlikely to cheer. In decertification elections, unions are likely to lose more often than ever.

Economists ignore the reality of class conflict. *The Share Economy* cheerfully assumes that the existing division of corporate revenues among workers, managers, and stockholders is acceptable to workers. In a sop to unions, he suggests that they might bargain for a larger labor share. The very possibility recalls us to the realities of this decade. In industry after industry, leading corporations have been engaged in concerted anti-union drives. A thriving industry of consultants—lawyers, psychologists, public relations wizards, and specialists in labor relations—devises tactics of resistance to union organizational efforts and strategies to expel unions where they now represent groups of workers. Not so long ago, it was fashionable to postulate the presence of a new maturity in the better boardrooms, an acceptance of unions as legitimate institutions with a constructive role to play in harmonious industrial relations. No longer.

Here is how matters stand in the Reagan era. Strikebreaking is popular and illegal immigrants play the role that earlier in our history new European immigrants and native blacks did in bitter, often violent industrial conflicts. As the *Wall Street Journal*[33] cheerfully told the story,

> Happily for industry, illegals keep not only wages but unions under control. Some auto-parts manufacturers have moved illegals into their work forces as part of a strategy "to weaken union strength, keep wages low and promote competition among workers of different race and citizenship," according to an academic paper presented last February at a meeting of the Los Angeles Business-Labor Council.

There was even better news for managers and stockholders:

> Illegals, where necessary, have functioned as effective strikebreakers as well. Last year, about one hundred members of the Hotel and Restaurant Employees and Bartenders Union walked off the job when Mission Foods, Inc., a tortilla maker for Taco Bell Restaurants, Safeway Stores and others, cut entry-level wages to $3.75 an hour from $5.25 to meet competition from other manufacturers employing illegals.

For some, the ending was happy: "Seven months later, with illegals helping to man the production lines at Mission Foods, the union caved in."

In Reagan's first year, the president signaled his anti-union attitude—first, by the appointment of Raymond Donovan as Secretary of Labor, a New Jersey contractor viewed as antilabor by the AFL-CIO and subsequently indicted on bribery and conspiracy charges; and second, by the spectacular mass firing of striking air traffic controllers. Ironically, their union and the Teamsters were the only labor organizations to endorse Mr. Reagan in the 1980 presidential election. He has appointed to the National Labor Relations Board attorneys and others with records of pro-management sympathies. Performing as expected, they have increased managerial power to fire union activists, hire strikebreakers, and intimidate with the threat of layoff workers who might consider unionization. Possibly the agency's most effective anti-union tactic has been delay. Even when workers discharged illegally for union activity win their cases before the board, decisions arrive years later. The lesson for other workers is starkly plain: you can get fired right now,

## After Reagan . . . Still More Reagan

and in the sweet bye and bye your employer may be compelled to pay you back wages less whatever you have managed to earn in the meantime. The risk for workers is great, for anti-union employers small. NLRB chairman Donald L. Dotson judges that collective bargaining, which his agency is by statute charged with promoting, implies "the destruction of individual freedom and the destruction of the marketplace."[34]

Despite my own inclinations and a good deal of less emotional evidence, I cannot identify the Reagan administration as the single source of all political evil. During the two decades, 1960-80, which preceded its ascent to power, ". . . the number of charges of all unfair employer labor practices rose fourfold; the number of charges involving a firing for union activity rose threefold; and the number of workers awarded back pay or ordered reinstated to their jobs rose fivefold."[35] By 1980, "one in twenty workers who favored the union got fired." Lane Kirkland has publicly wondered whether unions would be better off without the National Labor Relations Board than with it as presently constituted. Younger labor organizers increasingly bypass board-sponsored union-representation elections, recruit members as secretly as possible, and confront employers with faits accomplis. As in the 1930s, strikebreakers are popular. Labor thugs (compliance counselors?) and union spies (data collectors?) lurk in the wings.

What can unions do to reverse a decline which threatens to reduce their membership to a tenth of the labor force by the end of this decade? One strategy is reinvigoration of labor alliances with other groups. Liberal Protestants and Jews and especially Roman Catholics have been traditional friends. The Catholic bishops' much-discussed pastoral letter on the economy vigorously emphasized the importance of trade unions, as has Pope John Paul II in many homilies to the faithful. The women's movement is another source of strength. The drive for payment by comparable worth has predictably aroused the derision of Reagan officials and the opposition of most economists in thrall to their usual obsession with hypothetical free markets. Union leaders have supported comparable worth, and in state after state politicians have actually readjusted or moved toward readjusting compensation in predominantly female occupations. Some unions are attempting to organize the illegals and thus diminish their appeal to employers as reservoirs of cut-rate labor.

Alarm may be premature. An earlier spell of deunionization in the 1920s was followed by the union surge of the New Deal. It occurred with the help of a sympathetic national administration but evoked the opposition of far more violent employers within the context of unemployment that was triple the current rate. There is no assurance, of course, that after Reagan the political winds will blow into office another pro-labor president and Congress.

Unions are toying with the alternative strategy of joining those whom they despair of defeating. Early in 1985, the AFL-CIO executive council, meeting as usual in Florida, endorsed a searching self-study which candidly revealed labor's internal weaknesses and the urgency of action to correct them. The report, "The Changing Situation of Workers and Their Unions," asserts that better-educated workers are "less likely to see work as a straight economic transaction providing a means of survival and more likely to see it as a means of self-expression and self-development."[36] As the veteran labor journalist Abe Raskin summarizes the document, "It discloses the results of a poll taken by Louis Harris and Associates showing that most unaffiliated workers do not view labor as pursuing an agenda drawn from the needs and desires of its members. Nearly two-thirds of the nonunionists questioned said they felt unions forced members to accept decisions they didn't like, and almost as many expressed the belief that union leaders, not the rank and file, decide whether a strike should be called. More than half of the nonunionists thought unions increase the risk of a company going out of business, stifle individual initiative and fight change. Among the population at large, fully 50 percent think most union chiefs no longer represent the workers in their organizations."[37]

What is to be done? Here the report's authors are less persuasive therapists than they are diagnosticians. They suggest movement toward mediation and arbitration instead of strikes wherever employers are willing to play. They endorse quality-of-life experiments that offer workers a voice in decision-making. "To further satisfy the computer-age desire for individual expression, the federation advises that in some bargaining situations unions ought to abandon effort to write detailed rules, negotiate minimum guarantees, and leave members at liberty to bargain on their own merits for pay and benefits above the common floor." Could employers ask much more?

One must wonder whether the prescription is worse than the ailment. In their generally favorable estimate of unions, Freeman and Medoff praise them for narrowing white-collar–blue-collar differentials, as well as sex and age differentials. What sort of common action will be stimulated, if any, by situations in which some workers are encouraged to swim and others are allowed if not to drown to do no more than hold their heads above water? Anti-union employer actions and anti-union sentiments among the unorganized labor majority derive stimulus from the emphasis upon self-enrichment never far from American consciousness but deliberately encouraged in the Reagan era. Little may be gained financially for unions by embracing the values of their opponents. Much will be lost if the sometimes wavering but persistent attachment to social justice is surrendered in a fruitless effort to turn unions into more efficient agents of individual greed.

That unions are imperfect organizations needs no demonstration. That they have in the past served progressive causes for communities larger than their own membership and that they may do so again ought to be equally platitudinous. That it is a controversial claim measures still again the powerful impact of reactionary ideology upon American consciousness.

Privatization, militarization, persistent unemployment, de-unionization, middle-class shrinkage, and the triumph of plutocracy threaten, in alliance with phenomena yet to be considered, to transform American society, a prospect that darkens the next chapter.

## Chapter 5
# America Rearranged

THE TIME HAS come to contemplate the myths resurrected, the prejudices reignited, the avaricious interests additionally legitimated, and the weak appropriately punished for their lack of power and all-round wimpishness. Pause briefly for a respectful nod to the judiciary, whose crucial role up to now has been slighted. By the end of his final term of office, Ronald Reagan will have appointed at least two-thirds of the membership of the federal courts, at the district and appeals levels below the Supreme Court, some of them of such appallingly low quality that nominations have been rejected by the Republican Senate. At least one was an outright racist. Another commended the John Birch Society. Particularly after Mr. Meese became Attorney General, the single and sufficient qualification for nomination to the federal bench has been utter loyalty to the social agenda of the far right.

Much to the distress of conservatives, the Burger Court did little more than nibble at Warren Court liberal decisions. On abortion rights, Justice Blackmun's landmark *Roe* v. *Wade* ruling was more "activist" even than the Warren Court's liberal majority. In mid-1986, however, the high tribunal was populated by grizzled veterans older than the fabulous Nine Old Men (a sexually inaccurate description of the current body), who were Franklin Roosevelt's favorite targets. The roster included Thurgood Marshall (a Lyndon Johnson selection), William Brennan (an Eisenhower miscalculation), Harry Blackmun (a Nixon nominee but a miraculously born-again liberal), and John Paul Stevens (President Ford's single opportunity but a switch hitter as often as not located in the company of

Blackmun, Brennan, and Marshall), who persevere at ages that reassert the hope of human immortality.[1] The Burger Court, whose members include now Chief Justice William Rehnquist and Lewis Powell (two more Nixon choices), Byron White (John Kennedy's salute to football renown and old friendship), and Sandra Day O'Connor (a Reagan pick locked into a tight race for reactionary laurels with her Stanford Law classmate William Rehnquist), has not edged further away from the enlightened Warren Court only because of the intellectual mediocrity of the conservative majority and the ineffectual leadership of the Chief Justice.

A change for the worse now seems inevitable. Warren Burger's retirement allows his replacement by William Rehnquist, possessor of a superior mind, a more collegial disposition, and the most consistently reactionary principles of any Supreme Court Justice since the 1930s. Antonin Scalia, promoted from the Court of Appeals to Associate Justice, has been described as the strongest enemy of the First Amendment among sitting jurists. He is a vigorous fifty-year-old who will be doing his ingenious best to curtail individual freedoms, unleash the police, defend presidential power, shrink the powers of business regulators, and otherwise return the country to the joys of untrammeled capitalism, well into the next century.

The lads in waiting—Robert Bork, who fired Archibald Cox in the glorious Watergate era, and Richard Posner, who firmly believes what he has profusely written, namely, that law is economics and economics is the free-market theology enshrined by Milton Friedman—both possess intellects operating at higher wattage than the dim bulbs whom they salivate to supplant, as does their soulmate Antonin Scalia. Blessed with the physical and mental vigor of veritable Gorbachevs, they can be counted upon, granted the chance, to institutionalize Reagan era attitudes.

Practicing Reaganites invariably favor government authority over individual rights and liberties wherever conflict occurs. By the end of Ronald Reagan's first term, the Court had nibbled at the exclusionary rule by creating a so-called good faith exception for dim-witted cops who were unaware that they were violating the rights of suspects; upheld the installation of a crèche on public property in Providence, Rhode Island, on the shockingly sacrilegious ground that it was indistinguishable from Santa Claus, reindeer, and other symbols of rampant holiday merchandising; retreated significantly on the affirmative-action hiring front; and otherwise indicated disaffection with much of the Supreme Court's record in the 1950s, 1960s, and opening years of the 1970s. At the start of Reagan's final four years, Justice O'Connor upheld a conviction based upon a confession made in police custody while the suspect's attorney was desperately trying to find out where her client was being held. Mendaciously, police authorities withheld this vital information. But that was not enough to invalidate the evidence for six members of the Court. The majority—everybody except Stevens, Marshall, and Brennan—rejected the notion that arresting authorities had to inform suspects "of any and all information" helpful to them. Stevens's dissent scathingly complained that "Today, incommunicado questioning is embraced as a societal goal of the highest order that justifies police deception of the shabbiest kind."[2] Increasingly, the Supreme Court registers Reagan hatred of government action in social and educational policy and admiration for the agents of law and order. Big government is only to be commended when it unleashes men who carry guns at home and abroad. Everywhere else it feeds bureaucracy, undermines individual initiative, and perpetuates poverty.

Just as Defense Secretary Caspar Weinberger has never encountered a weapon he disliked[3] or a statistic he was incapable of fudging, the Department of Justice, the Federal Trade Commission, the Federal Communications Commission, and, increasingly, the courts find it harder and harder to identify corporate takeovers and mergers that pose threats to competition. Almost anything goes in the name of laissez-faire. Even liberal economists, like Lester Thurow, appear to regard the asset reshuffling in vogue in financial markets as efficient redeployments from less to more efficient auspices. That most mergers disappoint bondholders and stockholders in acquiring companies, that more frequently than otherwise conglomerates operate inefficiently, and that in numerous instances acquisition in short order is followed by divestiture deters few celebrants of agglomeration. The merger and acquisition game enriches most lavishly its players—promoters like T. Boone Pickens and

Carl Icahn, arbitrageurs like Ivan Boesky, investment bankers, Wall Street law factories, and the proprietors of golden parachutes unfolded for the benefit of the very executives whose actions had invited friendly or hostile takeovers. Managers preoccupied with the shuffling of paper have neither time nor personal interest in long-term investment in technologies that just might stimulate productivity, raise living standards, and improve American competitiveness in world markets.

Merger madness might evoke only moderate alarm in the context of Reagan catering that spreads before an anesthetized public a banquet of lethal policies, were it not for the spread of size and consolidation to the sensitive arena of free expression, the arena in which the First Amendment, much battered, still sets operating rules. Diversity of opinion is ill served when small, independent publishers are swallowed by larger rivals who in turn sell out to conglomerates. Small magazines of opinion on the political left find it harder and harder to survive as mailing charges steadily rise to levels that begin to exceed printing costs. Their right-wing counterparts enjoy easy access to funding from sympathetic foundations and millionaires. Fewer and fewer independent newspapers remain, more and more operate as units of huge chain enterprises.

As for television, freight scales are not required to weigh the courage of network news executives. ABC found it expedient to issue an apology to the White House for allowing a Soviet commentator seven precious minutes to castigate the president's State of the Union address at the start of 1986's political season. Just bad luck that the network had time unsold to commercial sponsors. Nevertheless, the nightly news is certain to become even more inconsequential, commentary still more conservative, and documentaries part of history, in an atmosphere poisoned by the empire-building of the Rupert Murdochs and Ted Turners. Independent newspapers, often attacked by the right for their dangerous "liberalism"—above all the *Washington Post* and the *New York Times*—have drifted further and further into the political center, the terrain not so long ago of the political right. While deploring new landings of marines in Nicaragua, both newspapers take it editorially for granted that it is appropriate for American politicians to meddle in the internal affairs of another country and install a democratic pluralism suitable to American tastes, even when the champions of civil liberties turn out to be former Somicista national guardsmen. Neither paper objected in mid-1985 to a proposed reduction from 50 to 35 percent of the top tax rate applied to large personal incomes. Nor were editorial voices raised against even more favorable treatment of capital gains. Although New York's major politicians—Governor Cuomo, Democratic senator Daniel Patrick Moynihan, and his Republican colleague Al D'Amato—have vociferously attacked the Treasury's proposal to end deductibility of state and local taxes from federal returns, the *Times* initially waffled on the issue and only grudgingly and belatedly signed up in the Cuomo crusade. This is to say the most allegedly liberal of the major media increasingly define themselves according to their own financial interest. As communications conglomerates—owners of TV and radio outlets, other newspapers, and periodicals—the *Post* and the *Times* concern themselves with after-tax profits and the value imputed to their securities in financial markets, just like your favorite local conglomerate.

In the case of the *Times*,[4] decreasing attention is paid to the black and Hispanic communities and more and more space and devotion are lavished upon upscale, yuppie urbanites and suburbanites who constitute the market for the advertisers who make the cash registers ring. The *Times* clung to Westway to the bitter end, even though or possibly because the project became less a highway than a real estate scam. This purportedly courageous paper criticizes alert local politicians who protest the more outrageous proposals of Manhattan's voracious developers. It abruptly fired as a columnist Sidney Schanberg, an outspoken critic of Westway, real estate developers, and a number of his newspaper's favorite politicians. If the paper had the courage of its opinions, it would make public its private detestation of rent controls.

With transparent favoritism to Mayor Koch, the *Times* all but ignored the intelligent 1985 primary campaign waged by City Council president Carol Bellamy against an incumbent who had shamelessly exacerbated racial tensions while doing little to improve city services, but a great deal to enrich the Trumps and their peers in the development community. In gratitude, an appealing human sentiment, they have contributed generously to the Koch campaign chest. As soon as Koch was safely reelected, a series of revelations began to expose the corrupt practices of Koch appointees. That the mayor himself did not profit hardly excused the extortions of which he was culpably ignorant. No confession of error in endorsing Koch, no second thoughts about ignoring preelection charges by the critical *Village Voice* that city contracts, zoning variances, and tax abatements flowed most readily to contributors to Koch's enormous reelection fund. The *Times* enjoys virtual immunity from the criticism of politicians, writers, musicians, and artists, who justifiably fear reprisals from the paper's reviewers and editorial writers.

In general, TV naturally does far worse. Serious documentaries have all but disappeared from network programming. For occasional criticism of American icons, viewers early in 1986 could do no better than inspect Gore Vidal's adoption of the novel *Dress Gray* on commercial television.[5] CBS won its case against the rather pathetic General Westmoreland but has aired nothing as abrasive as its Vietnam exposé since then. Bill Moyers, the most enlightened major TV newsman, rarely gets airtime on CBS. The official commentators on rival evening news programs are the omnipresent conservative-for-all-seasons George Will on ABC and the raving moderate John Chancellor on NBC. On public television, "The MacNeil-Lehrer Newshour" often provides serious analyses of single issues, but it almost exhausts public television's contribution. Most of its public-affairs programming is either grimly balanced between participants slightly to the right of center and those minimally to the left or clearly conservative, as in the case of William Buckley's enduring "Firing Line" or "The McLaughlin Report." The heirs of Edward R. Murrow are as invisible and unheard as so many mute, village Miltons.

Ours are times of inappropriate reaction to genuine problems of social policy, nowhere more glaringly than in our expensive, inequitable, and erratically competent health-care nonsystem. Hospitals are in trouble. As a result of relentless Washington pressures against supposedly unneeded hospitalization or unduly prolonged stays, and parallel efforts by health insurers and major corporations, room-occupancy rates declined from 77 percent in 1965 to 72 percent in 1983 and 67 percent in 1984. Admission rates dropped between 1983 and 1984 by 4 percent, or 1.5 million patients.[6] To hospital boards, medical administrators, and other prudent types, the obvious recourse is joining the marketing celebration that has already enrolled lawyers in need of clients, dentists short of customers with aching teeth, and doctors with low billings.

The case of the pampered nobleman exemplifies the new ethic of health-care marketing. Featured is the One South luxury wing in Bethesda's Suburban Hospital. As this vacation tale runs, "The Italian count checked in unnoticed by the other guests. He settled into a two-room suite where he was served gourmet meals on the finest china and crystal. A pink rose arrived with breakfast. He called London frequently, and when he left he was whisked away in the private elevator. In the midst of all that, the count was undergoing major surgery."[7] Hospitals, once pledged to the ideal if never the reality of equal treatment of all patients, now clutter the airwaves with pitches for the luxury accommodations, superb food, gracious surroundings, tape decks, and videocassettes of the newspaper's Living and Style sections. Survival for health providers now is seen to require the same market segmenting, the same differential pricing, the same ploys of product differentiation that in happier days were scorned by proud health professionals as the domain of hucksters. The national response to the health crisis of the 15 percent of mostly working Americans totally uncovered by Medicaid, Medicare, or private health insurance is fancier care for the affluent.

As with health so also with the federal role in job training. When an approximation of decent job training against the odds wins political favor, its life continues to be precarious. In October 1984, the Department of Labor issued the following statement, evidently before the administration had decided to eliminate the Job Corps.[8] The 1987 budget reiterated the administration's aspiration to terminate a successful program for, evidently, an ill-regarded clientele. Someone in the Department of Labor had not checked signals with the budget warriors esconced in OMB. Hearken:

## JOB CORPS HELPS DISADVANTAGED YOUTHS

Michael Perez was living in an abandoned building and was a leader of a street gang when he walked into the South Bronx Job Corps Center in October 1980.

During his months at the Labor Department's Job Corps, he threw away his gang clothes and learned carpentry skills. He designed and constructed the center's library, founded its security cadet program, and earned his high school equivalency degree. Today, he is an assistant foreman for a New York construction firm.

Perez is one of approximately 60,000 young men and women who receive job training and basic education each year in the Job Corps, the nation's only residential program for economically disadvantaged youths needing special attention to get that all-important start in life.

For some, it's the last, best hope to join the societal mainstream. The average participant is an eighteen-year-old high school dropout who reads at the elementary school level, comes from a poor family, is a minority group member and has never held a regular job.

"We take the more severely disadvantaged," says Frank C. Casillas, Assistant Secretary of Labor for employment and training, "and ask, 'Where are you going now?' They're growing up and they decide they've got to do something."

Since 1965, when the Job Corps opened its first center, more than 800,000 people have been helped by the program. . . . Residential living distinguished the Jobs Corps from all other federal employment and training programs. There are 107 residential centers in forty-two states, the District of Columbia and Puerto Rico. . . . There are over one hundred vocational offerings. . . . Discipline at the centers is strict. . . . Corps members are also taught living skills at the center. . . . Corps members also learn about civic responsibility. . . . In various locations, corps members have built firehouses, conducted blood drives, held community clean ups, cut forest trails and rehabilitated townhouses . . . The Job Corps recently observed its twentieth anniversary. Looking to the future, Casillas says the program will be taking a closer look at the changing nature of the job market, and how that relates to corps members' training. That may mean less training in such fields as stenography and keypunching, and more emphasis on data entry and word processing skills and health service occupations.[9]

Casillas, an innocent soul, evidently did not know that back at the ranch, the folks at the Office of Management and Budget were totting up the numbers and concluding that the Job Corps had failed its cost-effectiveness test. What an outrage that it costs as much in a year to rescue a drifting ghetto youth as to send an upper-class youngster to Harvard!

These phenomena illustrate the complementary principles that propel Reagan zealots. The first, of course, is doctrinaire affection for presumably competitive markets, or at least markets that operate as though they actually were competitive. The second is an equally powerful thrust toward greater social control. If public services continue to be privatized and voucher mechanisms more widely substituted for direct provision of housing and medical services, the outcome amounts to filling in the details of an American portrait sketched in outline by two Reagan presidential terms.

Markets first. Economic life is a struggle between competition and monopoly. Flesh-and-blood businessmen compete the better to become monopolists. That monopolies tend to be transitory—either because new technology renders them obsolete or their profits soar to exorbitant enough heights to allow would-be rivals to gamble huge capital entry costs for a share of a lucrative market or, in time past, because the antitrust division of the Department of Justice and the Federal Trade Commission policed the more egregious anticompetitive ploys of dominant players—should not conceal the certainty that so long as monopolies endure they misallocate resources, distort consumer choices, and reward inefficient performance. If continued, present official attitudes toward mergers, bids to take over TV stations and entire networks, and privatization of public services will dramatically alter the mixture of private, public, and nonprofit voluntary activity. In communications, both public television and public radio, starved for funds, have been compelled to rely more heavily upon corporate sponsorship and such entrepreneurial, profit-seeking ventures as they can dream up. One tempting source of immediate help but later decline is exchange of a Very High Frequency channel for an Ultra High Frequency substitute. The much weaker UHF signal, of course, sends programs into fewer homes. For this loss of viewers, the compensation is anything up to $200 million, the sum reportedly offered to Channel 13 in New York City, probably a bargain for an entrepreneur in search of a new money-making machine. In the post-Reaganite future, even "MacNeil-Lehrer," mild fare at best, may vanish along with National Public Radio's occasionally irreverent evening news program, "All Things Considered."

Before the 1930s, government funded almost no services for children and their parents. Since the New Deal, these services have continued to be delivered by secular agencies like New York City's Community Services Society and such religious organization's as Catholic Charities. However, much of the funding has come from government. In the Reagan period, the cash flow from Washington has diminished. The administration's 1985 tax proposals hit hard at alternative revenue sources. Exclusion of state and local taxes as federal deductions was designed to intensify tax competition among local jurisdictions, for the loss hurts upper-income, itemizing taxpayers in high-tax jurisdictions like New York, California, and Massachusetts. Such taxpayers have the resources to move into contiguous lower tax states. To retain the prosperous, generous states may be coerced into lowering taxes, funding for public services, and subsidies to private charitable organizations. Much as the Reagan administration extols voluntarism, its policies threaten to undermine private nearly as much as public social action.

Private altruism, the remaining source of support, is also discouraged by the Treasury's proposal to set a 2 percent floor before an itemizing taxpayer can subtract gifts and to junk any deduction for the nonitemizing majority. Fortunately, folks make gifts out of human sympathy, religious obligation, or special experience without first consulting their accountants. It is reasonable to anticipate, however, that such contributions will diminish in size, if not necessarily in number, simply because givers will feel less able to afford them. The outlook, then, is elimination or reduction of services—counseling, adoption, job training, psychiatric, and others—for those unable to pay for them.

For health care, the prospect is, if anything, even bleaker. The ongoing growth of for-profit hospitals, immediate-care facilities, nursing homes, and dialysis centers proceeds at the expense of both public and voluntary alternatives. As municipal and voluntary hospitals close or are acquired by the health conglomerates, provision for the medically needy but financially insolvent will become sketchier and sketchier as the burden of care falls upon fewer and fewer emergency rooms and outpatient clinics. Where cities contract with Humana or Hospital Corporation of America for the care of low-income patients, it will be within the context of ever-narrower service segmentation now altering the character of health service delivery. To put the point with appropriate bluntness, the poor will be treated as charity patients, separated from prosperous fellow citizens. For medical purposes, more and more families will be defined as poor. Reliance on markets is the equivalent of reversion to the practices and attitudes of the nineteenth century, when few questioned the propriety of minimal care for their social inferiors. In a plutocracy, social inferiority corresponds to financial status.

Education during the Reagan years has proven amazingly resistant to privatization. Recurrent proposals to offer parents vouchers exchangeable for their children's education at either private or public schools have attracted little support. Congress has rejected tuition tax credits in aid of parents who now send youngsters to fee-charging schools. Nor has it been willing to terminate Title I grants to schools in low-income neighborhoods. And although the Department of Justice routinely intervenes against school-busing plans, these have for the most part survived in communities grown accustomed to them, and unwilling to endure the probable turmoil attendant upon their disruption. It is reasonable to expect that in a post-Reaganite future these will be major items on an unfinished social agenda. Consistent with free-market ideology will be still sharper curtailment of loans and grants to college students than Congress so far has countenanced.

Conservatives have already imposed their ideology upon labor markets. There is logic and coherence in their rejection of an affirmative action and comparative worth as grounds for public intervention. Both principles challenge the legitimacy of market operations. For those who accept the market's verdicts as unimpeachable, government meddling must generate consequences inferior to those of the unhampered interplay of supply and demand. For admirers of Herbert Spencer's social Darwinism, the news is equally good on the union front. As union membership shrinks, unions are forced to adopt two- or several-tier pay arrangements certain to generate bitterness between veterans and newcomers. For employers, the gap between union and nonunion wages and working conditions has steadily narrowed. Huge deficits in federal budgets and international trade have combined to sabotage export and domestic markets for manufactured goods. Manufacturing jobs have been permanently lost, multinationals have shifted facilities abroad, and pressure upon wages and benefits in the older industries where unions are most strongly entrenched has mounted. The momentum toward a union-free environment is powerful. But if the future resembles the present, it may make comparatively little difference to employers whether or not their workers are organized. Indeed, insofar as chastened unions can be converted into adjuncts of managerial control, they can be transformed into assets rather than liabilities. At their strongest and most enlightened, unions promote worker solidarity, narrow inequalities within the plant, and modify market outcomes. Where they are weak, they perforce increasingly yield to managerial preference to hire and fire people much in the way materials and products are bought and sold. Old-fashioned capitalism esteems human beings as interchangeable, products as fungible as raw materials.

Social control characterizes and defines organized societies. Even in the more benign utopias, such as Edward Bellamy's *Looking Backward*, William Morris's *News From Nowhere*, and the land of the enlightened horses in Jonathan Swift's *Gulliver's Travels*, social roles must somehow be at least gently suggested, if not actually assigned. Public opinion and the wish to maintain the esteem of neighbors and friends can be as coercive as outright police action. In some societies, notably Japan, shame operates powerfully enough on occasion to induce suicide. Our own history can be understood as a record of tension between the demands of social order and the claims of individualism. In popular mythology, heroes are fearless and independent, from Daniel Boone to the Gary Cooper of *High Noon* and the *Rambo* of Sylvester Stallone. So engaging is the image that that rather unlikely figure Henry Kissinger imprudently confided to an interviewer that he fancied himself in the role of the lonely cowboy.

Possibly because individualism is so potent an American ideal, the reaction to it can be equally intense. If in the 1960s and even the 1970s gays emerged from their closets, interracial couples became commonplace, and unwedded bliss competed on equal terms with the marital variety, the 1980s recorded a sharp public reaction registered in the clamor for more homework, emphasis on basics, and more classroom days in the schools; increases in the age of legal drinking; routinization of executions in more and more states; mandatory sentencing for crimes; rampant vocationalism on the campuses; and a new popularity of careers in the military and the CIA, whose recruiters attract few protests even on Ivy League campuses. Buckle-up seat-belt statutes; drug testing for athletes, federal workers, and corporate employees; literacy tests for experienced teachers—all are miscellaneous signs of new popular indulgence of government restraints on individual choice. Judges impose longer jail terms.

The popularity of social control has its bizarre side, notably television cop and private-eye dramas in which the good guys and gals are indistinguishable from their evil counterparts. They share similar tastes for violence, blow away approximately the same number of bodies, and speak in the same street vernacular. Social scientists endlessly quarrel over the impact of TV violence. Does it discharge violent aggressions safely short of temptations to reenact TV fantasy in real life, or does it promote imitation and better-informed shopping for lethal weapons? Both on TV and in daily life the individualistic ideal and the passion for tight, even vindictive control of bad people merge into the archtype of the solitary enforcer.

Thus far (how much longer?), red-baiting has been comparatively muted although far from absent. Liberal Democrats in Congress agonize over Central America, MX missiles, B-1 bombers, and numerous other questionable weapons, fearing to vote their convictions lest they be charged with softness on Communism, a sin against recrudescent machoism akin to wimpishness itself. That the administration has thus far sponsored no Commie or Commie-symp hunts testifies less to any secret passion for civil liberties than to the acute implausibility

## America Rearranged

involved in locating dangerous reds at a time when spy scandals revolve around avaricious servicemen, one of whom devoted what time remained after his naval duties and espionage to recruiting new members for the Ku Klux Klan.

Post-Reagan America will be a playground for the wealthy, a mean society for the poor and vulnerable, and a place of constant struggle for a shrinking middle class to maintain living standards. The gap between poor and rich will continue to widen as it has since 1981. The percentage of the officially poor will continue to rise. The gamut of respectable politics will range from moderately conservative to wildly reactionary. Prayer will come back to public schools. As it was before the Supreme Court's landmark decision, safe abortion will become again a prerogative of prosperous women. Policemen and soldiers will surge in general esteem. Foreign policy will edge closer and closer to the Soviet model. The CIA and KGB will be in a position to exchange training manuals without loss of national security in either country. Once more the unfortunate will perforce depend upon the altruistic impulses of better-financed fellow citizens. The delights of imperialism and plutocracy will become, even more than they already are, the staples of mass entertainment.

*Chapter 6*

# Neolibs, Technocrats, and Yuppies

WALK NORTH ON a balmy weekend evening from Lincoln Center in Manhattan along Columbus Avenue for fifteen or twenty blocks and treat yourself to a vision of youth à la mode. No costume is outré when clothes are expected to project personality, to make statements comprehensible to peers if not to touring cultural anthropologists and marveling senior citizens, and to assert individuality within safe social limits. Boutiques and sidewalk cafés, sanctuaries of gelati, tofutti, and premium ice cream, jostle each other. Chinese and Japanese restaurants compete with Mexican, Thai, Indian, and Italian rivals. Lines form in front of particularly popular "in" establishments like Ruelles, where the sounds of soft rock entice customers into a Gay Nineties interior whose walls feature buxom female nudes. Overheard conversations conduct themselves in the educated tones of the college-credentialed. Topics are those of *New York* magazine, the *Village Voice,* and the Living, Style, Home, and Weekend sections of the *New York Times*—movies, dance, theater, food, furniture, apartments, exercise, clothing, and, inevitably, jobs. Loud along the boulevard resonates the psychobabble of relationships, getting in touch with one's feelings, personal growth, transference and countertransference, how to get through the summer while the analyst is away, and other verbal evidences of the vulgarization of austere Freudian doctrine. If a classical Freudian survives and keeps the faith, he or she will in moments of carefully rationed utterance tell a patient yearning for happiness that the best psychoanalysis offers is enhanced capacity to cope with ordinary, human misery. Not at all a palatable message for the optimistic young.

With minor variations, this yuppie scene is protean. On the beaches of Fire Island and the Hamptons, summer weekends feature the same young and not-so-young virtuosi of self-presentation. On a smaller scale, similar sights and sounds are to be seen or heard in Seattle, San Francisco, and Portland, Maine, as well as other reasonably prosperous urban centers. Outposts spring up in unexpected locales. A street or two in St. Cloud, Minnesota, an hour northwest of Minneapolis, contains restaurants and menus indistinguishable from those of Northampton, Amherst, or for that matter Columbia, Missouri, where the state university is headquartered, and Greenville, South Carolina, where that bastion of biblical inerrancy, Bob Jones University, wages total war against sinful hedonism. The look-alike ferns in look-alike brass fixtures hang from look-alike loft ceilings almost anywhere in the happy land.

Who are these young urban professionals? What do they do, think, portend for the national future? There is no official definition of the group and no known coiner either of yuppie or of yumpie—young, upwardly mobile urban professional. *Business Week* advised its addicts that as of the New Year, yuppies were "out," along with economists, consultants, Theory Z, synergy, and junk bonds.[1] Seventy-five million Americans were born between 1946 and 1966, the yuppie generation, slightly less than a third of the nation's population in the middle of the 1980s. Obviously not very many of them qualify for these labels redolent of mingled envy and derision. The cohort includes high-school dropouts; drug addicts; street criminals; welfare mothers; clerks; craftsmen; farmers; white-, pink-, gold-, and blue-collared workers; career members of the armed services; and hordes of small businessmen and women, civil servants, and housewives. Nothing new here, of course. Cultural and political phenomena invariably define themselves in the polemics and behavior of vanguards, some of them as tiny as the group around Lenin who turned czarist and Kerensky calamities into Bolshevik triumph. Not, one hastens to add, that yuppies have such subversive notions in mind.

The uncertain fraction of the seventy-five million who possess convincing claims to genuinely elite membership share appropriate educational credentials. At the least, they possess college degrees. The lawyers and aspiring executives among them have presumably earned or at least received marketable credentials from law factories and schools of business administration. They are associates or, more lucratively, junior partners, in the major Wall Street and midtown law firms—Sullivan and Cromwell; Davis, Polk; Dewey Ballantine; Gotshal, Menges; Simpson, Thatcher; Finley, Wagner, Heini, Underberg, Myerson, Manley & Casey; and so multisyllabically on. In famous litigations, the particularly privileged among them may get to carry the briefcases of their seniors. The stacks of documents they sedulously check generate revenues priced at $80 to $100 per hour. Yuppies, of course, deal in many other varieties of symbols and abstractions—as stock analysts, management consultants, editors, computer programmers, loan officers, forecasters, designers of advertising and marketing campaigns, and shapers of images for politicians and other performers. Yuppie politicians consult David Garth for image implants, for that famous nonyuppie sees deeply into yuppie psyches.

Yuppies, unlike old-fashioned intellectuals who are similarly removed from the mundane sphere of physical production, specialize only in those varieties of the intangible that promise financial profit, and by habit and preference comfort themselves with the application of technique to data. They are the adepts of the age of information. No doubt connections exist between their daily labors and the quantity and quality of food, clothing, living space, cars, and consumer appliances that ordinary folks aspire to, but they are singularly elusive. Strategic planners generate strategic plans. Public relations wizards put spins on media perceptions of their clients. Space buyers distribute advertising budgets among competing print and TV media. Humbler, blue-collar types work with machines and their own hands to fill the tangible needs of, among others, yuppies themselves. In Marxist terms, yuppies inhabit the superstructure atop an ever-narrowing base in which fewer and fewer factory operatives produce usable, physical commodities.

Prophets of the information age, notable among them Harvard sociologist Daniel Bell and the late Princeton economist Fritz Machlup, accurately forecast the occupational restructuring of the labor force: the minority of men and women who produce products and services continues to decline as the proportion of information or misinformation workers increases. With some exceptions, mostly related to new computer-related occupational specialties, yuppies in their offices occupy themselves more modishly in ways familiar to their predecessors. A young lawyer may plug himself into Lexis, a data base that simplifies the laborious search for precedents. Consultants lengthen or shorten their tasks with personal computers. Financial experts "access" themselves to spread sheets, but the quality of their output is no more altered than is this manuscript because I have used a word processor instead of a typewriter or a quill pen.

To be a real yuppie one must think and act like one. Saints excepted, we are all creatures of self-interest. Most religions and ethical codes do their best to mitigate the primacy of ego. The yuppie code is distinctive, for it appears to be the first article of the yuppie faith that nothing is more natural and even commendable than narcissism. To be obsessed with self is commonplace among the young and far from unique among the middle-aged and elderly. There is, accordingly, nothing unprecedented in yuppie displays of ego, any more than in their passion for the latest fads in food, house plants, furniture, physical-fitness recipes, watering holes, summer weekend locales, audio and video equipment, movies and music, and the multitudinous artifacts of personal adornment. The celebration of self in our culture differs from time to time and place to place in expression, but not in essential psychic quality.

Yet there is something distinctive about this decade's yuppie phenomenon, suggested by a pair of contrasting stereotypes, the first of them William H. Whyte, Jr.'s, *The Organization Man*, a best seller of the Eisenhower era; and the second, Charles Reich's coronation of youth, *The Greening of America*, an evocation of the ethos of the wild 1960s. Whyte's title entered the language of common discourse, but he cannot fairly be charged with admiring the behavior he analyzes. Organization men—the corporate culture of the 1950s furnished no powerful role for women—conformed. If IBM favored white shirts, sober ties, and gray-flannel suits, executive trainees dressed to suit and dutifully ate no-martini lunches. IBM holds fast to its tradition: he or she who drinks at lunch is advised not to return in the afternoon to his or her desk. If success demanded conformity in conduct and expression as well as mere apparel, one gladly obeyed, for, as Whyte put it, middle-class careerists shared "a belief in the group as the source of creativity; a belief in 'belongingness' as the ultimate need of the individual; and a belief in the application of science to achieve the belongingness."[2]

In Whyte's drab universe, the large corporation substitutes for religion and politics. Success defines itself as upward movement in its bureaucracy. It is David Riesman's other-directed gladhanders—not inner-directed souls still responsive to the Protestant ethic—who rise. Whyte detested the spiritual sterility of those who worked, married, and lived according to the organizational code. He savagely caricatured the suburbs in which young families huddled for mutual protection against the contamination of thoughts, beliefs, actions, and people different from those of the organizational imperative.

Reread three decades later, Whyte's polemic seems to describe Japanese corporate culture better than it does our own. Sony and Hitachi confer lifetime jobs on faithful employees, unlike *Fortune*'s five hundred largest industrial operators, one hundred major banks, or two hundred giant retailers. In Japan, but certainly not here at home, it is bad form to change employers.[3]

Conferences between Japanese and Americans baffle at least the latter because at meeting's end it is still mysterious who on the Japanese side is in command and what has been decided. Japanese value group consensus and mutual respect. Americans glorify decisive executives and clear hierarchical definitions of authority. The Iacoccas, Geneens, and Hennesseys dominate their colleagues, humiliate them at will, and rejoice in volcanic eruptions of temperament. Japanese executives drink, golf, and play together. Japanese wives and children place a distant second to devouring corporate demands. One of this decade's unfolding dramas features the success or failure of the Japanese ethic in Fremont, California, where General Motors and Toyota embrace in a joint venture, as well as in, of all places, Detroit, where Mazda has negotiated on its own terms with the United Automobile Workers.

## Neolibs, Technocrats, and Yuppies

General Motors's Saturn project breaks still more abruptly with standard American corporate tradition. Its brand-new small-car factory in Spring Hill, Tennessee, GM's last-ditch multibillion dollar attempt to compete with Japan's thundering herd of Hondas, Nissans, and Toyotas, substitutes cooperation for confrontation on the factory floor and management-union committee substitutes for the traditional top-down, hierarchical style of the auto industry and most other manufacturing enterprises. The contrast is dramatic. In a typical 1985 GM plant, supervisors/foremen (ninety per shift) report to general supervisors (fifteen per shift) who answer to production superintendents (five per shift) who salute a single general superintendent who owes allegiance to a production manager who communicates with the man at the top, the plant manager. When Saturns begin to roll off the assembly lines in 1989, they will be artifacts of a very different set of social relationships. At the bottom of the factory's hierarchy will be work units, teams of six to fifteen men and women who elect a UAW "counselor" to lead them. A work-unit module—three to six work units—will be headed by a company-selected "work-unit adviser." A business unit to coordinate plant-wide operations will include company representatives and specialists and also an elected union adviser. Union representatives will sit on the manufacturing advisory committee overseeing the entire Saturn operation and also on the strategic advisory committee charged with conducting long-range planning. Workers will be paid salaries. Four-fifths of them will be covered by lifetime employment guarantees, save in the occurrence of "catastrophic events." Such symbols of privilege for managers as executive dining rooms and reserved parking slots will be eliminated.[4] However, wages will average just four-fifths the pay of other UAW workers. As in Japan, Saturn employees will be encouraged to supplement wage guarantees with productivity bonuses. In still another sharp break with union tradition, job classifications are practically abolished. All production workers will be enrolled in a single category. Managers will acquire complete flexibility to switch people from one task to another.

Saturn's imitation of Japanese practice and its actual organizational expression in mainland America impose fascinating pressures upon corporate behavior, and agonizing choices for yuppies. Should they bet their career prospects on sagely calculated shifts from one employer to another or is corporate loyalty the new ticket to promotion, stock options, titles of escalating significance, and perquisites, however suitably disguised, of transcendent spiritual fulfillment? Will the psychobabble of the imminent future be translations from the Japanese? Will particularly eager yuppies actually learn to speak and comprehend the language of the masters of international markets?

Before we explore the many mansions of yuppie heaven, let us resurrect another, wildly contrasting vision, that of a nearly forgotten prophet of the 1960s, Charles Reich. Reich's subtitle to *The Greening of America* was *How the Youth Revolution Is Trying to Make America Livable*. His dedication read, "For the Students at Yale, Who Made This Book Possible, and for Their Generation." Hard upon these words followed the song lyrics of Woody Guthrie and Chet Powers invoking love of country and fellow man. For those whose age enables or compels them to recall the intoxicating mixture of drugs, revolution, spiritual exaltation, and instantaneous epiphany of fashionable college campuses in the 1960s, this paean to youth and call to brotherhood was a sanitized version of Woodstock, Berkeley, and Columbia.

In our national landscape of perpetual youth and well-preserved senior citizens, best-selling gurus have traditionally tended to impart virtues to the young whose absence they uneasily deplore in themselves. But even if one is a forty-three-year-old law professor, as Reich was when *The Greening of America*'s vision of a New Jerusalem shimmered before his eyes, one can enlist as an auxiliary of liberated and liberating youth. Indeed, Reich's own transformation is almost as startling as the salvation of America that is the stuff of his book-length sermon. At Yale, he was esteemed as an extraordinarily gifted teacher of law, of all implausible subjects, and beyond the boundaries of New Haven as the author of exceptionally provocative law-review articles, occasionally cited with approval by members of a Supreme Court spectacularly different from that of the 1980s. These essays on property, government regulation, and twentieth-century feudalism contain the roots of the assault upon the corruptions of organizational power that endures as the most satisfactory portion of this book.

"The New Property,"[5] the most celebrated of these articles, focused upon governmental "largesse" as the dynamic of alteration in property relations. Under this rubric, Reich listed numerous benefits conferred by government upon groups of citizens, among them welfare, Social Security, and veterans' pensions; government jobs; occupational licenses; bus, trucking, airline, and taxicab franchises; subsidies to farmers, shipbuilders, and an ever-lengthening list of other supplicants; access on indulgent terms to grazing, mining, and lumbering on public lands; subsidized commercial mail delivery; cut-rate savings-bank and home-construction insurance; and free technical information for farmers and corporations.

Elected representatives and public functionaries perceive largesse as so many acts of grace, to be as legitimately recalled as compassionately extended. Beneficiaries, understandably, come quickly to esteem each boon as similar to older varieties of property as inalienable as acres of land and the structures erected upon them. Reich's own distinction between largesse, the new property, and more traditional property entitlements focuses upon a danger to new-property claimants. In general, private property originates in the economic activities of private markets. By contrast, largesse both reflects and reinforces existing distributions of political power and influence.

Public largesse enriches the wealthy and tightens the grip of the powerful. Large commercial farmers collect the bulk of agricultural subsidies. In the 1950s and 1960s, FHA loan guarantees financed middle-class flight to the suburbs. In depopulated cities, urban renewal (in black circles bitterly translated into charges of black removal) diminished inventories of low-cost rental housing in exchange for convention halls, new hotels, and luxury flats. At New York's Columbus Circle the Coliseum, an architectural horror, displaced low-income renters and the dry cleaners, grocers, shoemakers, launderers, and bankers who served them. Only fair that in the mid-1980s developers plan to demolish the Coliseum and erect two much larger towers on the site. When Reich wrote his book and the articles which preceded it, he noted that California's tax and fee structures combined to generate subsidies for middle-class college students financed mostly by regressive taxes levied upon their financial inferiors, for it is a law of public largesse that acute social need accompanies small political power. From that law flows an ineluctable corollary: the powerful, never the needy, collar a disproportionate percentage of the cash. Lyndon Johnson's war on poverty in short order became a jobs program for middle-class professionals.[6]

Nor in Reich's view was this the worst of the tale. By definition, largesse can be capriciously granted and removed at the pleasure or displeasure of administrators endowed with alarming discretionary power either by congressional design, congressional inattention, or the natural disposition of bureaucrats to interpret statutes in ways that widen their own sphere of action. Communications policy exemplifies the general condition. In their wisdom, courts have ruled that the Communications Act, which created the Federal Communications Commission, awarded no property right to radio- or TV-station operators. Licenses are mere privileges, initially granted for three-year terms and, subsequently, renewed or revoked by FCC decision. That they are also licenses to print money is beside the legal point. Congress originally may have intended license limitation as pressure upon broadcasters to meet minimum criteria of public service. But in the Nixon-Agnew era, the source of most of Reich's "horribles," as in the age of Reagan, such precariousness of tenure impressed timid network executives as sufficient reason to tone down news comment, deemphasize documentaries critical of establishment institutions, and confine the guest list on discussion programs to responsible souls slightly to the left or slightly to the right of the amorphous, dearly beloved center. Reich's point remains sharp: the networks retain enormous opportunities for profit on condition that they barter away at least part of their First Amendment right to free speech. As in the Middle Ages, property amounts to a grant conditioned upon loyalty to the sovereign. Nor does it much matter that Americans change their sovereigns at four- or at most eight-year intervals. Fear of sovereign displeasure is a constant.

Reich warned that such coercive powers of government over individual access to largesse are extensive and growing. With few signs of popular opposition, Congress decreed that "Any person shown by evidence satisfactory to the Administrator to be guilty of mutiny, treason, sabotage, or rendering assistance to any enemy of the United States or of its allies shall forfeit all accrued or future benefits under laws administered by the Veterans Administration."[7] Yet we do not take money away from disloyal millionaires. What warrant justifies shearing a veteran of benefits earned by past service because of poor behavior at some date after his honorable discharge from the armed services? Once again application of public largesse involves threat by sovereign power to personal freedom.

Reich wrote at the end of a period when a Supreme Court led by strong liberals—among them Chief Justice Earl Warren, William Douglas, Arthur Goldberg, Thurgood Marshall, and William Brennan—moved cautiously away from definition of welfare grants to indigent families as largesse or gratuity and toward enunciation of a right to public assistance. The distinction is crucial. The awesome constitutional protection of due process envelops "rights." In the case of public welfare, one Supreme Court decision required welfare administrators to accord beneficiaries fair hearings *before* termination or reduction of benefits. Another threw out a New York statute which imposed a twelve-month state-residency requirement for benefit eligibility. A third prohibited midnight raids on the apartments of welfare recipients in search of adult males cohabiting in violation of eligibility rules. For a time, the Supreme Court seemed to be nerving itself to proclaim something akin to a right to life translatable into a governmentally guaranteed income large enough to impart reality to that right.

In an instance too late to be included in Reich's volume, the vagaries of the Supreme Court on issues of property, entitlement, and largesse were highlighted by abrupt reversal of movement on welfare terrain. In 1971, Mr. Justice Harry Blackmun, not yet the born-again liberal he was soon to become, delivered the majority opinion in *Wyman* v. *James*.[8] Barbara James, a New York City welfare recipient, rejected home visits by her caseworker as an invasion of her Fourth Amendment protection "against searches without warrants based on probable cause," as the lawyers phrase American expectations that no governmental official can legally knock on a door and demand entry without the backing of a judge. Be it ever so humble, a person's home is his castle. Nevertheless, New York's Department of Social Services sought to terminate benefits because Mrs. James persisted in her refusal to welcome her caseworker.

Justice Blackmun rejected the notion that such visits were the sort of searches the framers of the Constitution had in mind and then proceeded to justify the visits as reasonable even if they were construed as searches. The public had an interest in the welfare of Mrs. James's child and in the appropriate use of tax funds, as well as in the rehabilitation of adult welfare recipients. Caseworkers ought to be regarded by their clients as friends, not cops. However, the most mischievous argument from the standpoint of Reich's new property merits direct quotation:

> One who dispenses purely private charity naturally has an interest in and expects to know how his charitable funds are utilized and put to work. The public, when it is the provider, rightly expects the same. It might well expect more, because of the trust aspect of public funds, and the recipient, as well as the caseworker, has not only an interest but an obligation.[9]

In this passage, the Court turned away from welfare as an emergent right and retreated to welfare as an act of sovereign grace, to be conferred on terms defined by government.

In a typically vigorous dissent that explicitly cited Reich, William Douglas defined "the central question" as "whether the government by force of its largesse has the power to 'buy up' rights guaranteed by the Constitution."[10] Why, he asked, should welfare recipients be treated differently from other beneficiaries of public programs? In his pointed language,

> If the welfare recipient was not Barbara James but a prominent, affluent cotton or wheat farmer receiving benefit payments for not growing crops, would not the approach be different? Welfare in aid of dependent children, like Social Security and unemployment benefits, has an aura of suspicion. There doubtless are frauds in every sector of public welfare whether the recipient be a Barbara James or

someone who is prominent or influential. But constitutional rights—here the privacy of the *home*—are obviously not dependent on the poverty or the affluence of the beneficiary. It is the precincts of the *home* that the Fourth Amendment protects; and their privacy is as important to the lowly as to the mighty.[11]

As the elderly are currently learning, Douglas was prescient in his inclusion of their benefits among those stigmatized and thus subject to revision or revocation. In 1984, Congress for the first time made a portion of Social Security pensions taxable for relatively prosperous recipients. The next year the House and Senate treated themselves to a lengthy wrangle over keeping or suspending for a year annual cost-of-living adjustments. By the beginning of 1986, the whole country had adopted for Medicare patients a system of prospective reimbursement to hospitals according to 468 diagnostic-related groups (DRGs). Hospitals, as we have already had occasion to note, that spend less than the amount allowed get to keep the difference. Those that exceed the prescribed amount must absorb the bulk of the excess.

The system is a cost accountant's dream and a doctor's nightmare. Here is an example of its slightly psychotic taxonomy. In Omaha, a case of uncomplicated asthma for a patient under age eighteen is labeled DRG 98 and assigned a weight of .4275. That weight, multiplied by $2,888.76, equals $1,234.94 as prospective payment. If, by bad luck for patient and hospital, actual costs run above 150 percent of this sum, or $1,852.41, Medicaid calls the case an "outlier." The hospital must absorb the $617.47 difference and 40 percent of costs in excess of $1,852.41. Obviously DRGs will discourage hospital admission and treatment of outliers—sickly, expensive, cranky types unlikely to be ready for discharge after stays of average length for their DRG.

Inevitably, institutions that serve low-income clienteles will suffer the worst pressure either not to admit or prematurely to discharge patients lest they sink rapidly into bankruptcy.[12] DRGs soon to be extended by health insurers to most of the rest of the population complete the shift from the treatment of sick people as patients to their evaluation as potentially profitable medical commodities. The more successful hospitals are in discharging patients in periods shorter than those stipulated by the DRGs, the greater the prospect that in succeeding years DRGs will be readjusted downward. DRGs echo old-time piecework standards. Energetic employees who raise their take-home pay by harder work soon discover that standards are revised and that they must work still harder merely to meet new norms.

A generation ago Reich epitomized such situations as revivals of an exceedingly dangerous version of feudalism. His analysis was prophetic, for increasingly property and benefits get linked to status and status is conferred either by the state or, still more insidiously, by a small number of very large private organizations that act as loosely regulated agents of the state, among them corporations, foundations, and universities. The moral?

> If the individual is to survive in a collective society, he must have protection against its ruthless pressures. There must be sanctuaries or enclaves where no majority can reach. To shelter the solitary human spirit does not merely make possible the fulfillment of individuals; it also gives society the power to change, to grow, and to regenerate, and hence to endure. These were the objects which property sought to achieve and can no longer achieve. The challenge of the future will be to construct, for the society that is coming, institutions and laws to carry on the work. Just as the Homestead Act was a deliberate effort to foster individual values at an earlier time, so we must try to build an economic basis for liberty today—a Homestead Act for rootless twentieth-century man. We must create a new property.[13]

Reich's publisher, Basic Books, anticipated so little public interest in Reich's expansion of his analysis into a volume that its first printing was a mere five thousand copies. Yet this high-pitched screed turned its author into an instant celebrity. Reich extended the themes of his law-review essays and celebrated his own rebirth as a child of the new consciousness. He warmed up with a catalogue of New Left charges: American society was very nearly terminally corrupted by "disorder, corruption, hypocrisy, war"; "poverty, distorted priorities, and law-making by private power"; "decline of democracy and liberty, powerlessness"; "the artificiality of work and culture"; "absence of community"; and "loss of self."[14] The heavy indictment is every bit as justified today when few care as in 1970 when the country listened.

Such a society invites radical change. As always, a successful revolution requires revolutionaries. Enter the young as vessels of new revelations and heightened consciousness. Their parents and grandparents, alas, are mired either in Consciousness I, the atavistic remnants of frontier individualism, or Consciousness II, the charcoal-gray spirit of the organizational mentality, bureaucracy incarnate, Whyte's corporate purgatory. Odd and sad that Ronald Reagan won two elections as a celebrant of Consciousness I, and hordes of young men and women crowd classrooms in which the mysteries of accounting, financial management, computer science, and corporate law presumably are explained, the better to prepare true believers for updated versions of Consciousness II. Sadder still that so many of the 1960s celebrants of Consciousness III now earn comfortable livings as management consultants, lawyers, and investment bankers. One of them, co-author of a best-selling exposé of the Kennedys, revealed in print that in 1984 he had voted for Reagan out of repentance for his contribution to the wild 1960s.

How entrancing, only a few decades ago, was the Consciousness III challenge to ersatz cowboys and prisoners of three-piece suits! The converts to the new ethos contemptuously dismissed both the asserted inevitabilities and the purported rewards of hierarchical organization. For them, they substituted new and inalienable entitlements to joy, love, friendship, infinite openness to experience and sensation, immediate communication, and warm, oh so warm, community. As Reich barely refrained from saying in the quaint patois of the time, like oh wow!

Rejecting hierarchy, competition and the routines of daily, dull jobs, how could the children of the new age hope to inherit the earth, as Reich was certain they would and should? Not to worry. The approaching revolution was advertised as a gentle event, a matter of demography and peaceful persuasion, for externally imposing as it might appear to the uninstructed eye, the Establishment really was little more than a hollow shell. The generals, executives, politicians, financiers, and university presidents who pretended to run institutions lacked conviction and purpose. They were ever more vulnerable targets of infiltration as the number of infiltrators steadily rose. As the fifty-year-olds died, declined into their dotage, or occasionally joined the revolution, their juniors in age and superiors in consciousness succeeded them in the seats of the mighty. At the instant of liberation, Consciousness III promised to transform the institutions that oppress us all and to liberate even the bureaucrats. In the utopia struggling to be born, organization and technology, today's enemies, will enlarge individual personality and enhance human experience. Somehow the universe of work and the private cosmos of individual sensation will be rejoined and the ancient pangs of alienation at last relieved. Astonishingly meek in Reich's idealization of them, the young will lay gentle hands upon their birthright. Much as Marxists believed that the state would wither away in the wake of socialist revolution, Reich envisaged the defeat not of capitalist exploiters but of slaves to outmoded states of consciousness. It sounded, and of course was, too good to be true.

As ever, social reality is messier than the abstract categories of scribblers. In today's yuppies Consciousness III survives, albeit less as a sense of community than as a stage of consumer culture. The yuppie version of Consciousness II combines the vocationalism of Whyte's organization men with claims to individual autonomy that remind one of the 1960s. If one strains, even Consciousness I reappears in the entrepreneurial aspirations of many yuppies. Yuppies' distrust of government interference in personal lifestyles and their aspiration to property and wealth echo at considerable distance Reich's insistence on individual autonomy. Yuppies, as New Hampshire license plates boast, aspire to live free, but alas for Reich, not in communes furnished mostly by warm emotion, altruism, and a relentless sense of community. If the Japanese work ethos sweeps over America, Whyte's world-class bore, the organization man and woman, may stage a strong comeback. His home base incorporates consumer items unknown to Whyte's organization man: Jacuzzis, VCRs, exercycles, and compact-disc players. But the spirit of consumption and the ethos of conformity endure.

### YUPPIES AND NEOLIBERALS

Confusion is the fate of the young. Consciousness III lingers from the 1960s as hedonism shorn of Reich's apocalyptic aspirations. Little in the realm of sensation offends trendsetters: drugs, X-rated movies, abortion, pornography, and of course sex, straight or kinky, with or without benefit of matrimony. Yuppies crave success and money as any old Consciousness II young fogey might, but according to one of their admirers, "They are imaginative and original," display "little tolerance for boredom," expect "interesting work and satisfying emotional relationships," and anticipate "psychic and social stimulation on the job." They are very likely to consider themselves "underutilized and yet oversupervised." Their distinct preference is to "manage themselves," since "taking orders . . . insults their intelligence and often results in a creative shutdown."[15]

Nor has Consciousness I ceased to influence the conduct of the young. The fashion at elite schools of business administration is entrepreneurship. Start your enterprise in emulation of the heroes of Route 128 and Silicon Valley and become rich and independent. Or, second best, join the large organization which pretends to be entrepreneurial by setting up quasi-independent small units under its umbrella, a process dubbed with the unlovely sobriquet "intrapreneurship," in the enormously popular *A Passion for Excellence*.[16] Self-expression, perspicaciously deployed, translates into money in the bank.

No wonder psychobabble is the popular yuppie dialect. But the yuppie horde—true yuppies, fellow travelers, aspirants, and mere followers—constitutes a political prize of enormous value. Whoever speaks most convincingly to the largest percentage of their generation may well be Ronald Reagan's successor. If a single value unites them, yuppies are pro-choice—in their careers, lifestyles, and political representatives. In 1984, Gary Hart was their favorite candidate. His youth, energy, craggy good looks, indeed his very boots proclaimed affiliation with the baby boomers' passion for jogging, pumping iron, grazing, and fashionably consuming. Hart proclaimed himself the prophet of new ideas. On inspection, their origins were either neoconservative or derivative from industrial policy, itself a tendency of ambiguous intellectual sponsorship. Individual Training Accounts, as an application of vouchers in place of government programs, date back of course to Milton Friedman's advocacy of them in education. Why shouldn't individual workers choose the type of training they prefer and the vendor—corporate, government, religious, or collegiate—most attractive to them? And why shouldn't the resources poorly employed by bureaucrats be released to the competition of free markets and the tastes of the customers?

In his campaign volume, *A New Democracy*, Hart endorsed the Business Roundtable scheme developed by its economist Pat Choate. Individual Training Accounts are designed to be jointly financed by employer and employee contributions. They are portable: an employee who shifts jobs will take with him his own and his employer's contributions plus accumulated interest, much as migrating academics take their Teachers' Insurance and Annuity pension accumulations with them when they change universities. The federal role is ideally limited to certifying eligible institutions, just as in the wake of World War II the Veterans Administration certified colleges and other educational institutions as places where veterans could spend GI Bill grants. Nothing, of course, prevents Congress from sweetening the pot, but freedom of choice by individuals will continue to be enhanced by market competition. In a general way, another prominent neoliberal, Senator Bill Bradley, has endorsed the notion, indicating in a *New York Times* essay that "one way [to help workers upgrade skills] might be to create an insurance program under which workers displaced by technology or foreign competition could cash in their policies and use the money to acquire new skills."[17]

In their reliance upon markets, distrust of "big government," and emphasis upon growth instead of equity, neoliberals and neoconservatives converge if not coincide. Both tend to ignore an interesting fact: the federal government's share of gross national product has actually risen during the Reagan years, partly because Social Security pensions have been paid to more recipients as the population has aged, but mostly because defense expenditures and the interest costs of servicing the enormous deficits caused by them and reckless, supposedly self-financing supply-side tax cuts, have ballooned. One of the reasons why income is distributed still more unequally in 1986 than in 1980 is the enormous transfer of resources from ordinary taxpayers to the collectors of interest on the federal debt, most of them far better off than those whose taxes flow in their direction.

Neolibs, like neocons, dislike the skewed growth of the 1980s. Its emphasis is military and much of its financing is foreign. Neos fret over comparisons with the thrifty Japanese and West Germans. They have turned to tax policy as encouragement of better saving and investment attitudes. In the past, Gary Hart advocated a consumption tax. One avoids paying such a tax by saving more and spending less. More saving means more funds for productive investment. Congressman Leon Panetta's Tax Simplification Act would tax all income at a single 18 percent rate. Senator Bradley and Congressman Richard Gephardt have offered a scheme which closes some loopholes, collects the same revenue, and pushes most personal tax rates down to a maximum of 30 percent. These proposals have in common diminished emphasis upon the hunt for the liberal white whale—a truly progressive tax structure which extracts rising percentages of income as the amount of that income increases. No differently from supply-siders, the neos have convinced themselves that lower tax rates promote growth, and growth is the best assurance that free markets will lift the poor out of their poverty and provide resources for government to alleviate the plight of the shrinking minority still below the poverty line.

Parenthetically, it is remarkable how little evidence validates the efficacy of tax policy as a stimulus to investment and saving. The only serious study of the impact of Reagan tax breaks upon corporate expenditures over the 1981–84 period inspected the investment record of 259 of our largest and most profitable nonfinancial corporations. Not only was there "absolutely no correlation between tax 'incentives' and improved capital spending or job creation," but "the forty nonfinancial companies in the survey that paid no federal income taxes at all—or received net refunds—over the four years actually performed far worse than the forty-three highest taxed companies, each of which paid at least 33 percent of its domestic profits in federal income tax." The delinquent first group cut capital investment by 4 percent and reduced employment by 6 percent while actually collecting $2.1 billion in tax rebates as a supplement to profits of $53.6 billion. Among the more prominent offenders were Boeing, Dow Chemical, and W. R. Grace & Co. Oddly the highest taxed enterprises, among them Whirlpool, Campbell Soup, and R. J. Reynolds, paid $18.2 billion taxes on $49 billion pretax profits but somehow succeeded in hiring 4 percent more men and women and enlarging investment by 21 percent. A skeptic might wonder whether the best way to stimulate investment is to tax corporate profits more heavily,[18] as indeed 1986's sweeping tax revision appears to ensure.

On some issues the neos split. In Congress, neoliberals share nearly flawless civil rights records with traditional liberals of the Tip O'Neill–Ted Kennedy stripe. Nevertheless, implicit in their diagnosis of poverty as largely the consequence of slow growth and inadequate labor market skills is quiet endorsement of the Thomas Sowell position in the endless argument over the relative importance of race and class as explanations of the perpetuation of a large black underclass. Rapid growth encourages employers to accept and train less qualified and less literate workers, following the precedent of World War II. The payoffs for education and marketable skills in an expanding economy similarly encourage teenagers to stay in school and out of jail. Black pathology cures itself in the benign atmosphere of high employment. The pro-market bias of the neolibs inevitably tells against cultural and political interpretations of brutally high rates of unemployment in the black community and inordinately high percentages of female-headed black families subsisting in poverty. The heritage of racism and its continuing manifestations tend to be discounted as explanations of the black plight.

Then there is that ideological wild card, industrial policy, whose advocates are to be found on an ideological spectrum running from *Business Week*'s corporate version on the right to the neo-Marxist prescriptions of Samuel Bowles, David Gordon,

## Neolibs, Technocrats, and Yuppies

and Thomas Weisskopf in their *Beyond the Wasteland* on the left. For good neoliberals, the most influential voice has been that of another, quite differently inclined Reich. Robert Reich, currently at Harvard's Kennedy School of Government, a Yale-trained lawyer, senior analyst at the Federal Trade Commission during the Carter interregnum, prolific journalist and lecturer, wrote just in time for the 1984 electoral follies *The Next American Frontier*, a polemic admired by both Walter Mondale and Gary Hart but scarcely used by either one.

Greatly tempted, 1984's Democrats shied away from Reich because the chap undeniably and shamelessly believes in planning. As he asserted in September 1982, "A neurotic can't see the world as it is because of these paradigms that keep wandering around in his head. . . . No matter how much you explain and reveal that there was *never* a free market in this country, these people won't believe it." All the same, "Government intervention sets the boundaries, decides what's going to be marketed, sets the rules of the game through procurement policies, tax credits, depreciation allowances, loans and loan guarantees, a thousand different schemes." No chance at all that government will cease to intervene. Sensible folks will endeavor to make that intervention coherent and associate it with business and labor as full partners.[19] The business community needs to realize, scolds Reich, that education, medical services, and job training and retraining are investments in productive human beings, just as important, if not more so, than resources devoted to plants and equipment. For their part, liberals must overcome their contempt for the private sector and recognize it as the major source of jobs and hope for rising living standards. Hart's proposed investment, job, and wage compacts between corporations and unions are stabs at translating cooperative planning into arrangements in which unions make concessions in the interest of productivity and corporations become centers for the delivery of social services.

Industrial policy is vague, controversial, and possibly because of, rather than in spite of, this characterization, also amazingly durable. For the older industries of the Midwest rust belt and the major unions which negotiate steadily less lucrative contracts with them, industrial policy amounts to more protection against foreign, especially Japanese, competition and access on preferential terms to federal credit. The highly successful federal bailout of Chrysler owed something to Lee Iacocca's managerial charisma, more to federal loan guarantees, and most to quotas that limited the sale of Japanese cars in the American market. It is a vintage example of ad hoc industrial policy.[20]

In the hi-tech variant of industrial policy, older industries are consigned to their fate: portions of them will sink, others will survive. Large integrated steel operations may disappear. Mini-mills using scrap as raw materials and modern electric furnaces may prosper. Industrial-policy planners ought to place their bets on winners, essentially high technology in which an American comparative advantage over rivals here and there still survives. Felix Rohatyn, widely credited, not least vocally by himself, with a major role in saving New York City from bankruptcy in 1975, has persistently advocated enlargement of the Big Apple's invention, the Municipal Assistance Corporation, to national size. As he and others have noted, his proposal has antecedents in the Depression-era Reconstruction Finance Corporation. MAC forged unlikely alliances among bankers like Citibank's Walter Wriston, District Council 37's Victor Gotbaum, local and state politicians, and federal regulators. For Rohatyn, industrial policy is, candidly, planning by elites in the public interest as defined by members of those elites.

The critics of industrial policy include traditional conservatives, supply-siders, neoconservatives, unreconstructed Keynesian liberals, and victims of ideological confusion. Charles Schultze, Lyndon Johnson's budget director and Jimmy Carter's Council of Economic Advisers chairman, a moderate Keynesian now in exile at the Brookings Institution, has been one of industrial policy's severest critics. With the skepticism of an alumnus of bureaucratic warfare, he doubts government's "ability to do anything at precise targets,"[21] particularly to separate business winners from business losers. During the 1970s, he informed a congressional committee that poultry farming headed the list of the twenty fastest-growing industries. "Who," jeered Schultze, "was going to pick that as a winner?" Rohatyn's revived Reconstruction Finance Corporation has drawn the fire of Michael Kinsley, editor of *The New Republic* (about which more later), a neoliberal with occasional deviations into concern about equity in the distribution of income and wealth characteristic of older liberals. He termed Rohatyn's cozy direction of investment policy by a tight, elite circle "fascism."[22] Former California governor and quondam presidential candidate Jerry Brown possesses as good a claim to the neoliberal label as any other politician. He trashed Rohatyn's scheme as "technocratic planning beyond public accountability in any sense."[23] On pragmatic grounds, George Eads, a former member of the Carter Council of Economic Advisers, argues that "Any entity created by the Congress, given access to large amounts of government funds, and asked to deal with matters having great political importance could not be 'nonpolitical.' "[24]

Definitionally promiscuous though industrial policy is, all major versions share common properties. The first is reliance upon mild planning designed to encourage voluntary cooperation among major players. The second is guidance of investment presumably in directions distinguishable from those occurring in the absence of industrial policy. A third is creation of some sort of financing agency to give practical effect to the investment priorities set by some sort of board or council. Finally, all the advocates implicitly or explicitly concede that actually existing markets, whatever the claims of economists' ideal constructions, do a poor job of deploying machines and people in the most productive directions.

Robert Reich, probably the most enthusiastic and optimistic of industrial-policy advocates, has persuaded himself, at least— though few businessmen and policy intellectuals—that both conservative businessmen and liberals of all varieties will arrive under the pressure of reality at the realization that education and training as well as expenditures upon nutrition and medical care should not be praised by liberals merely out of compassion and condemned out of hand by conservatives as raids upon the public treasury by the lazy, immoral, and wicked. In reality, in Reich's words, "I don't think social justice is a charity that can be traded off against economic growth. . . . I think it actually *undergirds* economic growth." And, for their part, liberals must acknowledge the job and growth-creating role of the private sector. It is more than time, proclaims Reich, to abandon the machismo models of sports, litigation, and political horse races: "People throw up their hands and say, 'America is not Japan! Frontier! Cowboy! and all that sort of stuff'. . . . Not only can it change, but we are changing in accepting the values of collaboration, cooperation, and interpersonal caring. We are getting away from the baseball-lawsuits-politics paradigm."[25] Reich may be correct, but evidence for his position is hard to locate.

On the whole, neolib politicians and their gurus prefer markets to bureaucracies. Yet as their continuing flirtation with industrial policy reveals, they lack the conservative supply-side faith that markets can be trusted always to work efficiently without some sort of public intervention. As far as social policy is concerned, the neolib stance is complex. Gary Hart, among others, prefers an economic to a regulatory approach to environmental protection. Why not charge escalating emission fees, after the example of the West Germans, for the discharge of noxious wastes into water or atmosphere, instead of invoking the cumbersome regulatory model and its invitation to interminable delay in definition of standards and endless legal wrangles over their application?

In their rational, affectless fashion, neolibs share numerous goals with old-style libs. They do favor a decent welfare state, but their position entails no commitment to a national health program, an official Democratic position as recently as 1980. They fret over unemployment, but successfully control latent nostalgia for public jobs programs to alleviate it and never, never refer to that legislative embarrassment, the Humphrey-Hawkins Balanced Growth and Full Employment Act of 1978. Their attachment to civil rights seems to be consistent with skepticism over the more aggressive varieties of affirmative action. And their general pro-choice posture on abortion is flexible enough to accommodate Representative Gephardt, who, representing a conservative constituency, opposes abortion under almost any set of contingencies. Like conservatives and Democrats of the hard-line Henry Jackson school, they are anti-Soviet and pro-defense. They have researched strategy and procurement as thoroughly as taxes and energy policy. The chairman of the House Armed Services Committee, Les Aspin, an MIT Ph.D. in economics, is a leading light among the neolib defense intellectuals, something of a specialist in the crafting of intricate compromises between his colleagues and

## Neolibs, Technocrats, and Yuppies

the White House over the production of MX missiles, resumed manufacture of nerve gas, and Star Wars funding. His objective is thriftier bangs from fewer bucks.

The old-fashioned rhetoric of social justice, equality, redistribution, empowerment of the weak, and full employment does not trip easily from the tongues of the Bradleys, Aspins, and Gephardts. For them, politics seems less group conflict than the search for tax, regulatory, and mild planning initiatives that promote enough growth to soften the harsh edges of ancient struggles between rich and poor, black and white, males and females, the Sunbelt and the rust belt. If all of the above sketches a set of dull fellows, all too likely to glaze the eyes and turn off the hearing aids of their auditors, it is unfortunately closer to truth than to caricature.

What turns the troops on is emotion. As governor, New York's Mario Cuomo has reduced business taxes and levies on high-income families. He has been notably prudent in social-program funding. He vigorously supported Westway, a favorite of New York City's bankers and real estate developers. His policies, in other words, have not significantly differed from those of his Massachusetts colleague, Michael Dukakis, a stylish neolib, or his opposite number in New Jersey, Thomas Kean, a temperate moderate Republican. But millions of people in the summer of 1984 watched and heard him deliver a passionate keynote address to the assembled Democrats in San Francisco. It was a traditional liberal appeal for justice complemented by an equally traditional assault upon the Republicans as the party of the rich and privileged. The hardened politicians in the huge auditorium actually listened, cheered, applauded, and seem prepared to nominate Mr. Cuomo for president on the spot. The Cuomo hour was the highlight not only of the nominating convention but of the entire dismal campaign.

Passion elects presidents. Jimmy Carter, an apparent exception to the rule, won narrowly in 1976 because his opponent, Gerald Ford, displayed even less emotion and aptitude for public speaking than did Mr. Carter. He lost in 1980 to a virtuoso prestidigitator of traditional symbols—patriotism, individualism, opportunity, freedom from meddling government—not terribly different from Carter's 1980 themes. Indeed, for three national campaigns in a row, Democrats and Republicans, whether incumbents or challengers, have run against big government, just as though they did not yearn to head it.

If, in the the second half of the l980s, a single periodical exemplified both neoliberal attitudes and ambiguities it was *The New Republic*, under the joint and sometimes clashing leadership of editor Michael Kinsley and owner Martin Peretz.[26]

On social and economic policy, *The New Republic* is less conflicted because the temptations of market ideology are strongest. Thus, with true enthusiasm, Kinsley endorsed the breakup of AT&T as opening telecommunications to the brisk breeze of wholesome competition. The journal acclaimed both the original and the revised versions of tax reform sponsored by the Reagan administration. It gave space to Charles Murray, who, in *Losing Ground*, a volume nearly as celebrated in conservative circles as George Gilder's earlier *Wealth and Poverty*, argued that social programs not only had failed to eliminate poverty, but, worse, had so sabotaged the morale of the poor that they were worse off than they would have been in the absence of each and every New Deal and Great Society initiative. Just for good measure, the editors also printed a devastating critique of Murray in the same issue.

As though school busing were not adequately dumped upon in the conservative media, *The New Republic* of February 28, l983, featured George Higgins's "Why Busing Didn't Work," a meditation on Boston's violent experience of school integration. Prominent conservatives and neoconservatives like sociologist Peter Berger, a frequent *Commentary* contributor, appear as book reviewers. Congressman Jack Kemp praised the journal in these terms: "There is no question that TNR is moving in the, shall we say, right direction. If you believe we are in the middle of a fundamental realignment, as I do, *The New Republic* reflects much of it."[27] The encomium should have provoked—but evidently did not—an editorial crisis of conscience.

On the other hand, the magazine is also occasionally hospitable to Michael Harrington and Irving Howe, leaders of Democratic Socialists of America; Robert Kuttner; Robert McIntyre; Robert Reich; and other strong critics of Reagan social and tax policies or, in the instance of Kuttner and Reich, proponents of industrial policy and—Kuttner's term—"managed trade." On domestic policy, the magazine, some of whose editors apparently voted for Reagan in 1984, strives for compassionate social policy after a thus far inadequately specified fashion different from the New Deal and Great Society, admires the alleged efficiency of markets, and yet can't help wondering whether or not an industrial policy fix might improve their workings. If the FBI is still monitoring the journal, its analysts, uncomplicated patriots, must be hopelessly confused by the subtleties of Ivy League controversy.

Can a neolib make it to the White House next time around? It is not impossible. Charismatic is not the first or tenth adjective that even their admirers attach to George Bush, Howard Baker, Robert Dole, or even Jack Kemp. Hysterical is the word of choice for Alexander Haig. All but Kemp tried unsuccessfully to get the Republican presidential nomination in 1980, and in so doing encountered nearly universal popular apathy. No living soul can sensibly forecast the condition of the economy in 1988, but it is unlikely to be buoyant. Quite probably, recession in 1987 and 1988 will succeed the sluggishness of 1985 and 1986. As foreigners sour on American prospects, the flow of funds that in the first half of the decade financed rearmament, huge budgetary deficits, and equally unprecedented deficits in international trade is fated to slow. Interest rates accordingly will rise, push new homes out of the reach of middle-income families, and complete the destruction of independent farmers. Deficits, unless, implausibly, a hastily patched-up version of Gramm-Rudman is permitted to wreck its mindless destruction of federal activity, will have compelled the White House to accept new taxes. Yuppies, who now find themselves in industries like data processing, computer services, banking, law, advertising, and public relations, will be especially vulnerable to recession. Many of them, now nearing forty, are parents and homeowners, burdened by debt and kept barely financially afloat when both spouses are employed. Not only is Ronald Reagan constitutionally unavailable as a third-term candidate; his popularity, come 1988, could well sink to Carter levels and Democrats rather regret his departure to the golden West.

Far more valuable in 1988 than it was in 1984, the Democratic presidential nomination stirs the aspirations of such senators as Gary Hart; Bill Bradley; Dale Bumpers; Joseph Biden,

George Will's favorite Democrat; and Daniel Patrick Moynihan. Governors in office or just out of it sense the call of public service—Arizona's Bruce Babbitt, Massachusetts's Michael Dukakis, and Virginia's Chuck Robb, among others. The very March 24, 1986, issue of *Newsweek* whose cover was occupied by a portrait of a brooding Mario Cuomo also featured Michael Dukakis, regarded by his fellow state leaders as our most effective governor. What is the man like? He is "impatient with small talk, maladroit at humor, short, slope-shouldered and buys his suits at Filene's basement."[28] What has he done? He has cut taxes and encouraged welfare recipients to work and educate themselves. Cooperation with business and universities is the statehouse watchword. Arizona's Bruce Babbitt, another *Newsweek* pinup politician, favors means tests for federal benefits and taxation of Social Security pensions. In his opinion, "Voters have begun to demand problem-solving abilities and administrative competence on the part of their governors. . . . Partisan politics just isn't as important anymore."[29] Reagan at least entertains the populace, a feat not within the grasp of our efficient governors.

Here fantasy lures us into the following scenario. Democratic moneybags upon whom all the contenders depend weed out sure losers and thus starve out most of the field. By May 1988 the race narrows down to Mario Cuomo and Gary Hart. Although the razor-tongued Cuomo cuts up Hart in ninety-three of the ninety-seven debates that precede the nominating convention, Hart does sufficiently better in the caucuses and primaries to corral a majority of the delegates. Cuomo's indifferent record as a governor catches up with him. Women and blacks note that his administration has given them rather more sympathetic rhetoric than funding for favorite programs. Yet that very rhetoric makes yuppies uneasy, for it reminds them of the old liberalism of the allegedly failed Great Society, and of the high taxes supposedly needed to finance its programs. Bored in his third term as New York City's mayor and depressed by revelations of pervasive corruption among his appointees, Ed Koch does what he can to undermine his old rival by endorsing first Moynihan, then Hart. Hart keeps the yuppies who supported him in 1984 and then to their subsequent regret switched to Reagan. Although by now Hart is fifty, he seems a generation younger than Cuomo and much closer to aging yuppies than the New Yorker who is further handicapped by covert anti-Italian prejudice. Moreover, Hart's positions on taxes, environmental regulation, and trade attract considerable support from a business community by now long soured on Reaganomics. It is a safe rule of thumb that the investment community loves their president as long as the stock market booms and, fickle souls, hunts for new political partners very soon after bust supersedes boom.

Though vigorously asserting his utter lack of interest in the second spot on the ticket, Mario Cuomo, after taking counsel with his wife, Matilda, and his son Andrew, brooding deeply and publicly upon his responsibilities to all Americans, and responding filially to the inferred encouragement of his long-deceased immigrant father, yields to the importunities of Democratic potentates, poll findings that the Hart-Cuomo duo are by far the strongest team, and a strong personal appeal from Hart himself. In their single televised debate, he demolishes Congressman Jack Kemp, Bush's running mate. Kemp is reduced to challenging Cuomo to a game of touch football.

In the November 1988 election, Hart easily beats George Bush, who is badly damaged by primaries in which Kemp, Dole, and Baker deride him for changing his position on supply-side economics, abortion, and the Equal Rights Amendment in slavish conformity to President Reagan and the Moral Majority. George Will's 1986 denunciation of him as a lap dog is distributed by the hundred thousands. His uncharitable rivals portray or caricature him as a man who left no footprints as head of the CIA, envoy to China, member of Congress, chairman of the Republican National Committee, or vice-president. Just to make his situation even more uncomfortable, Hart saddles him with the failed tax and spending policies of two Reagan administrations. In televised debates, Hart locks his hapless opponent into Mondale's 1984 dilemma: whether to stand loyally by his chief's unpopular policies or claim private disagreement with them. Loyalty wins few votes when it is to discredited politicians, and protestations of private disagreement invite derision, demands for evidence, and proof that the potentate in the Oval Office paid heed to his subordinate's representations. Restored in 1986, the Democratic Senate majority swells and the party's edge in the House approaches New Deal size.

Then what? The time is January 1989. President Hart's Inaugural Address carefully echoes the inspirational tone of John F. Kennedy in 1960. There is a notable difference: Hart strikes a dovish note in his references to the Sandinistas in Latin America and the Russians everywhere. After Vietnam and Lebanon, only hard-line cold warriors hunger for holy wars against godless, materialistic Communists. Then comes the flood of details in the State of the Union, budget, and economic messages. The new president's initial appointments presage his inclinations. To a man or woman, they are reasonable, temperate in expression, cool like their president, technically qualified, well-disposed to free enterprise, and quite willing to give entrepreneurs a nudge from time to time in the right direction.

The major economic appointments are well-received. Alice Rivlin, director of economic studies at the centrist Brookings Institution, former head of the Congressional Budget Office, and a past president of the American Economic Association, takes the key position at the Office of Management and Budget. Aside from David Stockman, making his fortune on Wall Street and hustling his memoirs in bookstores and on talk shows, no one commands the details of the federal budget as well as Rivlin. A mildly liberal Democrat, she frets over deficits and favors cost-benefit analysis and other analytical tools of quantitative analysis. MIT's Lester Thurow, a strong advocate of industrial policy, heads the Council of Economic Advisers. Felix Rohatyn becomes Secretary of the Treasury; Robert Reich, Secretary of Commerce; and Donald Elphin, Secretary of Labor. All three belong in the industrial policy camp. As vice-president of the United Automobile Workers, Elphin has worked closely with General Motors in its efforts to substitute cooperation and a degree of shop-floor democracy for traditional authoritarian management. He was the key union negotiator of the Saturn agreement. Widely popular in responsible business circles, he is for that very reason distrusted by the membership of his own union.

Other notable Hart selections include: at Defense, Congressman Les Aspin, chairman of the House Armed Services Committee; Henry Aaron, also at Brookings, at Health and Human Services; and New York University's well-publicized president, former Indiana congressman John Brademas, at Education. Aspin, with his MIT Ph.D. in economics and as a long-time critic of Pentagon management and strategy, has built his reputation upon the proposition that the Pentagon can provide more security per megabuck. He seizes the opportunity to prove his point. During the Carter administration, Aaron, a Harvard product, served as Assistant Secretary in what was then the Department of Health, Education and Welfare. Charged by Carter with preparing a comprehensive welfare-reform measure, he presided over an effort titled Program for Better Jobs and Incomes. Like Nixon's earlier attempt at welfare reform, the Family Assistance Program, it failed in Congress, although it was in several ways an improvement over its predecessor, notably in its training and public-jobs provisions.

A mild surprise is the new man at the helm of the Federal Reserve. He is John Reed, Walter Wriston's Citibank successor and that rarity among big-time bankers, a Democrat. Esteemed by his peers as supremely competent, Reed at the Fed leaves the financial markets calm and reconciled to the retirement of Paul Volcker. The economy imposes a challenge and a constraint upon the administration's experts. Unemployment is already above 8 percent, and the prime interest rate up to 13 percent, and both are rising. The deficit, if unchecked, will grow to $300 billion by the end of the 1980s. In a deeply resented insult to American self-esteem, the International Monetary Fund offers the Treasury a substantial loan on condition that it accept an austerity plan like those IMF routinely imposes on the Brazils and Argentinas of the Third World. Hart's first budget responds to the malignant numbers on both the revenue and expenditure side. Tax indexing is suspended until the deficit shrinks to 2 percent of the gross national product. To the anguish of motorists, car dealers, and others, gasoline taxes go up twenty-five cents per gallon and to the horror of Southern Democrats, the president, a nonsmoker, adds an additional levy of 50 cents per pack on cigarettes. Bankruptcy vies with cancer as a threat to tobacco addicts. The president promises to send Congress before the end of 1989 a comprehensive tax-reform measure designed to encourage investment and saving and increase Treasury receipts. Breaking all Pentagon precedents, Aspin's first budget axes a number of weapons systems and actually asks Congress for 5 percent fewer dollars than it appropriated in the final year of the Reagan regime. Other savings are proposed in water projects, farm subsidies, and synthetic fuels.

In the context of a slumping economy, this abrupt fiscal-policy shift threatens to convert contraction into a mini-depression reminiscent of the 1981–82 Reagan episode. The administration accordingly enlists the cooperation of the new man at the Fed. Reed informs Congress that the first Hart budget, in combination with much unused factory capacity and many unemployed men and women, justifies monetary ease. Accordingly he raises the Fed's money-supply targets in order to push interest rates down and encourage business revival as well as consumer spending.

Fortunately, the administration's new initiatives require little or no new spending. With much fanfare the president announces the appointment of a new commission, on the bipartisan model of the Reagan panels on Social Security and Central America, to define no later than January 1, 1990, a bright, shining industrial policy designed to restore American competitiveness in world markets and reverse Japanese inroads into American banking, fast foods, financial planning, and yuppie cuisine, for by 1989 Japanese hegemony reaches far beyond VCRs, memory chips, robots, TVs, and microwave ovens. The commission is headed by Lee Iacocca, industrialist, best-selling author, and Democrat. The new Attorney General, Constance Baker Motley, a liberal black veteran federal judge, announces a sweeping review of Reagan civil-rights enforcement policies, strict interpretation of antitrust statutes, and a search for more severe criminal penalties against corporate criminals. She practically eliminates FBI political surveillance and advises her fellow Cabinet members that lie detectors diagnose mostly nervousness. For good measure, she shares scientific evidence that urinalysis is almost equally unreliable as a device for screening of the clean from the unclean. What, after all, ought one to think of an "infallible," "scientific" test that registers positive for an unfortunate consumer of bagels sprinkled with poppy seeds? Ralph Nader, who unexpectedly

## Neolibs, Technocrats, and Yuppies

accepts appointment as chairman of the Federal Trade Commission, pledges himself to coordinate FTC policy with the Department of Justice and urges President Hart to sponsor federal incorporation of all business units employing one thousand or more workers. At Housing and Urban Development, Henry Cisneros, the well-regarded former mayor of San Antonio, Texas, promises to seek authorization of additional subsidized low-income housing and also to expand, as budgetary conditions allow, Reagan voucher experiments.

Hart's slogan—New Ideas and New Leaders for a Better America—gains added credibility in foreign policy. His new Secretary of State, Stephen Solarz, until his selection represented a Brooklyn constituency in the House of Representatives. He is young, the first Jew in the position since Henry Kissinger, a player in the ignominious exit of Ferdinand and Imelda Marcos, and among the most astute critics of Reagan adventures in Angola and Central America. Solarz announces immediate support of the Contadora process, initiates talks with the Sandinistas, endorses tough sanctions against South Africa, and appoints George Kennan senior adviser on Soviet-American relations. He and Defense Secretary Les Aspin agree as a token of urgency in arms-control negotiations to make Star Wars a fully negotiable agenda item, still another significant departure from Reagan intransigence.

Hart's modest social-policy agenda contains a surprise, White House support for enterprise zones, a measure long advocated unsuccessfully by Congressman Kemp. The administration proposal coordinates special tax and financing help in the zones with focused low-income housing construction and rehabilitation initiatives. To no one's amazement, the president urges Congress to take early action on Individual Training Accounts. At the same time, he asks extension of the duration of unemployment-compensation benefits and the opportunity to take unemployment benefits as a lump sum as a stake to start new enterprises.

Editorialists and syndicated pundits greet the new administration quite predictably. The *Washington Post* considers it unfortunate for the "peace process" in the Middle East that a Jew will again head the State Department but takes some solace from Kissinger's capacity to befriend Anwar Sadat and do business with other "moderate" Arabs. Evans and Novak denounce Solarz's appointment as an affront to the Muslim world and encouragement of Israeli obstinancy. In *Commentary*, the magazine he has long edited, and on the Op-Ed pages of major newspapers, Norman Podhoretz denounces Hart's foreign and defense policy and warns that Finlandization is imminent. The usually silent Finnish ambassador promptly protests that the world contains a great many political arrangements immensely less satisfactory than Finland's. Joining Podhoretz's funereal groans over American surrender of world power to the Soviets, *Wall Street Journal* editorialists extract what solace they can from the absence of major spending novelties. At least, concludes one pained essay, liberals have learned something about domestic policy whatever their dangerous blindness to Soviet machinations. Temperate conservatives are quietly grateful. Not a whisper about national health. No large public job programs. Limited increases in publicly assisted housing. True still to supply-side faith that lower taxes solve all economic problems, the editorial page—Herbert Hoover preserved in aspic—deplores Hart's plan to sponsor a version of European value-added levies, but concedes that the scheme refrains from reviving the soak-the-rich ideology of old-style liberals. It teeters on the brink of apoplexy at the identity of Hart's National Labor Relations Board chairman. He is none other than Philip Sipser, whose law firm specializes in representation of unions in collective-bargaining negotiations.

The White House gets its best press on the new budget. The *Washington Post*'s Hobart Rowen and the *New York Times*'s Leonard Silk agree that Hart's effort to get the deficit under control is serious and credible, a welcome departure from the shadow boxing between Congress and the president of the second Reagan administration and the folly of Gramm-Rudman. Economists hold their breath, for the time of testing has arrived. With the exception of a wistful band of supply-siders, respectable practitioners had endlessly reiterated the argument that federal deficits pushed interest rates up, attracted huge capital flows from the rest of the world, and raised the value of the dollar measured in other currencies so high that imports flooded the American market and fatally handicapped the most efficient of American exporters. Would the dollar now obediently decline against the yen and mark? Would the American trading deficit, annually in excess of $150 billion, shrink? Would American machinery, semiconductors, agricultural implements, even consumer electronics regain ground lost to relentless foreigners? Can these essential adjustments take place without severe recession in the United States and new troubles for major debtors in the developing countries? Can policies as subdued as those of the new Hart administration improve productivity, diminish unemployment, alleviate the plight of the poor and homeless, and renew deferred hope of rising living standards for typical working- and middle-class families?

## CAN NEOLIBERALISM SUCCEED?

By themselves, yuppies are not numerous enough to elect a president. Nor do they share single allegiance either to neoliberal ideology or neoliberal contenders. Hart's triumph was made possible by the lowered expectations of traditional Democrats, inveterate Republicans, and a drifting mass of weakly affiliated or nonaffiliated voters. Chastened by the Reagan administration's mixture of hostility and indifference to their aspirations, blacks were moved to support almost any Democrat capable of recapturing the White House. In 1984 their overwhelming support of the Mondale-Ferraro ticket had in the South called into being a backlash of white, conservative registration which more than counterbalanced black registration gains.

Recognizing the mood of his troops, Jesse Jackson, after making loud, threatening noises, decided not to repeat his 1984 candidacy and to endorse Hart. The National Organization of Women, not yet recovered from the failure of the Equal Rights Amendment campaign, was as comfortable with Hart, whose record on freedom of choice, ERA, funding of food stamps and child nutrition, and other issues central to NOW's agenda was flawless, as with any of the other major Democrats. From any Democrat militant women had learned to expect, except under intense pressure, little more than pro forma endorsement of their priorities. Even so minor a boon promised a refreshing change from the right-to-life, male-supremacist fixations of good Reaganites.

The union role in Hart's victory was inevitably subdued. An overvalued dollar, anti-union crusades by numerous industries, creative deployment of bankruptcy to discredit unions by unilateral reduction of wages and benefits, lack of success in organizing service workers, pervasive two-tier wage schemes well calculated to pit veterans against new workers, and blatant sabotage of collective bargaining by an employer-controlled National Labor Relations Board had combined to drive down the union share of the labor force to its lowest figure since the 1920s. Its Mondale fiasco taught the AFL-CIO to avoid early endorsement of any Democrat, and although many unionists preferred Cuomo to Hart, they had no trouble choosing Hart over Bush or any of the other Republican lightweights. At best, Hart was half a loaf. His version of industrial policy was unlikely to be as protectionist as the AFL-CIO's major industrial unions wanted, and his hi-tech image and support made them uneasy about the intensity of his commitment to the rescue of the industrial Midwest. Still, Hart's early appointments, his initial judicial selections to vacancies on the federal district and appeals benches, and the replacements he seemed poised to choose for retiring or dying Supreme Court veterans reassured unions that at the least the new boys and girls, unlike their predecessors, listened to Lane Kirkland and shared many union aspirations. They rested their hopes for better organizing prospects and lifting of the state of siege under which they had been living partly on the shift in Washington atmospherics but mostly on a resumption of economic growth at rates high enough to diminish unemployment.

The second half of Reagan's final term had dampened conservative euphoria. The religious right threatened to sit out the 1988 election or, worse, nominate their own candidates. Pat Robertson, a thriving TV evangelist who heals the sick and speaks in tongues, had offered himself in Republican primaries as the Christian savior. George Bush averted a third-party run by Robertson only by painting himself into a still tighter corner on pornography, drugs, school prayer, pure textbooks, and right-to-life. Frustratingly for Falwellites and Robertsonians, Congress managed to smother anti-abortion and pro-prayer constitutional amendments. The Supreme Court adhered to its decision in *Roe* v. *Wade*. Although Ronald Reagan spoke as eloquently as ever against abortion and in celebration of prayer, Moral Majoritarians could not help noticing that Nicaragua, the Pentagon budget, and the threat of higher taxes all seemed higher priorities for Mr. Reagan than the piety of school children and the lives of the unborn. With the exception of George Gilder, Paul Craig Roberts, and the *Wall Street Journal* editorial page, scarcely a supply-sider was to be heard in the sullen land.

The national mood was sour, but not hopeless. For a space, the public seemed prepared to wait for the benefits of experiments in industrial policy, substantial shifts in tax and spending priorities, and modest voucher, enterprise-zone, and training-accounts experiments. In 1982, at the depth of a mini-depression, Ronald Reagan had appealed to the voters to stay the course. On the whole they had done so. Republicans retained Senate control and lost only twenty-odd House seats, little more than the midterm average for the party in control of the White House. The precedent comforted the new administration.

Would the public be equally patient with a president less endowed with Reagan's inexplicable but genuine grip on public affection, at least during the first six years of his presidency? Hart's political chips were bet on three risky propositions. The first was the hope that the shift to fiscal restraint, even though mitigated by easy credit policy by the Federal Revenue, would not plunge a weakening economy into deep and prolonged recession. The second was the prospect of quick returns on new economic policy in the shape of a cheaper dollar and a better balance between imports and exports. Still more problematic was the restructuring of the American economy initiated in the automobile industry in Fremont, California, where General Motors's joint venture with Toyota was under way, in Detroit where Mazda had made a deal with the UAW, and in Tennessee where General Motors seemed to be betting its future on the success of a $3.5 billion gamble on Saturn. Was this the model for the industrial policy recommendations of the Iacocca commission? Were rearranged exchange rates, managerial renewal, and a new spirit of cooperation between labor and corporations enough to restore the bloom of health to the sallow countenance of American capitalism? Affirmative answers to these queries all but guaranteed a second Hart term, continued Democratic control of Congress, and reaffirmation of the neoliberal vision of America—its unemotional compassion, preference for free markets in lifestyles as well as consumer goods and public services, and caution in foreign affairs.

In American politics almost anything, aside from outright socialism, is possible. It may be that in the wake of the most ideological president in our history, the public gratefully welcomes neoliberal emphasis upon technique and process and suspension of crusades at home and abroad. Particularly if the economy's readjustment is brief and not too painful, neoliberalism fits comfortably into the tradition of pragmatism. For unknowing disciples of William James, the important question to ask of any human effort is, Will it work? If vouchers improve the quality of education, increase the quantity of low-income housing, and widen access to medical care for the poor, let millions of vouchers bloom. As with vouchers, so with pollution metering instead of legalistic regulation, contracting out of public services to low-bidding, profit-making bidders, Individual Training Accounts in place of government-sponsored programs, and, even possibly, for-profit medical care in preference to public or voluntary alternatives. One carefully evaluates the costs and benefits of different routes to politically defined objectives.

Numerous successful politicians have been playing neoliberal games. They are almost as skeptical about the efficacy of large-scale government action as Ronald Reagan himself. Unlike him, they also identify in their constituents a yearning for the sort of public intervention that protects peace-loving citizens from criminals, environmental damage, unemployment, nuclear accidents, catastrophic medical bills, indigence in later life, and so on, with as little intrusion by fussy officials as possible. The apparent contradiction between enthusiasm for a great many government services and income-maintenance efforts and generalized distrust of government can be resolved by breaking the link between financing and delivery of traditional public services. Medicare and Medicaid pay a high percentage of Hospital Corporation of America's and Humana's bills. If the users of for-profit hospitals judge that they are better treated as customers of profit-maximizing enterprises than as patients of nonprofit institutions, then the former deserve to expand their market share and the latter to shrink in importance unless or until they shape up and match the amenities of their rivals.

Health care, however, highlights a major neoliberal defect. Social Security survived eight years of a president with an earlier record of strong opposition to it because pension benefits flow to nearly everybody and above all to the vast, amorphous middle class. Universal entitlements create enormous constituencies in favor of their continuance. The neoliberal approach is tacitly hostile to national health, comprehensive welfare reform, large-scale job and public-housing ventures, and similar national solutions on grounds of principle and political practicality. Yet American and British experience makes it abundantly clear that services for low-income and otherwise vulnerable groups will be second-rate or unavailable whenever and wherever access to them is means-tested. In laissez-faire Victorian England, public health legislation was enacted only after it became clear that the plagues of the poor spread on an equal-opportunity basis to the affluent. Then and only then did London purify its water and install sewer systems. In the next century, free medical care for miners, a reform jointly sponsored by Lloyd George and Winston Churchill, was generally inferior to that available to the middle class and affluent. It took a universal program in the wake of World War II, the British Health Service, to raise standards for the poor. In the United States, public housing from its inception in the 1930s has been closed to all but low-income families. Council homes, the British equivalent, have been open to middle-income as well as poorer families. No surprise that council housing has a generally good reputation and public housing does not. Means-tested benefits inflict stigma; universal benefits are popular entitlements.

By now the process should be drained of mystery. Segregate any group as the objects of public charity. Tempt conservative politicians and media allies to stigmatize them as cheats. Make sure that a constant flow of anecdotes, accurate or apocryphal, reminds the respectable that their tax dollars support lazy and immoral leeches upon the body politic. Target welfare, Medicaid, food-stamp, and public-housing recipients for frequent investigation. Subject them to complex and humiliating qualification requirements, frequently baffling even to those who administer them. Then discover that some overpayments have been made. Conceal the news that numerous clients have received *less* than they are entitled to. Then whenever Congress or a state legislature needs to cut spending, start with means-tested programs.

At the end of July 1985, in a meeting with Senate Republican leaders on the budget deficit, President Reagan, advancing a tradition he had done so much to celebrate, regaled his case-hardened guests with yet another anecdote illustrative of welfare cheating. Seems that a woman had to miss her federally financed medical exam because she was busily buying tickets for an expensive holiday in Hawaii.[30] At least the president has stopped telling his story of the food-stamp recipient taking her change in vodka or the welfare queen driving from welfare center to welfare center in her Cadillac, collecting multiple checks.

Unlike their opponents on the political right, neoliberals do not by preference stigmatize the poor. They recognize the legitimacy of decent social provision. All the same, their distrust of large-scale, universal programs and attraction to market mechanisms lead ineluctably to segmented service delivery. Yet again, health care is paradigmatic. Endorsement of for-profit hospitals, nursing homes, dialysis centers, and health maintenance organizations also sanctions a hierarchy of accommodation and inevitably nursing care that trails downward from luxury suites, ordinary private rooms, semi-private accommodations, and wards of varying size, according to the financial resources of individual patients. The economic approach to health care assimilates it to any other commodity or service in the marketplace. Naturally, the rich will fare better than the poor. They will enjoy wider choice of physicians and superior hospital care. The hospital chains will gladly contract with the federal or local government to treat the medically indigent on terms that simultaneously economize on public expenditures and pay suitable dividends to stockholders. Under the cloak of rationality, the functional equivalent of old-time charity medicine completes a comeback begun by Reagan.

This is to say that what remains of the welfare state after eight years of Reagan reaction will be threatened by the social accounting of neoliberals. Viable social arrangements, public or private, flourish in an ideological atmosphere of solidarity. Human solidarity enlists familial affection, solicitude for neighbors, and concern for still larger and more distant groups. If their marriages endure, husbands and wives do not cast monthly accounts of the extent to which the larger of two incomes subsidizes the recipient of the smaller one, nor do they set monetary values upon cooking, cleaning, and other household duties. Departments of accounting, management, and computer science subsidize colleagues who teach unpopular courses in philosophy, foreign languages, and art history. Law faculties earn profits for universities that harbor them. Some of the money supports graduate programs in the humanities and social sciences. Sensible members of fashionable departments moderate their grumbling partly out of fellow feeling for colleagues and partly out of the sense that a university bereft of concern for culture, history, and the roots of human conduct is indistinguishable from a trade school.

As with families and university faculties, so with the communal enterprise of popular government. The principle of progressive taxation requires affluent citizens to contribute more substantially than the less prosperous. Federalism entails complex patterns of state contribution to Washington and equally complicated flows of subsidies and other expenditures from Washington to states and local jurisdictions. With much encouragement from politicians eager to score local points, citizens in Iowa are led to wonder why they should underwrite New York City's buses and subways. New Yorkers reflect that food prices would be lower if a portion of their taxes were not devoted to propping up markets for Iowa's corn and wheat. New York's senior senator, Daniel Patrick Moynihan, has been computing his state's "balance of payments" with Washington. In 1984, he reported, New Yorkers paid $55.4 billion in federal taxes but got back $2.1 billion less. Ergo, New Yorkers were subsidizing folks west of the Hudson in ways difficult to trace.[31]

Calculation is fatal to comity. Families, voluntary associations, professional societies, and political entities quarrel and disintegrate when they focus narrowly upon who pays and who benefits. Harmony requires peaceful acceptance of cross-subsidization and the humility to realize that in most lifetimes most individuals at some times are subsidized and on other occasions contribute to subsidies for others. Young workers whose Social Security deductions have alleviated the poverty of their elders will in time collect retirement benefits financed by workers who are young when they are old. Thus far, a bit more than half a century since that August 14, 1935, when Franklin Roosevelt signed into law the Social Security Act, all retirees have been collecting far more in benefits than the actuarial value of their own and their employers' payments to Social Security trust funds.

The Reagan administration's alarmist cries over impending "bankruptcy" of Social Security have shaken the confidence of younger workers that they will collect full benefits twenty, thirty, or more years hence. In truth, the more prosperous of Social Security beneficiaries have during their working careers contributed enough to pay the least affluent retirees most generously of all. Younger workers have made intergenerational transfers to senior citizens, some of whom are far more prosperous than they are. The payment and benefit pattern has endured both because at least until recently the young expected to gain from it in due time and because few were inclined to examine in the close detail necessary exactly who was subsidizing whom. So examined, Social Security is unfair on both the revenue and expenditure side. Payroll taxes are regressive. Since a single rate applies to wage and salary income and does not apply to earnings above $40,000, the corporate vice-president paid $400,000 is assessed the same amount as a colleague much further down the executive ladder collecting a mere $40,000. As a percentage of salary, his tax is one-tenth that of his hierarchical subordinate. Moreover, the larger the individual income, the more substantial the proportion of it derived from dividends, interest, and capital gains, not a dollar of which is subject to Social Security levy.

On the expenditure side, Social Security benefits replace higher percentages of earnings as those earnings move downward. A pensioner who gratefully retires after four decades of steady but ill-rewarded work will receive monthly checks that are a much larger proportion of his recent earnings than will better-paid retirees. In other words, the system is progressive in its outlays: the more lucrative your working career, the less significant a part of your golden years resources will Social Security be. There is less logic than political wisdom in these arrangements. That they have endured so long testifies to public acceptance of the system.

It should be glaringly clear that tampering with either side of the ledger risks an open season of interest-group conflict. Well-paid professional and managerial workers will judge that they could earn much higher rates of return from their and their employers' contributions if they were allowed to invest these sums in common stocks or real estate.

The social costs of rational investment are heavy. An individual retirement account option would at a stroke destroy the universal character of the present system. Retirement rewards will be strictly associated with income performance. Low-paid workers will require supplements to the amounts they have earned either from the Social Security trust fund or their own small IRAs. In effect, welfare will supplant current, dignified income-maintenance provision, much as Medicaid, to the dismay of many middle-class patients, finances long-term nursing home care only *after* assets have been all but dissipated in order to establish eligibility. As conservatives indignantly charge, Social Security does embody an element of income redistribution. Indeed, this is one of its major contributions to decency. Practically everyone gets more than the actuarial value of lifetime contributions, and low-income families benefit most. There is an intergenerational transfer and probably another between affluent and less affluent beneficiaries.

I have lingered upon Social Security because here as elsewhere neoliberal, like neoconservative, logic draws upon the wrong social science, economics instead of sociology. Economists proficiently calculate costs and benefits for individuals operating in efficient markets. Insofar as the scholarly imperialism of economists is allowed or actually encouraged by politicians to reshape social policy, it is almost certain to ratify and reinforce existing distributions of income and wealth. Lacking any old-fashioned passion for social justice and possessing far too rational attitudes toward public policy, neoliberals are quite capable of reshaping policy in much the same direction as supply-siders and neoconservatives, not out of ideological fervor but out of solicitude for efficiency, international competitiveness, faster economic growth, and intellectual tidiness.

Neoliberalism perpetuates Reaganomics by other devices. It continues to tear at the frayed fabric of group harmony. As industrial-policy emphasis upon readjustment and identification of winners implies, losers will continue to have a hard time. But, worse still, neoliberal intervention is unlikely to succeed in good part because rewards are directed to groups which constitute a good part of the problem. The plain fact is that corporate managers have been excessively compensated for nearly two decades of demonstrated incompetence. Policies that further reward them dangerously miss the point. Japan has prospered without lavishing million-dollar salaries and multimillion-dollar compensation packages upon its executives. To rival Japan requires devotion to educational achievement and sharing of collective aspirations and rewards in ways alien to the individualism legitimated as much by neoliberalism as by its conservative rivals.

On several grounds, neoliberalism is preferable to the nightmare of four, eight, or more years of Reaganism, the premise of an earlier chapter. Crusades against abortion and for public school prayer no doubt will continue but without White House encouragement. Defense policy should be less expensive and foreign policy less chauvinistic. Blacks and Hispanics will not be totally ignored because no Democrat can become president without substantial minority support. Electoral calculation will inevitably modify economistic impulses. Neoliberalism is less a nightmare than a recipe for uneasy sleep, an interlude between right-wing activism, Reagan-style, and, just possibly, revival on the political left.

*Chapter 7*

# New Wars of Religion

NOT SO LONG ago, it was conventional wisdom among experts, some of whom deplored and others of whom applauded their findings, that the kinetic energies of modernity were everywhere undermining the influence of religion upon individual standards of morality, personal conduct, and public policy. Pundits, glutted by survey data and the behavior of their own children, chimed in chorus that the lure of the artifacts of mass culture—blue jeans, Bruce Springsteen, Michael Jackson, Sly Stallone, Madonna (and names not yet on the horizon as this book goes to press), junk food and health food often indistinguishable from each other, television and videocassettes, the apparatus of physical fitness, the manifold marvels of personal electronics, and much, much more—was, in obedience to Marshall McLuhan's metaphor, turning the peoples of the world into a global village. The strongest of faiths, let alone the attentuated versions of Christianity and Judaism in vogue in the West, could not long resist the inexorable tug of fatally enticing diversions and compelling appeals to immediate gratification of the senses. Few were immune from these temptations. Young Moslems, young Hindus, young Buddhists, perhaps young African animists, responded little differently from young Catholics, young Jews, and young infidels. The future for the developing countries of the southern hemisphere was ripe for inspection in the readily available experience of North America and Western Europe. So ran a tale conclusively buttressed by the entire social science apparatus of stratified public opinion sampling, focus panels, longitudinal studies, cross-sectional comparisons, factor analysis, and techniques still less comprehensible to the laity.

Unfortunately for the reputation of sociologists and political scientists, a minor consideration, and the physical safety, personal liberties, and mental health of large numbers of Lebanese, Iranians, Pakistanis, Iraquis, and citizens of allegedly more advanced societies, religion has revived, generally speaking, in its most absolutist, least tolerant variants—the Ayatollah's version of Islam, the authoritarian orthodoxy of Israel's Likud, and, in First Amendment America, Jerry Falwell's Moral Majority, renamed in 1986 the Liberty Federation.

Among advanced industrial societies, precisely those in which technology, the gospel of high consumption, and the cult of self might have been expected most completely to supplant theism, the United States by every quantitative measure is the most avowedly religious. No need for the moment to examine the reciprocal relationship between commerce and creed. On that score, it suffices to recall Jerry Falwell's assertion that wealth is God's way of rewarding those who put Him first. The pollsters report that 94 percent of their respondents believe in God; 88 percent esteem the Bible as divinely inspired; 90 percent call themselves Jews, Catholics, or some brand of Protestant; and 89 percent claim the habit of regular prayer.[1] Even if these numbers include some unknown quantum of puffery, they signify at the least the popularity of religion and the sense abroad in the land that atheists, skeptics, and secular humanists, whoever they might be, are as out of step in Reagan's America as a chapter of the American Civil Liberties Union would be in Iran.

As a product—perhaps service is the better word—religion is a hot item, a double platinum platter to pitch its claims modestly. A good way to be excused from service on a jury even in sinful New York City is to refuse to take an oath and insist on affirming. Lawyers on both sides of the case will jostle each other to disqualify any individual willing to separate him or herself in open court from the theistic consensus of the community. Such oddballs are likely to prolong jury deliberations and almost certain to make verdicts even more unpredictable by lawyers than they already are. In 1985, Congress signified its detestation of secular humanism while prudently refraining from definition of the corrupting doctrine. It excused school authorities from devoting federal funds to the teaching of this pernicious doctrine, however local educational officials might identify it. The United States, as politicians and TV preachers habitually boast, is a Christian country. Sensitive pols compliment the voters as heirs of Judeo-Christian revelations, particularly in communities where Jews are numerous.

A minor entertainment of the otherwise enervating 1984 presidential campaign was a flap over Armageddon, according to the *Oxford English Dictionary* "the place of the last decisive battle at the Day of Judgment." How many prisoners did the Lord plan to take? What should one pack for the trip? How near was judgment day? How many Jews would at last accept Jesus as their Savior and thus be transported in ecstacy to eternal bliss? Possibly to the consternation of some of his constituents, President Reagan revealed that he had himself brooded over such theological issues but hastened to reassure them that any conclusions he might have reached did not influence American foreign policy. The news, one hopes, consoled the Soviet Union's dying leader Constantin Chernenko in the final months of his life and subtracted one item from the agenda of his successor, the vigorous Mikhail Gorbachev. A former editor of *The New Republic*, Hendrik Hertzberg, was moved amiably to protest as a genuine Judeo-Christian (half Jewish, half gentile), "Where is it written that if you don't like religion you are somehow disqualified from being a legitimate American? What was Mark Twain, a Russian?"[2]

No doubt many Americans, not unlike their president, applaud religion more extravagantly in words than in individual observance. In 1958, some forty-nine million Americans attended churches or synagogues during the week before the census enumerator visited their homes. Out of an increasing population, that number declined steadily to a mere forty million in 1983.[3] A stray secular humanist could legitimately wonder whether many of his fellow citizens considered religious observance more wholesome for the neighbors than for themselves. Cynics may be unfair, of course, to the millions who tuned their TVs to Pat Robertson, Jimmy Swaggart, Jerry Falwell, Robert Schuller, and lesser paladins in the unceasing battle against sin. In 1980, Falwell estimated his TV audience at twenty-five million faithful viewers of his "Old-Time Gospel Hour."[4] One of his aides cheerfully doubled that figure to fifty million.

However, neutral Arbitron calculations for February 1980 reported that the audiences for the sixty-six religious programs cluttering the airwaves combined added up to considerably less than twenty-five million. Included in that number were gluttons who for their souls' sake watched two or more of the sixty-six. The top six were Oral Roberts (2,719,250), Rex Humbard (2,409,960), Robert Schuller (2,069,210), Jimmy Swaggart (1,986,000), Jerry Falwell (1,455,720), and James Robison (464,800).[5] Moreover, of the six, Roberts, Humbard, and Swaggart are "fundamentalist and flamboyant, but not particularly political." Schuller is an apolitical mixture of mainline Protestantism and Norman Vincent Peale's positive thinking. Only two programs in the top religious ten, Falwell's "Old-Time Gospel Hour" (number six) and Jim Bakker's "PTL Club" (number nine) are closely identified with the religious right.[6] As a liberal Protestant critic derisively comments, "Alan Alda is still the leading preacher in America, even in reruns."[7] True to American commercial culture, large helpings of hype surround the fundamentalists' claim for an enormous and increasing audience for their message of selective scripture, free-enterprise economics, Christian meanness to the poor, and foreign-policy chauvinism.

Public piety, of course, lacks novelty. The Eisenhower regime evoked from an unsympathetic Protestant minister and journalist a series of articles entitled "Piety on the Potomac." Ike was alleged to have glanced around the table at his first Cabinet meeting and solicited a blessing from the senior religious official present, who turned out to be Agriculture Secretary Ezra Taft Benson, a Mormon bishop, considerably higher in rank than the pious Secretary of State, John Foster Dulles, a mere Presbyterian elder. In due course, in his mid-eighties, Mr. Benson became head of the Mormon church and a candidate for American Express television commercials.

Ministers, priests, and rabbis preface sessions of Congress, legislatures, and political conventions with invocations of the Almighty. That the ensuing deliberations rarely plausibly comport with divine inspiration may attest to no more than human difficulty in fathoming the plans of the Deity, technical defects in the invocations, the Lord's nasty sense of humor, or David Hume's conjecture that a committee of gods concocted the universe. Public school pupils prior to the Supreme Court's outlawing of religious ceremonials in classrooms were likely to encounter Bible reading, prayer, recitation of the Ten Commandments, and in the Christmas season the singing of carols stuffed full of religious references. Catholics displeased with the King James version of the Bible either suffered in silence or sent their sons and daughters to parochial schools. Jews and secularists had even fewer alternatives because, for one thing, the best and most expensive private schools practiced even more intrusive varieties of Protestantism. Particularly in the South and the rural Midwest, public schools were Christian academies.

Herbert Hoover's 1928 landslide owed much to anti-Catholic prejudice against Al Smith, who, according to legend, sent the Pope an eloquent, one-word telegram in the wake of the election, "Unpack." In 1960, John Kennedy had to persuade West Virginia hardshell Protestants in a crucial primary and Texas clergymen traditionally opposed to popery that his Catholicism did not threaten the wall of separation between church and state, or in practical financial terms promise federal subsidies to parochial schools. As president, Jimmy Carter shared his religious feelings in season and out with his constituents. At the 1984 Dallas renomination celebration of Ronald Reagan's first term, the Reverend Jerry Falwell conveyed God's endorsement of the Republican ticket. The following year, he expanded his activities to South Africa. After a six-hour session with that country's dour president, he emerged with blessings upon Mr. Botha's "reforms" of apartheid; harsh, un-Christian criticism of Bishop Desmond Tutu as a "phony"; conclusive evidence that blacks interviewed by him opposed foreign disinvestment; and plans for a campaign to persuade Americans to buy more Krugerrands and boycott those corporations which withdrew from the South African economy. New York's mayor, Edward Koch, who conducts an active foreign policy of his own, deplored Falwell's pronouncements and relocated him in the moral minority.

One needn't rummage very hard or long in American

political history to collect instances of our penchant for mixing religion and politics. It was, after all, the Women's Christian Temperance Union that deserved much credit or blame for Herbert Hoover's "noble experiment," the Eighteenth Amendment to the Constitution which between 1919 and 1933 made drinking delectably illegal and delightfully profitable for gangsters, saloonkeepers, local politicians, and policemen on the take. Religious influence has been particularly potent at the many intersections of politics and personal morality. For decades, the Catholic Legion of Decency exerted de facto censorship over the movie industry. The National Organization for Decent Literature, another Catholic group, harried booksellers and news dealers who sold allegedly obscene books and periodicals. That devout Protestant Anthony Comstock was triumphantly responsible in the nineteenth century for the definition of birth control manuals as obscene literature, unfit to be delivered by the postal service.

All this recalled, the 1980s do appear to offer unusual evidence of religious involvement in politics, national and local, as well as education, the practice of medicine, and public exhibitions of religious symbols. On the last score, the Supreme Court's affirmation of the right of Pawtucket, Rhode Island, to display a crèche on public property should have comforted neither advocates nor opponents. The latter failed to prevent the display but the former won their victory on the ground that Christmas had become a festival of commerce in which religious symbols amounted to little more than competitive advertising. Some at least of the faithful might have preferred defeat to victory on grounds so demeaning to religious faith.

As one would expect in our national marketplace of ideas, the religious players are numerous and some of the alliances among them unexpected. At varying distances right of center there are Protestant fundamentalists, main-line Protestant economic conservatives, neoconservative Catholics, and *Commentary*-style Jews. Located left of center are Protestant social-action groups still at home in the National Council of Churches, the respectable Catholic left of the National Conference of Catholic Bishops, out-of-season Jewish liberals (surprisingly numerous though less hysterical than Jewish conservatives),[8] the threatening left of liberation theology, and, a wild card in the theological deck, radical evangelicals represented best in print by the monthly journal *The Sojourners*.

How does one distinguish left from right? The publicly religious focus on three significant groups of issues. The first, war and peace, embraces Pentagon budgets, nuclear freezes, relations with the Soviet Union, sanctions against South Africa, and American intervention in Central America. The second, primarily economic, includes social spending, tax equity, unemployment, the appropriate relationship between government and private enterprise, and the degree of enthusiasm brought to the celebration of American capitalism. In recent politics, it is the third set of issues—abortion, pornography, gay rights, feminism, and prayer—that has aroused strongest passion.

Start with conservative fundamentalism. According to Richard Neuhaus, a Lutheran pastor, frequent contributor to *Commentary* and *The National Review*, and an informed and sympathetic observer, fundamentalists share several beliefs or "fundamentals":

> the inerrancy of Scripture (the Bible contains no errors in any subject on which it speaks); the virgin birth of Jesus (the Spirit of God conceived Jesus in Mary without human intervention); the substitutionary atonement of Jesus Christ—on the cross he bore the just punishment for the sins of the entire world; his bodily resurrection; the authenticity of the biblical miracles; and premillennialism.[9]

As Neuhaus points out, "In the past it was generally thought that premillennialist Christians would be politically passive, because there wasn't much point in trying to change the world before Jesus returns to set everything right."

Reagan's first Interior Secretary, the vociferous James Watt, vented a version of this sentiment at his 1981 nomination hearings when he somewhat casually informed a Senate committee that the importance of federal policy toward national parks and public lands was substantially diminished by the possibility that the Lord might repossess them at any time. Under such theological circumstances, long-range planning was wasted effort. After all, mused Mr. Watt, "I do not know how many future generations we can count on before the Lord returns," but in the meantime, "My responsibility is to follow the Scriptures, which call upon us to occupy the land until Jesus returns."[10] Who could better further the Lord's agenda, as thus defined, than coal miners, oil-well drillers, lumbermen, resort developers, stock grazers, and other predators for the Lord?

Today's conservative fundamentalists certainly do not limit their agenda to the salvation of individual souls. As an Alameda, California, fundamentalist preacher put it, "When I was growing up, I always heard that churches should stay out of politics. Now it seems almost a sin *not* to get involved."[11] Their agenda features legalization of prayer and Bible reading in public schools (declared unconstitutional by the Supreme Court in its 1962 *Engel* v. *Vitale* decision); abolition of legal abortion either by constitutional amendment or Supreme Court reversal of its 1973 *Roe* v. *Wade* decision; legal restrictions upon pornography (however defined); an end to state "harassment" of Christian schools; opposition to feminist and gay rights legislation; reinterpretation of the Constitution to favor religion against skepticism, agnosticism, atheism, and "secular humanism"; larger appropriations for the Pentagon; careful screening of nominees to the courts so as to guarantee appointment of pro-life, pro-"family," pro-prayer jurists; termination of social programs that assertedly undermine individual responsibility and increase the dependency of the poor; and, of course, resistance to a "secular humanism" that allies itself with feminists and gay advocates, promotes free choice, embraces anti-family doctrines like comparable worth, and insults Holy Writ by teaching innocent children the evolutionary heresy of Charles Darwin.[12]

In foreign policy, "right" connotes vigorous anti-Communism, high defense appropriations, and intervention in Nicaragua and any other place where the red menace threatens to advance. As far as the economy is concerned, "right" enlists the Deity as a strong supporter of free enterprise and fervent opponent of "statism," "planning," and regulation.

On matters of individual morality, "right," quite in contrast to its economic attitudes, is interventionist on abortion, prayer, pornography, public displays of Christian symbols, medical treatment of severely handicapped newborn infants, the qualities of candidates for judicial posts, and the contents of school textbooks. Shakespeare is routinely bowdlerized in school texts.

Publishers who want their biology texts adopted in Texas had best give equal space to "creation science" and evolution, preferably without mentioning the name of Charles Darwin.

Manifestly, conservative fundamentalists are "right" on all three scores. Although they may occasionally differ, as on South Africa, where a group of far-right congressional conservatives led by Representative Newt Gingrich support sanctions and the Reverend Jerry Falwell vociferously opposes them, this is a rare exception to a cohesiveness of opinion unusual among conservatives and unimaginable among liberals and radicals. Conservatives themselves, of course, fight bitterly over distinctions minute to the comprehension of outsiders. But they unite in celebration of Ronald Reagan as a president after their own heart, a chief executive who publicly proclaimed the Soviet Union as the Evil Empire that true Christians have known it to be since 1917, the man who in 1981 terrorized Congress into slashing appropriations for the idle poor and cutting taxes upon the productive wealthy, the partisan of market capitalism who appointed to regulatory commissions such opponents of regulation as Anne Gorsuch Burford at the Environmental Protection Administration and James Miller as successively chairman of the Federal Trade Commission and director of the Office of Management and Budget, and the exponent of public morality who has tried but failed to translate appropriate rhetoric into effective action on the abortion and prayer fronts.

Their position is considerably strengthened by support on many if not all issues by orthodox Jews and Catholics. Not so long ago Catholics and fundamentalists profoundly distrusted each other. As a haven of immigrants, the Catholic Church, not without justification, regarded itself as beleaguered by intolerant Protestant majorities. At heavy financial cost to pious, working-class parents, Catholic parochial schools were established as much to protect impressionable children from Protestant influence in public schools as to provide appropriate Catholic religious formation. Catholic parents involuntarily helped pay for the education of their neighbors' progeny as well as their own.

Franklin Roosevelt's New Deal coalition enrolled its most reliable troops out of urban concentrations of blue-collar Catholics. In the ensuing half century, Democrats lost more and more presidential elections partly because increasing percentages of Catholics were turning Republican. Catholics now are as prosperous as other Americans and by no particular coincidence securely located in the mainstream of national politics. They elected a president in 1960. An Italian Catholic woman was Walter Mondale's vice-presidential selection. No one discounts Mario Cuomo as a Democratic presidential possibility. The occupational distribution of Catholics—professional, technical, managerial, clerical, and blue-collar—approximates the national norm. Thus, papal and episcopal endorsement of unions addresses itself to communicants who in decreasing numbers possess union cards and increasingly work for large corporations hostile to collective bargaining. Nor do pronouncements in support of public job creation, planning, progressive taxation, and so on command, to speak gently, the automatic deference of Catholic entrepreneurs and millionaires.

All of which is to say that despite important theological differences among orthodox Jews, fundamentalist Protestants, and conservative, lay Catholics, the three groups can and increasingly do cooperate amicably on issues that range from abortion, through taxation and deregulation, to foreign policy and defense appropriations. Much as Catholic liberals and radicals pick as they choose from official Church teachings on contraception, abortion, and other issues, equally self-confident religious conservatives freely differ particularly upon judgments of capitalist performance and the policy consequences of contrasting judgments. On election day, November 4, 1984, a self-appointed lay commission of financiers, politicians, and academics issued a manifesto, *Catholic Social Teaching and the U.S. Economy*. The lay commission's report, composed in the main by Michael Novak, drew upon such standard secular sources as Walter Lippmann, *The Federalist Papers*, Alexis de Tocqueville, and the speeches of Abraham Lincoln, as well as government statistics and suitably conservative contemporary economists and sociologists. But many of the lay letter's authorities were Catholic, among them Saint Thomas Aquinas on the nature of God: "God is pictured as Providence, allowing contingent causes to work in all their humanly baffling contingency, empowering human beings as free agents; compelling no one, but ordering all things sweetly and from within their own natures and liberties. . . . God is the God of liberty and contingency, of the random and lawlike, Who respects the individuality of every lily in the field, every blade of grass, every singular human being."[13] Building assertedly on this interpretation of Aquinas, the report justifies capitalism in these terms: ". . . we value free markets because they allow for fresh insight, for new initiatives, for astringent criticism of their current deficiencies, and for new courses of action to bring about newly desired results. . . . Markets, in short, allow for self-correction. Markets are a 'rational' device, but not as small groups of experts are 'rational.' "

Appropriately interpreted by the lay commission, Pope John Paul II also sides with capitalism. The lay commission evokes encouraging exegesis from the Pope's discussion of planning:

> As we view the whole human family throughout the world, we cannot fail to be struck by a disconcerting fact of immense proportions: the fact that while conspicuous natural resources remain unused there are huge numbers of people who are unemployed or underemployed and countless multitudes of people suffering from hunger. This is a fact that without any doubt demonstrates that both within individual political communities and in their relationships on the continental and world levels there is something wrong with the organization of work and employment, precisely at the most critical and socially most important points. . . . These observations hold true most of all in those parts of the world in which markets do not function, individual intelligence is repressed, and human providence is frustrated.

True, John Paul II does call for "overall planning" but warns that "it cannot mean one-sided centralization by the public authorities. Instead, what is in question is a just and rational coordination, within the framework of which the initiative of individuals, free groups and local work centers and complexes must be safeguarded."[14]

Ignoring the Pope's dislike of economic inequality and his weakness for planning, Novak et al. "welcome" his warning against centralization and his "reliance" upon individuals. Picking and choosing among papal pronouncements, they find much of comfort in support of capitalist endeavor and numerous salutary cautions against government action. No need to linger upon the present pope's frequent criticisms of Western capitalism's materialism, failure to alleviate domestic poverty, inequitable distribution of income and wealth, and exploitation of the impoverished societies of the Third World. No need also to remind the faithful of Aquinas's unfortunate lapses as an economist. Even saints fall short of perfection. Their man did vilify interest as usury. Even more erroneously, he advocated a doctrine of just price which required, horrible to recall, controls to protect consumers from exploitation by greedy merchants. Hard as it might seem to enlist the saint in the American Enterprise Institute, the authors of the lay commission report have succeeded, to their own satisfaction at least, in doing so. After their cosmetic surgery, Saint Thomas Aquinas remarkably resembles Saint Milton Friedman.

Far better than any other set of human arrangements, capitalism pursues "the lay task of co-creation," in the spirit of John Paul II's encyclical *Laborem Exercens*: "Man is the image of God partly through the mandate received from his Creator to subdue, to dominate the earth."[15] Capitalism, an efficient agent of dominion, is also and above all in America the guarantor of dignity and freedom: "Only a market system allows economic agents regular, reliable, ordinary liberties. Only a market system respects the free creativity of every human person, and *for this reason* respects private property, incentives (rather than coercion), freedom of choice, and the other institutions of a free economy."[16]

Critics erroneously attack market capitalism for selfish concentration on individual advantages. In fact, "A market system obliges its participants to be other-regarding, that is, to observe the freely expressed needs and desires of others."[17] Successful entrepreneurs rejoice in risk-taking on new methods, products, and services. For the poor, the best hope that some day they will prosper resides in the job-creating dynamism of men and women who risk their resources in pursuit of new opportunities. Despite his regrettable lapses, John Paul II does from time to time see this point, as in his Milan speech in 1983 to a business group: "The degree of well-being which society enjoys today would be unthinkable without the dynamic figure of the business man, whose function consists of organizing human labor and the means of production so as to give rise to the goods and services necessary for the prosperity and progress of the community."[18]

Profit generates progress. It is not to be confused with the corruption of greed. Greed brings its own retribution for "Firms that use profits unwisely, for the selfish gains of a few, typically injure their own long-term prospects."[19] It is odd retribution upon the greedy that stockholders lose money and innocent employees their jobs. The greedy have been known to take the money and run, leaving their mismanaged enterprises to sink or swim.

The lay commission does not indulge in such wimpish complaint because its members have still more to say in praise of profit. Profits fund universities, medical research, voluntary hospitals, museums, and charities, religious and secular. Catholic prosperity in the United States is an excellent case in point:

> One of the reasons why the American Catholic Church has become in less than two centuries a dominant financial force in the universal Church springs directly from the free-market profit system. In diocese after diocese, beautiful properties and great buildings have been contributed to the Church, by Catholics and non-Catholics alike, directly out of their own liberty and profits. Cathedrals, convents, colleges, hospitals, magnificent estates, recreational areas and many other properties have been freely given, quite apart from state control or fiat. The liberty of the American Catholic Church is directly owed to a free-market profit system, which permits both economic creativity and liberty of conscience in the disposal of wealth earned.[20]

Multinational corporations, often assaulted as exploiters of poor nations, no doubt have been guilty of "some abuses" but "On the plus side, multinational corporations bring badly needed capital investments, technology transfers, import substitutions, training, infrastructure, employment and wages, taxes, and important economic contacts to LDCs."[21] Indeed, the multinationals have been the product of

... moral and material necessity. They extend the creative breakthroughs of entrepreneurships which occur within one nation to other nations. They promote international interaction, the reduction of barriers between nations, and cultural interpretation from one to another part of the human race. They benefit the home nation by expanding its employment in new ways (not without some dislocation). They benefit recipient nations by indispensable transfers of ideas, methods, capital, and other benefits; they expand the total world economy.... [I]f they did not already exist, the critical needs of human kind would require that they be invented.[22]

Just possibly, Union Carbide's Bhopal victims might utter a dissent. ITT's role in the overthrow of Allende in Chile helped install the durable General Pinochet. Elsewhere, multinationals have meddled in local politics, rarely on the side of democracy, almost invariably in support of Jeane Kirkpatrick's tolerated authoritarians. The lay commission's vision does not focus on such disagreeable historical episodes.

Capitalism befriends the poor. The first thing to be said is that living standards rise fastest and poverty shrinks most encouragingly in South Korea, not North Korea; West Germany, not East Germany; Kenya, not Ethiopia; Hong Kong, not mainland China; Taiwan, not Vietnam; and Australia, not Argentina. Somewhat obliquely the report concedes that not all of these success stories are models of civil and political freedom: "Capitalism seems to be a necessary, but not a sufficient, condition for political and civil liberties and also for economic development."[23] On neither side of the comparisons do embarrassing countries like Chile and the Union of South Africa appear. Apparently they are deplorable exceptions. In Chile a brutal military regime presides over a free-market economy notably unsuccessful in improving the living standards of the population. The more successful South African economy continues barbarous policies of racial segregation akin to the Nazis' Nuremberg laws. In South Korea thriving entrepreneurs comfortably coexist with authoritarian generals. Strikes in the small, thriving Asian economies are to all intents and purposes illegal. Nosy bureaucrats do not impede progress by attention to environmental hazards and threats to the health and safety of workers.

The lay commission does concede that our blessed land falls short of absolute perfection. The family urgently requires support, as the "first teacher of social justice."[24]

The report's authors "object to those base forms of commerce—in abortion, pornography, prostitution, and drugs—which make direct war upon the virtues of family life and on the necessary moral strength of any free Republic."[25] However, unlike the fundamentalist right, they stop short of censorship and urge "leaders of public opinion . . . to emphasize the importance for the life of the Republic of such basic human virtues as self-respect, honesty, loyalty, chastity, fidelity, integrity, and the like."[26] No bad thing, either, for "business leaders to become critically aware of the moral impact . . . of their own advertising and of the entertainments they support."[27] One wonders, as this document does not, that so many enterprising capitalists specialize in moral corruption, just as though capitalism were ethically indifferent instead of spiritually uplifting.

Do we do enough for our own poor? Hell, yes: "The generosity of the American people in wishing to help the poor, by supporting legislation targeted on the needs of the poor . . . has been immense."[28] Wise policymakers of course carefully distinguish between indigent souls who are capable of self-reliance and those who because of age, disability, or chronic ill-health can be excused from the obligation of self-support. Care must always be taken to target aid to the first group in ways that do not prolong dependence. Appropriate aid helps the poor clamber out of their condition. For blacks, poverty is in part the lingering heritage of slavery. For blacks and whites, it is a cultural condition. Hence, intelligent policies will emphasize not alone or even primarily more money. What is needed is "person to-person" efforts, which take Christian account of the "need one human being has for respect, attention, and realistic love from another."[29] That poverty which is of the spirit can never be cured by the best-intentioned of public policies.

For the rest, the text recommends that "the habit of saving should once again be taught as a virtue crucial to the building of the future."[30] Government should set an example by restraining its own spending, curbing deficits, and exercising "intense vigilance to prevent inflation."[31] The report exhibits no curiosity about an uncomfortable paradox: capitalism depends upon saving and investment but devotes skilled advertising and marketing effort to separating the customers from as much of their money as possible and luring them into heavy debt.

For Catholics, particularly Catholic bishops, the moral is plain and reiterated. Capitalism, particularly in its American version, has been good for Catholics: "We American Catholics are privileged to have received two precious legacies: Catholic faith and citizenship in the United States."[32] Thus, ". . . we feel immense gratitude toward this nation's Founders, who first imagined . . . the fundamental humanistic instincts embodied in the U.S. economy. Committed to liberty and justice for all, this economy has freed millions of families from poverty, given them an unparalleled domain of free choice, taught them virtues of cooperation and compassion, and unloosed upon this earth an unprecedented surge of creativity, invention, and productivity."[33] Of course the story is incomplete. Defects linger, but despite them American capitalism has something to teach Catholicism just as Catholicism has much to teach capitalism. Recommendations for improvement ought to be made in a generous spirit of acknowledgment of how much American capitalism has done to enhance freedom, raise living standards, and lift the curse of poverty from so many. Capitalism is Catholicism's best friend. Sensible Catholics, accordingly, will oppose government regulation, burdensome taxation of corporations and entrepreneurs, and other meddling in the free markets that have served all Americans so well. It is always pleasant when religious faith and material self-interest coincide. Seldom has such coincidence been more complete than in the lay commission's demonstration that God is an American capitalist.

In this period of shifting alliances, Jewish attitudes also are fluid. In 1984, Jews preferred Mondale-Ferraro to Reagan-Bush by a two-to-one margin. Only blacks and low-income voters excused themselves from the Reagan celebration in greater percentages. Superficially, it might seem that Jews, though even more affluent than Catholics, set their immediate economic interests aside and remained faithful to the liberal agenda of concern for the vulnerable, social programs in aid of the poor, faithful adherence to First Amendment separation of church and state, and minimal government interference with the personal choices of consenting adults, however outré.

Jewish behavior puzzled students of electoral politics. Reagan's tax cuts; deregulation of banking, securities, airlines, and trucking; and the special favors lavished upon real estate and other interests all as surely benefited Jewish as non-Jewish entrepreneurs, property developers, and investors, as well as the legal, accounting, and other professional specialties associated with them. Moreover, administration opposition to affirmative action responded to Jewish fears that affirmative action equaled quotas and quotas entailed the sort of discrimination against Jews in universities, professional schools, and corporations that middle-aged Jews had themselves experienced. Assistant Attorney General Bradford Reynolds had dedicated his four years in office to reopening affirmative action settlements between his predecessors and municipalities. As reconstituted by presidential appointments, the Civil Rights Commission took a similarly hard line against affirmative action agreements that set numerical and chronological targets for the hiring and promotion of women and minorities.

This was the very issue that, with the possible exception of policy toward Israel and the PLO, had most sharply set traditionally allied blacks and Jews against each other. Many blacks seemed not merely to lump Jews with other whites, but to target them for special resentment as faithless friends. The increasing number of Jewish parents who enrolled children in their own religious schools presumably endorsed Reagan's support of tuition tax credits and school-voucher experiments. Moreover, since relatively few families lived in the low income school districts to which federal Title I subsidies flowed, they suffered little from administration curtailment of education budgets.

On Israel, Reagan policy was ambiguous, but no more so than that of other presidents. During his brief tenure at the State Department, Alexander Haig apparently gave a green light to the Israeli invasion of Lebanon. Certainly the president himself uttered few criticisms. Economic and military aid increased and the two countries edged closer to military cooperation just short of outright alliance.

All in all, the Reagan record on issues of Jewish concern might reasonably have justified stronger support than the president received, all the more so because influential Jewish neoconservatives enthusiastically endorsed the Republican ticket. Irving Kristol, Norman Podhoretz, and Milton Himmelfarb, among other publicists associated with *Commentary, The Public Interest*, and the *Wall Street Journal*, strongly advised Jews to behave like other groups. Without noticeable compunction, American ethnic, religious, professional, and business groups routinely favor politicians who best represent their interests. They vote for them and contribute to their campaigns. Why should Jews act differently? A strong America was good for American Jews. It was good for Israel. Martin Peretz's *The New Republic*, though frequently critical of administration domestic policy, applauded its defense buildup and, more waveringly, its anti-Soviet bellicosity in Central America. In the end, hawks hoped, Reagan's military buildup might induce the Soviets to release less famous prisoners of conscience than Anatol Scharansky and allow more refuseniks to emigrate to Israel or the United States. Certainly Carter's less confrontational policy had been ineffective. Moreover, Jews could only benefit by spreading their bets more evenly between the major parties. So long as they stubbornly voted for Democrats, Republicans in office owed them few favors. Indeed, Jews, like blacks, risked being taken for granted by Democrats and ignored by Republicans. It was, after all, the Republicans who in 1984 made the gesture at their Dallas convention of approving a resolution against anti-Semitism and the Democrats who failed to take similar, symbolic action, possibly out of fear of alienating Jesse Jackson and his supporters. Mondale perforce treated Jackson carefully and muted criticism of his difficult ally's lapses into anti-Semitism. Republicans enjoyed the luxury of unqualified condemnation of Jackson's description of New York as "hymietown" and his belated disavowal of Louis Farakhan's outright anti-Semitism and approval of Adolf Hitler.

Yet Jewish electoral behavior, closely analyzed, was far from irrational and quite closely connected with group interests. Take Israel first. In Lebanon, Defense Secretary Caspar Wein-

## New Wars of Religion

berger's instructions to American forces briefly stationed in Beirut and elsewhere seemed deliberately designed to avoid any suggestion of cooperation between Israelis and Americans. Several unpleasant disputes about demarcation lines between the two forces halted just short of actual bloodshed. Against intense Jewish lobbying, the administration pushed through Congress sales of AWAC planes to Saudi Arabia and continued a flow of advanced ordnance to Jordan. The administration's 1983 peace plan struck most Israelis and many American Jews as a dangerous departure from the Camp David process and a gratuitous American attempt to create some Palestinian entity, possibly in confederation with Jordan. Although the administration at least formally honored Henry Kissinger's 1975 pledge not to negotiate with PLO representatives until the PLO explicitly acknowledged the legitimacy of the Jewish state and accepted UN resolutions 242 and 338, it all but openly regretted the promise and privately evaded it.

American policy toward South Africa and Central America posed ethical problems. The security and prosperity of the South African Jewish community may be linked to the preservation of white rule. Israel and South Africa trade with each other and exchange military information, to the discomfort of many American Jews. For apartheid and de facto American indulgence of its continuation offended Jews as much as they did most other Americans. Israel had sold arms to the Somoza regime and other repressive governments in the region. The PLO publicly supported the Sandinistas in Nicaragua and possibly sent them weapons. Most Jews were not prepared to follow Israel on a course morally repugnant to them, even when they were disposed to make special allowances for Israeli necessities.

On the social agenda, the president's fervent advocacy of public school prayer rendered Jews uneasy, particularly within the context of reiterated statements of America as a Christian community. Occasional references to the Judeo-Christian roots of individual morality sounded too much like afterthoughts to be reassuring. Just as quotas reminded Jews of the period not that far in the past when they excluded Jews, prayer recalled the compulsory Christian religiosity of the same era. And although on the abortion issue, Orthodox Jews allied themselves with fundamentalists, Catholics, and Reagan loyalists, most Jews were pro-choice.

Atmospherics may in the end have been most influential. Unlike Carter, Ford, and Nixon, President Reagan surrounded himself almost entirely with white, overwhelmingly male, and utterly Christian advisers at senior staff levels. The echoes are those of the country club locker rooms in which good old boys trade good old-time anti-Semitic and anti-black stories and epithets. Although Jewish spokesmen were unhappy with Mondale's cautious handling of Jesse Jackson, they valued his long record of public support.

Jerry Falwell, Reagan's devout admirer, also embraced Israel fervently, but the terms of endearment embarrassed many American Jews. True, Jews were among those to be lifted to glory come Armageddon, but only those among them who acknowledged in time Jesus Christ as their savior. For the remainder, the outlook was decidedly sticky. Mutual tributes to each other by Falwell and Menachem Begin added nothing to the joy of secular Jews already distressed by Begin's encouragement of orthodox fundamentalism in Israel. America has done well by Jews, but the overt anti-Semitism mostly of the past and the covert anti-Semitism of the present frequently express themselves in terms of religious derogation.

Jews have prospered financially and professionally as doctors, lawyers, businessmen, scientists, and university professors in a secular society. Doors opened for young Jews because of Supreme Court decisions, secular organizations like the American Civil Liberties Union, and the horrifying lesson of the holocaust that anti-Semitism at its extreme equals extermination of hated human targets. Certainly opposition to anti-Semitism ranks low if anywhere on the agenda of fundamentalist denominations. Catholic teachings until recently encouraged anti-Semitism on grounds that reached back to the Jewish role in the crucifixion of Jesus. On the playgrounds of America a generation ago, the epithet "Christ killer" too often was yelled by children from Christian homes at Jewish classmates. For Jews with memories, religiosity is bad news and the worse for presidential embrace of its more extravagant demands and loudest voiced prophets.

Jews and yuppies share ambivalences. Yuppies, like a majority of Jews (the categories overlap), are libertarians in their attitudes to sex, pornography, drugs, prayer, and abortion. They are grateful beneficiaries of Reaganomics. In 1984, yuppies overlooked, discounted, or ignored the administration's anti-libertarian sentiments on moral issues and voted their perceived financial interests. Most Jews made the opposite decision.

Presidential politics in 1988 require reconciliation for both parties of the clashing priorities of interventionist religionists and libertarian yuppies. Reagan economics unite traditional conservatives, prospering Jews and Catholics, and yuppies. These same groups reject the moral authoritarianism implicit in the Reagan social agenda. Secular and observant Jews are equally unlikely to fare well in an aggressively Christian America. Ronald Reagan's unique political charisma sufficed to keep comparatively intact the coalition of disparate allies that in 1984 carried forty-nine of the fifty states.

No other Republican is likely to do as well, but a winning formula for Democrats is just as elusive. Whatever twists and turns our politics take, the fundamentalist right and its free-market allies will exert continuing influence in at least one branch of the federal government—the judiciary. By the end of the Reagan era, half or more of the federal judiciary will be Reagan appointees, carefully screened for "correct" views on abortion and prayer, civil rights, and free-market economics. The White House has nominated young, vigorous activists likely to be busily rewriting earlier, liberal judicial findings well into the twenty-first century. A second valuable Reagan legacy to the political right is fiscal disorder. Enormous federal deficits and the swelling annual interest costs of servicing a national debt that far more than doubled under Mr. Reagan have shifted congressional attention from social to budgetary issues. Whether or not this fiscal policy was deliberately conceived to tic the hands of more generous subsequent presidents and Congresses, it will have that effect. It will take a courageous presidential nominee, after the Mondale fiasco, to advocate tax increases. Yet these are essential to repair Reagan damage to social services, let alone advance toward universal health services, decent quantities of moderate-priced housing, and public-job creation. On economic issues, conservatives have probably won for the rest of this century. Or so it seems in 1986.

## THE RELIGIOUS LEFT

Fortunately, a good deal more is going on in the community of the religious than the activities of the right. Its opponents might be encouraged by the appearance of Jerry Falwell on the front cover of the September 2, 1985, issue of *Time*.[34] The newsmagazines are notorious for their celebration of trends and personalities soon after they have peaked in importance. Not that the numbers in early 1986 support the application of this generality to the fundamentalists. A thousand or so of the country's 9,642 radio stations are religious in programming, the bulk of it evangelical or fundamentalist.

Several qualifications need to be added to those earlier made. Although the more numerous evangelicals, one of whose most notable figures is Billy Graham, share fundamentalist certainty about the inerrancy of scripture, evangelicals are far more willing to cooperate with more liberal Protestants than are fundamentalists. Graham himself has taken a far softer line on disarmament and relations with the Soviets than Falwell. And just for variety, the religious right also harbors seven million Pentecostals, whose TV spokesman Pat Robertson commands an audience comparable to Falwell's. Pentecostals indulge themselves in faith healing, speaking in tongues, and prophecies purportedly emanating from God, all practices disapproved of by both fundamentalists and evangelicals. Abundant occasions for dissension manifestly exist on the religious right, cooperative as its major spokespersons may be upon many issues.

Media fashion has amplified the sufficiently loud voices of the apostles of the religious right. But their opponents on the left are no forlorn band, no partisans of lost causes. They include radical evangelicals, mainstream social gospel Protestants, liberal Jews, and on two of the identifying left-right positions—economics and foreign policy—most of the American Catholic hierarchy.

Because of the Church's hierarchical organization, it is convenient to start with official Catholicism. In his tireless tours of the globe, Pope John Paul II has made it utterly clear that Latin American liberation theology in any version that endeavors to combine elements of Marxism, notably the central significance of class struggle, with Catholic doctrine is as abhorrent to him as polygamy, birth control, headhunting, witchcraft, cannibalism, abortion, and infanticide. Father Ernesto Cardenal, the poet and Sandinista minister of culture, has been suspended from priestly functions as punishment for his refusal to resign his government position. At the same time, the Pope decries with moving sincerity glaring inequities in the distribution of the world's goods within Third World societies in particular and capitalist economies in general. His analysis of the Third World's exploitation by the United States and Western Europe parallels in effect if not in rhetoric that of secular radicals, many of them influenced by Marxism.

John Paul II's distrust of capitalism is also cultural, a critique formerly associated with secular friends of high culture like *Partisan Review*. His distaste for materialism, the consumer society, the ethos of profit maximization, and the threat to individual autonomy of unchecked corporate power all make him in American terms a practicing radical, the best efforts of Simon, Novak, et al. to the contrary notwithstanding. To emphasize, as the Pope routinely does, the Church's preferential option for the poor is at minimum to criticize capitalism for doing less than it ethically should to improve the condition of those who somehow exist on the margins of prosperous societies.

The lay letter does not challenge the legitimacy of collective bargaining between unions and corporations, but its enthusiasm is decidedly muted. Yet from Leo XIII's *De Rerum Novarum* through John XXIII's *Mater et Magistra* to the current pontiff's own *Laborem Exercens (On Human Work)*, a century of authoritative Roman utterances has commended unions as protections of working people against exploitation and as opportunities for communal protection. Squirm as they do, the authors of the lay letter simply cannot enlist John Paul II in their crusade for free markets. Speaking of unions, the Pope declared, "The experience of history teaches that organizations of this type are an indispensable element of social life, especially in modern industrialized societies."[35] Insofar, and it is very far indeed, as Catholic doctrine emphasizes social solidarity and the reciprocal obligations of rich and poor, employers and their employees, young and old, it contravenes the ethos of free markets where most things, if not quite yet everything, are bought and sold.

Therefore, the bishops' pastoral, prudently released just after instead of just before the 1984 presidential election, is in content not especially surprising. It is no more than the latest in a series of pronouncements on the American economy, the first of which, *Problems of Social Reconstruction*, appeared in 1919. That document vigorously advocated maintenance and even extension of wage gains made under pressure of World War I labor shortages. Its call for "prevention of monopolistic control of commodities, adequate government regulation . . . and heavy taxation of incomes, excess profits, and inheritances" invited predictable denunciation from the National Association of Manufacturers, which labeled the bishops' support of unemployment insurance and collective bargaining "partisan, pro–labor union, socialistic propaganda."[36]

*Plus ça change, plus c'est la même chose*. The well-known sociologist Peter L. Berger, a trifle less intemperately, regretted that "the Catholic bishops are increasingly sounding like the left wing of the Democratic party gathered for prayer." They are in the bad company of "official mainline Protestantism." Worst of all is the virulent combination of Swedish heresy and misguided American Protestant liberalism (radicalism?): "If their pastoral letter reads in places like a translation from the Swedish, it is also, minus a few papal quotations, reminiscent of the social action pronouncements of the United Methodist Church."[37] It is all "profoundly sad," although "One should be grateful for small favors: far better an American Catholic document that reads like a translation from Swedish than from Albanian."[38]

What do the deluded prelates actually say in their sixty-one closely printed triple-column pages down which march 333 numbered paragraphs, buttressed by four pages of citations of sources sacred and profane? The cover page of *Catholic Social Teaching and the U.S. Economy* identifies as "Three priority principles" "fulfillment of the basic needs of the poor" as "highest priority"; "increased participation in society by people living on its margins takes priority over the preservation of privileged concentrations of power, wealth and income; and meeting human needs and increasing participation should be priority targets in the investment of wealth, talent and human energy."[39]

By these criteria, the lush American economy does not rate high: "The fact that more than 15 percent of our nation's population lives below the official poverty level is a social and moral scandal that must not be ignored." Moreover, "The distribution of income and wealth in the United States is so inequitable that it violates the minimum standard of distributive justice. In 1982 the richest 20 percent of Americans received more income than the bottom 70 percent combined. The disparities in the distribution of wealth are even more extreme."[40] And, "Our nation has a moral obligation to help reduce poverty in the Third World."[41] Again, "The most urgent priority for U.S. domestic economy policy is the creation of new jobs with adequate pay and decent working conditions. ... Current levels of unemployment are morally unjustified."[42]

If only the bishops had halted with theology and exhortation, their open letter would have been universally ignored, the sad fate of so many of its predecessors. However, these overweening prelates proceeded to enter flagrantly the realm of politics, economics, and social action sacred to economists and other credentialed experts. Infuriated critics attacked most vehemently the bishops' arrant, unapologetic endorsement of redistribution, an issue forever identified with George McGovern's gallant 1972 loss to Richard Nixon. Since human needs are unmet, "The condition establishes a strong presumption against inequality of income or wealth as long as there are poor, hungry and homeless people in our midst. It means that all persons must be prepared to come to the aid of those who are deprived, primarily through a system of taxation based on assessment according to ability to pay." True, the bishops hedge their position: "This presumption can be overridden only if an absolute scarcity of resources makes the fulfillment of the basic needs of all strictly impossible or if unequal distribution stimulates productivity in a way that truly benefits the poor."[43] But no hedge weakens pastoral conviction that if the private economy cannot generate enough jobs, it is government's responsibility to create additional slots for the unemployed.

In this document, government's social responsibility looms unfashionably large. For dutiful students of Catholic doctrine, the "basic norm" harks back to Leo XIII's *Rerum Novarum*: "if, therefore, any injury has been done to or threatens either the common good or the interests of individual groups, which injury cannot in any other way be repaired or prevented, it is necessary for public authority to intervene."[44] In our time, "Government, therefore, has a moral function: that of enabling citizens to coordinate their actions to protect basic rights and ensure economic justice for all members of the commonwealth."[45] So, "We recommend that the nation make a major new policy commitment to achieve full employment. We believe that an unemployment rate in the range of 3 percent or 4 percent is a reasonable definition of full employment in the United States today."[46] Back, in other words, to the standard set by John Kennedy's economists a quarter of a century ago.

Nor is this the end of the document's efforts to resurrect liberalism. The bishops advocate welfare reform, deplore an existing "patchwork arrangement marked by benefit levels that leave recipients poor; gaps in coverage; inconsistent treatment of poor people in similar situations; wide variations in benefits across states; humiliating treatment of clients; and frequent complaints about 'red tape,' and reprove our punitive attitude toward the poor."[47] Bad enough for true-blue free-marketers and celebrants of the *Rambo* ethos. Worse follows. Mild though their language is, careful as they are to oppose "statism," the bishops are planners. They simply do not trust free markets to employ all the employable, succor all the vulnerable, and embrace all the marginalized. They aver that "In an advanced industrial economy like ours, all actors in society, including government, must actively and positively cooperate in forming national economic policies."[48] The context makes clear a preference for some variety of industrial policy, indicative planning, or mechanism for establishing and advancing national priorities.

In the bishops' eyes, the unchecked play of the market inflicts malignant side effects here at home. In the Third World, uncurbed markets have inflicted vastly more damage. Blame for the international-debt burdens of poor countries is distributed among OPEC, American commercial banks which practically shoveled OPEC deposits in the 1970s to Latin American and other clients, and International Monetary Fund loan-guarantee policies that "usually fall most heavily on the poor through reduction of public services, consumer subsidies and often wages."[49] Necessary repairs include "serious consideration to some forgiveness of such debts owed to it," American pressure on the IMF to modify its policies, and more generous foreign aid from industrialized to developing countries.[50] There is urgent need for a new international order: "To restructure the international order along lines of greater equity and participation will require a far more stringent application of the principles of affirmative action than we have seen in the United States itself."[51] Not content with endorsing pernicious affirmative action in the United States, the bishops seek universal application of this unpopular intervention into private choices.

The pastoral scrupulously eschews the rhetoric of class. No echoes of conflict between rich and poor, owners and workers, resonate painfully in Rome to remind the Curia of the proscribed tunes of liberation theology. The planning contemplated is to occur within the ambit of American politics and the disorderly play of the usual organized interests. The tax revisions the bishops apparently have in mind would not expropriate the wealthy. At most they might restore the mild progressivity of the pre-Reagan tax code. Unemployment targets in the 3–4 percent neighborhood were widely accepted as centrist policy in the 1960s and in 1978 incorporated into the Humphrey-Hawkins Balanced Growth and Full Employment Act.

The pastoral poignantly reminds its readers just how reactionary American politics have become. During his first presidential term, Richard Nixon of all people made a serious effort to reform welfare and convert the patchwork of state programs into a single federally financed and administered benefit. His Family Assistance Program would also have supplemented the low incomes of the badly paid working poor. Yet radical is one of the few derogatory adjectives not applied to our most notorious ex-president. Until the mid-1970s foreign aid flowed to the Third World in amounts whose restoration (in current dollars) the bishops would surely welcome as a vast improvement over recent appropriations. The war on poverty was a Democratic innovation, but it was the Nixon administration that vastly enlarged appropriations for education, food stamps, job training, Medicare, Medicaid, nutrition supplements for pregnant women and infants, and a long list of other benefits sponsored undeniably by Democrats but accepted with varying degrees of enthusiasm by Republicans in a spirit perhaps not noticeably different from that of Democrats in 1981, who clambered hastily onto the Reagan bandwagon and endorsed tax and benefit cuts only recently alien to their party's posture as friend of the needy and critic of the rich and powerful.

Nevertheless, those who stay where they are while the parade marches past them define themselves by their relative isolation, and, if they don't define themselves, their critics will gladly undertake the task of relabeling. Peter Berger justifiably located the bishops in the company of the Democratic left wing. No matter that at least on domestic policy, members of that wing, who do their best—such is the temper of the days—to elude so dangerous a designation, not so long ago swam comfortably in mainstream politics. Nor is it relevant that Berger's epithet "Swedish," used to evoke admiration for an efficient society which simultaneously combined full employment, a lavish menu of social protections, a high standard of living, and heavily taxed capitalists who, contrary to the teachings of supply-side economists, continued to sponsor research and development and invest heavily in their commercial applications. That "left" is where the personally conventional, frequently Republican American bishops are located testifies not to their change of mind or heart but to the rightward migration of most Americans, Catholics emphatically included.

## JEWS OF THE RELIGIOUS LEFT

Jews, as I have had occasion to note without joy, are prominent among conservative intellectuals who first prepared a policy agenda for Ronald Reagan and then devoted their considerable skills to justifying its application and consequences. Irving Kristol and Nathan Glazer of *The Public Interest*, Norman Podhoretz of *Commentary*, and their stable of contributors, many of them also Jews, do their best to convey the impression that intelligent Jews, whatever the radical indiscretions of their youth, have matured into the sort of conservatives who identify the prosperity and security of themselves and Israel with low-tax, free-enterprise, and military-buildup Reagan policies. James Atlas in the August 25, 1985, *New York Times Magazine*, placed that newspaper's imprimatur on the rightward drift of the intellectual community, Jewish and gentile. His piece was adorned by a full-page portrait of Norman Podhoretz in a grim mood. At a guess, more university types read small journals of Marxist persuasion than Kristol's and Podhoretz's only slightly more widely disseminated periodicals. At a second conjecture, the combined readership of ideological journals, left and right, is a small fraction of the horde who scan the pages of the *Chronicle of Higher Education* and the Sunday *New York Times* ad pages on the hunt for job openings.

One shouldn't underestimate the importance of sheer hype. *Commentary* has fewer subscribers now than it did in the 1960s when its pages harbored such inveterate disturbers of the peace as Norman Mailer, Paul Goodman, Norman Brown, and Edgar Friedenberg. But the mainstream media ignore Marxists except in Central America and occasionally cite *Commentary* and company. How thrilling that Ronald Reagan was moved to elevate Jeane Kirkpatrick first to the United Nations and then to the lecture circuit after reading her *Commentary* disquisition on the eternal iniquity of Marxist regimes and the transitory nature of their authoritarian counterparts.

It is only just to concede that in the 1980s Jewish conservatives make more noise than their radical opponents. Inevitably, the novelty of Jewish conservatism becomes one more story for newsmagazines and serious newspapers of large circulations. The evidence, nevertheless, is scant to nonexistent that Jews have moved right on social policy and most foreign policy issues as their incomes have risen and their alliance with blacks has fractured. In 1984, TV exit polls revealed that Jewish voters preferred Mondale to Reagan by approximately two-to-one margins. They projected the national total from small samples of Jewish voters. The American Jewish Congress, searching for more accurate measurement, surveyed Jewish voters in eighty-five different locations around the country. Respondents totaled 2,932, five or six times the number interrogated by TV.[51] Seventy-one percent went Democratic and only 27 percent Republican. Educated and presumably more prosperous

Jews voted still more heavily Democratic. And although the gender gap was wider than in the electorate at large, men preferred Mondale to Reagan by a 62 percent vote. Their wives, daughters, aunts, cousins, mothers, and grandfathers, wiser in their generation than Jewish males, cast an astonishing 77 percent of their ballots for the Democratic ticket. Jesse Jackson's casual anti-Semitism and his reluctance to disown his supporter Louis Farakhan's virulent form of the disease strongly influenced a third of the Reagan voters, but three-fifths of the Mondale majority reported that they were quite sensibly more disturbed by the president's reiterated advocacy of a close relationship between religion and government.

Jews who have flourished in a generally secular society understandably doubt that they will fare equally well in a Christian America. They proved able to distinguish between the minor threat posed by a black presidential candidate to whom Mondale reacted with perhaps excessive caution, and the substantial danger to themselves and their children implied by de facto establishment of a state religion. If preference for a secular state correlates with other positions, these tend at least for Jews to be liberal. Twice as large a percentage of Jews as of the general population (41 vs. 20) indentify themselves as liberal and a mere 17 percent of the former admit to conservatism. Translated into attitudes on a range of issues, 43 percent think government does too little for blacks and Hispanics and only 10 percent judge that too much is done; 89 percent oppose a ban on abortion; 71 percent oppose increased defense spending; and 90 percent oppose public school prayer. Moreover, nearly four-fifths of Jews favor more government action against unemployment and 86 percent would devote more federal money to education.[53]

The undeniable prosperity of the Jewish community evidently has not diminished its members' attachment to the traditional agenda of liberal action. Five percent of Jews had incomes below $10,000, less than a third of the national figure. At the other end of the income distribution, two and a half times as many Jews enjoyed incomes in excess of $50,000 than was true of their fellow citizens.[54] Jewish conservatives who supported Ronald Reagan argue that their opponents fail to understand their own interest. The point is arguable. It may be that liberal Jews judge their long-range financial interests more acutely than conservative Jews. Those interests are best served by social and political stability. To such stability black and Hispanic poverty constitutes an implicit threat. A large, disaffected underclass is vulnerable to the temptations of urban riots and the scapegoating of Jewish merchants and landlords as traditional targets of opportunity. The funds and programs that improve education and career alternatives for young members of ghetto populations reduce property-insurance rates; diminish robberies and burglaries; shrink instead of enlarge the South Bronxes and Bedford-Stuyvesants of urban America; and reduce the cost of prisons, policemen, and the rest of the criminal justice establishment. So to say is not to deny the persistence of ideals of social justice. It is to suggest that many Jews are capable of connecting such ideals with their own personal and financial security. Indeed, in such potential connections or reconnections is located the hope of liberal revival in the community at large.

As befits their educational and economic status, Jews are politically sophisticated enough to reject the simplistic equation of hard-line anti-Communist attitudes and huge military appropriations with the security of the state of Israel. A June 2, 1985, resolution of the American Jewish Congress, for example, urged "the Congress and the Administration to substantially cut defense spending in the proposed fiscal year 1986 defense budget and reorder our national priorities to ensure the health and welfare of our nation and its economy." The sacred cause of Israel for the Jewish majority simply does not legitimate policies and groups otherwise repugnant. Thus, as early as October 4, 1981, the governing council of the American Jewish Congress phrased its judgment of the Moral Majority in these sharp terms:

> We are mindful that many leaders and spokesmen for the Evangelical Right vigorously defend and support the State of Israel. We acknowledge that support, but this consideration is irrelevant to our assessment of their domestic programs. The damage done by their efforts to curtail domestic freedom is not made less by the soundness of their views on Israel. Although we welcome their support

for Israel this will in no way cause us to mitigate or modify our opposition to the many policies and practices of the Evangelical Right with which we disagree.[55]

Although the American Jewish Congress is among the most liberal of Jewish organizations, its policy positions evidently command support from many other Jewish groups. Each year the National Jewish Community Relations Advisory Council, which coordinates eleven national and 111 local Jewish organizations, issues a "Joint Program Plan" as a guide to its member bodies. The 1984–85 document focused on the continuing problem of poverty and deplored administration budget cuts in programs addressed to low-income families. It questioned the rate of increase in military spending and expressed alarm at presidential support of constitutional amendments designed to ban abortion and allow public school prayer. On affirmative action, possibly the most divisive issue between Jews and blacks, the NJCRAC struggled hard to accommodate traditional Jewish opposition to quotas with recognition of the special history and needs of black Americans. Although "We regard quotas as inconsistent with principles of equality; and as harmful in the long run to all, including those groups, some individual members of which may benefit from specific quotas under specific circumstances at specific times," at the same time "We recognize the need for numerical data and statistical procedures to measure and help assure the effectiveness of affirmative action programs."[56] These are the very techniques that the Reagan administration seeks to eliminate as valid measures of the success of affirmative action for government contractors.

In 1984, "Jews returned to a 'normal' 'Democratic distance' of about twenty-five points between their presidential voting and that of the general population."[57] Jews vote even more overwhelmingly for Democratic congressional candidates. As Earl Raab and Seymour M. Lipset, two respected political scientists, also note, "Jews may have become more affluent but they still do not belong to the same social network as the middle- and upper-class white Protestants who form the backbone of the Republican party."[58] Many Jews apparently voted not so much against a president perceived as deliberately hostile to them as for their traditional party and their traditional friends. Subliminally, a good many Jews sense more anti-Semitism in the Republican than in the Democratic party. Raab and Lipset's upper-class Protestant social network operates to exclude Jews. The line is fine if not invisible between such exclusion and polite or less polite social anti-Semitism. In sum, Jews have kept the liberal faith because their traditions and their interests are clearly identified with secular social justice.

## MAINLINE PROTESTANTS

Mainline Protestants do not speak in tongues. They interpret scripture as genuinely the word of God, but not the literal denotation of each syllable of both Testaments as strained through history, several languages, and the textual corruptions unavoidable in so complex a literary enterprise as the transmission of words composed two millennia ago, long before Gutenberg's movable type and the era of computers. The pious can believe that an omnipotent deity commits no typographical errors without imputing similar beatitude to fallible mortals. Mainstream Protestants seem to derive guidance and inspiration from the twentieth century: the social gospel of its early decades, the neoorthodoxy of Karl Barth, and the Christian realism of Reinhold Niebuhr. As coordinated by the National Council of Churches in the United States and the global World Council of Churches, Protestant mainliners support social reform, racial justice, less inegalitarian distribution of income and wealth, full employment, comprehensive health protection, environmental safety and preservation, cooperation with Catholics and Jews, redirection of budgetary priorities away from the Pentagon and toward social initiatives, sanctions against South Africa, a nuclear freeze, abstention from intervention in Nicaragua, and genuine arms-control negotiations with the Soviets. Peter Berger did not libel them when he lumped these Protestants with the soft-on-Sweden Catholic bishops.

Official Protestants share most policy preferences with official Jews. With varying nuances, they differ on Israel. Protestants of the left favor recognition of the PLO as the official representative of Palestinian aspirations and the creation of an independent Palestinian state. Only a minority of Jews agree, although the size of that minority probably is growing. Again, Protestants accept with fewer reservations affirmative-action schemes that some Jewish groups deplore as tantamount to quotas. With even liberal Catholics, Jewish dissent focuses on abortion and birth control, issues upon which John Paul II's adamant attitude controls his church's position. Mainstream Protestants accept "artificial" techniques, including the Pill. Catholics officially (Catholic practice approximates that of the non-Catholic majority) decry all "unnatural" techniques of population control.

Thus, on a substantial range of issues, most or many *organized* Protestants, Jews, and Catholics agree. These include funding for social programs, more equitable taxes, high-employment policies, a low-calorie diet for the Pentagon, a nuclear freeze, and restraint in the holy war against Marxists either where they are strong as in the Soviet Union or weak as in Central America.

How representative of lay opinion these Protestant religious organizations are, is open to serious question. The National Council of Churches and the World Council of Churches increasingly are under siege both from religious conservatives and from their own communicants. Within the denominations, defections to fundamentalist sects are numerous enough to cause serious concern. That concern is intensified by the increasing number of congregations which, while remaining within official denominations, select spiritual leaders sympathetic to fundamentalist positions. Episcopalians, once the richest and most self-confident of Protestants, steadily have declined in membership. Suffering from an identity crisis, they waver neurotically among Bishop Paul Moore's social activism, the social quietism of respectable, suburban congregations, and their own charismatics. Complacency comes harder these days to Episcopalians than ever before.

Then there are the respectable Presbyterians. Not quite as rich as the Episcopalians, they are numerous enough to be divided into southern and northern branches only recently reconciled as "the Presbyterian Church (U. S. A.)." In 1983 and 1984, they decided to prepare a document whose ultimate title, "Toward a Just, Caring, and Dynamic Society," enunciated

## New Wars of Religion

concerns similar to those of the Catholic bishops' pastoral. In this worthy enterprise, Presbyterians were handicapped. They drew upon a smaller body of less-settled theology than did their Catholic brethren. Scripture was naturally available on an equal-opportunity basis, but Catholics could cite in addition Church Fathers, papal encyclicals, and an American Catholic tradition of social concern for vulnerable groups. Moreover, the Catholic mode of church government remains abidingly authoritarian. Although the bishops heard assorted economists, among them Herbert Stein and Charles Schultze, chairmen respectively of Nixon's and Carter's Council of Economic Advisers, and other social scientists before they issued their document, they were under no obligation to consult the opinions of lay Catholics nor in any systematic fashion did they do so. Save briefly and sporadically in the wild 1960s, college teachers by and large do not design course curricula in collaboration with students. No more do bishops share their teaching responsibility with those whose appropriate role is gratefully to make themselves available for instruction.

In conformity to their own tradition, Presbyterians proceeded to solicit the views of the laity. Their Committee on a Just Political Economy, a diverse assortment of clerics, lawyers, academics, business executives, and social activists, mostly but not entirely Presbyterian in affiliation, met *en banc* for two-day sessions in 1982, 1983, and 1984. Numerous smaller meetings heard from economists and other experts of varying perspective. A national teleconference late in 1983 drew into participation lay groups in many cities. Finally, on January 22, 1985, the committee issued a 124-page report addressed to the Advisory Council on Church and Society of the United Presbyterian Church.

What an odd document it turned out to be, a mouse timidly peering out of a paper mountain and every now and then emitting an imitation of a roar. Heeding the differing interests and political views of the laity as revealed by the teleconference and research evaluation of its significance, the authors of the report concluded that the world is a complicated place, simple solutions seldom were available, public policies often led to unexpected and unwelcome consequences, and caution almost invariably was advisable. As the introduction put it,

> ... the major part of our report consists of an interrogative exploration of complex and inter-related issues, seeking to stimulate continuing discussion and exploration rather than to foreclose it [sic!]. We have sought to ground our own exploration of these policy issues in a framework of the values we believe to underlie our Christian vocation in the society, and to carry on our discussion in each area in a deliberate dialogue between those values and the economic and political choices that confront us in the formation of social policy.... These policy issues are in our everyday conversation as citizens and participants in the political and economic structures. We are persuaded that such everyday conversation should include the question of what values should shape our economic and political policy choices.

Hard upon this stupefying prose followed twenty-nine pages of platitudes. There are reminders of biblical calls for fairness and justice, inevitable reference to Madison's acceptance of diverse interests in *The Federalist Papers*, endorsement both of individualism and community, affirmation of the legitimacy of government, emphasis upon the role of voluntary organizations, and exhortations to the business community to look beyond narrow obedience to law and toward wider ethical responsibility.

Then came exercises in complexity. What should be done about Mireille Cadeau, a Haitian detained for fourteen months, now employed as a Brooklyn house cleaner? Or Angel and Emily Vargas, who both work hard at low wages, save as much as they can, take no vacations, haunt discount stores, and still cannot afford to buy a house in their neighborhood because interest rates are so high? Then there's Arnie Hatfield, who used to earn $10 an hour at Firestone in Pottstown, Pennsylvania. When the plant shut down in 1980, he got an $8.50-an-hour job as a machine-shop foreman. That lasted six months. Now Arnie works twelve hours a week in a garage at little more than the minimum wage. He would like to send his teenage sons to college but the family needs their earnings for fuel oil. Arnie's wife earns so little as a teacher's aide that her bimonthly checks don't even cover mortgage payments. But "Arnie considers himself one of the lucky ones. Many of his neighbors face mortgage foreclosures, crumbling marriages, untreated illnesses, and developing alcohol problems."[59]

What ought a just society to do? Give money through the church to the Arnies and Mireille? Or should the church open a soup kitchen or establish a college scholarship fund for children of laid-off workers? Perhaps Presbyterians should agitate for laws regulating plant closings? Are training programs for displaced workers the answer? What about employee participation in management or worker ownership as clues to motivation, efficiency, and enhanced competitiveness? Should government create jobs fixing deteriorating roads, bridges, sewers, and water systems? Then there is macroeconomic policy. Lower interest rates would make mortgages cheaper and American industry more competitive. No end of dilemmas for the conscientious.

"Well," sighs the report, "that's quite a laundry list." Who pays? What form should payment take—taxes, tithes, voluntary contributions? Will Presbyterians who have done well in the world and benefited from Reaganomics sacrifice valuable interest and property-tax deductions or subject more Social Security benefits to taxation? Are the faithful able to accept even more government action? Soon the text broods over the complications of the world as an international economy in which "some economic policies that are good for some people are bad for others."[60] Hence, "Some political economic issues require major rethinking and new ways of understanding. Our fundamental moral beliefs will not change, but the way we apply them has to change because the world has changed."[61]

How do such weighty musings apply to distributive justice? Like Catholic bishops, the Presbyterian drafters worry about the marginalized who are "excluded from any role in making economic decisions, directly or through the political process, even economic decisions that can drastically change their lives."[62] They are "deeply distressed by the attitudes held by many Americans, including some Presbyterians, about poverty and economic justice. These attitudes seem to blame the poor for being poor, minorities for being discriminated against, the elderly for being old, and women for trying to earn a fair wage."[63] Hence, "Our focus must be on improving the way our economy works for all of us. We need to change this harsh, punitive economy into a caring economy."[64] The poor in particular need help. Federal programs did reduce the incidence of poverty. Lower unemployment rates would be enormously effective in further reductions. The effect of Reaganomics—cuts in social programs, tax changes that cost the poor money, and the mini-depression of 1981 and 1982—reversed earlier progress.

Blacks are in particularly bad shape. Affirmative action "does indeed force many employers to pay more attention to hiring minorities than they otherwise would" but "it is hard to enforce" and "can steal the pride of accomplishment from minorities who get jobs based solely on their qualifications." Still, "we strongly support affirmative action for one simple reason: we know of no better way to keep up the pressure to break down the barriers."[65] And needless to say, justice for Hispanics, Asians, Native Americans, and women as well as blacks "cries out for moral and spiritual leadership in our churches, our communities, and throughout our nation."[66] Lapsing as the text from time to time does into controversial policy, it endorses the concept of comparable worth but hastens to add the caveat that "a sudden upward shift of certain wages throughout the economy might involve massive disruptions." Thus, "Adjustments over time may be appropriate, but action is necessary."[67] If anticlimax remained possible it was contained in this unstriking conclusion: ". . . we propose a serious, in-depth discussion of the issue, one that involves the entire country in an effort to build a consensus on what is fair, and to encourage men and women to enter all occupations."[68]

Fair is fair. Social Security reforms here endorsed will cost Presbyterians money, particularly the most affluent. In a rare instance of specificity the drafters call for increasing the Social Security tax base to $60,000 and including investment income. Social Security benefits should become fully taxable for the prosperous. If the Social Security trust fund runs out, it is perfectly acceptable to copy European practice and supplement trust-fund receipts with general tax revenues. Among the improvements in the lot of children that "we should consider are more public assistance, larger contributions from fathers, more federal funding for day-care, and drastic reorientation" of adoption and foster care. And it should go without repetition that "If handled with Christian care and love and seasoned with economic reality, the relationship between all racial and ethnic groups in the U.S. can be a creative, expansive, and joyful experience for all of us." Best of all, "Then our economy will be able to run on all cylinders."[69]

Before Presbyterian duty is done, there's the rest of the world to fret over. When the American economy falters or Congress erects barriers against the exports of poor countries, its impact upon "a poor child of a large landless family engaged in the plantation or in the export-oriented sector of a low-income family . . . may easily result in a deterioration of income of 50 percent or more . . . severe health and nutritional problems . . . higher risks of infant and child death."[70] Growth and equity can be reconciled: "this Committee believes that greater income equality than we now have can, if accomplished in the right way and accompanied by appropriate economic policies, create [sic!] more and stronger growth than we now enjoy, while directly improving the lives of many of our neighbors."[71] But, pray tell, what is the right way?

The huge budget deficit and the swelling national debt raise issues of stewardship for Presbyterians. They also complicate the pursuit of equity. Taxes must be raised. Rich Presbyterians should pay more, for "The federal tax cuts passed in 1981 and 1982 would have done the Sheriff of Nottingham proud."[72] There is no justification for special tax treatment of capital gains. Inheritance levies should rise. A progressive consumption tax would be both fair and an incentive to save. Military spending ought to decline and skilled scientists, engineers, and technicians be redirected to productive civilian tasks.

Unemployment entails both human and material waste. So, "We need some kind of full employment policy. Better yet, a full employment commitment. A commitment that is shared by us all."[73] Government must devote more money to job creation and job training. The Swedes have kept unemployment low during world recessions by an active labor-market policy that emphasizes training, relocation, job creation, and careful placement. It's not easy to emulate Swedes, for care must be taken to avoid trading one problem for another: "If we fail to design the training and job creation activities carefully and just step hard on the economy's accelerator, we might reduce joblessness, but we also run the risk of setting off a burst of inflation."[74]

The document winds up by debunking five myths: "The operation of 'the market' will correct itself and deal with our problems of justice if it's not interfered with"; "government is our enemy and our biggest problem. Government doesn't do anything useful and can't do anything well"; "The issues are too technical for ordinary people; we should leave it to the experts"; "The best way to serve the common good is for every individual to seek their own goals and welfare"; and, finally, "Individuals can't do anything about these matters. We're helpless against the big interests and the big power."

The anguished caution of the Protestant statement does not quite obscure important similarities between Presbyterians and Catholics. The two groups are not far apart on taxation, social spending, military budgets, and policy toward the Third World. Although the Presbyterians do not embrace planning, they are hospitable toward industrial policy, at least as one more topic for further discussion. Both endorse full employment, though the Presbyterian document does not specify the 3–4 percent unemployment adopted by the bishops as a practical definition of full employment. As the introduction to the Protestant statement avers, cooperation seems perfectly possible on numerous items on the congressional agenda.

Substantial differences persist. The pastoral letter link between theology and specific recommendation is strong. For the Presbyterians it is weak partly because less theology appears relevant to the Committee but for additional reasons as well. The first is the economist's concern with complexity and the unpredictability of second- and third-order effects. The other influence is divergent definitions of mission. With all their professions of deference to expert testimony, the bishops are secure in their teaching role. Catholic communicants owe an obligation to guide their behavior according to authoritative hierarchical pronouncements. Because Presbyterians want to learn as well as instruct, they are obliged to make their messages acceptable to members of their denomination and they cannot avoid qualifications that weaken strategic recommendations. And because some Presbyterians do embrace one or more of the five myths at the document's conclusion and many have benefited from Reagan policies, the report is a transparently negotiated document. Quite remarkably, the bishops' pastoral does not convey the same impression. It could actually have been composed by a single human being, imbued with eloquent passion against poverty, inequality, unemployment, and injustice. The pastoral is almost free of cop-outs: references to other committees and bodies, professions of uncertainty, and invitations for further discussion and study. The bishops look at America and find it flawed. So do the members of the Protestant committee. The bishops take the next step: they advocate specific measures without the crippling reservations and tepid rhetoric of the Presbyterians.

## PROTESTANT RADICALS

Neither Catholics nor Presbyterians venture into the dangerous territory of class. For Catholics, of course, specific emphasis upon capitalists and workers as separate social groups entails the deadly risk of papal displeasure as tantamount to liberation theology and indulgence of Marxist heresy. Too many good Catholics and Presbyterians are capitalists to encourage the framers of either statement to go much further than identify differences of immediate interest between rich and poor and argue that properly formulated public policy will unite these opposing groups in common enjoyment of economic growth, empowerment of the marginalized, and equitable prosperity.

Yet liberation theology overlaps the mainstream liberal social concerns of Catholic bishops and Protestant commissions. Liberation theology, not quite totally condemned by the Vatican, applies class analysis, implicitly or explicitly Marxist, to the maldistributions of income, wealth, and power deplored by mainstream religious liberals. It substitutes calls for structural change for appeals to the conscience of the politically and financially powerful. In Central America, some of its proponents have sanctioned revolution as the only remedy available to the oppressed. Class struggle is endorsed as the only route to social justice. In Nicaragua, Father Cardenal has been deprived of priestly functions but he remains a priest, and, according to his own lights, a faithful son of the Church. There are, especially in foreign affairs, additional parallels between liberals and liberation radicals. Methodists, Presbyterians, members of the Disciples of Christ, the American Lutheran Church, the United Church of Christ, and even some Baptists have endorsed the sanctuary movement, which in defiance of official State Department policy shelters illegal aliens seeking refuge from persecution in El Salvador and other Central American states supported by the White House.

Most distressing to conservative critics is the generalized assault by religious liberals and radicals upon American arms programs, nuclear weapons, support of repressive but fervently anti-Communist regimes, and readiness to intervene against governments suspected of Marxist inclinations. To the editorial writers of the *Wall Street Journal*, who benignly countenance Jerry Falwell's brand of political meddling, church critiques of American capitalism are misinformed and misguided, and church opposition to American foreign policy edges perilously close to actual disloyalty to the United States. Presbyterians who have been in the forefront of the sanctuary movement earn the newspaper's special wrath.

Within the Catholic fold, liberation theorists urge the Church itself to become poor, for, as the Catholic lay critics of the bishops' pastoral sharply noted, the Catholic church is itself a large property owner, heavily dependent on the gifts of its wealthier communicants. There is similar Protestant ferment. Radical Protestants, notably the Sojourners, group themselves in frugal communities, similar in spirit to base groups established by Catholics outside of this country. Not many radical evangelicals have followed the example of the Sojourners group in Washington, D.C. Its fifty-odd members live and work in a slum, distributing food, organizing tenants, and offering family programs. Those who join the community surrender their assets to it, share living costs, and get along on $5,000 per person per year.

Yet signs of the group's growing popularity are visible. Sojourners founder Jim Wallis edits a well-written, slick periodical, *Sojourners Magazine*, among whose contributing editors is Republican Senator Mark Hatfield. Hatfield describes Wallis as a person who "comes on like a shy hick from an Amish community in the Midwest, but he's actually an extremely artful communicator."[75] Many evangelical radicals adopt simple living styles and, like Georgia attorney George Reid, head of the North Carolina Baptist Convention's Christian citizenship-education program, give away large percentages of their incomes. The Reids contribute 20–30 percent of their combined $30,000 income.[76] Radical evangelicals have circulated a pledge of civil disobedience or support for it in case of an American invasion of Nicaragua that by May 1985 had enlisted 62,000 signers.

Like conservative evangelicals, their radical brothers and sisters believe in biblical inerrancy and sexual morality and oppose abortion. But their interpretation of the Bible is sufficiently different from Jerry Falwell's to evoke from Mr. Falwell the verdict that "these men are theological liberals," not genuine evangelicals. At the least, the evangelicals, no differently from Catholics and fellow Protestants, are split. The Sojourners find common ground with liberal Catholic bishops, Protestant peace groups, and Catholic Workers. On practical issues of public policy, they are almost entirely at odds with the free-market, hard-line anti-Communist attitudes of the Moral Majority.

## WHO WILL WIN?

That religion will in the foreseeable future influence politics and play a significant role in the election of candidates for public office, high and low, seems safer than most prophecies. Fundamentalist contributions mightily aided Senator Jesse Helms in his successful 1984 reelection campaign against a popular, moderate Democratic governor.

But by no means are all Protestants or even all evangelicals fundamentalists. As the *Oxford English Dictionary* grapples with the definition of evangelical beliefs, its lexicographers center upon "the doctrine of salvation by faith in the atoning death of Christ ... [it] denies that either good works or the sacraments have any saving efficacy." In smaller type, the *OED* observes that "Other features more or less characteristic of the theology of this school are: a strong insistence on the totally depraved state of human nature consequent on the Fall; the assertion of the sole authority of the Bible in matters of doctrine, and the denial of any power inherent in the Church to supplement or authoritatively interpret the teachings of Scripture; the denial that any supernatural gifts are imparted by ordination; and the view that the sacraments are merely symbols, the value of which consists in the thoughts which they are fitted to suggest."[77] In this sense, Methodism has been particularly influenced by evangelical doctrine. Nothing in the evangelical tradition dictates an imperialistic foreign policy, antipathy to social programs, prayer in public schools, or total prohibition of abortion. Evangelicals and fundamentalists venerate biblical authority. Evangelicals stop short of taking literally each word of scripture, recognize that God's word is transmitted by fallible human beings in several languages, and do not condemn the biblical scholarship that beginning in the nineteenth century analyzed the historicity of biblical texts. Nor do they share the premillennialism of fundamentalists.

Fundamentalists have their own troubles. Even so strong a fundamentalist stronghold as the Southern Baptist Conference has been bitterly torn over appropriate definition of "inerrancy." When scripture speaks of sexual roles, natural events, botany, or geography, is it to be taken as infallible? Jerry Falwell put the matter vividly: "Ask an evangelical whether or not he believes there are really flames in hell, and after a thirty-minute philosophical recitation on the theological implications of eternal retribution in light of the implicit goodness of God, you will still not know what he really believes. Ask a fundamentalist whether he believes there are really flames in hell, and he will simply say 'Yes, and hot ones too.' "[78] All parties, including Falwell, who professes inerrantly to be interpreting inerrant scripture, read sacred documents selectively. Acts 2:44–45 strongly implies that the early Church was no free-enterprise model: "The faithful all lived together and owned everything in common; they sold their goods and possessions and shared out the proceeds among themselves according to what each one needed." The Sojourners and the Catholic base communities in Latin America have taken this passage to heart. There is no indication that free-market fundamentalists have recently returned to it or for that matter remembered that an essay in *The Fundamentals* argued that "a genuine Christian profession" was entirely compatible with personal advocacy of socialism.[79]

Divisions are sharp within most religious communities. On the economy, lay and official policy preferences frequently clash. Although the Church speaks authoritatively on matters of personal morality, notably abortion and contraception, the resemblance of Catholic birth rates to national figures registers substantial lay deviation from papal teachings. Even at the hierarchical level, there are conflicts between theological conservatives such as New York's Cardinal O'Connor and Chicago's Cardinal Bernardin over linkage between prohibition of abortion and nuclear freezes. Cardinal O'Connor puts the anti-abortion crusade at the head of his agenda. Cardinal Bernardin links abortion, arms control, and anti-poverty measures as elements of concerted Church action in support of a right to life.

Methodists, Episcopalians, members of the United Church of Christ, and other mainline Protestants continue to pass resolutions and issue policy documents critical of American foreign policy and friendly to traditional social programs. But as the painful experience of Presbyterian consultation with their communicants demonstrated, it is questionable how high a percentage of these denominations read, let alone endorse, such positions. Much the same holds true for the relationships between individual Jews and the generally liberal official positions of the American Jewish Congress and the American Jewish Committee, themselves somewhat anachronistic testimonials to divisions early in this century between assimilationist German Jews and less educated and less prosperous newcomers from Eastern Europe. If the 1984 voting pattern persists, Jews will remain heavily Democratic so long as Falwell fundamentalists strongly influence Republican policies, appointments, and postures. Should the next Republican presidential candidate distance himself credibly from the Moral Majority on abortion, prayer, and the intrusion of religion more generally into public affairs, Jews will conceivably vote their economic interests, much as non-Jews of similar professional and financial situation did in 1984. If the economy is reasonably buoyant in November 1988, Republicans will presumably fare better than they did four years earlier.

How religion and religiosity will play themselves out is a

fascinating puzzle. Consider it first as a Republican dilemma. Can the party identify a nominee who smothers fundamentalists in public sympathy but winks reassuringly at young and aging lawyers, financial analysts, managers, and miscellaneous urbanites whose lifestyles contrast abruptly with the precepts of the religious right? Evidently these yuppies overwhelmingly supported Ronald Reagan in 1984 out of a reassuring conviction that the old charmer would continue to substitute words for deeds. But Ed Meese's agenda at the Department of Justice may give them pause. Far more aggressive than his placid, equally conservative predecessor, William French Smith, the Attorney General in 1985 boldly asked the Supreme Court to reverse *Roe* v. *Wade* and put the legality of abortion up for grabs in state legislatures. His hard line on drugs and soft line on white-collar peculation will presumably frighten cocaine sniffers and reassure designers of bad-check schemes, cheaters on product-safety tests, and pharmaceutical company employees who neglect to report fatal side effects from new drugs. The two groups—druggies and white-collar criminals—overlap, but presumably the first is larger.

Probably more to the political point, fundamentalists are becoming restive. In 1981 they were persuaded to be patient while the White House concentrated on its tax- and benefit-cut program. The mini-depression of 1981 and 1982 compelled Congress and the White House to react to economic events. But why have anti-abortion and pro-prayer constitutional amendments gone nowhere in 1983, 1984, and 1985? Could it just be that neither the president nor Republican congressional leaders sincerely support the agenda of the religious right? Such suspicions have spread among the faithful. As potential contenders in 1988, none of the leading Republicans—Bush, Baker, Kemp, or Dole—impresses fundamentalists as their spiritual brother. Could any one of the quartet place his hand on his heart and attest to the absolute inerrancy of scripture? Would anyone believe him if he tried?

Just possibly (a thought to make Tip O'Neill even happier than do the royalties from his autobiography) the hard religious right will desert the Republican party and run their own candidate, presumably Senator Jesse Helms or TV evangelist Pat Robertson, much as in 1948 Strom Thurmond, then a

Democrat, ran as a States Rights candidate. The South, in recent elections solidly Republican, would then split three ways to the benefit of Democrats. In other regions, a well-financed third party could quite plausibly subtract enough conservatives from the Republican ticket to tip states to the Democrats. Third parties never win in American politics but their role as spoilers can be substantial. Al D'Amato is New York's junior senator because in 1980 a majority of voters divided their ballots between the Democratic nominee and the veteran Jacob Javits, who, defeated in the Republican primary, drew enough votes on the Liberal line to deny victory to Elizabeth Holtzman. In a sluggish economy, a presidential race between, say, Gary Hart and George Bush, two uncharismatic politicians, might plausibly turn on the conduct of disaffected extreme conservatives, secular or religious. Even in the absence of a third-party entry, a sufficient number of them might stay home on election day to ensure a Democratic victory. Neither major party now contains a potential Reagan, a human phenomenon of fortunate rarity in American politics.

There is a less attractive possibility. The yuppie generation includes settled families trembling on the edge of early middle age, young born-again Christians, precariously employed factory workers, ill-paid couples in fast-food service and dead-end clerical slots, single mothers, and old-style macho males, in numbers far larger than the tiny percentage of expensively educated and well-paid urban lawyers, financial analysts, and assorted manipulators of words and symbols who are celebrated by advertisers as big spenders. Most of the yuppie generation are not particularly prosperous. Wives work because husbands earn less than their fathers did. The traditional families beloved of conservatives are fewer not necessarily because women seek, much less find, fulfillment bagging groceries, keypunching data, assembling computers, or processing Medicare forms but because access to something like the standard package of American consumer goods requires two incomes.

An enduring hope of liberals and radicals is the expectation that financial adversity shifts political attitudes leftward. On occasion, notably in the 1930s, such movement does occur. I shall in the next chapter survey the signs of possible repetition in 1988 and afterwards. But it is at least equally possible that the large legion of disappointed adults will turn for satisfaction to sports, patriotic display, and the old-time religion that sanctions concentration on personal salvation, old-fashioned morality, and the combination of aggression abroad and laissez-faire at home that has defined the Reagan era. Less fervent than Falwellites in crusades against abortion, homosexuality, pornography, and secular humanism, they might well settle for disapproving rhetoric on the part of a George Bush, Robert Dole, or Jack Kemp. Resigned to their meager financial rewards, skeptical of help from any government program, they could plausibly vote nearly as heavily for a Republican presidential nominee in 1988 as they did in 1984. Such an outcome is especially likely in the absence of a clear and convincing Democratic program designed to create new jobs and rising living standards.

Nor is even a serious crisis of the economy any guarantee of an important alliance between religion and liberal, left-liberal, or outright radical politics. Father Coughlin's anti-Semitic, quasi-fascist radio sermons were enormously popular in the worst periods of the Depression. Particularly in the Midwest, Protestant varieties of xenophobia and anti-Semitism flourished. Liberals and leftists blame economic disaster on large corporations and conservative politicians. Farmers and small businessmen in financial distress tend to revert to the worst features of populism—racial and religious scapegoating and paranoid fantasies of conspiracies among Jews, Rockefellers, the Council on Foreign Relations, and the Trilateral Commission.

What of the religious left? With all its divisions on abortion, public school prayer, homosexuality, and pornography, there is considerable agreement at hierarchical or official levels on foreign policy and the economy among Catholics, Jews, and Protestants. On the first score, support for serious arms-control efforts, opposition to nuclear weapons, and dissent from the Reagan administration's Central American policies unites mainstream groups. The Catholic bishops' pastoral has evoked considerably milder Protestant responses, but even so timid a document as the Presbyterian effort registers dissent from Reaganomics and support for more generous funding for social programs. It may be that the religious left, less demoralized than its secular counterpart, will serve as a rallying point and a program resource for Democrats in increasing need of issues more appealing than budget deficits and tax reform of conjectural benefit to their constituents. The pastoral's firm emphasis upon public-job creation, welfare reform, universal health coverage, redistribution, and mild planning may not at the moment command the adherence even of observant Catholics. Yet the time may come when it will be perceived as a landmark of liberal revival.

*Chapter 8*

# The Secular Left: Hope or Fantasy?

FOR SECULAR LIBERALS and radicals, frequently suspicious of organized religion and contemptuous of its doctrines, it is humbling to realize that the religious left in this decade runs a better show than the embarrassingly dejected and intellectually fatigued performances of liberal Democrats, let alone those of social democrats and outright socialists further left.

Times are bad for serious critics of American society. Save in periods of severe economic stress, they are never good. Foreign observers—friendly, derisive, or hostile—have traditionally emphasized American optimism, an element in Ronald Reagan's temperament that contributes to his popularity, just as Jimmy Carter's perceived pessimism subtracted from his popularity and political support. Don't knock, boost, is an always popular admonition.

Here is how one astute visitor viewed American politics. In 1904, Werner Sombart, the German economic historian, at the time sympathetic to the Marxists of his own country, visited the United States, toured factories, conversed with workers and managers, and discussed politics with American radicals. Two years later he wrote *Why Is There No Socialism in the United States?*. His answer is startlingly cogent more than three-quarters of a century after he offered it. America, to begin with, was blessedly free of the curse of feudalism. Class lines were sharper in Europe where the descendants of serfs still deferred in un-American fashion to landowners and new men of power who owned factories and controlled the lives of those

## The Secular Left: Hope or Fantasy?

who worked in them. No doubt, Sombart conceded, class divisions persisted in the land of the free and the home of the brave, but a powerful myth of equality governed social intercourse almost as though these distinctions were inconsequential. Factory owners were indisputably richer than steelworkers and sewing-machine operators, but no one touched his hat or curtsied when the master strolled into the factory or workshop. Sombart marveled at the use of first names by the managed and their managers in casual conversation. Inconceivable in Germany! Where capitalists and workers treat each other as human equals, class bitterness is minimized, especially when many employees plan to become capitalists in the near future.

Radicals had a hard row to hoe for a second reason. American living standards were already higher and steadily rising at a faster rate than in Europe. Reefs of roast beef and mountains of apple pie discouraged political activism. In Sombart's judgment, socialism fed on the European combination of class antagonism and economic deprivation. To be a class-conscious proletarian required acceptance of permanent membership in the working class for oneself and one's children.

Matters were otherwise ordered in the new land. True, immigrants discovered immediately that the streets were not paved with gold. Early in this century, economist Milton Friedman's mother worked in a garment-center sweatshop. Families huddled in wretched tenements. Fathers educated in Orthodox Polish Yeshivas groaned under heavy packs as they made door-to-door sales pitches or operated pushcarts on slum streets. The Bronx was one generation and Scarsdale and Great Neck were two generations in the future. Elsewhere, coal miners and thugs hired by mine operators fought pitched battles in Kentucky and West Virginia. Violence is as American as Sombart's high-cholesterol diet of roast beef and apple pie. American capitalists belatedly, reluctantly, and, as the 1980s revealed, only temporarily accepted unions as legitimate organizations. Well into the 1930s, such anti-union industries as coal mining, steel, and autos deployed company thugs, labor spies, blacklists, yellow-dog contracts, and sympathetic judges as weapons against unions which were perceived as trespassers on the sacred ground of managerial autonomy and the supreme principle of private property itself.

Nevertheless, as Milton Friedman's renown strikingly demonstrates, ambitious and talented children of the poor can reach the heights. Income, occupational, and social mobility does exist, even though its extent is generally exaggerated and children are well advised to select affluent, educated parents. Poor boys and girls simply must work harder than luckier middle-class agemates. *Ad astra per aspera.*

Prescient as Sombart turned out to be, socialism in the early years of this century was a politically significant force. In 1912 the Socialist party rejoiced in the charismatic leadership of Eugene V. Debs. In that presidential year, nearly 6 percent of the vote—879,000 ballots cast by a still all-male electorate—was Socialist. Victor Berger, a Wisconsin party member, sat in the House of Representatives. Many declared Socialists were state legislators. Socialist mayors presided over the affairs of Flint, Michigan; New Castle, Pennsylvania; and Saint Marys, Ohio. Socialist publications were numerous, some in English, many in foreign languages. For the faithful, five English dailies and eight in other languages offered instruction, inspiration, and occasional intellectual sustenance. There were in English alone 262 weeklies and ten monthlies. This flood of print lapped over the doorsteps of as many as two million families. The circulation of the Kansas weekly *Appeal to Reason* averaged 750,000, a figure to conjure with in a population of less than ninety-two million.[1]

Socialists were a wildly diverse crew. Many were Christians who drew their inspiration from the Bible. To take seriously the Old Testament Exodus narrative[2] is to decry extremes of wealth and poverty in all places and at all times. John Wesley, the great Methodist revivalist of the Industrial Revolution, wrote in his journal for February 8, 1753, "In the afternoon I visited many of the sick; but such scenes who can see unmoved? There are none such to be found in a pagan country. If any of the Indians in Georgia were sick (which, indeed, exceedingly rarely happened until they learned gluttony and drunkenness from the Christians), those that were near him gave him whatever he wanted. Oh, who will convert the English into honest heathens!"[3] Such sentiments echoed Old Testament prophetic outcries against the wealthy.

Wisconsin radicals were influenced by the temperate Marxism

## The Secular Left: Hope or Fantasy?

of German social democracy. Immigrant Jews in New York, embittered Oklahoma tenant farmers, and sporadically violent Western syndicalists interpreted socialism in wildly different ways. Some believed in the victory of socialist ideas through peaceful electoral processes. Others were certain that nothing less than revolution could overcome entrenched capitalism and substitute a workers' economy. Advocates of the Protestant social gospel had little in common with Marxists of any stripe, any more than Yiddish-speaking New York socialists empathized with radical farmers and revolutionary western miners.

It is unlikely that even the powerful personality of Eugene Debs could long have held together in one party immigrants and old settlers as divided by culture, language, geography, occupation, and doctrine as the 6 percent who in 1912 preferred Debs to Woodrow Wilson, William Howard Taft, and Bull Mooser Theodore Roosevelt. After 1912 the party declined. Socialists made many tactical mistakes and overdosed upon the factional squabbles endemic to fringe groups. Their principled opposition to American participation in World War I cost them dearly, just as their inability to come to terms with the New Deal later reiterated socialist status as a permanent sectarian minority.[4] The horrors of Stalinism quite unjustly tainted the most democratic of socialists. The tendency of nasty Third World regimes to call themselves socialist has added to the tribulations of believers in an alliance of democracy and enlightened economic substitutes for corporate control.

All this said, socialism probably would not have fared much better if the political judgment of Eugene Debs and Norman Thomas had been as astute as that of Franklin Roosevelt. For reasons deeply embedded in personal as well as national history, Americans distrust government, glorify individual initiative, admire rather more than they envy those who strike it rich, and distrust collective action of the kind that in Europe and neighboring Canada fosters comprehensive health care, generous unemployment benefits, and subsidized housing for low- and moderate-income families.

Yet from time to time, pragmatic Americans accept specific radical proposals. For once, Ronald Reagan had his history straight when he complained that Karl Marx advocated progressive income taxation. Wisconsin Socialists pioneered the

## Visions and Nightmares

devices that in 1935 were written into the Social Security Act. America is the land of cooptation. Sensibly humble democratic socialists accordingly take care to separate utopian vision from political practicality. They can and should imagine better societies in which workplace democracy flourishes, public education is infused with altruistic instead of materialistic ideals, and popular culture is undefiled by the rampant materialism of a dominating business community, because politics of any variety are dreary if they are driven by nothing more than the immediate self-interest, narrowly defined in financial terms, of the political players. Ronald Reagan's grip upon American affections is not entirely, nor even mostly, his promise of larger after-tax incomes to the electorate. Large numbers of Reagan voters in 1984 must have realized that their financial situation failed significantly to improve between 1980 and 1984 and in numerous instances actually deteriorated. They responded, nevertheless, to the optimism, promise of opportunity, and simple patriotism projected by the president. The most reactionary of politics, a regime welded to the desires of the affluent, succeeds only as it acquires the sanction of aspirations beyond the merely material.

What then is an American radical—socialist, left liberal, social democrat, populist, or unclassifiable—to do? The path of undeviating principle guarantees enduring frustration, not only at the polls but also in the mass media. In the TV era, failure to make the local newscasts is tantamount to nonexistence. Thus, each spring a thousand or more wistful souls, self-identified as socialist scholars, convene in New York City and just as regularly the city's newscasters and the *New York Times* totally ignore their existence. On the painfully balanced "MacNeil-Lehrer Newshour," "Nightline," and other TV fora, very occasionally a democratic socialist, usually Michael Harrington, will be an invited participant, but for the most part tedious discussion attempts to differentiate those slightly to the left from others slightly to the right of an amorphous center itself drifting to the right. Scrupulous journalists concerned about the reputation of their informants, or possibly about their editors' reaction to the quotation of radicals, carefully relabel such folks as liberals, progressives, or, daringly, left liberals.

Not that radical purists lack opportunities to express their

## The Secular Left: Hope or Fantasy?

views. Marxist journals such as the venerable *Monthly Review* and *Science and Society* and many newer organs clutter the shelves of urban bookstores and newsstands in the vicinity of Columbia, Berkeley, the University of Wisconsin, and Harvard. Trouble is that their circulation is in the low thousands, rarely touching even five thousand, and their readers consist of the already converted. Congressional committees seek no counsel from radicals. Reed Irvine's Accuracy in Media has initiated a new right-wing project, Accuracy in Academia, which encourages right-minded students to listen carefully to radical instructors, take good notes, and convey them to the proper authorities. To its credit, the Reagan administration has not sponsored a full-scale red scare, possibly because, even including paid-up FBI informants, the Communist party, Socialist Workers, Socialist Labor, and still more minute grouplets succeed better at frightening one another than in alarming Ed Meese's politically alert Department of Justice.

Yes, Virginia, there are real Marxists in American universities and exceptionally, as at New York's New School for Social Research and the University of Massachusetts in Amherst, they are numerous enough to constitute a significant presence, as in the economics departments of these institutions. But far more numerous, particularly among economists, are social scientists whose politics range from stolid center to far right. Following the advice of Irving Kristol and William Simon, corporations and affluent individual donors are establishing chairs of democratic capitalism, free enterprise, and so on and seeing to it that their occupants faithfully represent the views of those who pay their salaries and fund their research. Young scholars, out for the main chance, heed the far-from-subliminal message that access to data, research assistance, and paid time off from teaching are all benefits available from conservative sources. Not to publish is surely to perish in academia. Those who facilitate publication and eventual tenure cannot avoid evoking the gratitude of their favorites, as much in the expectation of future benefits as in appreciation of those already conferred.

The very word *left* is vague. If Ted Kennedy, routinely identified with the liberal wing of congressional Democrats, constitutes in his person the outer reaches of political respectability, then left in the United States as a pragmatic position entails little more on the domestic scene than defense of past civil rights gains, preservation of social programs targeted at low-income families, cautious restraints on Pentagon budgets, fiscal responsibility, willingness in selected areas such as air travel and trucking to substitute market mechanisms for regulatory agencies, and, when the reaction against Reaganism takes hold, a return to the agenda of the 1960s—comprehensive health care, full-employment policies, federalization of welfare, low-income housing, and equitable taxation. Not a single item on this list seems a likely goal during the remainder of the Reagan era. A European might in a kind mood identify this agenda as mildly social democratic, for it does not challenge the primacy of market capitalism or the equity of the distribution of income and wealth generated by its operations. With the possible exception of the Thatcher regime in England, conservative governments in Western Europe accept social, income, and employment protections considerably more generous to recipients and far more onerous to employers than anything contemplated seriously by the Democratic left.

On the socialist fringe, disagreement is substantial, if anyone aside from the polemicists cares. Distrust of the market and outrage at enormous concentrations of wealth and power are easy points of agreement. But on the central issue, markets versus planning, a cacophony of voices registers radical discord. Easy enough to utter the word *planning*, much harder to describe mechanisms that promise inspiring combinations of efficiency and equity, social control and workplace democracy, individual initiative and social solidarity, and public, private, community, and employee ownership. If the timid, liberal Democratic agenda lacks immediate political plausibility, the aspirations of democratic socialists must sadly endure the label of utopianism.

### WHY DON'T THE PEOPLE RISE?

Have I been excessively lugubrious?

There is hope available in portents of popular radicalism that do not register themselves adequately either in the mass

## The Secular Left: Hope or Fantasy?

media or in conventional politics. Call them incipient or actual movements and, to anticipate the argument, recall how often in American political history movements have eventually transformed politics. The abolitionists contributed to the emancipation of the slaves. Prohibitionists actually outlawed the sale of alcohol for a decade and a half, at least by legitimate merchants. In more recent times, environmentalists placed on the statute books clean-air and clean-water strictures on factory operations. Martin Luther King, Jr., with the indispensable aid of Southern bigots like Sheriff Bull Connor and George Wallace in his racist phase, led Congress, the public, and two presidents to accept major civil rights legislation for the first time in nearly a century. In New York City, an ad hoc community group founded and led by Marcy Benstock, a Ralph Nader disciple, stalled and ultimately defeated in 1985 the massive Westway project, a combined real estate and highway construction bonanza, enthusiastically supported by banks, real estate developers, construction unions, and the politicians, including the mayor and governor, to whose campaigns these powerful institutions had generously contributed.

Our political arrangements are hostile to the emergence of influential third parties. The American affection for quick results, the nation's traditional distrust of government, and its exaltation of voluntary action collude to explain the extraordinarily empty content of our politics. In 1984, President Reagan offered no agenda for his second term and his opponent promised nothing more inspiring than a tax increase. Neither foreign nor social policy sullied the candidates' vacuous utterances. In 1985, Governor Kean, a moderate Republican, won an enormous plurality over a youthful Democratic challenger whose major complaints against the incumbent were that he had failed to lower property taxes and had moved too slowly to clean up New Jersey's unrivaled collection of toxic-waste sites. Congressional Democrats are advised by Les Aspin, one of their more influential members and chairman of the House Armed Services Committee, not to oppose too many weapons systems, whatever their absence of merit, lest they be portrayed as weak on defense and soft on Commies. Both parties in the autumn of 1985 embraced an utterly nonsensical proposal to reduce the budget deficit to zero between 1986 and 1991 by, in effect, surrendering to the president Congress's constitutional obligation to determine expenditures and levy taxes. Although liberals feared damage to programs targeted at low-income families and conservatives trembled at potential assaults upon the Pentagon budget, everybody agreed that action had to be taken even if it were undesirable on legal, economic, social, and ethical grounds. The public, so the omnipresent pollsters agreed, demanded that the budget be balanced in their lifetime.

To dwell upon these examples of political frivolity, drawn from a much larger universe, is to suggest that the sources of change are located in social movements, not political platforms. Jerry Falwell's Moral Majority, Phyllis Schlafly's Eagle Forum, and lesser conservative advocates of old-time values, rabid anti-Communism, and the demolition of the wall less and less effectively separating church and state, are creations of private citizens whose skilled use of television, direct mail, and sophisticated polling and pressure has had a powerful impact upon the politics of both parties. That in recent years it has been the reactionary right which has played movement politics far more successfully than its liberal and radical opposition does not blunt the major lesson for the left: it is a strategy that in the past has worked as effectively for progress as it now does for reaction.

One message for the left is as old as Saul Alinsky's organizing strategy or the tactics of successful teachers facing groups of sketchily prepared, reluctant adolescents. It is to start where people are, identify the grievances that afflict them, and act practically to alleviate their causes. The scarcely literate high school student, the only marginally more proficient community college inmate, harbor justified rancor against the schools and the society that have equipped them so badly to compete for legitimate careers and middle-class incomes. Liberal mainstream politicians who succeed in empathizing with their anger in ways that do not inflame more satisfied, psychologically better-settled groups rise to ever higher office.

In this decade, Ronald Reagan has been the beneficiary of the grievances, disappointments, and insecurities of groups that add up to a national majority. Because the disaffected dislike each other rather more than they do their corporate

## The Secular Left: Hope or Fantasy?

and political oppressors, it is possible for a charismatic president who is the century's most effective agent of concentrated wealth and power to represent himself plausibly as an enemy of special interests and a celebrant of the general welfare. Charisma, as the *Oxford English Dictionary* defines it, is "a free gift or favour specially vouchsafed by God."[5] Evidently God is as free to confer this gift upon the uneducated, the unread, and the prejudiced as upon intellectuals or liberal politicians reasonably conversant with the English language. In the 1984 election, Ronald Reagan ran strongly in South Boston, an area once represented in Congress by John F. Kennedy and still populated by numerous Irish Catholics loyal until recently to the Kennedy family and its current head, Senator Ted Kennedy. What shattered that loyalty, what imperiled the physical security of a Kennedy who ventured into the area, is a tragic illustration of warfare over the crumbs of power between two mistreated groups. It is a warning to optimistic carpenters of liberal coalitions.

The Boston tragedy began on June 21, 1974, when Arthur Garrity, a federal district judge, issued his desegregation order for the Boston public schools.[6] That the Boston schools were severely segregated was not in doubt. In Roxbury they were black. In Charlestown, an Irish enclave, they were white. In both low-income areas, schools were old and badly maintained, academic standards were low, dropout rates high, and success measured by social and athletic prowess rather than scholastic achievement. Few of these young men and women went on to college. Nevertheless, Irish families took fierce pride in their high school and regarded it as a precious community possession.

If, as the first Coleman Report on the condition of public education argued, black pupils benefited from association with middle-class whites, little educational gain could realistically be anticipated from mingling lower-class adolescents of different colors, even if all parties had been friendly or resigned to the experiment. What might have transformed black prospects was the sort of metropolitan solution ruled out by the Supreme Court, busing of middle-class whites into Roxbury schools and busing of lower-class blacks into the affluent suburbs from which the whites came. Of course, working-class white Bostonians were anything but friendly or resigned to the massive school reassignments that went into effect for eight schools on September 12, 1974.

For most of the schools, opening day came and went quietly. Not so at South Boston High School, where furious whites welcomed blacks arriving on buses with shouts of "Niggers, go home!" Six hours later, at the close of the school session, crowds pelted buses returning blacks to Roxbury with "eggs, beer bottles, soda cans, and rocks, shattering windows and injuring nine students."[7] As the school year began, so it continued. A Haitian maintenance worker who made the mistake of driving into South Boston to pick up his wife who worked in a laundry was attacked and beaten until a policeman rescued him. In Roxbury, black students in reprisal stoned cars and assaulted stray whites. Very soon, Governor Francis Sargent summoned the National Guard. This is not the occasion to summarize the sad tale of the disastrous impact of a well-intentioned jurist's attempt to apply the mandate of the Supreme Court as solemnized in its 1954 *Brown* vs. *Board of Education* decision, a unanimous holding that virtuous Northerners innocently assumed applied only to wicked Southern descendants of slave owners.

The moral extends far beyond Boston. Judge Garrity, the lawyers who fought segregation, and most of Mayor Kevin White's staff who were involved in applying racial integration lived comfortably in Boston's prosperous suburbs. Their children attended excellent public schools, staffed by carefully selected and well-paid teachers, and watched over by Ivy League parents engaged in the practice of law, medicine, academic administration, and similar well-paid pursuits. If an occasional black youngster shared these suburban classrooms, he or she was almost certain to be the child of middle-class, upwardly mobile parents, close in all but color to white neighbors. Not uniquely in American history, upper-class folks with their hands on the levers of power applied uplifting remedies at no personal cost to themselves but a great deal to their social, educational, and financial inferiors. Judge Garrity's legally correct and meticulously argued decision built no new schools, hired no new cohorts of highly qualified teachers, and did nothing to

## The Secular Left: Hope or Fantasy?

transform Roxbury's and Charlestown's dilapidated buildings into equivalents of Wellesley or Newton affluence.

Blacks and Irish Americans, who had coexisted comparatively peacefully so long as each group controlled its own turf, exploded in mutual rage, violence, arson, assault, and gang warfare when outsiders wrested from them power over one of the few institutions where once their writ had run. No wonder bitter Irish families excoriated Ted Kennedy as a deserter of his own kind, a traitor to those who had supported his brothers and himself, a convert to the two-toilet, rich Irish who could afford to patronize blacks whatever the damage to Irishmen with names other than Kennedy. Save for different colors of the combatants, South Boston uncannily resembled Northern Ireland.

Boston's trauma helps explain the political weakness of the majority entitled to answer negatively Ronald Reagan's repetition of the question he used so effectively in 1980 against Jimmy Carter: are you better off today than you were four years ago? The casualties of Reagan's war against the vulnerable are the troops in any successful Democratic coalition effort. Their diverse interests, ignorance of each other's lives, and mutual prejudice present the same challenge to a successful liberal presidential candidate as in their various ways Franklin Roosevelt, John Kennedy, and, briefly, Lyndon Johnson encountered and overcame.

### A PARADE OF LOSERS

Reagan losers are heavily female. It is a measure of their good sense that women in 1984 did give a smaller proportion of their votes, though still a majority, to Ronald Reagan than did their obtuse husbands and brothers. Mondale's principal appeal to women was that he was not Reagan, a war cry scarcely powerful enough to arouse the enthusiasm of the politically inactive, particularly since many of them admired the president, his consort, or both.

Women are a majority only arithmetically. The differences are as wide between welfare mothers and suburban matrons, blue-collar factory workers, their pink-collar clerical sisters and dressed-for-success women lawyers and corporate executives, black high school dropouts and Ivy League MBAs, as the gulf between similarly contrasting males. Nevertheless, the Reagan administration had done one or several things to displease or enrage a great many women of assorted colors, ages, education, and financial status.

Well-educated, professionally ambitious women benefited substantially from the civil rights policies of pre-Reagan administrations. Affirmative action increased female representation in elite business and professional schools, compelled the stuffiest of law firms to recruit women associates, and integrated corporate boardrooms.

Who would have believed in the 1950s, when men were men and women specialized in cooking, consolation, and child-rearing, that one's twenty-seven-year-old niece (my very own relative, if only by marriage) would be invited to manage J. C. Penney credit card operations in the western half of the United States? Federal insistence on equal facilities for women athletes in college has enriched leading female golfers and tennis players. The Reagan administration notoriously has sabotaged affirmative action.

Lower and far more numerous in the occupational pecking order, nurses, secretaries, female administrative assistants, and elementary school teachers have a strong investment in the court-aborted comparable-worth movement. The Reagan administration's assault upon affirmative action in the courts and its derision of comparable worth are, of course, consistent with its opposition to the Equal Rights Amendment, a measure mostly of symbolic importance, but precious precisely for that reason to both supporters and opponents. Administration policies in other areas are hostile to the interests of the large majority of women in the work force at nearly every financial level. The Congressional Budget Office has done its considerable best to limit federal funding of day-care facilities. The tax-reform measure presented to Congress in 1985 tilted proudly in favor of what Communications Director Pat Buchanan called "traditional" families, that new minority in which husbands bring home the bacon to grateful wives who care for the children, prepare proper meals for the head of the household, and devote leisure time to church activities. The trouble is, too little bacon can be bought with a single paycheck in many millions of working- and middle-class families. One wonders whether President Reagan with a straight face could have fired a male Secretary of Health and Human Services while announcing that he was promoting him to an ambassadorship—to Ireland. Such, however, was the fate of Margaret Heckler in the summer of 1985—poor reward for a politician who had done her best to wreck family planning, reduce Medicaid funds, and implement hospital cost-containment regulations menacing to the health of all patients and particularly to low-income consumers of health services.

I have elsewhere described the selectively cruel impact of cuts in means-tested programs such as AFDC, food stamps, Medicaid, and WIC upon low-income women and children, a majority of them white but a disproportionate number black and Hispanic. In 1984, low-income adults who bothered to vote did favor the Democratic ticket. Blacks, accurately identifying the administration's racism, apparently cast 90 percent of their ballots for Mondale-Ferraro. In 1988, middle- and upper-middle-income white women will have good reason to support Democrats, particularly within the context of an economy either in recession or growing too slowly to fulfill the career aspirations of women already professionally employed or to offer decent entry-level positions to their daughters and younger sisters. It is not sexist to report women's powerful attachment to their children. As things now stand, nearly a third of those children are growing up in mostly female-headed families below the poverty line.

## THE ELDERLY

For familiar reasons I shall shortly reiterate, Social Security pensions have survived the Reagan years and evoked reluctant praise from the president's appointees. One does not expect in the 1985 *Economic Report of the President* approval of any social program. Since 1981, much of the leaden prose in these documents has been devoted to deploring the alleged extravagances of the welfare state and demanding that they be pruned. Yet the good, gray, reactionary economists who concocted the 1985 volume were moved to say, "Thirty years ago, the elderly were a relatively disadvantaged group in the population. This is no longer the case. . . . Today, elderly and nonelderly families have about equal levels of income per capita. Poverty rates among the elderly have declined so dramatically that in 1983, poverty rates for the elderly were lower than poverty rates for the rest of the population."[8] Even more euphorically, Daniel Patrick Moynihan stated the message of Harvard's Godkin Lectures, which he had delivered in the same year: ". . . having all but eliminated poverty among the aged, we surely could do something about its extraordinary relative rise among children."[9] As is his wont, the senator fell prey to hyperbole. A 1983 poverty rate of 14.1 percent falls more than a trifle short of near elimination of poverty, particularly in the light of official definitions designed to minimize its incidence. Nor is the difference between 14.1 percent and the 15.4 percent rate for the nonelderly particularly dramatic. Both numbers testify to the persistence of a national disgrace, the willingness of a complacent majority to tolerate deprivation, often actual hunger, in a rich community.

However, it would be churlish to deny that life has improved for the elderly, even though evidence is abundant that future progress will be extraordinarily difficult to achieve and that the more likely prospect is deterioration in the financial situation of the over-sixty-five cohort and especially of the so-called old-old, the rising percentage of men and particularly women over seventy-five. As a percentage of the population, it is the over seventy-fives who are increasing most rapidly. Those who care for them are mostly women themselves in their sixties.

One should do more than cherish a durable American success of social policy, for it is a rarity. There are lessons to be learned from Social Security's popularity. The 1935 Social Security Act, celebrated in numerous anniversary conferences in 1985, also inaugurated unemployment compensation benefits and Aid to the Families of Dependent Children. Our provision for the unemployed is meager by the criteria of benefits, eligibility, and duration of coverage in comparison with Western Europe. In 1985 only a quarter of the unemployed actually received benefits, averaging about a third of wages from previous

## The Secular Left: Hope or Fantasy?

employment. The media blow up welfare abuse and President Reagan has notoriously made "welfare cheaters" the butt of vacuous anecdotes. In short, of the many provisions of the landmark 1935 legislation, only Social Security itself has been persistently popular.

Why has it even survived two administrations of the radical right? When our Ronnie was a wandering minstrel of free enterprise on the General Electric banquet circuit, he regularly condemned Social Security as an infringement of personal liberty and an erosion of individualism much in the spirit of Barry Goldwater, whom he fervently supported in the former's 1964 presidential race. True to his past, President Reagan, in the initial year of his first term, sought severe benefit reductions. The Senate all but unanimously rejected them. Now the man nominates himself as the world's best friend of the elderly and indignantly refutes allegations that he ever harbored notions of substituting private for social insurance or allowing individuals to opt out of the Social Security program. True, the man majored in economics, not history, at Eureka College.

To start with the obvious: as a nearly universal benefit, Social Security is enormously popular with the vast, amorphous middle class and until recently with their adult children as well. In due time, the latter expect to collect larger benefits than those of their seniors out of the proceeds of economic growth. Meanwhile, young and mature families are relieved of financial responsibility for the maintenance of retired, frequently ailing mothers and fathers. The rarity of three-generation households registers the capacity of the elderly to finance separate residence, usually to the gratification of themselves and their children. One of Ronald Reagan's more destructive enterprises has been the undermining of the expectations of the young. More than once he has expressed his doubt that they will actually collect anticipated benefits.

Public approval of Social Security has been enhanced by the benign myth that Social Security levies on wages and matching employer contributions suffice to fund pensions for the elderly much in the fashion of an annuity purchased from a private insurance company. In fact, all pensioners receive several times the actuarial value of the sums they and their employers paid into the Social Security trust fund during their working lives.

Social Security has represented an intergenerational transfer from the young and middle-aged to the elderly, a benign Ponzi scheme.

The myth memorializes FDR's political acumen. Wilbur Cohen, a twenty-one-year-old research assistant on Franklin Roosevelt's Committee on Economic Security, which in little more than six months in 1934 drafted the Social Security Act, recalls that the president settled a wrangle among the committee's members over funding by insisting that "financing the program by earmarked payroll taxes would ensure that a future president and Congress could not, morally or politically, repeal or mutilate the entitlement character of the program."[10] In *The Republic*, Plato advised wise rulers to use noble lies in governing the uneducated rabble. He might well have accepted encouragement of the public perception that Social Security benefits were earned as a splendid demonstration of his technique's efficacy.

Complacency about the future is unwise. Social Security already has been wounded, though not yet mortally. Under cover of the president's Greenspan Commission, bipartisan congressional majorities for the first time taxed a portion of the benefits of the affluent, quickened the pace of payroll-tax increases, and slowly increased the age at which full retirement benefits were to be paid. The legislators thus allayed the administration's contrived panic over the alleged insolvency of the Social Security trust fund. The temporary gap between payroll-tax receipts and disbursement could readily have been closed by a small contribution from general tax receipts, the practice of many other countries. Nevertheless, young workers were not necessarily reassured that the trust accounts were actuarially sound until—pick a date: the year 2000, 2025, or 2035. By the second of these dates, the retirement age will have risen to sixty-six, the very moment that a wage-earner who is twenty-six in 1985 would expect to collect his first check. For middle-aged members of the labor force in 1985, the year 2000 is not that distant. The lie becomes less noble, the myth less benign when currently employed Americans fret that general revenues will be unavailable to supplement trust-fund receipts.

There is another reason to reject complacency. As aging

## The Secular Left: Hope or Fantasy?

yuppies narrowly inspect Social Security, they may come to realize that although up to now Social Security has been an excellent deal for almost all of its beneficiaries, it has helped some more than others. In general, the smaller one's lifetime earnings the larger is the percentage of those earnings replaced by Social Security. Yuppies, future yuppies, and the senior auxiliary of contemporary yuppies just might identify this situation as one of cross-subsidization between themselves and less-prosperous types, and on this ground welcome opportunities to substitute individual retirement accounts for Social Security benefits. Some would be prepared to gamble that equity investments in common stocks will return them substantially more in retirement than does Social Security. Yuppies are nothing if not self-confident.

Families of average income already pay higher payroll than personal income taxes. Come 1989, the sum of employee deductions and matching employer contributions will reach 12.4 percent. Payroll taxes are regressive, for the ceiling on taxable income is relatively low and receipts from dividends, interest, rent, and capital gains are untaxed for Social Security purposes. Blue- and white-collar types may become increasingly restive over these rising subtractions from their paychecks, particularly since, for families earning less than $15,000, Social Security tax increases between 1981 and 1985 more than wiped out tax savings from the famous Kemp-Roth three-year, 25 percent slash in personal income tax rates. Yet any recommendation to raise income subject to Social Security levy to $60,000 and include in that sum returns from investment—as advocated in 1985 by the Presbyterian Committee on a Just, Caring, and Dynamic Economy—risks furious opposition from upper-middle-income professional and managerial types whose political support for Social Security, or at minimum acquiescence in its preservation, is vital.

Of more immediate concern is mounting evidence that the last two decades' improvement in the financial situation of the elderly is slowing and reversing. The Reagan administration has mounted a quite successful continuing assault against Medicare. The program now costs $80 billion each year and yet covers less than half of the medical costs of its beneficiaries. Still more strikingly, the elderly now pay out of their own pockets just about the same percentage of income on medical care as they did in 1964, the year before Medicare came into operation. A majority of the elderly feel constrained to supplement Medicare coverage with expensive private insurance company policies.

The old-old who require long-term nursing-home attention, not covered by Medicare, are now forced to spend down their assets until they are sufficiently indigent to qualify for Medicaid, inextricably tagged with the stigma of welfare. Late in 1985, maintaining an elderly person in a well-appointed domiciliary, a residence for aged men and women requiring only occasional medical and nursing assistance, cost approximately $30,000 annually. DRGs, proliferation of for-profit hospital chains and other medical facilities, and the closing or sale of municipal and voluntary hospitals all in their assorted ways menace the health and income security of the elderly. As the number of the old-old grows, it will require a far more enlightened public mood than any registered on short-term political weather forecasts to maintain even existing benefits.

The elderly have much to lose from continuation after 1988 of Reagan policies. Should the electorate choose as their next president a Republican to continue current policies, or even a neoliberal yuppie Democrat, most bets are off. A post-Reagan Republican administration would encourage further privatization of health care, segmentation of retirement plans, ever-greater pressure upon Medicare, and additional closings of emergency rooms. As for Senators Hart and Bradley, two Democrats certifiably more compassionate than any of the Republicans whose names have been dropped by the Great Mentioners, they do share a disquieting yuppie fondness for allegedly efficient technical solutions that tend to translate into devices like Individual Training Acts, intricate tax devices, and experiments with privatization. Governor Mario Cuomo, of whom more shortly, ought not to be confused with Saint Francis, but of the Democratic presidential possibilities for 1988, he seems to represent the best hope for preservation of existing Social Security benefits and, should the political winds shift sharply enough to nominate and elect him, even their extension. If only Franklin Roosevelt, comparatively blessed be his memory, had had the guts in 1935 to take on organized medicine and fight for the comprehensive health-care provision that his Committee on Economic Security sought to include in the Social Security Act!

Threats to Social Security pension entitlements have only temporarily subsided. But even if they are repulsed, the poverty level among the elderly will soon begin to rise unless the United States joins the remainder of the civilized world, and an amazing number of nations in the less civilized portions of the globe, and far too belatedly offers comprehensive health protection to every resident.

## BLACKS AND OTHER LOSERS

I shall resist temptation to examine in at least equal detail the adverse impact of the Reagan experiment in untrammeled corporate rapacity on other groups. Suffice it to say that ample documentation attests to widely dispersed losses. Low-income black families, and above all, those headed by women, have suffered from curtailments in means-tested programs. The precarious foothold of middle-class blacks in elite schools and high-prestige managerial and professional situations is threatened by contractions in federal funds for student aid and retreat from affirmative action in municipal, academic, and corporate employment. Persistent high unemployment impinges with special severity upon black teenagers. The shift from manufacturing to service jobs, accelerated by the dollar overvaluation that has been the direct consequence of huge deficits created by imprudent tax cuts and wasteful military expenditures, has diminished the number of traditional entry points into mainstream labor markets for sketchily educated young men and women.

Farmers are something less than 2 percent of the labor force, but the rural economy as a system of banks, merchants, farm-equipment dealers, and actual farmers enrolls a multiple of this 2 percent. Farm foreclosures have reached levels unapproached since the 1930s. The banks that hold their mortgages have been failing by the handfuls. Layoffs have been savage in the farm-equipment industry and the losses of sales by International Harvester, John Deere, and their peers have weakened the export performance of these companies as well. Although

Congress has rejected repeated White House efforts to trim farm subsidies, administration pressure to do so continues.

Small businessmen have as little reason to cheer Reaganomics. The Small Business Administration, each year on the OMB hit list, survives only by congressional grace. The Pentagon prefers to deal with General Dynamics, McDonnell Douglas, and similar giants rather than to open contracts to serious competitive bidding. The Department of Justice and the Federal Trade Commission seem unable to identify any merger or acquisition as a threat to competition. One of the items on Attorney General Edward Meese's lengthy agenda is comprehensive revision of the antitrust statutes with a view to making increasing economic concentration even easier. In the economic as in the physical jungle large animals prey upon smaller ones. The high failure rate of small businesses has several causes, but one of them is competition from enormous conglomerates able to take temporary losses the better to eliminate frequently more efficient small rivals whose existence depends upon sales of a single product.

As for the wage earners of the nation—white-, blue-, or pink-collared—their experience has been unique in this century. During four recovery years—1983, 1984, 1985, and 1986—their take-home pay steadily diminished. In the case of factory workers, this was a continuation of a trend that began in the 1970s. By the end of 1985, it was apparent even to economists that the faltering economic expansion depended upon continuation of the federal deficit generated by the military Keynesianism of an administration which once believed that it was engaged in an exciting experiment in supply-side economics and a continuing willingness on the part of average families to save less and less and plunge more and more deeply into debt. Such consumer conduct obviously utterly destroyed the central premise of the supply-siders—that lower taxes in particular upon the incomes of the affluent would stimulate both saving and investment. It turned out that, as an old-fashioned Keynesian might put it, the marginal propensity to consume of the prosperous was just about as high as that of their financial inferiors.[11] Prosperous viewers of "Dallas" and "Dynasty" simply bought more of the consumer artifacts modeled by the soap-opera characters than did poorer citizens. The failure of

## The Secular Left: Hope or Fantasy?

supply-side economics exemplifies still again the cultural contradiction between the hedonism endlessly stimulated by American popular culture and unheeded admonitions to save more money the better to compete with the calamitously frugal Japanese and Germans.

Not only is the American standard of life no longer the highest in the world, it is fated, in the absence of significant shifts in personal behavior and political sentiment, to continue its decline. Economic historians still quarrel over the reasons why England began its descent into genteel poverty a century ago. It may be that a century from now, economic historians will occupy themselves with similar questions about the decline of American productivity, competitiveness in international markets, managerial quality, and almost universal preference for immediate gain over sounder long-term returns.

For most Americans the Reagan years have been a period of financial deterioration, varying of course in severity according to individual occupational and geographical situation. Displaced factory workers and foreclosed farmers have been among the more spectacular losers. But even middle-class families who retained jobs, homes, autos, and other possessions sustained their standard of life mostly because more and more women supplemented male incomes and everybody borrowed dangerously large sums in relation to capacity to meet the monthly payments. The groups who in one way or another actually have registered losses—most women, almost all blacks, farmers, small businessmen, factory operatives, and clerical workers—add up to an overwhelming majority of the public. Defined as the huge 1986 majority earning more than $19,000 and less than $47,000, the middle class has been shrinking since 1978. Nearly twice as many of its earlier members have fallen into genteel or actual poverty as have moved upward into high-income status.[12]

Winners include a familiar cast of characters, among them top corporate managers; real estate developers; professionally trained yuppies; purveyors of legal, financial, and managerial services; and, of course, millionaires and billionaires. To them might be added defense contractors, anti-union consultants, and merger and acquisition specialists. When, in 1985, Pantry Pride, a food purveyor, gobbled up Revlon, a cosmetics hawker, the maneuver generated $70 million in fees to lawyers and investment bankers, payment for a socially useless rearrangement of assets. The usual sequel to agglomerations of ill-sorted enterprises is sale of some or all of the acquired units.

Reactionary ideology has also enriched conservative foundations, fundamentalist religious operators, and miscellaneous entrepreneurs on the right. This fervent, affluent minority exerts considerable influence upon politics not only through intimate associations with the Reagan Executive Branch but also because of a well-honed ability to trigger congressional fear and greed. The militant right alarms moderate conservatives and mild liberals by threats to mobilize money and people against them in elections. Its political action committees (PACs) dangle the succulent carrots of campaign contributions under the twitching noses of congresspersons, governors, and smaller political fauna, worried as always about the next election. Nevertheless, if one is naïve enough only to count noses, those attached to the faces of the winners from Reaganomics are far less numerous than the organs of the losers.

I have thus far strayed into an economist's typical fantasy, the assumption that adults vote their financial interests and that if they appear to do the opposite, it is only because they have inaccurately identified those interests, pending clarification from economists eager to set them straight. On the assumption that confession is good for the soul and encouraging to a person's opponents, I recall writing a powerful Op-Ed piece in 1972 which demonstrated conclusively that the groups likely to gain from a McGovern presidency were a comfortable Democratic majority in the Electoral College and those continuing to benefit from Richard Nixon's continued White House occupancy a decided minority. That I was utterly confounded by the Nixon landslide is a trivial incident of autobiography, but the reasons for my error and that of a good many other analysts merit analysis, for they bear directly upon the prospects of liberal or even, in American terms as always, radical revival.

### IS THERE HOPE?

According to one of Ronald Reagan's better one-liners, "They have a new version of Trivial Pursuit now, just for economists—

it has three thousand answers for one hundred questions."[13] With the usual allowance for exaggeration, the president's comment points to the politically pointless fertility of proposals, sensible and otherwise, presented in small-selling editions by well-intentioned authors who have collected large quantities of data, horrible examples of administration damage to the vulnerable, and tidy agendas for the future.

Although many differences of detail and substantial disagreements on principle divide members of the democratic left—let it extend in an ecumenical spirit from Kennedy Democrats to temperate socialists enrolled, all 15,000 of them, in Michael Harrington's Democratic Socialists of America—their diagnoses of American society tend to converge.

For the left it is axiomatic that American capitalism is as inefficient as it is inequitable. Income, wealth, and power are scandalously concentrated. If in the Soviet Union wealth—dachas, limousines, decent apartments, access to gourmet foods, forbidden artifacts of Western culture, opportunities to travel in the West, and even fashionable capitalistic male and female clothing—flows from power, the reverse is the case in the United States. As the saying goes, political contributors and their political action committees buy no more than access to the congresspersons whose election or, more often, reelection they subsidize. Even if access were the only prize (does anyone believe it is?), it is not one available to ordinary constituents, even the $5 and $10 contributors. Calls to congressional offices by unimportant folks are answered by minor staff persons or receptionists. An hour of the officeholder's time correlates strictly with the power, influence, wealth, and past and future campaign role of the applicant.

No longer, as in the time of Boss Tweed, can politicians be purchased, but they appear to be available on short term rental, issue by issue, on terms related to the political influence of an individual congressman or senator and the potency of the interest-seeking to enlist that influence. Facing no opposition in 1984, Congressman Daniel Rostenkowski amassed huge campaign contributions, particularly from PACs. Not to wonder. The man is chairman of the House Ways and Means Committee, designer of tax legislation capable of enriching in lesser or greater degree timber barons, oil drillers, purchasers of industrial machinery, real estate developers, and the grandchildren of the Gallo wine family. Even lesser members of this panel and its counterpart, the Senate Finance Committee, fare financially well whether or not they face tight races.

Because corporations wax larger and more powerful and unions decline in depressing symmetry, business leaders call the tune in labor negotiations and local politics still more peremptorily than in Washington. Fear of revived inflation and the Reagan administration's bigoted aversion to public-job creation, along with the trade deficit induced by years of an artificially strong dollar, have kept unemployment rates at recession levels throughout the Reagan era. Corporations have demanded wage give-backs, benefit reductions, and work-rule revisions—or else.

Threats to recalcitrant groups of workers routinely include bankruptcy-voiding contracts (the successful tactic of Continental Airline's Frank Lorenzo among others), plant closings followed by the opening of new installations in nonunion communities, the activities of labor consultants adept in the black arts of union decertification and sabotage of organizing campaigns, hiring of strikebreakers as permanent replacements, and outright discharge of union militants. Although victims of the last tactic might ultimately win a grievance filed with the National Labor Relations Board, the legal process is designed to stretch over several years and the penalty imposed on the corporation intended to be no more severe than restitution of lost wages and benefits minus other earnings and job reinstatement. Violation of labor laws entails at most minor business expenses.

Public officials vie for new installations. In 1983 and 1984, most of the nation's fifty governors bombarded General Motors with promises of tax concessions, zoning variances, construction of new roads and public facilities, and so on, if only the mighty corporation deigned to build its Saturn plant within the supplicant's state. The happy winner, bucolic Spring Hill in Tennessee, now wonders what hit it. Mayors become frantic when large corporate employers threaten to pull up stakes and migrate to locations where the business environment is superior. Translation: where taxes are lower, local officials unaggressive about environmental hazards, unions absent or docile, and unemployment high enough to keep wages low.

That capitalism is not always equitable is sometimes conceded by its more temperate friends. But what of the claim that trade-offs between equity and efficiency are the unavoidable price of the sort of economic growth that improves the situation even of equity's victims? Running an economy at high rates of unemployment is itself inefficient. So also are the vast diversions of expensive legal, accounting, public relations, and advertising talent to mergers and acquisitions. The inflated salary structure of corporate management should be, but seldom is, reckoned a market failure by economists. As corporate critics uncharitably note, by the test of performance in actual markets, domestic and foreign, these managers are vastly overpaid in comparison to their more successful Japanese and German rivals. The vast trade deficit testifies not only to an overvalued dollar but also to widespread managerial failure. This failure registers itself also in the evidence of pervasive corruption in the relations of defense contractors with government officials and their own subcontractors, the incidence of fraud in bank failures, and such schemes as E. F. Hutton's check-kiting activities. Bribery—"dash" is the African synonym—is often diagnosed as a sign of economic underdevelopment. Endemic defense-contract scandals, revival of old-fashioned municipal corruption, and pervasive tax cheating imply an embarrassing verdict upon the American stage of development. Thomas Puccio, the attorney for Bronx boss Stanley Friedman, defended his indicted client with the argument that he had done nothing forbidden by the rules of the municipal marketplace. Precisely. In Washington, New York, Chicago, Philadelphia, and elsewhere government contracts, tax abatements, zoning variances, and similar invitations to larceny are available to high rollers just as in presumably less advanced communities.

The left now toys with the thought that equity and efficiency just might be complementary. In this spirit, productivity has attracted increasing attention. For too long the right monopolized the issue. Supply-side tax cuts, coupled with business deregulation, were advertised as sovereign remedies for a disquieting slowdown which began before and has continued during the Reagan administration. Between 1977 and 1982 the American economy grew at an annual rate, after inflation, of 0.6 percent. Only Canada fared worse in the advanced-nation league. Corresponding figures for Germany were 2.1 percent; France, 3.0 percent; Italy, 3.6 percent; Japan, 3.4 percent; and somnolent Great Britain, 2.7 percent. In 1983, twelve months of rapid American recovery, productivity growth rebounded to 4.2 percent as it normally does when partially idle equipment is brought back into full-time service. All of our rivals, this time with the exception of Italy, did better. France, Japan, Canada, and Great Britain exceeded 6 percent gains and, closest to our performance, West Germany turned in a 4.6 percent figure. In 1985, American productivity actually declined.[14] In most of these countries, to reiterate the point, income and wealth are less inequitably distributed than in our own, and corporate managers are less lavishly rewarded.

Critics of the Soviet Union attack the special privileges of the "nomenklatura"—top politicians, bureaucrats, dancers, official writers, musicians, and chess champions—as a source of inefficiency as well as a betrayal of socialist ideals. Their point is well taken. When chief executive officers and presidents of major corporations translate their dominion over boards of directors and compensation committees into dazzling rewards for themselves, very frequently unrelated to the performance of the organizations they manage or mismanage, are they not using resources inefficiently? Do they not betray the capitalist ideal of pay for performance? Our society is more efficient than the planned Soviet model. How long will it remain so?

Wary of previous inaccurate forecasts, liberals and radicals hesitate to describe the American economy as in a crisis. They concur, however, in diagnosis of its deterioration and the dim prospects of revival without dramatic revisions of current public policies. Revision entails at the start economic planning in the usual guise of that cloudy term "industrial policy." Neither the phrase nor most of its connotations are novel. In the 1920s, John Maynard Keynes offered schemes to cushion the decline of Britain's textile mills, shipyards, and coal mines under the exact label. His industrial policy involved cartel combinations to limit output, special financing to encourage modernization, and the sort of tripartite supervisory arrangements contem-

## The Secular Left: Hope or Fantasy?

plated by, among others, Felix Rohatyn—authority shared by unions, corporations, and government. Roosevelt's National Industry Recovery Act, initially, though briefly, popular in the corporate community, featured industry codes that specified minimum wages, encouraged price-fixing, and discouraged "destructive" competition. As an important afterthought, all the codes affirmed labor's right to organize and bargain collectively. In World War II, as in World War I, industrial policy included rationing, price controls, direction of vital materials and appropriate financing to defense production, and sorting of the labor force through the mechanism of selective service. Since workers vital to the war effort won deferments, the draft amounted to a recruiting device for able-bodied pacifists who secured deferments by staying on farms or seeking appropriate employment in ordnance and aircraft factories.

An influential version of industrial policy emphasizes not, as in opponents' caricatures, efforts to select winners and hasten euthanasia for losers, but regular tripartite consultation designed to promote Japanese-style cooperation in place of the mixture of muddle, inconsistent public policies, and irrational confrontation between labor and management, and management and government. A brand-new federal agency, for example, might fund industrial research on promising new products or processes. Other governments try to reduce the cost of capital in part by encouraging saving and penalizing consumption. We do the reverse. Whenever government credit is deemed as an essential supplement to private capital, the government should turn it into an equity investment—an acquisition of voting stock.

Even in Japan, declining industries cause anguish and difficulties of adjustment. When, in the United States, textiles, steel, machine tools, and other troubled industries seek government help, they should get it on appropriate conditions. The first of them should be preparation of a plan to restore the competitiveness of the industry in international markets. Are workers willing to take wage cuts, possibly in tandem with participation in future profits? Are owners and managers prepared to make substantial new investments and accept limits on salaries and dividends? As Lester Thurow states the objective of this variant of industrial policy, "The goal of industrial policies is not detailed central planning, but a cooperative bubble-up relationship where government, labor, and industry can work together to create world-class competitive American industries."[15] Cooperation embraces the possibility of new modes of labor compensation: comparatively modest wages supplemented by bonuses tied to productivity or profit targets, another Japanese echo, or even an experiment with Weitzman's adjustment downward of wages (and prices) in the interest of additional employment and increased sales volume.

On the quasi-Marxist left, industrial policy shades into a design for worker control of factories and offices. Public support for democratic trade unions is a prerequisite to workplace democracy: "Workers also need to become directly involved in planning and decision-making about production."[16] To participate, workers need detailed information unlikely to be made available to them without something like a Corporate Disclosure Act, "mandating full disclosure of detailed firm information on finances, taxes, stock ownership, employment, environmental impact, and health-and-safety conditions. . . . Those corporations who refused to disclose covered information would be subject to fines and withdrawal of government contracts—and upon repeated violations, withdrawal of their right to conduct business in the United States."[17]

As in Sweden, workers should acquire rights to negotiate over investment, job specifications, and other aspects of production. When, again as in Swedish auto companies, cooperative work teams become primary units of production, empowered to divide work, significant productivity improvements ensue. Full participation requires employee influence upon ownership. The Swedish Meidner Plan, fiercely resisted by major employers, distributes shares of profits to group-owned wage-owner funds. The profits paid into the funds purchase voting shares in corporations. Industrial policy should also encourage alternatives to large, bureaucratic corporations: "We therefore propose a new policy emphasis on development of community enterprises . . . any registered corporation in which decision-making power is held by a board elected by all production workers, or by all members of the surrounding community, or by some combination of both."[18] Funding should come from government, union pension funds, employee investment funds, and community investment pools.

It is child's play to supplement these Japanese and Swedish adaptations with the prophet who refuses to vanish—John Maynard Keynes. The stagflation of the 1970s, the apparent failure of Keynesian demand management devices, and the new influence of monetarists, supply-siders, and old-fashioned neoclassical true believers in the "magic of the marketplace" all indubitably damaged Keynesian morale. Events have revived the spirits of true believers. The Federal Reserve's experiment in monetarism generated the deepest recession in 1981 and 1982 since the 1930s. The supply-siders' promises of vast new saving and investment, and enormous tax flows to the Treasury out of a rapidly rising gross national product, have been exposed as the folly they always were. The recovery that began in late 1982 was a typical Keynesian event. Just in time to avert an international financial crisis, the Fed relented, eased credit, and pumped new money into the economy. As tax cuts came into effect and military procurement began to accelerate, consumers spent more out of rising incomes and, somewhat later, corporate investment also increased. Three years of deficit spending by government have sustained a very modest expansion, a rate of growth in output too low to push unemployment below 7 percent, and productivity growth far too feeble to preserve, let alone improve, the performance of American exporters in international markets.

Radical Keynesians, influenced by the late Cambridge economist Joan Robinson, argue that current capitalist arrangements result in distortions in income distribution, financial markets, wages, and prices that require government correction. Liberal Keynesians, such as Yale's Nobelist James Tobin, argue that full employment remains a primary public-policy objective and that its achievement without inflation requires some mechanism of intervention into wages and prices, such as deployment of the tax system, to reward those content with modest increases, consistent with productivity guidelines, in prices and wages and to punish overreachers.[19] Liberal Keynesians, like their more radical brethren, are beginning to recall that Keynes himself favored government action partially to socialize investment and diminish existing inequalities of income and wealth.[20]

I may have been unnecessarily harsh in earlier comments on the confusions of industrial policy. Coherence and policy convergence are difficult, if not impossible, when no analyst can sensibly expect his proposals to be translated into public policy for the foreseeable future. Under the tent of industrial policy, many liberal and some radical aspirations find shelter, among them more effective public control of the enormous corporate beasts that thrash about in the jungles of free enterprise, humanization of factories and offices, profit-sharing and approaches to Japanese employment guarantees, improvement and rationalization of social programs, and diminished inequity in the distribution of income, wealth, and power. The politics of industrial-policy advocates range from the intelligently conservative to the unashamedly radical, in the shorthand of personality from Felix Rohatyn to the three authors of *Beyond the Wasteland*.

For Rohatyn, New York City's recovery from its 1975 near-bankruptcy offers a model for national policy. It required cooperative effort, mutual sacrifice, and a degree of institutional invention for a success celebrated in late 1985 by none other than Senator William Proxmire, who in 1975 and again in 1978, when the city sought federal loan guarantees, led the opposition to federal bailout of an allegedly profligate metropolis.

The oft-told story memorializes substantial layoffs of public workers, wage freezes, declines in public services, termination of free tuition at the City University, tax incentives for developers, fare and tax increases for ordinary residents, and above all unusual alliances among bankers, corporate leaders, union magnates, and elected officials. The institutional inventions for which Mr. Rohatyn takes and merits considerable credit were, of course, the Municipal Assistance Corporation and the Emergency Financial Control Board. Both provided shelter to mayors and heads of unions. Mayors could blame these supervisory agencies for crowded classrooms, dirty streets, and the Dantesque horrors of the subways. Unions could cool the tempers of the rank and file with word that generous contracts would be disallowed by the EFCB and, if by some chance, approved, entail additional layoffs. Sacrifice, as Rohatyn himself concedes, had its limits. The banks, whose improvident extension of ever-larger amounts of credit in return for ever-higher fees and interest charges that contributed mightily to the city's almost terminal fiscal ailments, got off practically scot-free, and developers like the ubiquitous Donald Trump harvested vast sums in tax incentives for the construction of luxury housing, glitzy shopping arcades, and flashy hotels. Construction of affordable housing for low- and middle-income New Yorkers ground to a halt and vacancy rates in the diminishing stock of rental units declined to almost zero. As 1986's rash of investigations and indictments revealed, rampant corruption and self-dealing were also folded into the price of municipal revival.

But even in Rohatyn's elitest model, elements of liberalism lurk. This investment banker is no enemy of social spending. He is sufficiently alarmed by the threat to social and business stability of a swelling underclass of young blacks and Hispanics to advocate subsidies to manufacturers who employ school dropouts who otherwise might never enter into lasting connections with legitimate employment. Historically, manufacturing has been the entry point for sketchily educated newcomers to the labor force. White-collar jobs demand social and linguistic skills which take a generation or two to develop. East European Jews fluent only in Yiddish did not at the turn of the century move immediately to West End Avenue or the Bronx's Grand Concourse, let alone Scarsdale and Great Neck. Some, but only a minority, of their grandchildren did so. To be an enlightened business advocate of industrial policy is to recognize connections among social policy, employment opportunities, the quality of public education, and a favorable environment for the pursuit of profit. It is also to accept the limitations of free markets, and corporate lib à la Reagan as recipes for either efficiency or equity.

The further left one drifts from Rohatyn the more important become issues of social control of investment, workplace democracy, and distributional equity. In the 1984 campaign, the two finalists, Gary Hart and Walter Mondale, both flirted with the advice of Lester Thurow and Robert Reich, the somewhat ambiguously liberal cum yuppie twin gurus of industrial policy whose views have reached widest public attention. Neither articulated consistently or, in the case of Mondale, at all a fully developed economic program premised upon some version of industrial policy.

Unfortunately, industrial policy serves as a convenient metaphor for the general disarray of the liberal wing of the Democratic party, the outer boundary of political respectability. Industrial policy, balanced budgets, tax reform, Individual Training Accounts, and similar Democratic cries do not lift spirits and unleash political energies in the manner of simplistic appeals to the traditional values of patriotism, family life, religion, and old-fashioned education. If, as I have been complaining, liberal, left-liberal, even radical prescriptions are diverse and often contradictory, it is because practicing politicians, almost all of them in the first category, have yet to translate them into sufficiently stirring direct appeals to public emotion.

In this season of diminished expectations, Marxists despair over the wearisome scandal of pervasively false working-class consciousness, and liberals mourn over the political ingratitude of groups that ascended into the middle class as beneficiaries of New Deal and Great Society initiatives. If hope of liberal restoration exists, it resides in the personality and rhetoric that connect less unenlightened domestic and foreign policies with the passions of the voters. Of the prominent Democratic neoliberals—Gary Hart, Bill Bradley, Richard Gephardt, Bruce Babbitt, and Charles Robb—none shows signs of this talent. Truth to tell, these are dull lads.

Of big-league officeholders, Mario Cuomo comes closest to a winning, comparatively liberal formula. When Cuomo speaks, folks listen, even the jaded Democratic delegates at the 1984 presidential nominating convention. With convincing sincerity, he uses the imagery of family to recall us all to civic virtue. Would the most selfish soul allow his brother or sister to go hungry, untreated in time of illness, not provided with warm clothes and adequate shelter? Are not all Americans members of a single patriotic family, some of whose members arrived quite a while ago and others just yesterday? Immigrants are notable celebrants, particularly if they are economically successful, of their new country. Cuomo, the son of hard-working, ill-educated, low-income immigrant parents, can persuasively recall personal history as testimonial to America, the land of opportunity.

His own odyssey through college and law school, working to support himself throughout, protects him from the aura of privilege which surrounds such scions of the wealthy as Jay Rockefeller and George Bush. Moreover, as a moderately successful professional baseball player, he can draw upon the same wells of machismo as more celebrated athletes-turned-politicians such as Kemp and Bradley. The electorate is wary of soft, sentimental, wimpish leaders. Cuomo's scramble up the professional and political ladder attests to appropriate manly qualities. So also does his virtuosity in debate, something of a blood sport. He won a narrow victory in 1982 over a well-financed Republican opponent in part by reason of quick wit, an ability to twit a solemn antagonist about his wealth, and a well-displayed instinct for the jugular.

As a candidate, this paladin just might steal the rhetoric of family, church, and country from a Republican party cruelly bereft of Ronald Reagan and compelled to depend upon personalities unlikely to enunciate these themes with Reagan's authoritative speciousness. For one thing, Cuomo is a devout Catholic who goes to church regularly, a habit presumably appealing to a country as officially Christian as the United States. But he carefully refrains as a public official from efforts to impose his own opposition to abortion upon his constituents. Such principled restraint should soothe Jews, non-Catholics, and infidels.

The man is an astute political moralist. His vehement opposition to the provision of the Reagan tax reform measure that would have ended the deductibility of state and local taxes on federal income tax returns began, in media terms at least, as special pleading for a high-tax state unwilling to emulate the frugality of Texas toward local losers. With considerable skill, Cuomo enlisted support particularly from local officials in conservative as well as liberal areas, for it dawned upon mayors and county executives that as soon as property taxes ceased to be deductible, their constituents would demand lower assessments, lower tax rates, or both. Schools, road maintenance, garbage collection, and fire and police protection—as dear to the hearts of conservatives as of liberals—would suffer if local taxes produced less revenue. For officeholders, the Reagan proposal then posed two unacceptable alternatives— continuation of existing property and sales tax rates that would have constituted, once deductibility was denied, an effective tax increase, or curtailment of the services most valued by respectable middle-class homeowners.

On foreign policy, our potential hero has said little. Governors need not have foreign policies of their own. But Cuomo supplied a blurb for an essay collection, *Cutting Edges*, by Charles Krauthammer, which praised the author's "penetrating and lucid prose." A *New Republic* writer, Krauthammer runs with neoliberals in domestic affairs and with Reaganites in foreign policy. A second blurbist turned out to be none other than the ubiquitous George Will, who asserted that "Charles Krauthammer is the best new, young writer on public affairs."[21] Admirers of Krauthammer take the Soviet threat seriously.

Cuomo's strategy is prudent. What holds coalitions together consists partly of yearning for power and perquisite, a pinch of shared ideology, and the indispensably emollient ambiguity of the chosen leader. Ronald Reagan's first presidential campaign stressed Carter's economic failures and the redemptive promise of his own succession. His second race celebrated the new strength, pride, national purposes, and economic vigor assertedly promoted by his initial four years at the ship of state's helm. The first time around only close observers might have predicted the savage attack on social spending upon which Mr. Reagan embarked in 1981. Nor did the feel-good 1984 Republican campaign hint that tax reform was to be the domestic preoccupation of 1985. In an unideological land, the most ideological of presidents takes pains to present himself as anything but an ideologue.

As president, Cuomo just might succeed in curtailing Pentagon gluttony without outraged shrieks of treason from politicians to the left of Jesse Helms, enter into genuine disarmament negotiations with the Soviet Union, keep Star Wars as a research project on a starvation budget, and pursue less bellicose foreign policies in Central America and elsewhere in the world than Reaganites. In such a mildly social democratic regime, industrial policy, public-job efforts, low-income hous-

## The Secular Left: Hope or Fantasy?

ing, and comprehensive health care could plausibly resurface once the president surmounted the hurdle of raising taxes. Cuomo is far too astute to repeat Mondale's tax blunder. Mondale foolishly reiterated the necessity of tax increases without associating them with benefits to any constituency group. Whether or not in an actual campaign Cuomo might be cornered into conceding the necessity of raising more federal revenue, he would surely couple higher taxes with the promise of good things for the vast, ill-defined middle class as well as for the poor. In the great American family, even millionaires are honored members.

For pessimists, myself customarily among them, several reminders are in order. Americans, admire the wealthy though they may, lavishly reward entertainers, athletes, and corporate manipulators without stint, though they do also respond to populist appeals from both the left and the right. A presidential contest between Kemp and Cuomo would match two populists. Kemp on the right opposes abortion, favors school prayer, sanctions American intervention in Central America, clings still to the supply-side faith which brought him into national prominence, and allies himself with Defense Secretary Caspar Weinberger's yearning for ever-larger military budgets. At the same time, he seeks to protect social programs and insists that their curtailment is not the path to a balanced federal budget. This is to say that like other right-wing populists, Kemp projects a vision of power to the people that is selective. As economic animals, individuals should pay fewer taxes, the better to make up their own minds about the disposition of what they earn. Stepping back from the economic arena, government should simply let the contestants for financial improvement struggle among themselves, at most promoting the process by giving the handicapped a few special breaks, such as the tax and other incentives embodied in enterprise-zone legislation for depressed communities co-sponsored in Congress by Kemp and Robert Garcia, a liberal Democrat who represents the South Bronx.

Left-wing populism flips the coin. The freedom it favors most strenuously is in the sort of conduct regulated by right-wing populists. Though personally opposed as a faithful Catholic to abortion, Cuomo refuses to impose his values upon a variegated constituency. He harks back to the separation of church and state envisaged by the founding fathers in his suspicion of efforts to mandate religious observation in public schools. And although, like any ambitious politician, Cuomo boasts that in his administration taxes on business have been reduced and New York has become increasingly hospitable to enterprise, he clearly favors extension rather than curtailment of social provision, and the sort of environmental, health and safety, and product-reliability protections that right-wing populists condemn as shackles upon enterprise.

In our history, populism has often mixed resentment of government oppression and the power of the wealthy with a nasty streak of racism and anti-Semitism. It is either good luck or a sign of popular enlightenment that the reactionary populism of Jerry Falwell's Moral Majority is officially innocent of either sentiment. Nor, aside from unpleasant local incidents of discrimination, has the influx of Asians generated anything like the anti-Irish passions of the mid-nineteenth century, possibly because so many Americans have not yet forgotten that their parents or grandparents were themselves newcomers to a land of promise. This is to say that even right-wing populism, late-twentieth-century style, represents an advance over earlier varieties.

If our politics truly register shifting emphases among the interests and the passions, the 1988 presidential winner will be the runner who most adroitly addresses the subconstituencies mobilized by an interest, a passion, or a passionately cherished interest. Interests and passions often conflict. The very farmers who clamor for federal subsidies passionately favor independent effort, free enterprise, low taxes, and small government. Auto workers whose economic interests painfully suffered during the Reagan years voted heavily for the president in 1984 in response to his appeals to an aggressive patriotism shared by many blue-collar workers. Earlier in this century, businessmen, unappreciative of Franklin Roosevelt's success in preventing the collapse of the economy, became the New Deal's most bitter critics. In the 1960s, organized medicine resisted Medicare on standard free-enterprise grounds, as an example of leaping socialism. Doctors, as even they came to realize,

## The Secular Left: Hope or Fantasy?

were major beneficiaries of the attractively indulgent reimbursement formulae written into the Medicare statute.

Many, perhaps most, working-class Americans think that the rich have disproportionate political influence. One explanation of low voting turnouts is the apathy attendant upon a sense of helplessness. In schools and colleges where working-class students are numerous, political indifference supplements ambitious efforts to secure skills and credentials capable of translation into lucrative careers. The challenges to left-wing populists are complex. Least of them is identification of economic interests. More important is sincere appeal to passions of morality and patriotism that avoid the chauvinism and intrusions into lifestyles of the political right. Finally, left-wing populists confront as their most severe political obstacle the sense among their natural constituents that politics change nothing important.

1988 should be an interesting year.

# Notes

## Introduction

1. *The New York Times,* July 19, 1984, p. 1.
2. In 1798, Thomas Robert Malthus argued that "At nature's great table, no places are set for some. These poor souls, in the great lottery of life, have drawn blanks."
3. Peter Behr in *The Washington Post,* July 10, 1983.

## Chapter 1

1. His *Disabling America* (Basic Books, 1984) is a blazing assault upon a so-called rights industry of legal scholars, public-interest lawyers, and compliant judges who arrogantly ignored settled constitutional law the better to substitute their own values and policy preferences.
2. See *Statistical Abstract of the United States,* 104th edition, 1984, U.S. Department of Commerce, Bureau of the Census, pp. 432, 493.
3. See *Economic Report of the President,* February 1984, p. 259.
4. Joseph A. Pechman, *Federal Tax Policy* (Brookings, 1983), p. 318.
5. Ibid., p. 306.
6. These and the numbers that follow are on page 370 of the 1984 *Statistical Abstract* previously cited, unless otherwise specified.

7. February 14, 1985, p. 33.

8. In Malthus's words once again, "the sorrows and distresses of life ... seem ... necessary to soften and humanize the heart, to awaken social sympathy, to generate all the Christian virtues, and to afford scope for the ample exertions of benevolence."

9. See *Selected Plays* (Dodd-Mead, 1984), pp. 229–30.

10. *Statistical Abstract*, 1984, p. 367.

11. Ibid.

12. Ibid., p. 376.

13. Ibid., p. 368.

14. Sar A. Levitan and Robert Taggart, *The Promise of Greatness* (Harvard, 1976), p. 21.

15. Ibid., p. 23.

16. Sheila B. Kamerman and Alfred J. Kahn, *Income Transfers for Families with Children: An Eight-Country Study* (Temple University Press, 1983).

17. See Robert Kuttner, *The Economic Illusion* (Houghton Mifflin, 1984), pp. 247–49.

18. *The Liberal Imagination* (Doubleday/Anchor, 1950), p. 5.

19. Ibid., p. 6.

20. One of Mill's utilitarian precursors engaged in a cost-benefit analysis of the pleasures and pains of sin. Potential sinners were advised to weigh transitory fleshly pleasures against the eternal flames of hell. Proficient moral calculators, it was clear, behaved like good Christians. Virtue paid big dividends.

21. *New Dimensions of Political Economy* (Norton, 1966), pp. 1–2.

22. See "The Social Pork Barrel." *The Public Interest*, Spring 1975, pp. 3–31.

23. P. 1.

24. P. 3.

25. See *The Public Interest*, Summer 1967, pp. 15ff.

26. Milton Friedman, *Capitalism and Freedom* (University of Chicago Press, 1962), p. 192.

27. In the 1930s, Harvard investigators discovered that Western Electric workers at a Hawthorne plant increased their efficiency when working conditions were improved but also when conditions worsened. The moral: people are grateful for individual attention.

## Chapter 2

1. *The New York Times*, March 11, 1985, p. A-1.

2. Vide, among others, Banfield and Murray.

3. Vide Moynihan, Sowell, Gilder, and again Murray.

4. David S. Broder, "Another Watt?" *The Washington Post*, February 24, 1985, p. C-7.

5. See *Mandate for Leadership II: Continuing the Conservative Revolution*, by Stuart M. Butler, Michael Sanera, and W. Bruce Weinrod (The Heritage Foundation, 1984), pp. 5–8.

6. See "Hospital Chains Battle Health Insurers, but Will Quality Care Lose in the War?" *The Wall Street Journal*, February 5, 1985, p. 33.

7. "Business-Minded Health Care." *The New York Times*, February 12, 1985, pp. D-1, D-20.

8. From a paper delivered to a Columbia University seminar on privatization.
9. *Economic Report of the President*, February 1985, p. 137.
10. Ibid.
11. Ibid.
12. Ibid., p. 136.
13. Ibid., p. 154.
14. Ibid., p. 155.
15. Ibid., p. 160.
16. Ibid., p. 174.
17. See John E. Schwartz, *America's Hidden Success* (Norton, 1983), p. 26.
18. Thomas Alcock, *Observations* (1752). Cited by Edgar Furniss, *The Position of the Laborer in a System of Nationalism* (Houghton Mifflin, 1920), p. 153.
19. Furniss, p. 155.
20. Ibid., pp. 114–15.
21. See David Capiowitz, *The Poor Pay More* (Macmillan, 1967).
22. *Economic Report of the President*, February 1985, p. 264.
23. Schwarz, pp. 34–35.
24. Ibid., p. 36.
25. Ibid., p. 37.
26. *Toward the Future: Catholic Social Thought and the U.S. Economy, a Lay Letter by the Lay Commission on Catholic Social Teaching and the U.S. Economy*, Quadlibetal Publications, Notre Dame, Indiana, November 1984, p. 36.
27. Ibid.
28. Hobart Rowen, "Continent Strives to Overcome 'Europessimism.' " *The Washington Post*, March 10, 1985, p. G-1.
29. *Payments to Individuals*, Office of Management and Budget, February 1983.
30. *Lay Letter*, p. 36.
31. Ibid., p. 38.
32. Sheldon Danziger, "How Income Transfer Programs Affect Work, Savings, and the Income Distribution: A Critical Review." *Journal of Economic Literature*, September 1981. Cited by Schwarz, p. 40.
33. "Hunger in America: Ten Years Later," report of the U.S. Senate Subcommittee on Nutrition, 1979. Cited by Schwarz, p. 44.
34. Ibid. (Schwarz, p. 45).
35. Danziger, p. 62.
36. *The New York Times*, February 27, 1985, p. A-12.
37. Ibid.
38. The Robert Wood Johnson Foundation, *Special Report on Access to Health Care for the American People*, No. One, 1983.
39. Ibid.
40. See *The Wall Street Journal*, December 16, 1985, p. 28.
41. Ronald Andersen et al., *Two Decades of Health Services: Social Survey Trends in Use and Expenditures* (Ballinger, 1976), pp. 8, 20. Cited by Schwarz, p. 46.
42. Schwarz, p. 47.
43. Ibid.
44. Bruce Headey, *Housing Policy in the Developed Economy* (London: Croom Helm, 1978), p. 198. Cited by Schwarz, p. 49.
45. Sar A. Levitan and Robert Taggart, *The Promise of Greatness* (Harvard, 1976), p. 142.

## Notes

46. Laura L. Morlock et al., "Long-term Follow-up of Public Service Employment Participants: The Baltimore SMSA Experience during the 1970s" (Johns Hopkins Health Services Research and Development Center, 1981), p. 44.

47. Garth L. Mangum and R. Thayne Robson, *Metropolitan Impact of Manpower Programs: A Four-City Comparison* (Olympus, 1973), p. 292. Cited by Schwarz, p. 55.

48. Schwarz, p. 55.

49. Irving Lazar, "Summary: The Persistence of Preschool Effects" (Community Services Laboratory, New York State University College of Human Ecology at Cornell University, October 1977). Cited by Schwarz, p. 56.

50. Lance Liebman, "Social Intervention in a Democracy." *The Public Interest*, Winter 1974, p. 17.

51. Who bothers to read careful statistical analyses of the failure of tax breaks to stimulate investment? In February 1986, Citizens for Tax Justice, a public-interest group, issued *Money for Nothing: The Failure of Corporate Tax Incentives 1981–1984*, a devastating demonstration that so-called supply-side benefits to corporations did nothing to stimulate investment in new technology and a great deal to enrich stockholders and top managers. Precious little media attention saluted this research. Newspapers and TV channels are owned by folks who profited from Reagan tax legislation and are supported by corporate advertisers in similar situations.

52. Robert Lekachman, "Paying for Progress," in *Alternatives*, ed. by Irving Howe (Pantheon, 1984), p. 100.

53. *Annual Report to the Congress*, Fiscal Year 1984, Office of Technology Assessment, Washington, D.C., p. 18.

54. *The Washington Post*, March 10, 1985, p. A-23.

55. Lekachman, "Paying for Progress," in *Alternatives*, p. 103.

56. Ibid.

## Chapter 3

1. See *The Decline of Radicalism* (Random House, 1963), pp. 18–19.

2. See "Khomeini's New Order in Iran." *The Nation*, March 1, 1986, p. 242.

3. Popular in California and allowed in some other states are private courts presided over usually by former judges who are well paid by the litigants for expeditious resolution of their controversies.

4. See "The Pillars of Social Welfare" by Martin Rein, privately circulated paper, March 20, 1985, p. 40.

5. "Welfare for Profit: Moral, Empirical and Theoretical Perspectives." *The Journal of Social Policy*, January 1984, p. 64.

6. See *The New York Times*, January 26, 1985, p. A-5.

7. Ibid.

8. Ibid.

9. "Public Hospitals Under Private Management," by William Shonick and Ruther Romer, cited in *The New York Times*, ibid.

10. Ibid.

11. Ibid.

12. See *The New York Times*, February 12, 1985, p. D-3.

13. Ibid., p. D-20.

14. Ibid.

# Notes

15. See *The New York Times*, April 2, 1985, p. D-2.
16. See *The New York Times*, February 11, 1985, pp. A-1, A-16.
17. Ibid.
18. Ibid.
19. Ibid.
20. Ibid.
21. "At McPrison and Burglar King, It's Hold the Justice." *The New Republic*, April 8, 1985, pp. 10–12.
22. See *The New York Times*, March 11, 1985, p. A-1.
23. Milton Friedman, *Capitalism and Freedom* (University of Chicago Press, 1982), p. 89.
24. Community control in operation often disconcerts its advocates. With some success, fundamentalists have been busily attacking elementary and secondary textbooks for their alleged advocacy of "secular humanism" and their failure to emphasize the role of religion in history. One fundamentalist activist takes the Bible literally, as "Any thinking person does." Another objected to a text which featured a little boy cooking and a little girl reading. The book "planted in the first graders' minds that there are no God-given roles for the different sexes." (My source is that secular humanist newspaper, *The New York Times*, February 28, 1986, p. A-19.)
25. See "Privatizing the Delivery of Social Welfare Services," by Marc Bendick, an unpublished paper presented in April 1985 to a Columbia University privatization seminar, p. 26.
26. Ibid.
27. Ibid., p. 28.

## Chapter 4

1. That steadfast British ally of private profit, *The Economist*, claims on behalf of privatization that "Everybody Is Doing It, Differently." The journal devoted a special section to the good news that "The selling of state assets—from airlines to jute mills—is captivating politicians everywhere, even in socialist Spain and Communist China." See the issue dated December 27, 1985, p. 7.
2. These are examples of lemon socialism, the drift into public ownership of bankrupt enterprises serving clienteles influential enough to demand and secure continuation of threatened activities.
3. Early in 1986, the Department of Health and Human Services proposed a relatively inexpensive plan to protect Medicare patients against the intolerable costs of catastrophic illness requiring prolonged hospitalization. Private health insurers immediately protested the scheme as a threat to their own sale of hospital insurance to the elderly. The administration agreeably put the HHS plan on hold and appointed a commission to study the issue. The incident is quite representative.
4. See *Statistical Abstract*, 1985, p. 33.
5. Ibid.
6. See *Economic Report of the President*, 1985, p. 265.
7. Ibid., p. 243.
8. See *Statistical Abstract*, 1985, p. 331.
9. May 19, 1985.
10. David Packard, a former Undersecretary of Defense, is an establishment

## Notes

critic not readily discounted even by generals, admirals, and their political protectors.

11. Congressional Budget Office data cited in *The Washington Post*, May 19, 1985, p. A-10.
12. Ibid., p. A-1.
13. See *Statistical Abstract*, 1985, p. 332.
14. Ibid., p. 335.
15. Ibid., p. 337.
16. See "The War for Star Wars," by George W. Ball, *The New York Review of Books*, April 11, 1985, p. 38.
17. Ibid.
18. Ibid., p. 39.
19. "The Military Payoff, a Report on the U.S. Government's Most Generous Pension Plan," by John Bickerman for the Center on Budget and Policy Priorities, February 1985.
20. See *Budget of the United States Government*, Fiscal Year 1986, pp. 5–13.
21. See *The Washington Post*, November 16, 1985, p. A-10.
22. See Richard B. Freeman and James L. Medoff, *What Do Unions Do?* (Basic Books, 1984), pp. 27–28.
23. Ibid., p. 36.
24. Ibid., p. 222.
25. Ibid., p. 215.
26. Ibid.
27. Ibid., p. 214.
28. Ibid., p. 208.
29. Ibid., p. 211.
30. Published by the Harvard University Press.
31. Martin L. Weitzman, *The Share Economy* (Harvard University Press, 1984), pp. 4–5.
32. Robert Reich's apt label for the mergers, acquisitions, and asset shuffles which have occupied more corporate energy than product research and development.
33. May 7, 1985, p. 10.
34. A. H. Raskin, "Labor Redivivus." *The New Leader*, February 11–25, 1985, p. 4.
35. Freeman and Medoff, p. 232.
36. P. 4.
37. Ibid.

## Chapter 5

1. Burger and Powell were born in 1907, Brennan in 1906, Blackmun and Marshall in 1908. The youngsters include Byron White, born in 1917; William Rehnquist, 1927; John Paul Stevens, 1920; and Sandra Day O'Connor, just yesterday in 1930.
2. See *Newsday*, March 11, 1986, p. 7.
3. With the honorable exception of the Sergeant York gun.
4. As the insider's gag runs, the paper is the nation's best newspaper, alas!
5. The program's unsparing critique of West Point was at the end weakened by the hero's decision not to resign honorably. As usual, the lesson

*Notes*

taught was that our institutions are okay. It's just that an occasional bad apple contaminates barrels stuffed with sound produce.

6. See the Special Health Section, *The Washington Post*, June 5, 1985, p. 12.

7. Ibid.

8. Reprinted by the National Committee for Full Employment, May 31, 1985.

9. A Labor Department press release reprinted by the National Committee for Full Employment, Washington, D.C., May 31, 1985.

## Chapter 6

1. The revelation was on the cover of the journal's January 20, 1986, issue.

2. See *The Organization Man* (Simon & Schuster, 1956), p. 7.

3. Not every ex-yuppie admires current practitioners. *Business Week* (March 24, 1986, p. 54) quotes a 1949 Harvard Business School alumnus to this effect: "These kids are smart. But I'd as soon take a python to bed as hire one. He'd suck my brains, memorize my Rolodex, and use my telephone to find some other guy who'd pay him twice the money."

4. See *Business Week*, August 5, 1985, pp. 65–66.

5. *Yale Law Journal*, 73, 1964.

6. Daniel Patrick Moynihan has recently argued semi-seriously that the distribution of anti-poverty money might actually have made income distribution slightly more instead of less inegalitarian. See his *Family and Nation* (Harcourt Brace Jovanovich, 1986), p. 79.

7. Quoted in *The Seventies*, edited by Irving Howe and Michael Harrington (Harper & Row, 1970), p. 75, in an essay "Between Apostles and Technicians" by Robert Lekachman.

8. See *Law and Poverty*, 2nd ed. (West Publishing Company, 1973), edited by George Cooper et al., pp. 318–35.

9. Ibid., p. 323.

10. Ibid., p. 328.

11. Ibid., p. 330.

12. See "DRG: The Counterrevolution in Financing Health Care," by Danielle A. Dolenc and Charles J. Dougherty, in *Hastings Center Report*, June 1985, pp. 19–29.

13. See Lekachman in *The Seventies*, pp. 76–77.

14. See *The Greening of America*, passim.

15. Quoted in a *Fortune* review by Andrew Hacker (June 24, 1985, p. 135) of *The Gold Collar Worker* by Robert E. Kelley (Addison-Wesley, 1985).

16. Tom Peters and Nancy Austin strangely echo Consciousness III. As one hostile reviewer summarized their recommendations to successful managers, "Workers are to be 'empowered to take possession' of their own achievements; 'radical decentralization' is to be brought about through a 'certain militancy.' At the same time, we read, ever larger numbers of 'brave souls' with 'lonely lives' are banding together in a move from 'tough-mindedness to tenderness,' and that the reactionary values of 'controlling and arranging' are to be replaced by a 'visceral form of spiritual energy' for 'beauty is universally available.'" (See *Commentary*, August 1985, pp. 66–67, for a review by Jules Cohn.)

*Notes*

17. Quoted by Randall Rothenberg in *The Neoliberals* (Simon & Schuster, 1984), p. 140.
18. See "Money for Nothing," a report of Citizens for Tax Justice, February 1986, p. 3.
19. See Rothenberg, 223.
20. Robert B. Reich and John D. Donahue tell the Chrysler story in their *New Deals: The Chrysler Revival and the American System* (Times Books, 1985).
21. See Rothenberg, p. 227.
22. Ibid., p. 229.
23. Ibid.
24. Ibid.
25. Ibid., p. 224.
26. The journal's schizophrenia is especially glaring in foreign policy. Its March 24, 1986, issue opened with a Kinsley column opposing aid to the contras and continued with a three-page editorial justification of that aid entitled "The Case for the Contras," pp. 4, 7–9. The next issue contained an attack on Kinsley by Charles Krauthammer, presumably the author of the editorial, and an article by still another member of the journal's staff sharply criticizing the contras and Reagan's insistence upon aiding them.
27. Quoted in "Marty Come Lately." *Policy Review*, Summer 1985, p. 37.
28. See p. 30.
29. Ibid., p. 31.
30. See *Newsday*, July 31, 1985, p. 17.
31. See *Newsday*, August 5, 1985, p. 15.

*Chapter 7*

1. Richard John Neuhaus, "What the Fundamentalists Want." *Commentary*, May 1985, p. 43.
2. See "Diarist." *The New Republic*, September 16 and 23, 1985, p. 50.
3. See *Statistical Abstract of the United States*, 1985, p. 52.
4. Alarmed or nauseated critics of the Reverend Jerry could take comfort from "the public's impressive distaste for him." According to one Republican pollster, only Khomeini gets higher negative ratings. See Murray Waas, "Falwell's New Name." *The New Republic*, March 31, 1986.
5. See *Quarterly Review*, Summer 1984, p. 19.
6. Ibid., p. 20.
7. Ibid.
8. Nicely illustrating divisions in the Jewish community, the American Jewish Committee, sponsor of *Commentary*, also subsidizes *Present Tense*, a liberal journal often critical of American foreign and defense policy and hostile to Israeli intransigence on the West Bank.
9. Neuhaus, p. 44.
10. See Robert Lekachman, *Greed Is Not Enough* (Pantheon, 1982), p. 51.
11. See *Time*, September 2, 1985, p. 49.
12. Cited by Robert Lekachman, "Personal Perspective." *Christianity and Crisis*, January 21, 1985, p. 508.
13. Ibid., pp. 44–45.
14. All the quotations appear on page 45 of the lay commission document.
15. Ibid., p. 18.
16. Ibid., p. 19.
17. Ibid.

## Notes

18. Ibid., p. 20.
19. Ibid., p. 26.
20. Ibid., p. 27.
21. Ibid., p. 29.
22. Ibid.
23. Ibid., p. 31.
24. Ibid., p. 35.
25. Ibid.
26. Ibid.
27. Ibid.
28. Ibid., p. 36.
29. Ibid., p. 39.
30. Ibid., p. 40.
31. Ibid.
32. Ibid., p. 6.
33. Ibid., p. 7.
34. See *Time*, September 2, 1985, p. 49.
35. See first draft of the Catholic bishops' pastoral letter on the American economy, p. 353.
36. See Vincent A. Carrafiello, *The Month*, February 1985, p. 1.
37. See *Commentary*, February 1985, p. 35.
38. Ibid., p. 33.
39. See *Origins*, NC Documentary Service, Vol. 14, No. 22/23, November 15, 1984, p. 337.
40. Ibid., p. 340.
41. Ibid., p. 341.
42. Ibid., p. 339.
43. Ibid., p. 352.
44. Ibid., p. 355.
45. Ibid.
46. Ibid., p. 361.
47. Ibid., p. 365.
48. Ibid., p. 369.
49. Ibid., p. 373.
50. Ibid.
51. Ibid., p. 375.
52. See *The Jewish Vote in the 1984 Presidential Election*, by Martin Hochbaum, American Jewish Congress, January 1985.
53. Ibid., p. 3.
54. Ibid., p. 4.
55. (American Jewish Congress, New York), *American Jewish Congress Resolution 1948–1986*, p. 703.
56. See "Joint Program Plan," 1985, p. 42.
57. See Earl Raab and Seymour Martin Lipset, *The Political Future of American Jews*, American Jewish Congress pamphlet, March 1985, p. 12.
58. Ibid., p. 13.
59. Ibid., p. 30.
60. Ibid., p. 36.
61. Ibid., p. 37.
62. Ibid., p. 40.
63. Ibid., p. 41.
64. Ibid., p. 43.

65. Ibid., p. 51.
66. Ibid., p. 58.
67. Ibid., p. 60.
68. Ibid., pp. 60–61.
69. Ibid., p. 67.
70. Ibid., p. 69.
71. Ibid., p. 70.
72. Ibid., p. 79.
73. Ibid., p. 93.
74. Ibid., p. 95.
75. See *The Wall Street Journal*, May 24, 1985, p. 1.
76. Ibid., p. 10.
77. See Volume III, p. 329.
78. See *Quarterly Review*, Summer 1984, p. 14.
79. Ibid., p. 15.

## Chapter 8

1. See Irving Howe, *Socialism in America* (Harcourt Brace Jovanovich, 1985), pp. 3–4.
2. See Michael Walzer's scholarly commentary on the Israelite exodus from Egypt and its subsequent impact upon religious radicals, particularly in seventeenth-century England, in *Exodus and Revolution* (Basic Books, 1985).
3. See *Journal of John Wesley*, ed. by Nehemiah Curnock (London: Kelly, 1909), Volume II, pp. 453–54.
4. Whatever the party did, its prospects were bleak. Alliance with Roosevelt in all probability would have been tantamount to absorption by the Democratic party.
5. Vol. II, p. 288.
6. I have used as a source J. Anthony Lukas's magnificent chronicle *Common Ground* (Alfred A. Knopf, 1985).
7. Ibid., p. 241.
8. See *Economic Report of the President*, February 1985, p. 160.
9. See *The Public Interest*, Fall 1985, p. 107.
10. See 50th Anniversary Edition, *The Report of the Committee on Economic Security of 1935*, National Conference on Social Welfare, 1985, p. 8.
11. The marginal propensity to consume is the disposition to spend out of an additional dollar of disposable income. Before Reagan, it ran between ninety-two and ninety-four cents out of each additional dollar. In the third quarter of 1985, it rose to 97.5 cents.
12. See Stephen J. Rose, *The American Profile Poster* (Pantheon Books, 1986), p. 10.
13. See Richard Parker's review of Lester Thurow's *The Zero-Sum Solution* in *The Nation*, November 16, 1985, p. 518.
14. Lester Thurow, *The Zero-Sum Solution* (Simon & Shuster, 1985), p. 49.
15. Ibid., p. 265.
16. See Samuel Bowles, David M. Gordon, and Thomas E. Weisskopf, *Beyond the Wasteland* (Doubleday/Anchor 1983), p. 311. I summarize their program in this and the next paragraph.
17. Ibid., p. 312.
18. Ibid., p. 318.
19. See James Tobin's "Keynes's Policies in Theory and Practice" in *The*

*Policy Consequences of John Maynard Keynes*, ed. by Harold L. Wattel (M. E. Sharpe Inc., 1985), pp. 3–12.

20. Robert Lekachman, "The Radical Keynes," in Wattel, ed., *The Policy Consequences of John Maynard Keynes*, pp. 30–38.

21. See *The New York Review of Books*, December 5, 1985.

# Index

Aaron, Henry, 191
ABC, 151, 153
ABM treaty, 123
Abortion, 86, 87, 148, 196–97, 212, 249, 250
Accuracy in Academia, 259
Accuracy in Media, 259
Affirmative action, 44, 221, 242
AFL-CIO, xlviii, 130, 134, 146, 196
Agricultural Adjustment Act, 26
AIDS, xxvi
Aid to Families with Dependent Children (AFDC), 56, 126, 268
Air traffic controllers, 144
Alda, Alan, 208
Alinsky, Saul, xlviii, 262
Allende, Salvador, 47, 218
Altruisms, private, vs. government services, 157
American Civil Liberties Union, 4, 224
American Correctional Association, 103
American Economic Association, 190
American Enterprise Institute, xlii, 98, 216
American Federation of Labor, 129–30
American Hospital Association, 99
American Jewish Committee, 249
American Jewish Congress, 233, 235–36, 249
American Management Association, 133
American Medical Association, 81

American Medical International, 80, 97, 98
American Telephone and Telegraph Co. (AT&T), 71, 186
America Works, 46
Amtrak, 118
Anderson, Gerard, 100
Anderson, Marion, 127
Anderson, Ron, 98
Anti-Catholicism, 25
Anti-Semitism, 25, 224, 234, 252
*Appeal to Reason*, 256
Aquinas, St. Thomas, 214–15, 216
Armor, David, 38
Aspin, Les, 184, 190, 192, 193, 261
Atlas, James, 233
Augustine, Norman R., 128

Babbitt, Bruce, xxii, 188, 286
Baker, Howard, xxxv, 187, 189
Baker, James, xxxvi, 8
Bakker, Jim, 208
Ball, George, 123
Baptists, 246
Barth, Karl, 237
Basic Books, 174
Beer, Samuel, 33
Begin, Menachem, 224
Bell, Daniel, 32, 164
Bellamy, Carol, 152
Bellamy, Edward, 159
Belli, Melvin, 90
Bennett, William J., 44
Benson, Ezra Taft, 208
Benstock, Marcy, 261
Bentham, Jeremy, 23

## Index

Berger, Peter, 186, 228, 232, 237
Berger, Victor, 256
Bernardin, Cardinal, 249
*Beyond the Wasteland* (Bowles, Gordon, Weisskopf), 181, 284
Biden, Joseph, xxii, xxiv, 187
Billig, Commander, 126
Biotherapeutics Corp., 60
Birch Society, John, 148
Birth control, 3, 238
Black, Hugo, 3
Blackmun, Harry, 148, 149, 171, 172
Black Muslims, 2
Black Panthers, 2
Blacks, 2, 10, 42; health care 59; housing, 61; poverty, 15–16, 53–54; as Reagan losers, 267, 273–74; and school busing in Boston, 263–65
Bliss, Douglas, 99
Blue Cross, xxi
Boeing, 180
Boesky, Ivan, 151
Boone, Daniel, 159
Boorstin, Daniel, 88
Bork, Robert, 149
Botha, P. W., 209
Boulding, Kenneth, 33
Bowles, Samuel, 180
Bradby, Dennis E., 103
Brademas, John, 191
Bradley, Bill, xxvii, 178, 179, 187, 272, 286, 287
Brennan, William, 148, 149, 171
Brenner, Harvey, 130
British Broadcasting Corp., 117
British Health Service, 77, 199
Brookings Institution, 182, 190
"Brothers and Strangers," 132
Brown, Jerry, 183
Brown, Norman, 233
*Brown v. Board of Education*, 264
Buchanan, Pat, 266
Buckingham Security, 104, 105
Buckley, William F., xl, 125, 153
Bumpers, Dale, 187
Bunzel, John, 33
Burford, Anne Gorsuch, 70–71, 213
Burger, Warren, 148, 149

Bush, George, xii, xxxv, xxxvi, 187, 189, 196, 252, 287
Business Roundtable, 178
*Business Week*, 80, 163, 180–81
Busing of Boston schoolchildren, 263–65

Cadeau, Mireille, 240
Campus unrest, in 1960s, 5
*Capitalism and Freedom* (Friedman), 109–10
Capital punishment, 87
Cardenal, Ernesto, 227, 245
Carter, Jimmy, xii, 7–8, 20, 81, 85, 89, 91–92, 118, 139, 185, 209, 222, 265
Casey, William, xi, xx
Casillas, Frank C., 155, 156
Catholic Charities, 157
Catholic Legion of Decency, 210
Catholics, xxxix, 213–20, 238; in Latin America, 245–46; of religious left, 226–32
*Catholic Social Teaching and the U.S. Economy*, xxxix, 214, 228
CBS, 153
*Cato Policy Report*, xx
Celeste, Richard, 46
Central Intelligence Agency, xi, xxi, 32, 47, 160, 161
Centra Units, 100
Chancellor, John, 153
"Changing Situation of Workers and Their Unions, The," 146
Channel 13, New York City, 157
Channell, Spitz, xxi
Chernenko, Constantin, 207
Children: poverty, 50; programs, U.S. vs. international, 18
Choate, Pat, 178
*Chronicle of Higher Education*, 233
Chrysler Corp., 182
Church and state, separation, 4
Churchill, Winston, 199
Cisneros, Henry, 193
Civiletti, Benjamin, 133
Civil rights, 5, 30
Civil Rights Commission, 221
Cleaver, Eldridge, 2
Coercive powers, government, 170–74

## Index

Cohen, Wilbur, 270
Coleman Report, 263
Coliseum, New York City, 169
*Commentary*, 32, 125, 186, 194, 222, 232, 233
Committee on Economic Security, 270, 273
Committee on a Just, Caring, and Dynamic Economy, 271
Committee on a Just Political Economy, 239
Communications, privatization, 156–57
Communications Act, 170
Communist party, 259
Community action programs, 29–30
Community Services Society, New York City, 157
Comparable worth, 242
Competition, in public sector, 39
Comprehensive Employment and Training Act (CETA) (1973), 65–66, 106
Comstock, Anthony, 210
Congressional Budget Office, 266
Connor, Bull, xxiii, xxxii, 261
Conrail, 118
Conservatives, 31–32; fundamentalism, 211–13
Continental Airline, 278
Contras, xi, xxiv
Coolidge, Calvin, 24–25
Corbett, Bernard, 101
Corporate Disclosure Act, 282
Corporations, taxes, 179–80
Corrections Corp. of America, 103–4
Cost-benefit analysis, 34–35
Cost: compensation of GM workers, 140; corporate lawbreaking, 133; defense, 120–22; education, 17; Great Society programs, 43–44; health care, 17; military retirement, 126; social programs, 12–14, 16–18; Veterans Administration, 126
Coughlin, Father, 252
Council of Economic Advisers, 27–28, 33, 182, 183, 190, 239
Cox, Archibald, xv, 149

Crime control, 87
Criminal justice system, 103–6
Culture of 1960s, 1–6
Cuomo, Andrew, 189
Cuomo, Mario, xxvii, li, 152, 185, 188, 189, 214, 272, 286–89
Cuomo, Matilda, 189
*Cutting Edges* (Krauthammer), 288

Daley, Richard, xxxi, 16
"Dallas," 132, 274
D'Amato, Alphonse, 152, 251
Danner Corp., 105
Darwin, Charles, 212, 213
Davis, Polk, 164
Debs, Eugene V., 256, 257
Defense Department, 105
Defense Intelligence Agency, 47
Defense spending, 73–77; and militarization, 118–28
Democratic Socialists of America, 186, 277
Deregulation initiatives, 39
*De Rerum Novarum* (Leo XIII), 227
Desegregation of Boston Schools, 263–65
Deunionization, 128–47
DeVries, William, 46
Dewey Ballantine, 164
Diagnostic-related groups (DRGs), 173–74
Disciples of Christ, 246
*Dissent*, 38
Dole, Robert, xii, xxxv, 187, 189, 252
Donovan, Raymond, 144
*Doonesbury*, xiv
Doss, Robert F., 120–21
Dotson, Donald L., 145
Douglas, William, 171, 172
Dow Chemical Corp., 180
*Dress Gray*, 153
Drugs, in 1960s, 2–3
Dukakis, Michael, xxii, xxiv, 185, 188
Dulles, John Foster, 21, 208
Dun & Bradstreet, 107
"Dynasty," 132, 274

Eads, George, 183
Eagle Forum, 262

## Index

Earned-income tax credit, 56
*Economic Report of the President*, 48–50, 267
Economics, neoconservative, 32–40
Economy, 1, 9–21; in crisis, 279–81; laissez-faire, 2–24; of Reagan years, 69–70
Education: compensatory, 29; costs and results, 17, 43–44; privatization, 158; school busing in Boston, 263–65; and vouchers, 110
Eisenhower, Dwight, 3, 21, 208
Elderly: poverty, 50, 54, 55; as Reagan losers, 267–73; *see also* Social Security
Election of 1988, fanasy, 187–90
Elementary and Secondary Education Act (1965), 16
Ellender, Senator, 61
Elphin, Donald, 190
Emergency Financial Control Board, 284
Employment: lifetime, 166–68; and unions, 137–38; *see also* Unemployment
Employment Act (1946), 27
*Encounter*, 32
*Engel* v. *Vitale*, 212
Environmental Protection Agency, xxxiii, 38, 70–71, 91, 213
Episcopalians, 238, 249
Equal Rights Amendment (ERA), li, 189, 195, 266
Eureka College, 269
Evangelicals, 248
Experimental Housing Allowance Program (EHAO), 111

"Falcon Crest," 132
Falwell, Jerry, 40, 206, 207, 208, 209, 213, 224, 246, 247, 248, 262, 290
Family Assistance Program (FAP), xxxiii, 37, 231
Farakhan, Louis, 222, 234
Farmers, as Reagan losers, 273–74
Federal Communications Commission, 150, 170
Federal Deposit Insurance Corp., 26, 70, 71

Federal Housing Administration, 29, 70, 71
*Federalist Papers*, 214, 240
Federal Reserve, 283
Federal Trade Commission, 150, 156, 181, 193, 213, 274
Feldstein, Martin, 33
Fellowship of Christian Athletes, 85
Field Foundation, 57
Finley, Wagner, Heini, Underberg, Myerson, Manley & Casey, 164
"Firing Line," 153
Fitzsimmons, Frank, 90
Flashner Medical Partnership Doctors' Officenters, 100
Food stamps, 56, 57–58, 108
Ford, Gerald, 7, 9, 20, 92, 135, 185
Ford Motor Co., 9
Foreclosures, farm, 273
*Fortune* magazine, 32, 133, 166
"Frictional" unemployment, 10
Friedenberg, Edgar, 233
Friedman, Milton, 31, 35–36, 38, 109–10, 149, 178, 216, 255, 256
Friedman, Stanley, 279
Fundamentalists, 211–14, 224, 248
*Fundamentals, The*, 248–49

Galbraith, John Kenneth, 76
Garbage collection, private, 48
Garcia, Robert, 289
Garrity, Arthur, 263, 264
Garth, David, 164
Geneen, Harold, 47
General Dynamics, 75, 104, 105, 134, 274
General Electric Co., xxxvii, 105, 120, 134
General Motors Corp., 9, 141–42, 166, 190; Saturn plant, 167–68, 197, 278
George Washington University, 97
Gephardt, Richard, xxii, xxiv, 179, 184, 286
Ghorbanifar, Manucher, xiii
GI Bill, 178
*Gideon* decision, 4
Gilder, George, xxxvii, 33, 186, 197
Gingrich, Newt, xxxv, 213
Ginsberg, Allen, 2
Glazer, Nathan, 33, 232

## Index

Goetz, Bernard, 87
Goldberg, Arthur, 171
Goldwater, Barry, 120, 269
Gompers, Samuel, 130, 134
Goodman, Paul, 233
Gorbachev, Mikhail, 207
Gordon, David, 180
Gore, Albert, xxii, xxiv
Gorham, William, 33, 34–35
Gotbaum, Victor, 182
Gotschal, Menges, 164
Government: defense spending, 73–77; health spending, 77–82; and private altruism, 157; privatization of social services, 45–51; social welfare, 1960s, 13
Grace & Co., W. R., 180
Grace, Peter, xl
Graham, Billy, 226
Gramm-Rudman Act, xxxvi, 119
Great Depression, 25–26
Great Society, 18, 29–31, 42, 65, 67, 70, 82, 135
Green, William, 130, 134
*Greening of America, The* (Reich), 165, 168
Greenspan Commission, 115, 270
Grenada invasion, xlvii, 84–85
Grumman, 75
*Gulliver's Travels* (Swift), 159
Gun control, 87
Guthrie, Woody, 168

Haig, Alexander, xv, 187, 221
Hakim, Albert, xiii
Hall, Fawn, xxi
Hallucinogens, 2
Harrington, Michael, 186, 258, 277
Hart, Gary, xxii, xxiv, 39, 177–78, 179, 181, 184, 187, 188–90, 195–98, 272, 285, 286
Hatfield, Arnie, 240–41
Hatfield, Mark, 246–47
Hayakawa, S. I., 7
Hayde, Barbara, 46
Head Start, 16, 29, 42, 66–67
Health care, 43, 153–54; costs, 17; DRGs, 173–74; for elderly, 272; government spending on, 77–82; and neoliberals, 198–99, 200; and poverty, 58–60; privatization, 39, 45–46, 97–103, 157–58; U.S. vs. international, 18, 199; and vouchers, 111–15
Health, Education and Welfare Department, 191
Health maintenance organizations (HMOs), 81–82
Health Service, British, 199
"Heart of Steel," 130–31
Heckler, Margaret, 267
Heilbroner, Robert, 33
Heller, Walter, 28
Helms, Jesse, 247, 250, 288
Heritage Foundation, xlii, 38, 45, 110, 125
Hertzberg, Hendrik, 207
Higgins, George, 186
*High Noon*, 159
High-Speed Anti-Radiation Missile (HARM), 121
Himmelfarb, Milton, 222
Hitler, Adolf, 222
Hoffa, Jimmy, 90
Holtzman, Elizabeth, 251
Homelessness, xxvi
Homeowners Loan Corporation, 26
Hoover, Herbert, xli, 26, 209, 210
Horn, Carole, 77
Hospital Corp. of America, 80, 97, 99, 158, 198
Hospital Cost Containment Board, Florida, 99
Hospital Research and Educational Trust, 99
Hospitals, privatization, 97–99
Hostages, in Iran and Lebanon, 85
House Armed Services Committee, 184
House Ways and Means Committee 277–78
Housing, 46–47, 61–62; and poverty, 55; and vouchers, 111
Housing and Urban Development Department, 108, 111
Howe, Irving, 38, 186
Humana Hospital Corp., xxxiv, 39, 45–46, 77, 97, 98, 100, 158, 198
Humbard, Rex, 208
Hume, David, 209
Humphrey, Hubert, 20

## Index

Humphrey-Hawkins Balanced Growth and Full Employment Act (1978), xlix, 92, 139, 184, 231
Huntington, Samuel, 33
Hussein, Sadam, xi
Hutton, E. F., 134, 279
Hypocrisy, 86–89

Iacocca, Lee, xxxiv, 182, 192
Icahn, Carl, 151
Immigrants, and strikebreaking, 143–44
Immigration and Naturalization Service, 105–6
Individualism: rugged, 24–25; and social control, 159–61
Individual Training Accounts, 39, 178, 193, 198, 286
Industrial policy, 180–84, 281–86
Infant mortality, and Medicaid, 60
Inflation, in 1960s, 10
Inouye, Daniel, xii, xvi
*In re Gault*, 4
Instant Care centers, 100
Interest on savings, 24
International Harvester, 273
International Monetary Fund (IMF), 191, 230–31
International Telephone and Telegraph Corp. (ITT), 47, 218
Iranscam, xi
Irvine, Reed, 259
Islam, 206

Jackson, Jesse, xxii, 195, 224, 234
Jackson, Michael, 205
James, Barbara, 171–73
James, William, 21
Javits, Jacob, 251
Jencks, Christopher, 33
"Jewel in the Crown, The," 132
Jews, 214, 220–25, 238, 249; of religious left, 232–37
Job Corps, 43, 107, 154–56
Jobs Partnership Act, 48, 106
Job training, 46, 48, 62–67; privatization, 106–7; and vouchers, 112
John Deere, 273
John Paul II, Pope, 145, 215, 216–17, 226, 227, 238

Johnson, Lyndon, 15, 17, 42, 81, 113, 123, 265; and Great Society, 28–31; vs. Reagan, 69–70
Johnson Foundation, Robert Wood, 58
John XXIII, Pope, 227
Joint Economic Committee of Congress, 28
Jones University, Bob, 163
Justice Department, 150, 156, 158, 193, 250, 259

Kean, Thomas, 185, 261
Kemp, Jack, xxxv, 92, 186, 187, 189, 193, 252, 287, 289
Kempton, Murray, xii
Kennan, George, 193
Kennedy, John, xxiii–xxiv, 10, 209, 263, 265
Kennedy, Ted, 259, 263, 265
Kerouac, Jack, 2
Kerr, Clark, 33
Keynes, John Maynard, xvii–xviii, xxiv, 27–28, 280, 283
Khomeini, Ayatollah, 94, 206
King, Martin Luther, Jr., xxiii, xxxii, 2, 261
Kinsley, Michael, 182–83, 186
Kirk, Grayson, 5
Kirkland, Lane, 130, 134, 196
Kirkpatrick, Jeane, xxxv, 40, 218, 233
Kissinger, Henry, 159–60, 193, 223
Knights of Labor, 129–30
Koch, Ed, 48, 152–53, 188, 209
Krauthammer, Charles, 288
Kristol, Irving, 32, 222, 232, 233, 259
Ku Klux Klan, 25
Kuttner, Robert, 186

Labor: and conservatives, 158–59; and industrial policy, 280–84; occupational restructuring, 164–65; as Reagan losers, 274–75; and unions, 136–37
Labor Department, 154
*Laborem Exercens (On Human Work)* (John Paul II), 216, 227
Laissez-faire, 22–24
Landrum-Griffin Act (1959), 135
League of Women Voters, 89

## Index

Leary, Timothy, 2
Lebanon, hostages in, 85
Left, 258–60; as Reagan losers, 265–76; religious, 226–37; socialists, 254–58
Legal Services Corporation, xxx, xxxiii, 4
Legion of Decency, 210
Lehrman, Lewis, xxxv
Leo XIII, Pope, 227, 229–30
"Letter from a Birmingham Jail" (King), 2
*Liberal Imagination, The* (Trilling), 21
Liberalism, 21–31
Liberation theology, 226, 231, 245
Liberty Foundation, 40, 206
Liddy, G. Gordon, 2
Liebman, Lance, 67–68
Liebow, Elliott, 33
Lifetime employment, 139–41, 166–68
Likud, 206
Lincoln, Abraham, 214
Lippmann, Walter, 32, 214
Lipset, Seymour M., 236, 237
Living standard, 275; and capitalism, 218–19
Lloyd George, David, 199
Local Initiatives Support Corp. (LISC), 46–47
Lockheed, 76
Long, Russell, 91
*Looking Backward* (Bellamy), 159
Lorenzo, Frank, 278
*Losing Ground* (Murray), xxxvii, 186
LSD, 2
Lutheran Church, 246

Machlup, Fritz, 164
MacArthur, Douglas, xiv, xv
"MacNeil-Lehrer Newshour," 153, 258
Madison, James, 240
Madonna, 205
Mailer, Norman, 233
Mainline Protestants, 237–45
Malcolm X, 2
Malthus, Thomas, 23
Management: failure, 279; and unions, 278
Manion, Daniel, 94
Marcos, Ferdinand and Imelda, 193

Marshall, Thurgood, 148, 171
Martin Marietta Corp., 105, 128
Marx, Karl, 33, 257
*Mater et Magistra* (John XXIII), 227
Mazda, 166, 197
McCarthy, Eugene, 6
McCarthy, Joseph, 21
McDonnell Douglas, 274
McFarlane, Robert, xii, xviii
McGovern, George, xxii, 6, 91, 229
McIntyre, Robert, 186
"McLaughlin Report, The," 153
Meany, George, 130, 133–34
MedCenter, 101
Medfirst clinics, 46
Medicaid, xxxii, 16, 17, 18, 30, 43, 49, 56, 81, 107, 113, 126, 135, 154, 173, 198, 272
Medical care. *See* Health care
Medicare, xxvi, xxxii, 12, 17, 18, 43, 81, 101, 107, 113, 135, 154, 173–74, 271–72, 290–91
Meese, Edwin, 33, 87, 148, 250, 259, 274
Meidner Plan, Sweden, 282
Melman, Seymour, 127
Memphis Baptist Hospital, 60
Mergers and acquisitions, 150–51
Methodists, 246, 248, 249
Middle class: and social programs, 1960s, 13–15, 29; and political process, 43; as Reagan losers, 275
Midwest Business Group on Health, 102
Militarization, xiv–xix, 118–28
Military-industrial complex, 126
Mill, James, 23
Mill, John Stuart, 22–23, 115
Miller, James, 213
*Miranda* decision, 4
Model Cities program, 30, 62
Mondale, Joan, 86
Mondale, Walter, xxix, 86, 181, 196, 214, 224, 265, 285, 289
*Monthly Review*, 259
Moore, Paul, 238
Morality, 3, 212–13
Moral Majority, xxxv, xxxix, 8, 40, 189, 206, 235–36, 247, 249, 262, 290
Morgan, Richard, 4, 5

311

## Index

Morris, William, 159
Motley, Constance Baker, 192
"Mountbatten," 132
Moyers, Bill, 153
Moynihan, Daniel Patrick, 15, 33, 37, 91, 152, 188, 201, 268
Multinational corporations, 217–18
Municipal Assistance Corp. (MAC), 182, 284
Murray, Charles, xxxvii, 56, 186
Myths, social, 89–90

Nader, Ralph, 192–93
*Nation* magazine, xxii
National Conference of Catholic Bishops, 210
National Council of Churches, 210, 237, 238
National Education Association, 129
National Guard, 264
National Health Care, 80
National Health Service, 112
National Industrial Recovery Act, 26, 281
National Institutes of Health, 43–44
National Jewish Community Relations Advisory Council, 236
National Labor Relations Act (1935), 61, 135
National Labor Relations Board, xxxviii, 144, 145, 196, 278
National Medical Enterprises, 100
National Organization for Decent Literature, 210
National Organization for Women, 195
National Public Radio, 157
*National Review*, xl, 125
National Rifle Association, 87
National Science Foundation, 43–44
National Security Agency, 47
NBC, 153
Negative income tax (NIT), 35–37
Neoconservative economics, 32–40
Neoliberals, xliii, 195–204; and yuppies, 177–95
Neuhaus, Richard, 211
New Deal, 29, 135, 213, 257, 290
*New Democracy, A* (Hart), 178
*New England Journal of Medicine*, 97

*New Republic*, 182, 186, 222, 288
New School for Social Research, 259
*News from Nowhere* (Morris), 159
*Newsweek*, 188
Newton, Huey, 2
New York City: near-bankruptcy, 284–85; Parking Violations Bureau scandal, 48; Social Services Department, 172
*New York* magazine, 162
*New York Post*, 152
*New York Times*, 139, 151, 152, 153, 162, 178, 233
New York University, 191
*Next American Frontier, The* (Reich), xliv, 181
Nidal, Abu, xiv
Niebuhr, Reinhold, 237
"Nightline," 258
Nixon, Richard, 7, 20, 28, 37, 91, 123, 229, 231
North Carolina Baptist Convention, 247
North, Oliver, xii–xvi, xviii
Norton-Kosair Children's Hospital, Louisville, 98
Novak, Michael, xl, 40, 214, 215
Nunn, Sam, xxvii, 120
Nutrition, evidence on, 57–58

Occupational Safety and Health Administration (OSHA), 38, 70
O'Connor, Cardinal, 249
O'Connor, Sandra Day, 149, 150
Office of Economic Opportunity, 43
Office of Management and Budget, 75, 107, 154, 156, 190, 213
Ohio Works, 46, 106
"Old-Time Gospel Hour," 208
O'Neill, Tip, 250
OPEC, 19, 20, 230
Oppenheimer, Robert, 125
*Organization Man, The* (Whyte), 165
Orshansky, Mollie, 52
*Other America, The* (Harrington), xiii
*Oxford English Dictionary*, 207, 247, 263

Packard Commission, 120
Palestine Liberation Organization (PLO), 222, 223, 237

# Index

Panetta, Leon, 179
Pantry Pride, 275
Parking Violations Bureau, New York City, 48
Parkland Hospital, Dallas, 98
*Partisan Review*, 227
*Passion for Excellence, A*, 177
Patton, George, xv
Peace Corps, xxiii
Pensions, military, 125–26
Pentagon, xvii, 47, 104; and defense spending, 73–77; and militarization, 118–28
Peretz, Martin, 186, 222
Perkins, Frances, 29
Physicians' Task Force on Hunger, 58
Pickens, T. Boone, 150
Pinochet, General, 218
*Playboy*, 89
PLO. *See* Palestine Liberation Organization
Podhoretz, Norman, 194, 222, 232, 233
Poindexter, John, xii, xviii
*Policy Review*, xlii, 38, 125
Political action committees (PACs), 266, 276
Politics, 6–9; and poor vs. middle class, 43; and religion, 208–10
Posner, Richard, 149
Poverty, 51–57; and capitalism, 218–19; and health, 58–60; and housing, 61–62; and job training, 62–67; and nutrition, 57–58; and political process, 43; programs, 1960s, 15–18, 29–30; stigmatizing, 199–200
Powell, Lewis, 149
Powers, Chet, 168
Pragmatism, 21
Prayer in schools, 86
Presbyterians, 238–45, 246
Presser, Jackie, 90
Prices, in 1960s, 9–10
*Principles of Political Economy* (Mill), 23
Prisons, privatization, 39–40, 103–6
Privacy, welfare recipients, 171–73
Privatization, xix–xxii, 39–40, 45–51, 94–107, 117–18, 157–58; U.S. vs. international, 117–18; and vouchers, 107–16
*Problems of Social Reconstruction*, 228
Protestants: mainline, 237–45; radical, 245–47
Proxmire, William, 284
Prudential Insurance Co., 102
Psychobabble, 177
"PTL Club," 208
Public assistance, U.S. vs. international, 18
*Public Interest, The*, xlii, 32–35, 38, 67, 222, 232
*Public Opinion*, xlii, 38
Public services, privatization, 94–107
Public television, 153
Puccio, Thomas, 279
*Pygmalion* (Shaw), 15

Quadaffi, Muammur, xix
Quaker Oats, 102

Raab, Earl, 236, 237
Racketeers, and unions, 133
Radical Protestants, 245–47
*Rambo*, xxxv, 159
Raskin, Abe, 146
Reagan, Ronald, xlvi, 20, 33, 85–89, 93; vs. Carter, 7–8; vs. Johnson, 69–70; and television, 40–41
Reconstruction Finance Corp., 182
Red-baiting, 160–61
Reed, John, 191, 192
Regan, Donald, 86
*Regulation*, xlii, 38
Rehnquist, William, xxxviii, 149
Reich, Charles, 165, 168–71, 174, 175
Reich, Robert, 181, 183–84, 186, 190, 285
Reid, George, 247
Reiman, Arnold S., 97
Religion, 4, 85, 205–8; conservative fundamentalism, 211–13; left, 226–37; mainline Protestants, 237–45; and politics, 208–10; possible winner of wars of, 247–53; radical Protestants, 245–47; right, 196–97; and television, 207–8

## Index

*Republic* (Plato), 89, 270
*Rerum Novarum* (Leo XIII), 229–30
Reston, James, xii
Retirement, military pensions, 125–26
Retton, Mary Lou, 84
Revlon, 275
Reynolds, Bradford, 221
Reynolds, R. J., 180
Ricardo, David, 23
Richardson, Elliott, xv
Riesman, David, 33, 166
Right-to-life fervor, 87
Right-to-work laws, 135
Rivlin, Alice, 190
Robb, Charles, 188, 286
Roberts, Oral, 208
Roberts, Paul Craig, 33, 197
Robertson, Pat, 196, 207, 226, 250
Robinson, Joan, 283
Robison, James, 208
Rockefeller, Jay, 287
Rockne, Knute, 85
Rockwell, 105
*Roe* v. *Wade*, 148, 197, 212, 250
Rohatyn, Felix, 182, 183, 190, 281, 284–85
Roosevelt, Franklin, xli, 26, 27, 29, 81, 93, 202, 213, 257, 265, 270, 272–73, 290
Roosevelt, Theodore, 257
Rosenberg, Steven, 60
Rostenkowski, Daniel, 277–78
Rowen, Hobart, 194
Ruckelshaus, William, 71
Rugged individualism, 24–26
Ryan, William, 72


Sacramento Metropolitan Utility District, 14
Sadat, Anwar, 193
Samuelson, Paul, 19
Sanctuary movement, 246
Sandinistas, 127
San Francisco State College, 7
Sargent, Francis, 264
Saturn rocket, 197
Saving, 23–24
Say, Jean Baptiste, 23
Say's Law, 23, 26

Scalia, Antonin, xxxviii, 149
Schanberg, Sidney, 152
Scharansky, Anatol, 222
Schlafly, Phyllis, 262
School busing, 158; and desegregation in Boston, 263–65
Schorr, Alvin, 33
Schuller, Robert, 207, 208
Schultze, Charles, 182, 239
*Science and Society*, 259
Scientists, and military technologies, 125
Seale, Bobby, 2
Secord, Richard, xi, xviii, xx
Securities and Exchange Commission, 70
Senate Finance Committee, 278
*Share Economy: Conquering Stagflation* (Weitzman), 137, 143
Shaw, George Bernard, 15
Sheehy, Thomas, 104
Shriver, Sargent, 43
Shultz, George, xi–xii
Silk, Leonard, 194
Silverdale Detention Center, 103–4
Simon, Paul, xxii, xxiv
Simon, William, xl, 259
Simpson, Thatcher, 164
Singlaub, John, xiii, xviii
Singleton, John, 105–6
Sipser, Philip, 194
Small Business Administration, 14
Small businesses, as Reagan losers, 274
Smith, Adam, 23, 103
Smith, Al, 209
Smith, William French, 250
Smoot-Hawley Tariff Act, 26
Social control, 159–61
Social Darwinism, 159
Socialist Labor party, 259
Socialist Workers party, 259
Social programs, 12–14, 17–18; U.S. vs. international, 18–20, 55–56, 72–73
Social Security, xxii, xxxii, xxxvii–xxxviii, 10–13, 49–50, 70, 71, 91, 202–3, 241, 242, 267, 268–71, 115
Social Security Act (1935), 26, 81, 202, 258, 268–69, 270
Social services, privatization, 45–51

# Index

Social Services Department, New York City, 172
Social welfare costs, 19–20
Sojourners, 246–47
*Sojourners, The*, 211, 246
Solarz, Stephen, 193, 194
Solow, Robert, 33
Sombart, Werner, 254–55, 256
Southern Baptist Conference, 248
Sowell, Thomas, 33, 44, 180
Space shuttle, 123
Special military forces, xix
Special Supplementary Food Program, 111
Spencer, Herbert, 159
Spender, Stephen, 32
Springsteen, Bruce, 205
Stagflation, 19, 20
Stallone, Sylvester, 122, 159
Starr, Roger, 33
Star Wars, xvii, 119, 122–25, 193
Statistical communities, 88
Stein, Herbert, 239
Stevens, John Paul, 148–49, 150
Stockman, David, xlii, 31, 72, 190
Strategic Defense Initiative. *See* Star Wars
Strikebreaking, 143–44
Structural unemployment, 63–64
Students for a Democratic Society, 2
Student Nonviolent Coordinating Committee, 2
Sullivan and Cromwell, 164
Supplemental Security Income, 56, 91, 126
Supreme Court, 3–5, 148–50; and abortion, 148, 196–97, 212, 250; and public religion, 210; and *Wyman v. James*, 171–73
Sviridoff, Mitchell, 46
Swaggart, Jimmy, 207, 208
Swift, Jonathan, 159

Taft, Robert, 61
Taft, William Howard, 257
Taft-Ellender-Wagner Act (1951), 61
Taft-Hartley Act (1947), 135
Targeted Jobs Tax Credit (TJTC), 112
Taxes, 10–12, 28; negative, 35–37; and neoliberals, 179–80; and private altruism, 157
Tax Simplification Act, 179
Teachers' Insurance and Annuity, 178
Technocrats, 183
Television, 85, 153; and deunionization, 130–32; and elections, 40–41; and religion, 207–8
Tennessee Valley Authority, 26
Terkel, Studs, 62
Thatcher, Margaret, 72, 85, 117, 123
Theory Z, 163
Third National Bank, Ohio, 46
Thomas, Norman, 257
Thurmond, Strom, 250–51
Thurow, Lester, xliv, 141, 150, 190, 281–82, 285
*Time* magazine, 28, 226
Tobin, Dan, 90
Tobin, James, 33, 37, 283
Tocqueville, Alexis de, 88, 214
Toyota, 166, 197
Transportation Department, 118
Treasury Department, 152
Trilling, Lionel, 21, 22, 40
Truman, Harry, 81
Trump, Donald, 285
Tutu, Desmond, 209

Ueberroth, Peter, xxxiv, 84
Ullman, John, 127
Unemployment, 10, 243–44; benefits, 19, 268–69; blacks, 273; in Great Depression, 25–26; and Keynesian economics, 27–28; and military contracts, 122; in 1980s, 138–39; and wages, 142–43; and welfare dependency, 56–57
Union Carbide Corp., 218
Unions, 90, 159; decline, 128–47, 278; drive against, 142–44; and labor markets, 136–37; and neoliberals, 196; and racketeers, 133
United Automobile Workers, 9, 81, 141, 166, 167, 190
United Church of Christ, 246, 249
United Farm Workers, xxxi
United Methodist Church, 228

315

## Index

United Presbyterian Church, 239–40

Vance, Cyrus, xii
Vargas, Angel and Emily, 240
Veblen, Thorstein, xiii–xiv, xv–xvi, 142
Veterans Administration, 107, 126, 171, 178
Vidal, Gore, 153
*Village Voice*, 153, 162
Violence, 86, 87, 160
Volcker, Paul, 191
Voting rights legislation, 30
Vouchers, for private services, 107–16

Wage earners, as Reagan losers, 274–75
Wages, 91, 142–43
Wagner, Robert, 16, 61
Wagner Act, 61
Wallace, George, 261
Wallas, Graham, 29
Wallis, Jim, 246–47
*Wall Street Journal*, xii, 14, 60, 144, 194, 197, 222, 246
Walzer, Michael, 106
Wanniski, Jude, 33
War on poverty. *See* Poverty
Warren, Earl, 3–4, 5, 171
*Washington Monthly*, xliii
*Washington Post*, 151, 152, 193
Watt, James, 211–12
Wattenberg, Ben, 40
*Wealth and Poverty* (Gilder), 186
Weapons procurement, 119
Weinberger, Caspar, xii, xvi, 73–74, 119, 120, 150, 222–23
Weisskopf, Thomas, 181
Weitzman, Martin L., 137, 139–40, 141, 142, 143, 282
Welfare: abuse, 269; cheats, 199–200; reform, xxv, xl, 231–32;

rights of recipients, 171–73; U.S. vs. international, 18–19
Wesley, John, 256
Westmoreland, William, 153
Westway, xlviii, 152, 185
Wheeler, Raymond, 57–58
"When the Boat Comes In," 133
Whirlpool, 180
White, Byron, xxiii, 149
White, Kevin, 264
"Why Busing Didn't Work" (Higgins), 186
*Why Is There No Socialism in the United States?* (Sombart), 254
Whyte, William H. Jr., 165, 166, 175
Wildavsky, Aaron, 33
Will, George, 153, 188, 189, 288
Wilson, James Q., 33
Wilson, Woodrow, 257
Women: poverty in families headed by, 54–55; as Reagan losers, 86–87, 265–67
Women's Christian Temperance Union, 210
Workers. *See* Labor
Works Progress Administration, 26
World Council of Churches, 237, 238
Wriston, Walter, 182, 191
*Wyman v. James*, 171–73
Wyoming County Community Hospital, Warsaw, N.Y., 99

Xenophobia, 252

Yosemite National Park, 14
Young, Arthur, 51
Yuppies, xxii, xliii, 162–65, 175–77, 224–25, 251; and neoliberals, 177–95; and Social Security, 271

Zenith Corp., 102